DESISTANCE AND CHILDREN
Critical Reflections from Theory, Research and Practice

Edited by
Alexandra Wigzell, Claire Paterson-Young
and Tim Bateman

P

First published in Great Britain in 2024 by

Policy Press, an imprint of
Bristol University Press
University of Bristol
1–9 Old Park Hill
Bristol
BS2 8BB
UK
t: +44 (0)117 374 6645
e: bup-info@bristol.ac.uk

Details of international sales and distribution partners are available at policy.bristoluniversitypress.co.uk

British Library Cataloguing in Publication Data
A catalogue record for this book is available from the British Library

ISBN 978-1-4473-6911-0 paperback
ISBN 978-1-4473-6913-4 ePub
ISBN 978-1-4473-6912-7 ePdf

Cover design: Liam Roberts Design
Front cover image: Unsplash/ratushny

Contents

List of figures and tables   v
Notes on contributors   vi
Acknowledgements   xiv

Foreword   xv
Fergus McNeill

1   Desistance and children: setting the scene   1
        Alexandra Wigzell, Claire Paterson-Young and Tim Bateman

**PART I   Theoretical and conceptual perspectives on desistance
            and children**
2   'Child First' and desistance   37
        Neal Hazel and Stephen Case
3   Child time, adult time, fugitivity and desistance   57
        Diana Johns
4   Should desistance thinking be applied to children in the   73
        criminal justice system?
        Ross Little and Kevin Haines

PART II   The socio-structural dimensions of desistance
5   Young women and punishment within and beyond the   97
        penal system
        Gilly Sharpe
6   Supporting girls in care to desist from offending behaviour 112
        Jo Staines, Julie Shaw, Katie Hunter and Claire Fitzpatrick
7   Black and mixed-heritage boys: desistance through a   128
        co-creative Critical Race and postcolonial lens
        John Wainwright
8   Growing in maturity, growing in faith, growing out of crime: 147
        the role of children's and young people's faith in desistance
        Tim Rosier

PART III The application of desistance thinking to children
9   Desistance approaches in youth justice: conceptualisations, 175
        barriers and enablers
        Kathy Hampson
10   Summer Arts Colleges: using the arts to promote educational 194
        engagement and desistance
        Martin Stephenson

11   Desistance through participatory practice: involving children   212
      in decision-making processes in youth justice
      Sean Creaney, Samantha Burns, Anne-Marie Douglas,
      Andrew Brierley and Colin Falconer
12   Relationship-based work with children in the youth   228
      justice system
      Roberta Evans and Kirstine Szifris
13   Through a youth justice practitioner's lens: would a   245
      sentencing alternative to a criminal conviction be a small
      change with a big impact on children's desistance?
      Steven Carr
14   Innovative and theoretically informed intervention   261
      programmes for children who offend: The Compass Project
      Neema Trivedi-Bateman
15   What next for desistance and youth justice?   277
      Alexandra Wigzell, Claire Paterson-Young and Tim Bateman

Index   290

List of figures and tables

Figures

8.1	Faith, Spirituality and Religion model	148
8.2	Principles for reflection on religion and belief framework	161
10.1	Theory of Change	197
13.1	Social Discipline Window	248
13.2	Simplified schematisation of the changing shape of sentencing for children	250
13.3	Guernsey's OCC criminal offence referral and investigation workflow	252
13.4	Barcode of Desistance	258
13.5	Barcode of Desistance (with breach)	259
13.6	Barcode of Desistance (emphasising desistance gaps)	259

Tables

8.1	Fowler's Faith Development Model (1981) with additional insight about expected characteristics	154
14.1	The Compass Project topic strands and corresponding example activities	270

Notes on contributors

Tim Bateman was Reader in Youth Justice at the University of Bedfordshire. He has a background in youth justice social work and policy and has written and researched widely on issues across the youth justice landscape. He contributed the Youth Justice News section to *Youth Justice* journal for 20 years. Tim is a long-standing member of the Board of Trustees of the National Association for Youth Justice and has served as its Chair and Deputy Chair.

Andrew Brierley is Head of Access, Participation and Outcomes at Leeds Trinity with an extensive 15-year youth justice career. Qualifying in 2013, Andi worked with the most prolific and serious justice-involved children within the Intensive, Surveillance and Supervision Team. Andi has an array of practice experience in youth justice ranging from case management and secure settings to voluntary participation. Andi was instrumental in developing the role of the Child Looked After and Care Leaver Specialist at Leeds Youth Justice Service, leading on key initiatives that reduced the number of Leeds children in care being criminalised. Having the unique dual perspective of becoming a qualified youth justice professional and spending several years in custody and on probation himself in his youth prompted Andi to author three successful books on penology and criminology. Andi also sits on the strategic council for the Howard League for Penal Reform.

Samantha Burns is Lecturer in Criminology within the Department of Sociology at Durham University. Her research interests have focused on children and young people's participation and co-production in the youth justice system, fuelled from both academic learning and work experience. Samantha completed her PhD in 2020 within the Department of Social and Behavioural Sciences at City University in Hong Kong. Alongside her current role at Durham University, Samantha is Deputy Chair of the National Association of Youth Justice, an Advisory Board member for Peer Power Youth and member of the Risk-Work in Young Lives network.

Steven Carr is a youth justice practitioner with over 30 years' experience, dating back to before the implementation of Home Office national standards in 1991. He received his MA in Social Work from Exeter University and has worked in probation, at the Youth Justice Board and in both statutory and non-statutory settings. He was a part of the transition from youth justice to youth offending teams following the Crime and Disorder Act 1998 and has worked as a youth justice officer in London and every county in England starting with the letter 'B'; he has a specific interest in small island communities, having worked in the Shetland Islands and currently for the past 14 years as a youth justice officer in the picturesque Bailiwick of Guernsey and Alderney, where he experienced the implementation of the Office of the Children's Convenor.

Stephen Case is a criminologist in the Criminology, Sociology and Social Policy division at Loughborough University. His research and scholarship focus on the promotion of positive, 'children first', rights-based and anti-risk approaches to working with children in conflict with the law. In addition to over 60 academic journal articles, he has published numerous books including *Youth Justice: A Critical Introduction* (with Kevin Haines, Routledge, 2021), *Positive Youth Justice: Children First, Offenders Second* (with Kevin Haines, Policy Press, 2015) and *Understanding Youth Offending: Risk Factor Research, Policy and Practice* (with Kevin Haines, Routledge, 2009). Stephen has conducted funded research for the Youth Justice Board, the Home Office, the Welsh government, the Nuffield Foundation, the Economic and Social Research Council and the Leverhulme Trust.

Sean Creaney is a criminologist and Senior Lecturer in the School of Law, Criminology and Policing at Edge Hill University. His research interests include Child First justice, typologies, theories, models of participation and co-production and experiential peer support and mentorship in youth justice. Sean is a founding Advisory Board member of social justice charity Peer Power, an empathy-led charity focused on healing trauma and creating individual and system change. Sean was recently confirmed as an associate of the Children and Young People's Centre for Justice, acting as a champion for the Centre and contributing to practice, research and knowledge exchange activities over a two-year term. The appointment to the scheme, created to broaden and transform Scotland's youth justice knowledge base, was made in recognition of Dr Creaney's work improving justice for children and young people. Sean played a key role in establishing the knowledge transfer partnership between Edge Hill University, Chester University and Cheshire Youth Justice Services and currently sits as a voluntary member of the Cheshire Youth Justice Services Management Board. He is a member of the Editorial Advisory Board of the *Safer Communities* journal (Emerald) and was awarded Outstanding Paper in both the 2015 and 2021 Emerald Literati Network Awards for Excellence.

Anne-Marie Douglas's belief in the transformational power of empathy and personal experience of peer-led services led her to found the charity Peer Power Youth in 2015, which launched formally in 2016 at the House of Lords. Peer Power Youth works alongside young people who have experienced injustice, inequalities, trauma and childhood adversity. They work together to heal trauma and adversity through empathy and caring relationships and support young people to use their lived-experience voice to create real system change for their peers. Anne-Marie has worked in participation, youth justice and youth engagement for 25 years across support services in both voluntary and statutory sector roles. She is a Churchill Fellow, having travelled to the United States and Canada to research the role of empathy and lived experience in support services for children and young people, which resulted in The Empathy Report. Anne-Marie has written on empathy, youth voice and social action in numerous publications, has spoken in Parliament and is featured on podcasts and radio, such as the Radio 4 Four Thought episode, 'The empathy equation'.

Roberta Evans completed her doctorate in Youth Justice at Bedfordshire University, researching parenting and crime-prevention pathways. Her research and practice evolved into wider adolescent resilience and safeguarding, recognising the cumulative impact of political and contextual factors for young people in the justice system. She then created the tightrope,which is a toolkit for exploring risk and resilience with young people and presented a working paper to the Howard League 'What Is Justice?' conference in 2015. She has over 20 years of front-line experience in youth justice in London, was a youth justice manager for five years and is currently Associate Director for Family and Adolescents, which includes youth justice and adolescent safeguarding services. She delivers training and guest lectures on adolescent development, trauma-informed practice and youth justice policy in practice.

Colin Falconer is Director of InspireChilli, an innovation consultancy that specialises in asset-based training, quality assurance and development work for organisations from across the UK to Australia. Colin has led various education, health and quality-assurance programmes, including 14 years as director of innovation at youth charity The Foyer Federation, where he first introduced the concept of Advantaged Thinking in the youth sector. Colin has served as an advisor for Paul Hamlyn Foundation's Youth Fund and a mentor for young leaders through InspireChilli's Team Young People network. Colin is also a trustee at Sounddelivery Media Charity and chair of trustees for the award-winning We Belong, the UK's first youth charity set up and led by young people from migrant backgrounds. Credits range from a 2011 TEDx performance in Thessaloniki to a London theatre show in 2014, with various published pieces including the 'Advantaged Thinking program framework' (2019) with the Brotherhood of St Laurence, the 'Strength in solidarity' (2020) report for the Listening Fund, and the 'Connecting minds' (2021) evaluation for States of Mind.

Claire Fitzpatrick is Senior Lecturer in Criminology in the Lancaster University Law School and Youth Justice Lead for the Centre for Child and Family Justice Research. Research interests include: the criminalisation of children in care, gendered pathways between care and custody and exploring injustice at the intersection of welfare and punishment systems. Most recently, she led the three-year Nuffield Foundation-funded project 'Disrupting the routes between care and custody for girls and women'.

Kevin Haines has had a distinguished academic career for some 30 years. As Head of the Criminology Department at Swansea University, he led colleagues to successive REF success and the top rating in the *Guardian* league tables. His numerous books and articles have been widely read, resulting in considerable success in informing policy development for children in (or keeping them out of) the criminal justice system.

Kathy Hampson is Senior Lecturer in Criminology at Aberystwyth University, where she has developed both under- and post-graduate courses in youth justice. She worked for nearly a decade as a practitioner in a large city youth offending team as a case manager, during which she studied for her PhD looking at the emotional intelligence of children who have offended. After this, she worked in a hybrid strategic-research-advisor role looking at the resettlement of children coming out of custody across North Wales. Her research interests cover youth justice systems, custody and resettlement practice, Child First youth justice and participatory practice within the sector. She has provided training for youth offending teams across Wales in both desistance practice in youth justice and in Child First justice.

Neal Hazel is Chair of Criminology and Criminal Justice at the University of Salford. He has previously held posts as Director of the Institute for Public Policy and Director of the Centre for Social Research at the university. He has delivered more than 40 funded research projects, mainly in youth justice and family support, including several national surveys and evaluations. He specialises in providing useful policy and practice messages, most recently through his Beyond Youth Custody research and its 'Constructive Resettlement' framework for practitioners. In January 2018, Neal was appointed by the Secretary of State for Justice to the Youth Justice Board, which is responsible for overseeing the youth justice system across England and Wales. He has led the Board's policy development of 'Child First' as the guiding principle for the youth justice sector. He is also former HM Deputy Chief Inspector of Probation for England and Wales.

Katie Hunter is Administrative Data Research UK Research Fellow and Lecturer in Criminology at Manchester Metropolitan University. Her

Fellowship project involves using linked Ministry of Justice and Department for Education data to explore the intersections between ethnicity, care experience and youth justice involvement.

Diana Johns is Associate Professor of Criminology in the School of Social and Political Sciences at the University of Melbourne. She is a qualitative researcher who works predominantly with people who have been criminalised and/or imprisoned, young people and African Australian communities. Her work is focused on the effects of criminalisation, the impacts of imprisonment and the possibilities of restorative, relational and reintegrative justice practices. She is particularly interested in exploring experiences of transition, in-betweenness and liminality. Her first book, *Being and Becoming an Ex-prisoner* (2018), was published as part of Routledge's International Series on Desistance and Rehabilitation. Recent collaborative writing projects include two new books: *Place, Race and Politics: The Anatomy of a Law and Order Crisis* (Weber et al, Emerald, 2021) and *Co-production and Criminal Justice* (Johns et al, Routledge, 2022).

Ross Little is Senior Lecturer in Criminology and Criminal Justice at De Montfort University, Leicester, where he leads an undergraduate module focusing on young people and the criminal justice system. As a trustee, and former chair, of the National Association for Youth Justice, he brings together knowledge of research findings, practitioner perspectives, youth justice policy and children's experiences to improve understandings of how the youth justice system treats children in relation to their rights. His published work to date has primarily focused on children's education in custodial contexts.

Claire Paterson-Young is Associate Professor at the University of Northampton. She has extensive experience in researching the social impacts of social inequality and social disadvantage. Claire has experience in ethics and is a member of the West Midlands Police and Crime Commissioner Ethics Committee, Health and Research Association Research Ethics Committee and the University of Northampton Research Ethics Committee. She is an associate editor for the *Journal of Child and Family Studies* and has published in numerous international peer-reviewed academic journals.

Tim Rosier is Senior Lecturer in Social and Community Studies at the University of Derby. He primarily teaches on the BA (Hons) Youth Work and Community Development (Joint Negotiating Committee-recognised) programme and has particular responsibility for overseeing the Youth Justice (Youth Justice Effective Practice Certificate) and Radicalisation Pathways for final-year students. He also acts as the placements coordinator for the youth work and social work programmes, managing partnerships with a significant number of external agencies from across a range of disciplines including criminal justice. Tim previously worked as a probation officer in the East Midlands, during which time he undertook a secondment into the counter-terrorism-related arena, facilitating interventions with young people and young adults at risk of radicalisation. He was also a senior project manager for a faith-based charity overseeing outreach, non-formal education and chaplaincy work with young offenders in custody across 14 prisons in England. Tim continues to be involved with the National Association for Youth Justice and Alliance for Youth Justice and is a trustee for two faith-based prison/resettlement organisations.

Gilly Sharpe is Lecturer in Criminology at the University of Sheffield. Her research has focused on girls, young people and youth justice, persistent young offenders, community provision for women in the criminal justice system and qualitative longitudinal research examining desistance from crime and institutional stigmatisation in the penal and welfare spheres. Gilly's longitudinal work on criminalised young women and their transitions to adulthood has been published in two monographs by Routledge: *Offending Girls* (2012) and *Women, Stigma and Desistance from Crime* (2024). Gilly is a former youth justice social worker.

Julie Shaw is Senior Lecturer in Criminology at the Liverpool John Moores University Centre for the Study of Crime, Criminalisation and Social Exclusion. She is an experienced researcher, with interests that include the criminalisation of care-experienced children, the youth justice system and practitioner responses and child sexual and criminal exploitation. In addition, Julie is a former probation officer who has worked for both a youth offending team and with adults who were the subject of community and custodial sentences.

Jo Staines is Associate Professor in Youth Justice and Child Welfare in the School for Policy Studies, University of Bristol, with expertise in the care and criminal justice systems and the interconnections between these systems for children, their families and professionals. She was a member of the Prison Reform Trust's independent inquiry into the over-representation of care-experienced children in the justice system, chaired by Lord Laming, and was a co-investigator on the Nuffield Foundation-funded project 'Disrupting the routes between care and custody for girls and women'. Jo is a trustee of the National Association for Youth Justice and author of *Youth Justice* (Palgrave Macmillan, 2015). She was previously Senior Consultant in a national crime reduction organisation, working with the Youth Justice Board, youth offending teams and non-governmental organisations to support the development of policy and practice interventions.

Martin Stephenson has wide experience in education, youth justice and social care and has been involved in policy development, management and practice. He is a founding member of the Youth Justice Board, former Chief Executive of the charity INCLUDE, Senior Policy Advisor at the Department for Education and Skills, Director of ECOTEC Research and Consulting and Professor at Nottingham Trent University. He has been Non-Executive Director of Norfolk Primary Care Trust and Ormiston Academies Trust and a trustee of NACRO. Until recently, Martin was Chief Executive of Unitas, a national charity. Martin has written extensively on the educational engagement of young people in the youth justice system.

Kirstine Szifris has over ten years' experience doing research and evaluation in and around the justice system. She has previously worked at the Policy Evaluation and Research Unit at Manchester Metropolitan University and completed her PhD at the Institute of Criminology, Cambridge University. She currently works as Research and Evaluation Lead at SHiFT, a youth justice organisation based in the UK.

Neema Trivedi-Bateman is Lecturer in Criminology at Loughborough University. She completed her PhD in Criminology at the world-renowned Institute of Criminology, University of Cambridge. Neema's research expertise is in developmental psychology, including the causes and influencing factors behind a variety of behaviours. More specifically, she studies the development of moral rules and moral emotions and how they might influence aggression or delinquency. Her PhD thesis, entitled 'The roles of empathy, shame, and guilt in violence decision-making', explored the role of moral emotions in the decision to engage in acts of crime, using a combination of longitudinal quantitative data and qualitative in-depth interview data about persistent offenders' real-life violent events. Neema led a two-year project entitled 'A randomised controlled trial examining the effect of a morality-strengthening programme on positive behavioural outcomes and the reduction of crime' (British Academy Small Grant Funding, £9,989; University funding £32,000) at a youth work charity. Neema is Principal Investigator of 'SAT NAV Compass: striving for positive attitudinal and behavioural outcomes for school children in England using an innovative youth morality programme' (EPG Funding, LU, £28,600).

John Wainwright is Senior Lecturer in the School of Health, Social Work and Sport at the University of Central Lancashire (UCLan). John has several years' experience working with children, young people and their families in the care and youth justice system. His research expertise is in (anti)-racism, ethnicity, youth justice, children and young people in the care system, adoption and fostering. He is Director of the Global Race Centre for Equality at UCLan.

Alexandra Wigzell is Leverhulme Early Career Fellow and Affiliated Lecturer at the Institute of Criminology, University of Cambridge. She is currently Principal Investigator of a three-year project looking at 'care' and its ethical dimensions in child–worker relationships in youth justice. She completed her PhD at the Institute in 2020, which examined children's and practitioners' experiences of 'everyday' youth justice supervision in two English youth offending services. Prior to and alongside her PhD, Ali worked in policy and research in the youth justice field. She is currently a trustee of the National Association for Youth Justice and an Advisory Board member of Peer Power UK. She chaired the Standing Committee for Youth Justice (now the Alliance for Youth Justice) from 2016 to 2019. Ali is also a book review editor at the international journal *Criminology & Criminal Justice*.

Acknowledgements

This book would not have been possible without the support of many people and organisations. We are thankful to our colleagues at the National Association of Youth Justice (NAYJ), whose encouragement and enthusiasm over the past two years has enabled this collection to be realised. We are especially grateful for the generous donations from the charities Unitas and the NAYJ, which have made it possible to publish the book as Open Access, making all chapters freely available. We would like to thank the anonymous peer reviewers of the book proposal for their positive and constructive comments. We would like to express our gratitude to the team at Policy Press for their patience and guidance throughout the production of this book, particularly Grace Carroll, our editorial assistant, and Tim Page, our meticulous copy editor. And thank you to our contributors whose efforts have produced what we consider to be a stimulating body of work that will be of benefit to scholars, policy makers and practitioners.

Our final acknowledgement is to the children who come to the attention of the justice system. This book has been produced firmly with them in mind. Their extraordinary resilience and potential for change underpin the words that appear below even though many of them are unlikely to ever read them.

Foreword

Fergus McNeill

When I was first invited to write this foreword, I hesitated. As I explained to the editors, I no longer consider myself well informed about youth justice even in my home country of Scotland, let alone elsewhere in these islands. About 15 years ago, I realised I couldn't keep pace with developments in youth justice and in (adult) criminal justice simultaneously, particularly while trying to become more international in my outlook. Since I felt much more confident in my knowledge about (adult) probation, prisons and parole, that is where I decided to place my focus.

That said, there was a second and more important reason why I hesitated. I felt uneasy about the conjunction that forms the book's title: *Desistance and Children*. Does it make sense to talk about those two things together, or is desistance properly thought of as an adult affair? Would it not make more sense to talk about the development and wellbeing of children and to see any involvements with offending and desistance as very much secondary to those issues? What might be the risks of talking about and focusing on children's desistance?

Of course, once I started reading the manuscript, I realised both that 'desistance' had become a hot topic in youth justice in England and Wales and that the editors and contributors to this volume wanted to explore precisely these kinds of questions. The responses provided in this collection are as fascinating as they are diverse; and it has been intriguing for me, as someone who has written a lot about desistance and how we might best support it, to see how critical debates about desistance and youth justice have matured in the years since I stopped paying close attention.

But before reviewing those contemporary debates, it is worth recalling the policy and practice contexts in which desistance research and theory emerged at the start of this century. At that time, critical voices were bemoaning both an increasing punitiveness and a creeping 'correctionalism' in youth and adult justice systems (Goldson, 2001, 2002). The 'correctionalism' was associated both with the popularisation of 'what works?' research findings and with increasingly prescriptive and managerialised modes of practice.

Against that backdrop, desistance scholars added their voices to the call for a more expansive and considered conception of 'evidence-based' policy and practice, one that looked beyond evaluation evidence and engaged seriously with the emerging evidence about – and theories of – how and why people moved away from offending – especially persistent offending. Like several contributors to this volume, some desistance scholars also criticised research and practice that centred too narrowly on risk and that misconceived and misconstrued risk as an attribute of individuals.

Desistance researchers argued that it was crucial not just to understand 'what works?' but also to understand the processes of personal and human development involved in or associated with desistance. Notably, and perhaps in contrast to the preponderance of studies about desistance today, some of the first desistance studies that I read were, in fact, studies of children's and young people's experiences. Writing this foreword offers me a welcome opportunity to acknowledge that it was Janet Jamieson (then at the University of Stirling) who first introduced me to the term and who encouraged me to speak with Stephen Farrall. As well as Jamieson and colleagues' (1999) study of young people and desistance in Scotland, they both directed me to Graham and Bowling's (1995) influential study of young people and offending in England and Wales.

In most of what I read about desistance in those early days, whether focused on children, young people or adults, I found scholars repeatedly stressing the importance of attending to the socio-structural contexts within which these processes occurred. Looking back on my own (quite limited and early career) work on desistance and youth justice (McNeill and Batchelor, 2002; Batchelor and McNeill, 2005; McNeill, 2006; Barry and McNeill, 2009), I used the evidence I had found to insist that social 'contexts and relationships matter' (McNeill, 2006, p 125 [in the chapter title]) at least as much as the more psychological and intra-personal aspects of human development. The stress on relationships drew attention both to the significance of social relations in desistance and to the central importance of professional relationships in trying to support the process. Obviously, the twin stresses on contexts and relationships were very much intended and articulated as a corrective to the reductive conceptions of individual responsibility – and of individual change – associated then with 'what works?', with programmes, with risk technologies and with managerialised practices.

What I underestimated, of course, was the capacity of systems to absorb seemingly new and challenging concepts and ideas and to use them to re-package and re-legitimate existing practices. It is through these processes of absorption that, for example, 'supporting desistance' has sometimes been falsely reduced to a synonym of 'preventing offending'. Similar sleight of hand (or thought) also seems to allow some to hear the message 'contexts and relationships matter' not as a challenge first to change social contexts by pursuing social justice and second to invest in the relationships that matter to children and which provide developmental opportunities, but merely as a reason to train children to manage their pre-existing contexts and relationships differently. Both for policy makers unwilling to address structural injustices, and for practitioners who felt powerless to do anything about them, reverting to a focus on individual change and with it individual responsibilisation had (and has) an obvious attraction.

Of course, there were and are themes within desistance scholarship that have been more or less vulnerable to co-optation of this sort. The example that always irks me is Maruna's (2001) outstanding work which, in many ways, led the development of our appreciation of the importance of identity in desistance. Of course, for a while his work was quite hotly contested *within* the desistance field: some questioned the relevance and/ or necessity of identity change to desistance, preferring to lay the stress on 'structural turning points' (Laub and Sampson, 2003). The debate cooled, I think, when it became widely recognised that the importance of identity probably depended on the degree to which labelling had done its worst in terms of affecting people's sense of themselves and their life prospects (as the Edinburgh Study also made abundantly clear: see McAra and McVie, 2005). That said, it should perhaps have been obvious from the outset that since Maruna's account reflected an interactionist perspective, it was less about identity as it was experienced in the head of the persister or desister (as it were) and more about how the *social* dynamics of identity affected both personal narratives and social relations.

But again, these subtleties were, to some extent, lost in the translation from theory to practice. If policy makers weren't minded to address the harms of criminalisation, and if youth justice practitioners couldn't influence policing practices and/or community reactions to young people, then it is hardly a surprise that their focus narrowed to trying to address how young people see themselves and narrate their lives.

To be sure, researchers who seek to influence policy and practice have a responsibility to try to anticipate how their work is read and used and to attend to what it might legitimate and what it might marginalise. With this in mind, my own view is that the most potent critique of desistance research in this book is neither the mistaken claim that it neglects the social, nor that it focuses too much on identity (especially in the case of the still-forming identities of children). Rather, it is the argument that we should never have accepted the centring of 'offending' that desistance – even as a concept – continues to permit, least of all when discussing the development, treatment and support of children.

But perhaps that critique relies on the luxury of distance or the wisdom of hindsight. Looking back at it now, I can see in some of my own writing a pragmatic acceptance that youth justice policy makers (at least in the era of New Labour, anti-social behaviour orders [ASBOs] and parenting orders) were never going to be persuaded to displace offending from the centre of their agenda. Better then, I reasoned, to at least draw them away from narrow correctionalism and towards an awareness of the developmental processes involved in desistance, whether that meant the 'natural' desistance of the vast majority of children and young people (since some degree of offending is normative [see Chapter 1]) or the 'assisted' desistance of those whose behaviour was more persistent and problematic and who had (most likely) already been criminalised. If policy makers back then couldn't be persuaded to do the right things (avoiding criminalisation, supporting development, advocating for opportunities, for example) for the right reasons, like prioritising children's rights and taking 'Child First' approaches, then at least we could try to give them some instrumental reasons for doing some of the right things.

Reading this volume, it is heartening to see that the contributors are rightly determined to push us all further – towards doing the right things for the right reasons. In assembling these arguments, and articulating their basis in both evidence and principle, I think that this collection offers us a very rich repository of experience, research, ideas and proposals. I only hope that we can persuade those involved in children's services and youth justice at all levels to draw on the well provided here. If they do, they'll find refreshment I'm sure, and perhaps we'll all find hope that our policies, systems and practices might themselves grow up a bit in terms of how we respond to children at risk of criminalisation.

References

Barry, M. and McNeill, F. (eds) (2009) *Youth Offending and Youth Justice*, Research Highlights, London: Jessica Kingsley.

Batchelor, S. and McNeill, F. (2005) 'The young person–worker relationship', in T. Bateman and J. Pitts (eds) *The RHP Companion to Youth Justice*, Lyme Regis: Russell House Publishing, pp 166–71.

Goldson, B. (2001) 'A rational youth justice? Some critical reflections on the research, policy and practice relation', *Probation Journal*, 48(2): 76–85.

Goldson, B. (2002) 'New punitiveness: the politics of child incarceration', in J. Muncie, G. Hughes and E. McLaughlin (eds) *Youth Justice: Critical Readings*, London: Sage, pp 386–400.

Graham, J. and Bowling, B. (1995) 'Young people and crime', Home Office Research Study 145, London: Home Office.

Jamieson, J., McIvor, G. and Murray, C. (1999) *Understanding Offending among Young People*, Edinburgh: Scottish Executive.

Laub, J. and Sampson, R. (2003) *Shared Beginnings, Divergent Lives: Delinquent Boys to Age Seventy*, Cambridge, MA: Harvard University Press.

Maruna, S. (2001) *Making Good: How Ex-convicts Reform and Rebuild Their Lives*, Washington, DC: American Psychological Association.

McAra, L. and McVie, S. (2005) 'The usual suspects? Street life, young people and the police', *Criminology and Criminal Justice*, 5(1): 5–36.

McNeill, F. (2006) 'Community supervision: context and relationships matter', in B. Goldson and J. Muncie (eds) *Youth Crime and Justice*, London: Sage, pp 125–38.

McNeill, F. and Batchelor, S. (2002) 'Chaos, containment and change: responding to persistent offending by young people', *Youth Justice*, 2(1): 27–43.

Desistance and children: setting the scene

Alexandra Wigzell, Claire Paterson-Young and Tim Bateman

Rationale for the book

Since the late 1990s, 'desistance' – understanding how people move away from offending – has become a significant research focus and 'increasingly ubiquitous' in central policy (Maruna and Mann, 2019). Since 2014, with the introduction by the Youth Justice Board of a new assessment framework, desistance thinking has been progressively transplanted to youth justice in England and Wales from the adult justice system. Given that the desistance evidence base is primarily rooted in the experiences of adults who have a history of criminal behaviour, one might have expected this development to have been accompanied by some debate. Yet, discussion or examination of the relevance of desistance thinking to children in the justice system remains scarce, comprising a significant and important gap in scholarship.

While there is a limited, albeit developing, international knowledge base about the desistance pathways of children, these studies have typically focused only on children defined as 'serious' or 'persistent' 'offenders'. With desistance thinking increasingly applied across the spectrum of youth justice sanctions in England and Wales, it has become necessary to understand, and question, the relevance of desistance thinking with a much broader group of children. This is particularly pressing in light of the growing proportion of out-of-court disposals within youth justice caseloads, which comprise nearly half of supervision cases in some areas. And even among children on court-ordered community sentences, nearly 80 per cent now either have no or a minimal history of recorded offending (Youth Justice Board/MoJ, 2023). How might desistance theories apply given that most children's offending 'careers' are limited to adolescence (Moffitt, 1993) and, thus, desistance is largely normative?

Our starting point is that children's distinct needs, by virtue of their young age and ongoing development, together with their typically normative offending, raise important questions about the relevance and meaning of desistance thinking to their pathways away from crime. In light of this, our core guiding questions are:

- What helps children to move away from offending, and in what ways, if at all, does this vary by ethnicity, class and gender?
- To what extent is the concept and theorisation of desistance helpful when applied to children or does it, alternatively problematise rather than normalise children's behaviour?
- How is desistance thinking currently understood and implemented in youth justice policy and practice?
- What are the implications of the answers to these questions for youth justice theory, research, policy and practice?

The collection has been initiated by the National Association for Youth Justice (NAYJ), the only individual charity which campaigns exclusively for the rights of, and justice for, children in trouble with the law. The NAYJ believes that children who come to the attention of criminal justice agencies should be viewed individually according to their stage of development and treated as a child first and foremost (National Association for Youth Justice, 2019). The editors of this collection are all members of the NAYJ's Board of Trustees. Given that the charity is based in England and Wales, we have not attempted to give the book an international focus. However, it is likely that many of the chapters will be of international interest given that the role of desistance theory within youth justice is not restricted to a single jurisdiction.

Given the focus of the NAYJ's work, our philosophical position that children should be treated as distinct from adults, and the relative dearth of literature specific to desistance and children, the book deliberately, and unapologetically, restricts itself to discussion of individuals in conflict with the law who are under 18. In line with the ethos of the NAYJ, and international standards of children's rights, we refer throughout to these individuals as children, and the terms 'youth', 'juvenile' and 'young offender' are deliberately eschewed.

Aims of the collection

The volume aims to bring together a broad range of voices from research and practice to reflect critically on the relevance and application of desistance thinking with children. It has been a deliberate editorial decision to include a diversity of perspectives in this regard to reflect the fact that debate and evidence generation is at an early stage. As a consequence, contributors encompass *both* those who argue that desistance does not and should not apply to children, and those who contend that it does but critique its implementation and development insofar as children are concerned.

The collection is the first to explore the relevance and application of desistance theories with children. It explores the topic from multiple vantage points and through a range of highly pertinent themes. Youth justice in England and Wales lies at a pivotal stage as it attempts to employ desistance thinking in policy and practice with children. This publication aims to address the significant gap in scholarship as to how desistance should be conceptualised and is being experienced in youth justice. It seeks to advance the theorisation of desistance with children, to inform emergent desistance policy and provide a much-needed resource for youth justice practitioners.

The remainder of this opening chapter provides an overview of the existing evidence base on children and desistance through a review of the literature before describing the policy context within which desistance thinking has become central to youth justice in England and Wales. The chapter concludes by detailing the book's structure and the nature of the various contributions.

What is desistance?

'Desistance' has become so integral to the criminal justice lexicon during the current century that it may appear to require no introduction. But partly for that reason, and because the relevance of the concept for children is underexplored, references to desistance are frequently imprecise and act as shorthand for a number of explanatory models with variable implications for practice. 'Desistance' typically refers to the process by which people abstain from crime, in particular those who have an established pattern of criminal behaviour. It is widely understood as a journey rather than an event, characterised by wrong turns and false starts. For this reason, it is not easily defined or measured. For example, is it desistance if someone stops offending for a year, or shifts from serious offending to committing infrequent low-level crime? And from what point should desistance be measured? Furthermore, as Maruna (2001) has pointed out, the permanent cessation of offending can only be conclusively known posthumously (for a comprehensive discussion of such debates, see Maruna, 2001; Weaver, 2016). These are just some of the sticky questions and issues that arise in this field.

Maruna and Farrall (2004) contend that there are distinct phases to the desistance journey: primary, defined as a lull in offending; and secondary, understood as the assumption of a non-offender identity or role. This suggests a somewhat sequential process of change. More recently, McNeill (2014) has added the concept of tertiary desistance, which refers to recognition of one's change by others and accordingly integration into society. Nugent and Schinkel (2016) conceptualise these stages differently as 'act', 'identity' and 'relational' desistance. In line with this updating, Johnson and Maruna (2020, p 117) have noted that primary and secondary desistance 'likely develop together' rather than one preceding the other. Other studies have suggested that identity transformation is not necessary for cessation (Laub and Sampson, 2003, p 279; Godwin, 2022).

However, with some notable exceptions (for instance, Nugent and Schinkel, 2016), these widely used conceptualisations are largely based on research with adults. While it seems likely that there are similarities in the processes of change for children, there will inevitably be important differences too. These are explored in the course of this chapter.

Desistance and children: the evidence base

The genesis and development of desistance theories

The roots of desistance thinking can be traced back to American studies beginning in the 1940s, which sought to gather evidence on the causes of offending. These typically involved collecting data on large samples of children and continuing to do so over their life course (for instance, Gluecks and Gluecks' [1974] study of 1,000 boys). It was not until the 1980s, when some of these studies had been running for 30 years, that it was recognised that many of the study participants had significantly reduced or stopped their offending, and that considerable data had been amassed that could shed light on that phenomenon (Shapland et al, 2016, p 2). Thereafter, desistance research has become a growing area of interest, and understanding of the processes involved has developed significantly.

Early conceptualisations of desistance understood it as a natural activity correlated with ageing (Gottfredson and Hirschi, 1990) and associated physiological and psychological development (see, for example, Glueck and Glueck, 1974). This derived from evidence that offending typically begins during the teenage years, peaks between the late teens and early 20s and then rapidly decreases, a process known as the 'age–crime curve' (Graham and Bowling, 1995; McAra and McVie, 2017). Other explanations highlighted the role of agency, viewing crime and its cessation as the consequence of rational choices by those who broke the law (Cornish and Clarke, 1985). Later research focused instead on the relevance of social context to pathways away from offending. Such studies highlighted the importance of employment and family formation and consequent shifts in wider societal expectations associated with changing roles (Sampson and Laub, 1992; Laub and Sampson, 2003).

From the late 1990s, drawing on earlier social interaction theory, research began highlighting the importance of identity or cognitive change to desistance, emphasising the behavioural implications of how individuals see themselves (Maruna, 1997, 2001). A range of views have been advanced about the nature of identity change and the process by which it comes about. Maruna's (2001, p 87) research with adult ex-prisoners emphasises 'more self-reconstruction than amputation' of one's offending past: desisters exhibited 'redemption scripts', seeing themselves as essentially good persons, empowered to realise their true self, usually 'with the help of some outside force, someone who "believed in"' them. Desisters were also optimistic of their ability to control their destiny. Paternoster and Bushway (2009) propose that desistance requires that one's old identity is 'cast off'. By their account, desistance is motivated by 'a crystallisation of discontent' with offending, a desire to avoid a 'feared self', and an envisioned positive self (2009, p 1133). Grounded in adult women's narratives of desistance, Giordano et al's research (2002; see also Giordano, 2016) sees desistance as growing out of a cycle of cognitive changes – which interact with the individual's social context. These include a shift towards openness to change; exposure to 'hooks for change', which have subjective meaning for the individual; the creation of a conventional 'replacement self'; and a changed (unfavourable) perspective of offending (Giordano et al, 2002, p 1001).

Latterly, research has also drawn attention to the situational and spatial aspects of desistance, noting that stopping offending involves people spending time in different places from those in which they engaged in crime. The environmental fabric, in turn, both reflects and shapes how individuals view themselves and who they want to be (Farrall et al, 2014). While the specific emphasis on these issues has shifted over time desistance is now typically understood as interactional, such that cessation of offending in adults flows from a combination of maturation, cognitive and identity change, agency, relationships and social bonds.

Despite this evolution, there are aspects of desistance that remain underdeveloped. Most research in the field has been conducted with high-frequency offending White adult men, often post-custody, or with participants for whom an intentional resolve to change may be particularly pertinent (such as with those who have significant addiction; see, for example, Giordano, 2016). The period from the turn of the century has rightly seen growing attention, from a low baseline, to the desistance experiences of women and minoritised communities (Graham and McNeill, 2020). Desistance research with children is also underdeveloped. Interestingly, where children are the focus (see, for instance, Graham and Bowling, 1995; McIvor et al, 2004; Mulvey and Schubert, 2016; Droppelmann, 2017; McAra and McVie, 2022), there often appears to be less awareness, and citation, of the research, even within youth justice circles; findings from adult-focused research remain centre stage.

Such tendencies are perhaps understandable: lawbreaking and desistance is normative for adolescents, the vast majority of whom commit relatively minor offences and grow out of crime rapidly and without intervention (Rutherford, 1992). The study of children's desistance has therefore been seen as of questionable theoretical and policy relevance (Laub and Sampson, 2003; Kazemian, 2007). Farrall and Shapland's (2022) analysis of longitudinal data on 89 adult desisters of different ages, for instance, contended that 'there was almost no difference' in explanations for desistance by age or related factors such as length of criminal career, implying that there may be little value in exploring whether desistance is different for under 18s. Some scholars reject the application of the concept of desistance to children altogether (Case and Haines, 2020), arguing that 'desistance' is premised on a shift from an adult 'offender' identity and a long-term offending career and is thus irrelevant to children who are still, by nature, developing.

Conversely, as youth justice policy in England and Wales, and other jurisdictions (for example, Chile; Aldunate, 2022), increasingly embraces desistance thinking, it might be argued that understanding the relevance to children assumes added importance. As the NAYJ (2019, p 1) argues:

> Children are distinct from adults in important ways. Their cognitive and emotional functioning is less well developed, and they lack the fund of experience available to adults. ... Because children are continuing to develop, there is greater potential for criminal justice interventions to impair future prospects and adversely affect their identity.

Research on desistance and children

It should be acknowledged that some desistance research has focused on children or included under 18-year-olds within the sample, including several medium- to large-scale studies in England and Wales (Graham and Bowling, 1995), Scotland (McIvor et al, 2004; McAra and McVie, 2022), the United States (Mulvey and Schubert, 2016) and Chile (Droppelmann, 2017). A growing body of smaller-scale research has also provided rich insights into children's perceptions, and experiences, of desistance (Haigh, 2009; Murray, 2009; Panuccio et al, 2012; Bugnon, 2015; Nugent, 2015; Nugent and Schinkel, 2016; Johns et al, 2017; McMahon and Jump, 2018). Valuable evidence comes too from studies with young adult participants, including those undertaken by Barry (2006, 2010, 2017, 2019), Sharpe (2015), Nugent (2015) and Bottoms and Shapland (2016).

But the valuable insights this evidence provides have limitations which must be acknowledged if we are to improve understanding of children's pathways away from crime – and the relevance of desistance thinking to them. Much of the research relates to the Western world, particularly the UK and the United States, but studies which have been conducted in emerging economies (for example Bugnon, 2015; Droppelmann, 2017) suggest that children's desistance may be context dependent. Bugnon (2015), for instance, in a small-scale study of desistance among 'poverty stricken' children living in the favelas of Brazil, notes that criminality is frequently a professional activity woven into the fabric of their lives from an early age, motivated by material gain, in which they are deeply enmeshed and participate often on a daily basis. The context for children's desistance, and the implications which flow from it, is accordingly not universal but determined by factors such as socio-economic environment, cultural expectations, state provision for children and responses to crime.

The state of justice involvement is also significant (Wigzell and Bateman, 2024 forthcoming), an important consideration given that most research has focused on cohorts leaving custody or deemed 'serious or persistent offenders'. Such children are not representative of the youth justice population in England and Wales (Bateman and Wigzell, 2019). In the year ending March 2023, for instance, 54 per cent of children receiving a caution or conviction had no previous formal sanctions recorded against them (Youth Justice Board/Ministry of Justice, 2023).

Some of the qualitative studies involve small samples. This is not a criticism of such research, which often provides rich and detailed insights, but acknowledgement that this may limit the transferability of the findings to youth justice-involved children more generally. Participants are predominantly male, reflecting higher representation of boys in the youth justice system, with rare focus on the experiences of female children (for exceptions, see McIvor et al, 2004; Sharpe, 2012, 2015; Bateman et al, 2013). And there has been no consideration of ethnicity and desistance among children. Furthermore, most studies of desistance among children involve only retrospective accounts of their journeys away from offending and rarely involve follow-up as to whether desistance was sustained (with several exceptions: Mulvey and Schubert, 2016; Droppelmann, 2017; McAra and McVie, 2022).

Potential differences between adults and children and areas of uncertainty

Maturation

As noted earlier in the chapter, early desistance accounts focused on age- or maturation-based explanations for the cessation of offending. However, this vein of thought came under fire for describing the relationship between age and crime, rather than explaining the mechanisms by which age and maturation *shape* desistance (Maruna, 1997). As Sampson and Laub (1992, p 81) have argued, 'such theories fail to unpack the meaning of age'. In particular, the Gluecks' maturational reform theory was heavily criticised at the time for being tautological or circular insofar as it rests on the argument that maturation results in desistance and desistance is evidence of maturity (Bottoms and Shapland, 2016).

Research on the role of maturation in desistance has subsequently been long neglected. However, there has been renewed interest in the explanatory value of the concept with growing evidence demonstrating its significance. A consistent finding of empirical research with children and young adults is that they very often describe their shift towards desistance in terms of maturation (Graham and Bowling, 1995; McIvor et al, 2004; Beyond Youth Custody, 2017; McMahon and Jump, 2018), suggesting that children's understandings of desistance are associated with what they believe maturity to be. Mulvey and Schubert's (2016, p 135) longitudinal US study of 1,354 serious adolescent 'offenders' in two metropolitan areas in the United States provides evidence that such perceptions may have an objective foundation, since children who desisted from antisocial activity during adolescence showed significantly greater psycho-social maturity than those who did not, leading the authors to conclude that 'maturity (especially self-regulation) is an important developmental feature that accompanies the cessation of serious crime'. Farrall and Shapland (2022) have argued that 'social maturation', which they see as associated with mental and physiological functioning, may be a key variable. The transition from adolescence to adulthood status is for most children – at least in the Western world – associated with the most profound shifts in social context that they will experience in their lives. Empirically, therefore, it may be difficult to tease out differences between personal maturation and changes associated with social context.

Studies with young adults have provided valuable further insights into the dimensions of maturation. Bottoms and Shapland's (2016) Sheffield-based study with 113 young adult 'would-be desisters' found that maturation was a prominent feature in the narratives of participants, characterised by increased responsibility and improved self-control. However, they argue that it should be conceptualised as 'active maturation' to reflect that it is 'not simply an internal psychological matter [but] … continually shaped, prompted and/or inhibited by relationships with significant others' (2016, p 108). Coyle's research with 20 young adults (2019) observed that active maturation was critical to desistance journeys, but that desistance also involved a process of 'retrospective self-infantilisation' as a narrative tool that highlighted later maturity. This aligns with Maruna's suggestion that avoiding identification of bad behaviour with character traits or personality defaults is an important mechanism for maintaining a self-view of 'bad behaviours, but not bad selves' (2001, p 136) that guards against the internalisation of a criminal identity. Maturation is thus both an internal psychological and a relational process, with these two strands closely interlinked. This accords with evidence that children's experiences of relationships critically shape their emotional development and identity (Sroufe, 2005; Holmes and Slade, 2018; Brierley, 2021).

Socio-structural maturation

A long-standing focus of desistance research has been the role of the conventional social bonds associated with the transition to, and realisation of, adulthood. This includes movement away from 'delinquent' peers, family formation and employment (Sampson and Laub, 2003), or what might be termed 'socio-structural maturation' (Bateman, 2020). The evidence base paints a mixed picture. While some traditional socio-structural factors have been identified as important to desistance among this age group, these may apply differently to young men and women. The literature also suggests, perhaps unsurprisingly, that different types of socio-structural changes are likely to be associated with children's (and young adults') desistance, as distinct from older adults.

Graham and Bowling's (1995) research is the largest, and perhaps best-known, empirical study on desistance and children in England and Wales. It involved a survey of 1,721 randomly sampled 14–25-year-olds (and an additional 'booster' sample of 808 young people from minoritised communities) and life history interviews with 21 'desisters' aged 16–27 years (ten males and 11 females). The survey found that social factors reflective of the transition to adulthood – such as leaving school and home and having children – were strongly associated with desistance for young women but not for young men. Conversely, factors that were associated with young men's desistance were continuing to live at home into early adulthood, doing well at school and avoiding contact with offending peers, heavy drinking and illegal drug use. While this might suggest that desistance is more straightforward for young women, Sharpe's (2015) work with 19 young mothers aged 20–27 years has highlighted gendered barriers to desistance. She centres on the enduring stigma and intensified surveillance the young women experienced as not only former 'offenders' but also young mothers (Sharpe, 2015).

Notably, Graham and Bowling (1995) did not identify gaining employment – another characteristic of the transition to adulthood – as a significant influence on desistance for either young women or men. As the authors observe, these findings likely reflect the increasing remoteness – most clearly for young men – of meaningful opportunities to achieve adult status at the end of childhood, particularly starting work. This issue has likely only become more pronounced in the interim period. At the same time, interviews with 21 desisters suggested that where children and young adults do move away from offending, they often attribute this to meaningful activity, such as employment and voluntary work, that provides a 'sense of direction'. McMahon and Jump's (2018) study with 21 persisting and desisting children with histories of 'persistent and serious' offending, aged 13–17, echoes this finding. They reported that positive structural changes, such as education, employment and training (EET) and reparation of family relationships, play a dominant role in children's desistance (see also Paterson-Young et al, 2019, 2022). The authors also suggest that access to opportunities for positive socio-structural change may be especially important for adolescent desistance given that age and status may render teenagers less capable of exercising agency.

Both studies draw attention to the significance for children's desistance of repaired or positive relationships with parents and other family members, a finding shared by other research (Bottoms and Shapland, 2016). While supportive family relationships are widely recognised as a key mediator of desistance among adults, they may be especially central for adolescents transitioning to adulthood who are unlikely to be living independently. Conversely, the absence of such relationships might be thought relevant to explaining the over-representation of care-experienced children within custody (Day et al, 2020).

In this regard, it should be recognised that the adverse effects of de-industrialisation, and wider socio-structural inequalities, preclude opportunities to transition to adulthood (for example finding work) for some children, particularly those from deprived and minority ethnic backgrounds (Nugent and McNeill, 2016). Several scholars have argued that addressing such inequalities and structural barriers is fundamental to supporting desistance. Of particular note is Barry's (2016) empirical research with a sample of 60 justice-experienced young adults in Scotland. She argues that children offend due to a lack of 'recognition' consequent to emotional and physical neglect, abuse and societal marginalisation, including age-based and material inequalities. Barry (2016) further contends that enduring societal 'misrecognition' – that is, labelling and stigmatisation as 'offenders' (for example by potential employers) – is a key barrier to desistance as it compounds disempowerment, exclusion and marginalisation. The solution, accordingly, lies in 'transformative remedies' (Barry, 2016 p 103) that address structural barriers, marginalisation and misrepresentation.

Questions remain about how this can be achieved. Gray (2019) observes that despite the benefits of the 'Child First' approach evident in some youth justice services, practice continues to be hampered by a focus on individuals and families rather than alleviating socio-economic disadvantage. One potential solution lies in focusing on meeting children's entitlements – a concept used by the Welsh government to denote children's access to ten universal resources, including: education, training and employment, sport, health and housing, and consultation about decisions affecting them – to promote equality of opportunity and outcome (Williams and Daniel, 2021), but Gray (2019) questions whether youth justice services can work in more socially just ways when they are subject to offender management-oriented inspection and oversight frameworks. Perhaps the key message here is that desistance is not only a personal endeavour but a process wherein responsibility is shared with social agencies and society. Desistance does not just involve children making a conscious effort to change but requires that 'the society into which they wish to integrate also makes a conscious effort to welcome them. Desistance is a two-way process and must be recognised as such' (Barry, 2019, p 8).

Relationships

A consistent thread is the crucial importance of positive professional relationships in supporting children's hope and self-belief in their ability to desist from offending (Haigh, 2009; Panuccio et al, 2012; Bateman et al, 2013; Gray, 2013; Bugnon, 2015; Nugent, 2015; Beyond Youth Custody, 2017; Johns et al, 2017). In their paper on 12 'prolifically' offending adolescents in Wales, Johns et al (2017, p 18) found that a trusting supervisory relationship was perceived by children as the central factor in their movement away from crime, although intimate relationships and having a family were the 'biggest motivator'. Interview-based research with justice-involved children and young adults in the UK has found that having a worker who is felt to genuinely 'care' is a key determinant of engagement (Phoenix and Kelly, 2013) and desistance (Bateman et al, 2013; Nugent, 2015). A key theme of these latter studies is the critical role of such relationships in facilitating a sense of agency and optimism – through consistent and persistent emotional and practical support and a belief in the person's capacity to change – which in turn increases the likelihood of desistance. Fitzpatrick et al's (2015, p 179) UK-based study of personal goal aspirations among 14 boys under youth justice supervision found that prior experiences of powerlessness and victimisation resulted in significant uncertainty about the future, highlighting the 'crucial' importance of professionals in fostering agency and hope.

The relevance of professional relationships to desistance features in findings across jurisdictions. For example, Barry's (2017, 2019) comparative research with 85 children and adults aged 16–37 years in Scotland and Japan established the centrality to desistance of a respectful relationship with their supervisor for both groups. However, Japanese participants tended to emphasise social relational reasons for desistance, such as leading 'normal' lives and wanting to be accepted in social networks of family and friends, whereas Scottish participants focused on personal relations, including new partners and the responsibilities of parenthood (2017, p 11). Such findings accord with those of probation research studies, which have shown that the supervisory relationship is perceived by supervisees as the 'pivotal factor' in determining whether or not probation helps them to desist (Leibrich 1994; Rex, 1999; Healy, 2012). In this context, children's age-based vulnerability and marginalisation – notwithstanding the significance of their agency – combined with their formative stage of development, may mean that professional relationships are especially important for desistance in this age group. This may be particularly true for disadvantaged children who have fewer sources of relational support on which to draw (Day et al, 2020).

Professional relationships will not however deliver desistance in isolation. Although practitioners can motivate, and support, efforts to desist, children determine whether or not they give up offending. Moreover, social networks play just as an important, or greater, role (Farrall, 2002; McNeill, 2006; McNeill, 2009). Professional relationships do not moreover act 'as a substitute for addressing structural inequalities in society' (Burnett and McNeill, 2005, p 234) but instead underpin helping criminal justice intervention (McNeill et al, 2005).

Identity

There is a broad spectrum of views about the place and importance of identity shifts in desistance for under 18s (Haigh, 2009; Murray, 2009; Bugnon, 2015; Nugent, 2015; Beyond Youth Custody, 2017; Droppelmann, 2017; Johns et al, 2017; McMahon and Jump, 2018). Some studies have placed significant emphasis on the importance of identity shifts in the desistance process. As a case in point, McMahon and Jump (2018, p 9) reported that desisters 'explicitly discussed shedding "offending identities" and developing new, prosocial non-criminal identities'. Further, desisters had more hopeful narratives and underlined the role of agency in change, although, the authors note, the constraints of their life stage may render children less able to exercise it. The sample of desisters was however small (six children), and by focusing on children with significant offending backgrounds, and categorising them as either desisters or persisters, the study may have missed those who fall in-between (Maruna, 2001); those who desist without professional supervision, as frequently occurs (McNeill and Graham, 2020); or those with limited criminal justice involvement (Farrall and Shapland, 2022). Children with ambiguous or fragile identities, or who do not have entrenched offending identities (and thus move away from crime without support), are overlooked and little understood.

Another English study, involving interviews with around 100 young custody-leavers aged between 14 and 25, found that some described a 'very clear' shift to a 'new sense of self'. Yet, many were 'resistant' to the idea of 'shifts in identity', and others focused on the positive impact of significant relationships (Beyond Youth Custody, 2017, pp 18–23). However, participants often described the importance of maturation, discontent with criminal justice involvement and 'imagined future selves' (Paternoster and Bushway, 2009) in the desistance process, indicating that cognitive change played some part (Beyond Youth Custody, 2017, pp 18–23). Similarly, Haigh's (2009, p 308) Australian study of desistance among 25 young people (aged 14–24 years) found that 'subtle shifts in *their* interpretation' of their lives underlay all participants' attempts to desist such that external challenges to 'doing crime' and opportunities to change became 'relevant'.

In contrast, other research has suggested a more complex picture of the role of identity shifts in children's desistance pathways. Most recent is Droppelmann's (2017) short longitudinal study in Chile, which involved surveying a sample of 334 late adolescent 'offenders' aged 16–20 years at the beginning and end of a one-year period (waves 1 and 2) and interviews with a sub-sample of 35 young people at wave 2. A key finding of the research was that the participants did not adhere to the binary categories of persister or desister; instead, many 'oscillated' between crime and conformity. Forty per cent of those who were desisters in wave 1 were offending again at wave 2, while 31 per cent of those offending at wave 1 were desisting at wave 2. She further noted that desisters were often ambivalent about giving up crime, while persisters often demonstrated conformist values and aspirations (although slightly less so than desisters): '[F]or several desisters crime can always remain (or at least for extended periods of time) a possible alternative and for some persisters crime can co-exist with internal dispositions towards conformity' (Droppelmann, 2017). This was reflected in issues of identity: 50 per cent of persisters did not see themselves as 'delinquents', and 74 per cent did not see themselves as 'offenders' in the long term. Rather, they tended to construct a self that aligned with their future aspirational self, even if it was out of kilter with their current behaviour to 'maintain a current self that made sense for inconsistent forms of being at the present, in order to align themselves with their future conformist aspirations'.

Droppelmann's (2017) findings highlight the complex relationship between identity and behaviour, indicating that children can simultaneously be significantly involved in offending and not see themselves as 'offenders' or regard this as only a partial aspect of their identity. There are notable commonalities here with the findings of Bottoms and Shapland's (2011) study with 113 repeat offending young adult males in Sheffield. The majority did not perceive themselves as an offender, but importantly many acknowledged this was how they were regarded by others, for which they often felt shame and regret. The authors nonetheless observed that young men's efforts to live in line with conformist values entailed agency and cognitive transformation, indicating that desistance may not presuppose an offender identity, but cognitive change – and no longer being regarded by others as an offender – remains of particular relevance.

Cathy Murray's (2009) research with adolescents in Scotland offers some valuable insights and reflections on the practical implications in this regard. She sought to understand how both 'resisters' and 'desisters' maintained their avoidance of offending. Her research involved secondary analysis of interviews with 112 young people (62 resisters and 50 desisters) and primary research comprising peer-led focus groups with 52 resisters (aged 14–18, involving 28 girls and 24 boys). Of particular relevance to the discussion here, she identified three types of desister: the 'reformed' (who tell 'desistance tales' to explain their move away from offending), 'quasi-resisters' (who reject an offender identity) and 'desisters on the margins' (who are ambivalent about desisting and have paused rather than ceased) (Murray, 2009). Murray contends that for the latter two desister types, identity transformation does not apply. There are arguably also questions about the first group of reformer desisters because their offending may have been too short-lived or low level for an 'offending identity' to have been formed. However, identity remains a relevant consideration when working with such children: she interprets the quasi-resisters' denial or minimisation of their offending as a form of 'identity work' that enables them to retain an identity as a 'non offender'. She argues that interventions aimed at making children take responsibility for their offending are potentially counter-productive and advises that interventions may be best focused on their futures rather than getting them to acknowledge past crimes.

There are further links with the findings of Bugnon's (2015) life history interviews with 12 desisting young people aged 16–20 in two Brazilian cities. She identifies three different desistance pathways among the sample, which are related to their experience of offending and the system. These are the 'survivors', who have little social and human capital but whose desistance grows out of a strong emotional bond with their probation officer; the 'exemplary youths', so labelled by the system because they maximise the rehabilitative opportunities offered to them, in reflection of their pre-existing social and human capital, and desist through transferring their skills to conventional activities; and those who experience the system as labelling and desist despite its negative influences. Notably, identity transformation is only evident in the desistance narratives of the 'survivors', whose 'special relations' with their probation officer result in powerful identification with the system's values. However, identity work is likely to be relevant to the desistance pathways of the third group too, who somehow manage to sidestep the labels which others seek to attribute. Nevertheless, Bugnon contends that desistance in the 'survivor' form is likely to be 'much more infrequent and risky than desistance by skill transfer', noting that the future of young people in this 'group' remained 'extremely uncertain' because of the very limited resources available to them outside of the system.

Taken together, the research suggests that identity change may play a differing role in children's desistance pathways. It is worth noting that this finding is not limited to children and young adults but has been reported in some longitudinal studies with adult probationers (Farrall et al, 2014) including women (Godwin, 2022). Farrall and Shapland (2022, p 534) found that although explanations for desistance appeared to be age-invariant, individuals with limited criminal careers were an exception to this since they were much more likely to explain their offending as a 'one-off' or a 'phase' and 'did not see themselves as having a continuing identity as an offender'. Godwin (2022) has subsequently questioned whether the centrality of identity change in desistance has perhaps been overstated by the focus on high-frequency adult male desisters. Such findings suggest the importance of undertaking desistance research with diverse samples, in terms of age, gender, ethnicity, as well as by criminal justice involvement and offending profile. They also raise questions about the benefits of a practice focus on 'identity' and might indicate instead the value of nurturing the child's healthy long-term development (of which identity is just one part) and offering them the opportunities and support to realise it rather than trying to affect a shift (Wigzell and Bateman, 2024 forthcoming).

Resilience and desistance

The notion of desistance, as applied to children, is sometimes criticised on the basis of its negative ambition in the form of the cessation of offending. This focus tends to reinforce perceptions that the principal objective of youth justice intervention should be the reduction of recidivism – as is indeed implied by the statutory aim for the youth justice system, introduced by the Crime and Disorder Act 1998, of preventing offending rather than the long-term wellbeing and healthy development of children in conflict with the law (Bateman, 2020). Yet a genuinely Child First perspective (Case and Hazel, 2023), as currently espoused by the Youth Justice Board (YJB) and embedded in the latest iteration of national standards (Ministry of Justice/ Youth Justice Board, 2019), would entail a prioritisation of such wider outcomes. (The adoption of a Child First vision receives more attention later in this chapter.) In this context, a number of commentators have pointed to the merits of resilience as an alternative, or an adjunct, to that of desistance (see, for instance, Fitzpatrick, 2011; Robinson, 2016).

Fitzpatrick (2011, p 221) argues that while the two concepts have tended to develop separately, 'within different disciplinary contexts', there is considerable overlap, and there are some similarities in the strategies which they imply for working with children in conflict with the law. Resilience research has developed as part of academic debates in social work circles, and childcare in particular, and is now firmly embedded in practitioner narratives in those fields as an evidence base that attempts to understand why some children raised in adverse circumstances appear to have much better outcomes than others. A feature which the resilience literature shares with desistance is that there is considerable debate about how it should be defined, with one author terming it 'a slippery concept' (Houston, 2010, p 358). Early researchers tended to associate resilience with a set of qualities residing in the individual child that enabled them to counter risk (Gilligan, 2001). More recently, however, the focus has shifted to understanding resilience as a process 'encompassing positive adaptation within the context of significant adversity' (Luthar et al, 2000, p 544). Although the contours of the resilience process are delineated differently according to understandings of what constitutes positive adaptation in various contexts (Robinson, 2016), the potential parallels with, and the relevance for, the process of desistance are readily apparent.

Both resilience and desistance mark a shift away from a concentration on risk and, in this sense, both are future oriented (Fitzpatrick, 2011). Conversely, there is a sense in which resilience is conceptually related to risk, since it is defined in terms of better outcomes than might be expected given the levels of adversity which children have experienced (Rutter, 2012), whereas the relationship between offending and vulnerability, while commonly present, is empirical; it is not part of what desistance means. Children's agency, and perceptions of self, central to discussions of desistance, are increasingly recognised as features of resilience, as understanding of the latter has evolved from a focus on children's inherent qualities as protective factors to acknowledging the dynamic nature of pathways to healthy development (Patterson and Kelleher, 2005). Trusting relationships have also been identified as contributing to desistance and resilience (Taylor, 2006). The notion of tertiary desistance equally has a counterpart in resilience theory, which, in some elaborations, places considerable emphasis on social context and the ability or willingness of wider society to provide resources that facilitate positive longer-term outcomes for children surviving adversity (Ungar et al, 2008, cited in Fitzpatrick, 2011).

These similarities should however not be thought to imply that the concepts are interchangeable. Desistance is measured in terms of behavioural change since it logically implies a reduction in offending; resilience on the other hand is manifested through children doing better than might be anticipated, whether or not their behaviour changes (Fitzpatrick, 2011). Nonetheless, the commonalities might be sufficient to suggest that both resilience and desistance rely on the identification of similar mechanisms to achieving the respective desired ends. In the context of discussion of the application of desistance theory to children, and misgivings in some quarters about the continued focus on children's offending which this involves, resilience might accordingly be thought to widen the aims of legitimate youth justice practice to promote children's healthy development, which might reduce criminal behaviour as a by-product of that endeavour.

The youth justice turn to desistance

As noted earlier in this chapter, much of the evidence base for desistance derives from research with adults, but this has not precluded an increased orientation on desistance principles to inform youth justice practice from at least 2014 onwards (Wigzell, 2021). This shift represented a radical departure from reliance on what is frequently referred to as the 'risk' paradigm, a set of theoretical assumptions whose precepts had dominated youth justice discourse in England and Wales from the mid-1990s onwards. The paradigm sought to identify the risk factors that underpinned the child's offending and 'implement prevention methods designed to counteract them' (Farrington, 2007, p 606). Its centrality to youth justice practice was assured by the YJB through, among other mechanisms, the roll out of a mandatory assessment framework from April 2000, in the form of ASSET, which purported to operationalise risk theory (Baker, 2005); a series of Key Elements of Effective Practice (KEEP), standardised performance measures designed, it has been suggested, to 'circumvent the threat of the excessive discretion' associated with more welfare-inclined practice (Haines and Case, 2015, p 132); and the 'Scaled Approach', introduced in 2009, which prescribed that the nature and intensity of intervention should be linked to the assessed risk of reoffending (Bateman, 2011).

Although protective factors were theoretically part of the risk equation, their role was clearly subsidiary. The KEEP for 'Assessment, planning interventions and supervision', for instance, mentioned 'risk' 66 times but contained just nine references to protective factors (see Hampson, 2023, p 204). ASSET required practitioners to ascribe a numeric score to an array of 12 dynamic risk factors to generate an overall measure of risk of reoffending; protective factors were confined to a single 'evidence' box and attracted no quantitative value (Youth Justice Board, nd). Protective factors similarly played no part in determining the intensity of intervention under the Scaled Approach, the guidance for which contained no mention of such factors (Youth Justice Board, 2010).

To ensure consistent implementation, the YJB developed a range of dedicated training programmes including a Youth Justice Professional Certificate in Effective Practice and a Youth Justice Foundation Degree. These were designed to embed risk thinking into the youth justice workforce in a manner which, it has been argued, amounted to 'a hard schooling in risk' for practitioners (Hampson, 2023, p 304).

Over time, the risk paradigm was subjected to a sustained, and largely cogent, academic critique for a variety of shortcomings, which also served to highlight some of the advantages of the desistance literature by comparison. Conceptualising risk as a quantifiable factor reduces 'complex and multi-faceted' aspects of children's lives to a single statistic that fails to acknowledge children's individual experiences of, negotiations with and resistance to their environment (Case, 2023, p 59). It thereby treats children as 'crash test dummies' whose fate is largely determined by the risks they embody rather than as active individuals with a capacity to make choices, albeit that their options may be constrained by their socio-economic position. In reality, 'the active human agent may be a crucial determinant of any risk factor ... outcome' (Case and Haines, 2009, p 20). Moreover, the reductionist conceptualisation of children's realities entails that assessments of risk are frequently poor predictors of further offending (Armstrong, 2004; Bateman, 2011).

Risk-led interventions prioritise professional assessments over children's understanding of their own circumstances and the meanings they attach to them. As a consequence, the content of supervision is imposed on children with little consideration of their wishes or aspirations and without regard to how interventions will be subjectively received. In so doing, they undermine the potential for establishing meaningful engagement between children and professionals, despite long-standing evidence that relationships are pivotal to successful outcomes of youth justice intervention (Trotter, 2020). A focus on risk, moreover, directs practitioners' attention to correcting supposed, historical or current pathologies in the child rather than to the provision of future-oriented support and promoting strengths (Haines and Case, 2015). At the same time, because the risk paradigm targets the posited deficiencies of individual children rather than understanding their lawbreaking as a normalised response to the environment within which they grow up (Johns et al, 2017), it inevitably reinforces negative perceptions of children in trouble (Case, 2023) and locates 'the responsibility (blame) ... with the young person and their inability to resist risk factors, rather than examining broader issues such as ... social class, poverty, unemployment, social deprivation, neighbourhood disorganisation, ethnicity' (Haines and Case, 2015, p 103). In the process, it side-lines aspects of tertiary desistance highlighted earlier in the chapter and excuses authorities who have neglected to provide the necessary commitment, and resources, to tackle social inequality; 'responsibilisation' of children accordingly absolves agencies who have failed to provide requisite levels of support to those most at risk of criminal justice involvement (Bateman, 2020).

Criticism from academia was given additional impetus by practitioner concerns that ASSET was unwieldy and formulaic, and in 2010 the YJB announced a review of the assessment framework with the endorsement of the newly elected Coalition government. According to a recent insider account, by a previous Chief Executive of the YJB, the latter favoured a 'much less prescriptive approach to assessment', while senior figures at the YJB, increasingly influenced by desistance theory, were persuaded of the merits of strengths-based responses to children in conflict with the law (Drew, 2023, p 155). AssetPlus, which was rolled out on a phased basis to replace ASSET from 2014, aimed to incorporate desistance thinking into youth justice assessments. The YJB's rationale for the change made reference to the importance of identifying children's strengths and involving children and their families in the assessment process, although identification of risk was retained as an element that could not be 'completely ignored', albeit that it should 'be balanced alongside consideration of a young person's needs, goals and strengths' (Baker, 2014, p 5).

In 2016, HM Inspectorate of Probation (HMIP, 2016), which hitherto had been wedded to the risk paradigm, undertook a thematic inspection of desistance practice within youth offending teams (YOTs), a clear organisational acknowledgement of the adoption of desistance thinking among youth justice policy makers. The inspection explored the extent to which youth justice services were effective across eight different domains identified by the Inspectorate as being important in supporting children's desistance (HMIP, 2016):

- effective relationships and evidence of genuine collaborative working;
- engagement with wider social contexts, including family, peers and educational settings;
- management of 'diversity needs';
- effectiveness in addressing structural barriers;
- creation of opportunities for change and community integration;
- motivating children;
- addressing children's sense of identity and self-worth; and
- constructive use of restorative approaches.

The recognition of the importance of desistance to youth justice practice has subsequently been incorporated into the framework for youth justice inspections, although the influence of risk thinking has not, from this perspective at least, been excised. Indeed, in the latest inspection standards, effective from July 2021, references to risk continue to outnumber those to desistance (HMIP, 2021). Perhaps more significantly, within the rules and guidance documentation to assist inspectors to make judgements in relation to those standards, risk is mentioned more than three times as frequently as desistance, suggesting continued ambivalence on the part of the Inspectorate as to the extent to which the latter has supplanted the former rather than being appended to it (HMIP, 2022).

Child First and desistance

More recently, the youth justice policy landscape has shifted dramatically through the adoption by the YJB of 'Child First', 'a guiding principle and strategy for understanding children who offend and for shaping youth justice responses to this offending' (Case and Hazel, 2023, p 1). The principle that children in conflict with the law should be viewed as children first and offenders second had appeared in the All Wales Youth Offending Strategy as early as 2004 (Case and Hazel, 2023), but it did not extend to England until a government-commissioned review of youth justice by Charlie Taylor, published in 2016. This called for 'a shift in the way society, including central and local government, thinks about youth justice so that we see the child first and the offender second' (Taylor, 2016, p 3). The government's response acknowledged the need for reform to 'punish crime' but failed to endorse the review's philosophical position (Ministry of Justice, 2016, p 3). However, Taylor was appointed as chair of the YJB the following year, and while he was in that role, the Board committed itself to a 'Child First' model, first articulated in its Strategic Plan, published in 2018 (Youth Justice Board, 2018), a far cry from its original objectives which included the aspiration that children who offend should be 'identified and dealt with without delay, with punishment proportionate to the seriousness and frequency of offending' (Youth Justice Board, 2002, p 36).

To support the new framework, revised national standards were published in 2019 (Ministry of Justice/Youth Justice Board, 2019), followed by updated case management guidance in 2022. The former document set out four tenets of the Child First vision, subsequently expanded, as follows:

1. Prioritise the best interests of children recognising their particular needs, capacities, rights and potential. All work is child-focused, developmentally informed, acknowledges structural barriers and meets responsibilities towards children.
2. Promote children's individual strengths and capacities to develop their pro-social identity for sustainable desistance, leading to safer communities and fewer victims. All work is constructive and future-focused, built on supportive relationships that empower children to fulfil their potential and make positive contributions to society.
3. Encourage children's active participation, engagement and wider social inclusion. All work is a meaningful collaboration with children and their carers.
4. Promote a childhood removed from the justice system, using pre-emptive prevention, diversion and minimal intervention. All work minimises criminogenic stigma from contact with the system. (Youth Justice Board, 2021, pp 10–11)

There is explicit reference to desistance, and elements of desistance thinking are evident through the emphasis on strengths-based and future-focused intervention, supportive relationships and the promotion of pro-social identity, empowerment, engagement and participation. But it might equally be contended that Child First goes beyond desistance in important respects by prioritising the best interests of children, requiring that the work is child-focused, meets responsibilities towards children and enables them to fulfil their potential. Most commentators appear to assume that Child First implies, and is to some extent coterminous with, desistance (see, for instance, the contributors to Case and Hazel's (2023) recent collection on Child First). However, Stephen Case and Kevin Haines (2020, p 12), two of the most influential proponents of the Child First model, eschew the notion of desistance, contending that the concept cannot be applied to children and that Child First does not rely on it, since children are 'still growing, physically, mentally, emotionally for the first time so they cannot desist, they can only "become"'. Gray and Smith (2019) argue, in a slightly different vein, that desistance falls short of a genuinely Child First approach because, like the risk factor paradigm before it, it tends to prescribe individualised responses, such as promoting shifts in identity, to what are predominantly structural problems and imputes responsibility to children that is inconsistent with their age and social position. Wigzell (2021, p 14), on the other hand, suggests that a 'Child First desistance' may be possible.

Faltering desistance practice

Given that desistance within youth justice settings is in its infancy, relatively little is known about the extent to which it has been embedded in practice or the manner of its implementation. For the same reason, one would anticipate that some early teething problems would be encountered given the radical nature of the shift from one paradigm to another. The roll out of desistance will inevitably be in tension with, and have to overcome, what Williams (1997, p 121) calls 'residual' culture: assumptions, working practices and traditions associated with the risk paradigm that have become deeply embedded over time. The emerging evidence base suggests there is still some way to go before youth justice practice could be described as fully informed by desistance theory, let alone consistent with a Child First ethos (Wigzell, 2021).

HMIP's (2016) thematic review of desistance concluded that while there were pockets of effective youth justice desistance practice, the findings overall were disappointing. There was some evidence that children were being supported to address structural obstacles to desistance and there was a recognition, on the part of professionals and children alike, of the importance of trusting relationships to the desistance process. But children also reported that interventions frequently did not meet their needs and were critical of formal offending behaviour programmes, which, in general, they found unhelpful. Relationships with case managers were not always of the desired quality, and children complained of frequent changes of supervisor. Although self-assessment tools were completed in the majority of cases, evidence that these accurately reflected children's views was lacking, and children were not routinely involved in supervision planning.

While practitioners were for the most part aware of the concept of desistance, many had received little training on the topic and manifested a limited understanding of the theoretical underpinnings and implications for practice. Indeed, many case managers appeared to equate desistance practice with offence-focused work, suggesting that cultural hangovers from the risk paradigm were influential in determining the nature of intervention. This was, in some instances, reinforced through pressure from management to deliver such programmes, frequently at the expense of developing high-quality relationships (HMIP, 2016).

Hampson's research with youth justice practitioners in Wales confirms the general tenor of these findings. Her analysis of assessments, following the introduction of the revised AssetPlus framework, suggested that while

> plenty of positives and strengths were mentioned in passing … (198 identified by the researcher across all cases, constituting a mean average of over 14 each), these were not adequately reflected in 'factors for desistance' (mean average of under 3 per case, but with a median of 2 and a mode of 1; range 0–7). (Hampson, 2018, p 27)

Where positives were recorded, they were frequently tempered by obstacles to desistance. Almost twice as many negative factors were identified as strengths; moreover, they were frequently repeated in different sections of the assessment. As a consequence, positives were lost, and assessments were overwhelmingly deficit-focused. The 'Foundations for change' section, which invites comment on the opportunities within the community to support the child towards desistance, was frequently left empty or simply listed local agencies with no analysis of what support could be provided or how it would promote desistance. Feedback from practitioners acknowledged the difficulties of working in accord with desistance given that youth justice practice was deeply imbued with risk thinking. Ironically, given the criticism emerging from HMIP's thematic inspection, Hampson (2018, p 30) notes that subsequent inspections 'appeared to virtually ignore desistance as a pertinent methodology to be encouraged in YOTs'. Only two of 20 which had been published in the intervening period made any reference to desistance at all; an ongoing focus on risk reduction and the delivery of offence-focused work continued to dominate inspectors' judgements of effectiveness. Hampson suggests that such difficulties are exacerbated by the inspection framework and AssetPlus highlighting different aspects of desistance practice: the latter emphasises personal goals but does not invite reflection on trusting supervisory relationships; conversely, the Inspectorate stressed the importance of relationships but did not consider the significance of personal goals. In later writing, Hampson (2023) notes the continued centrality of risk thinking to the inspection process, which attempts to balance risk- and strengths-based modes of delivery. The 'blended approach', she argues, in fact leads to incongruity, undermining attempts to introduce a Child First ethos into service delivery given the importance attached to securing positive inspection ratings (Hampson, 2023, p 310).

Day's (2023) research also highlights a tension between HMIP's focus on risk and the YJB's Child First vision, a tension which continues to be reflected in front-line practice. Her analysis of practitioner perspectives confirms the ongoing influence of a risk adverse culture and the perceived benefits of offending behaviour work, even though this tended to be framed as 'negative stuff' that could be done early in the intervention to 'get it out of the way' (Day, 2023, p 66). While practitioners were aware that the introduction of AssetPlus was intended to stimulate a paradigm shift towards the adoption of a desistance approach, there was a consensus that changing paperwork was, in isolation, insufficient to address long-standing working practices and assumptions that tended to see, and assess, children in conflict with the law through a risk lens.

A recent analysis of local youth justice plans reveals a range of 'complex and sometimes contradictory' responses to the increased localised discretion available to youth justice services and the competing demands of different models of delivery. The authors discern evidence of a more child welfare-oriented focus than allowed by New Labour's 'tough on crime' philosophy but acknowledge that the language of "risk" is still alive and well in plans organised around principles of "targeting" interventions, based on assessments of the future likelihood of offending by identified young people' (Smith and Gray, 2019, p 566). While the analysis does not purport to ascertain the extent to which desistance principles infuse youth justice provision, the authors note that cessation of offending is a priority even for services that align themselves with a Child First ethos. The extent to which this priority involves adherence to the lessons derived from the desistance literature is unclear.

Where next for desistance and children? Concluding thoughts

A number of related themes emerge from this discussion. Desistance thinking has become increasingly important in narratives around how youth crime should be understood and how appropriate mechanisms for responding to it should be framed. Indeed, the centrality of the concept of desistance to youth justice, at least in England and Wales, is widely accepted, and, with few exceptions, the adoption of desistance as a functional replacement to the risk paradigm has gone largely unchallenged. At the same time, given that desistance theory encompasses a range of different – albeit overlapping – perspectives, each generating divergent implications for policy and practice, this paradigm shift, while it has often been described, has attracted remarkably little critical analysis.

It is of course early days. It may be too soon to assess the longer-term impact of the introduction of AssetPlus and the associated endorsement of youth justice practice formulated around desistance principles. A number of things are however clear. The finer nuances of applying desistance thinking to children have not been fully debated or thought through. The consequent lack of clarity is manifested in a lack of consistency in messaging emanating from the YJB and HMIP. Policy is accordingly not necessarily aligned to expectations of inspection, leading to a lack of coherence at best and confusion at worst. The relationship between desistance and Child First has yet to be fully articulated, leading in many quarters to an assumption that the two are interchangeable. Knowledge of desistance thinking among youth justice practitioners is uneven, and youth justice practice has yet to abandon all the trappings of risk-focused assumptions. Yet there has been limited consideration of whether, and in what ways, these two radically different approaches might be reconciled.

In our view, these conclusions highlight the relevance of the current book and the importance of stimulating increased understanding among the youth justice community of the complexities of introducing desistance models to working with children. We do not pretend that the collection provides answers to all of the questions posed in this introductory chapter, but we hope that it will help to begin the process of identifying where critical engagement is required to elicit those answers by exposing, and delineating the nature of, the (potentially) contested terrain.

Structure of the book

This edited collection is divided into three distinct but overlapping parts, with Part I containing chapters that consider and critique the relevance of desistance to children from a theoretical and conceptual perspective; Part II containing chapters that examine the socio-structural dimensions of desistance; and Part III containing chapters on the application of desistance thinking with children.

Part I: Theoretical and conceptual perspectives on desistance and children

Part I contains chapters that consider and critique the relevance of desistance to children from a theoretical and conceptual perspective. The opening chapter in Part I, Chapter 2, offers a critical analysis of the interplay between Child First and desistance by examining the potential and utility of the developing pro-social identity for positive child outcomes tenet as a 'theory of change' for Child First more generally and for its pursuit of desistance outcomes specifically. It examines the concepts of identity 'shift' and identity 'development' within Child First and whether tractional notions of desistance are applicable for children. Chapter 3 argues understanding child and youth temporalities allows for the development of appropriate responses to children in conflict with the law. Drawing on Bronfenbrenner's social ecological *chronosystem* and Moten's notion of *fugitivity*, this chapter explores desistance from the perspective that desistance is experience beyond and outside of the child's experience. It concludes that desistance frameworks have the potential to problematise children, which can limit growth and becoming. Chapter 4 offers a critique of desistance thinking in accordance with theory and practice with children in the criminal justice system. This critique is levelled at desistance as a theory and to the application of desistance thinking in practice with children subject to the criminal justice system. It covers individualism in desistance thinking, the role of social and environmental factors, retrospection in desistance thinking, absence of evidence and, more broadly, whether desistance theory is actually a theory.

Part II: The socio-structural dimensions of desistance

Part II contains chapters that directly and/or indirectly examine the socio-structural dimensions of desistance. The opening chapter in Part II explores the stigmatisation of working-class young women with a criminalised past. It argues that welfare retrenchment and conditionality, criminal records disclosure requirements and degrading cultural stereotypes create a harsh climate for girls and young women. This creates challenges for girls and young women who experience extra-legal judgement across state, welfare and health institutions, which, in turn, impedes opportunities and engagement with social and educational support. The chapter concludes by discussing the policy implications of this harsh climate, with recommendations for improving support. Further examining the experiences of girls and young women in the criminal justice system, Chapter 6 explores the roles of desistance in supporting care-experienced girls, including an exploration of the reasons care-experienced girls may be at risk of involvement in criminal activity and professionals' views on the obstacles facing care-experienced girls. It considers the impact of wider social responses to girls' experience, including the role of discrimination, stigmatisation and experiences of harm and victimisation in influencing behaviour. It concludes that supporting children in care with desistance is the responsibility of all relevant agencies.

Chapter 7 examines the experiences of Black and mixed-heritage boys in the community and criminal justice system. It explores the issues facing Black and mixed-heritage boys, including an exploration of the alternative types of provisions available for Black and mixed-heritage boys who are excluded from school. This leads to recommendations for developing strategies and approaches to investment in social, educational and psycho-social capital to provide attainable and sustainable support.

Chapter 8 examines the spiritual dimension of the whole person and recognises the innate power and potential of faith in the process of giving up crime. It acknowledges the role of the maturation process in helping children transition to adulthood, drawing on interactionist and situational theories. It also makes some recommendations to both policy makers and practitioners about ways to manage the unique challenges of considering faith with children and young people compared to adults, how to better engage with faith issues as a legitimate and positive desistance factor, the need to effectively link with faith communities as sources of support and the need for greater faith literacy and training to overcome potential biases, misperceptions and misunderstandings.

Part III: The application of desistance thinking to children

Part III contains chapters that directly and/or indirectly focus on the application of desistance thinking with children. The opening chapter in Part III, Chapter 9, examines desistance in terms of the conceptualisation, barriers and enablers. It examines the role of the YJB desistance model in creating clarity, or confusion, for the YOTs delivering services. It draws on the analysis of feedback from YOT practitioners following the delivery of specific training to inform recommendations for how the youth justice sector could adapt to conceptualise and operationalise desistance in youth justice. Chapter 10 offers further insight into relationship-based practice, with emphasis on the application of arts-based interventions with children in the youth justice system. It utilises a new theoretical model to explain how arts-based participatory projects can help children develop skills that promote agency. The development and application of desistance thinking and practice with children is not simply reliant on the development of adequate interventions but requires an understanding of the relationship dynamics between children and professionals in the youth justice system.

Chapter 11 examines the application of participatory approaches in youth justice, with emphasis on empirical evidence. It builds on limited research and theory on peer-led practices in youth justice including how and why peer-led practices can empower children and accumulate social bonds. Chapter 12 offers a reflection on relationship-based working with children in conflict with the law. It draws on empirical research and professional experience to examine the meaning of desistance in youth justice, with a focus on the relationships between children and adult professionals. Through the application of a reflective lens, this chapter concludes by considering how theories of trauma, dependency and professional approaches translate into practice. Chapter 13 offers a reflection on desistance from a youth justice worker. It considers the role of court orders on children's self-perception and the perception of youth justice practitioners as 'agents of social control'. It examines the youth justice practitioners' role in helping children navigate their identities, with emphasis on building relationships, reframing identities and promoting desistance. Building relationships and relationship-based working has a pivotal role in supporting children in conflict with the law, an area explored in the preceding chapter.

Finally, Chapter 14 explores the notion that adolescent desistance can be supported through psychological strategies to strengthen morality and associated emotions, including empathy, guilt and shame. It draws on a detailed literature review of moral emotions interventions and provides an in-depth description of one such intervention – The Compass Project, a novel morality-strengthening programme – which was piloted and subject to a Randomised Controlled Trial (RCT) with a sample of 11–17-year-olds in Cambridge. While analyses of the RCT data could not be undertaken at the time of writing, the chapter argues that such programmes offer clear potential to support morality and emotional development, and in turn desistance. Related to this, it offers the opinion that labelling children and pathologising their offending behaviour is not beneficial in achieving desistance.

References

Armstrong, D. (2004) 'A risky business? Research, policy, governmentality and youth offending', *Youth Justice*, 4(2): 100–16.

Baker, K. (2005) 'Assessment in youth justice: professional discretion and the use of Asset', *Youth Justice*, 5(2): 106–22.

Baker, K. (2014) 'AssetPlus rationale', London: Youth Justice Board.

Barry, M. (2006) *Youth Offending in Transition: The Search for Social Recognition*, Abingdon: Routledge.

Barry, M. (2010) 'Promoting desistance among young people', in W. Taylor, R. Earle and R. Hester (eds) *Youth Justice Handbook: Theory, Policy and Practice*, Cullompton: Willan Publishing, pp 158–67.

Barry, M. (2016) 'On the cusp of recognition: using critical theory to promote desistance among young offenders', *Theoretical Criminology*, 20(1): 91–106.

Barry, M. (2017) 'Young offenders' views of desistance in Japan: a comparison with Scotland', in J. Liu, M. Travers and L.Y.C. Chang (eds) *Comparative Criminology in Asia*, Cham: Springer International, pp 119–29.

Barry, M. (2019) 'A comparison of Scottish and Japanese young people's views of what works to reduce offending', *Confederation of European Probation*, 4(2), Available from: https://www.cep-probation.org/wp-content/uploads/2019/01/VOL-4.2-Scottish-and-Japanese-Young-Peoples-Views-FINAL.pdf

Bateman, T. (2011) 'Punishing poverty: the Scaled Approach and youth justice practice', *The Howard Journal of Crime and Justice*, 50(2): 171–83.

Bateman, T. (2020) 'The state of youth justice 2020', London: NAYJ, Available from: https://thenayj.org.uk/cmsAdmin/uploads/state-of-youth-justice-2020-final-sep20.pdf

Bateman, T. and Wigzell, A. (2019) 'Exploring recent trends in youth justice reconvictions: a challenge to the complexity thesis', *Youth Justice*, 20(3): 252–71.

Bateman, T., Melrose, M. and Brodie, I. (2013) '"Nothing's really that hard, you can do it": agency and fatalism; the resettlement needs of girls in custody', Luton: University of Bedfordshire.

Beyond Youth Custody (2017) 'Lessons from youth in focus: research report', London: Beyond Youth Custody, Available from: http://www.beyondyouthcustody.net/wp-content/uploads/Lessons-from-Youth-in-Focus-Research-Report.pdf

Bottoms, A. and Shapland, J. (2016) 'Learning to desist in early adulthood: the Sheffield Desistance Study', in J. Shapland, S. Farrall and A. Bottoms (eds) *Global Perspectives on Desistance: Reviewing What We Know and Looking to the Future*, Abingdon: Routledge, pp 99–125.

Brierley, A. (2021) *Connecting with Young People in Trouble: Risk, Relationships and Lived Experience*, Hook: Waterside Press.

Bugnon, G. (2015) 'Desistance from crime in Brazil: the impact of experience with the world of crime and the juvenile justice system', *Penal Issues*, July 2015, Available from: PI_2015_07.pdf (cesdip.fr)

Burnett, R. and McNeill, F. (2005) 'The place of the officer–offender relationship in assisting offenders to desist from crime', *Probation Journal*, 52(3): 221–42.

Carmona Aldunate, R.J. (2022) 'A new dawn? Exploring the Chilean youth justice system's underlying philosophies and principles through the lens of the children first approach', unpublished Master of Philosophy thesis, University of Cambridge.

Case, S. (2023) 'Challenging the risk paradigm: children first, positive youth justice', in S. Case and N. Hazel (eds) *Child First: Developing a New Youth Justice System*, London: Palgrave Macmillan, pp 51–82.

Case, S. and Haines, K. (2009) *Understanding Youth Offending: Risk Factor Research, Policy and Practice*, Cullompton: Willan Publishing.

Case, S. and Haines, K. (2020) 'Abolishing youth justice systems: children first, offenders nowhere', *Youth Justice*, 21(1): 3–17.

Case, S. and Hazel, N. (2023) (eds) *Child First: Developing a New Youth Justice System*, London: Palgrave Macmillan.

Clarke, R.V. and Cornish, D.B. (1985) 'Modelling offenders' decisions: a framework for research and policy', in M. Tonry and N. Morris (eds) *Crime and Justice: An Annual Review of Research*, Chicago: University of Chicago Press, pp 147–85.

Coyle, B. (2019) '"What the f**k is maturity?" Young adulthood, subjective maturity and desistance from crime', *British Journal of Criminology*, 59(5): 1178–98.

Day, A.M. (2023) '"It's a hard balance to find": the perspectives of youth justice practitioners in England on the place of "risk" in an emerging "Child-First" world', *Youth Justice*, 23(1): 58–75.

Day, A.M., Bateman, T. and Pitts, J. (2020) 'Surviving incarceration: the pathways of looked after and non-looked after children into, through and out of custody', Luton: University of Bedfordshire.

Drew, J. (2023) 'Developing Child First youth justice policy in England and Wales: a view from inside the YJB and Westminster', in S. Case and N. Hazel (eds) *Child First: Developing a New Youth Justice System*, London: Palgrave Macmillan, pp 137–67.

Droppelmann, C. (2017) 'Leaving behind the deviant other in desistance–persistence explanations', in E.L. Hart and E.F.C van Ginneken (eds) *New Perspectives on Desistance: Theoretical and Empirical Developments*, Basingstoke: Palgrave Macmillan, pp 213–40.

Farrall, S. (2002) *Rethinking What Works with Offenders: Probation, Social Context and Desistance from Crime*, Cullompton: Willan Publishing.

Farrall, S. and Shapland, J. (2022) 'Do the reasons why people desist from crime vary by age, length of offending career or lifestyle factors?', *The Howard Journal of Crime and Justice*, 61(4): 405–560.

Farrall, S., Hunter, B., Sharpe, G. and Calverley, A. (2014) *Criminal Careers in Transition: The Social Context of Desistance from Crime*, Oxford: Oxford University Press.

Farrington, D. (2007) 'Childhood risk factors and risk focused prevention', in M. Maguire, R. Morgan and R. Reiner (eds) *The Oxford Handbook of Criminology* (4th edn), Oxford: Oxford University Press, pp 602–40.

Fitzpatrick, C. (2011) 'What is the difference between "desistance" and "resilience"? Exploring the relationship between two key concepts', *Youth Justice*, 11(3): 221–34.

Fitzpatrick, E., McGuire, J. and Dickson, J. (2015) 'Personal goals of adolescents in a youth offending services in the United Kingdom', *Youth Justice*, 15(2): 166–81.

Gilligan, R. (2001) *Promoting Resilience: A Resource Guide on Working with Children in the Care System*, London: BAAF.

Giordano, P.C. (2016) 'Mechanisms underlying the desistance process: reflections on "A theory of cognitive transformation"', in J. Shapland, S. Farrall and A. Bottoms (eds) *Global Perspectives on Desistance: Reviewing What We Know and Looking to the Future*, London: Routledge, pp 11–27.

Giordano, P.C., Cernkovich, S.A. and Rudolph, J.L. (2002) 'Gender, crime and desistance: toward a theory of cognitive transformation', *American Journal of Sociology*, 107(4): 990–1064.

Glueck, S. and Glueck, E. (1974) *Of Delinquency and Crime*, Springfield, IL: C.C. Thomas.

Godwin, S. (2022) '"Keeping busy" as agency in early desistance', *Criminology and Criminal Justice*, 22(1): 43–58.

Gottfredson, M. and Hirshi, T. (1990) *A General Theory of Crime*, Stanford, CA: Stanford University Press.

Graham, H. and McNeil, F. (2020) 'Diversifying desistance research', in P. Ugwudike, H. Graham, F. McNeill, P. Raynor, F.S. Taxman and C. Trotter (eds) *The Routledge Companion to Rehabilitative Work in Youth Justice*, Abingdon: Routledge, pp 104–15.

Graham, J. and Bowling, B. (1995) 'Young people and crime', Home Office Research Study 145, London: Home Office, Available from: https://web archive.nationalarchives.gov.uk/20110218144139/http://rds.homeoffice. gov.uk/rds/pdfs2/hors145.pdf

Gray, E. (2013) 'What happens to persistent and serious young offenders when they grow up: a follow-up study of the first recipients of Intensive Supervision and Surveillance', London: Youth Justice Board.

Gray, P. and Smith, R. (2019) 'Governance through diversion in neoliberal times and the possibilities for transformative social justice', *Critical Criminology*, 27: 575–90.

Haigh, Y. (2009) 'Desistance from crime: reflections on the transitional experiences of young people with a history of offending', *Journal of Youth Studies*, 12(3): 307–22.

Haines, K. and Case, S. (2015) *Positive Youth Justice: Children First, Offenders Second*, Bristol: Policy Press.

Hampson, K.S. (2018) 'Desistance approaches in youth justice: the next passing fad or a sea-change for the positive?', *Youth Justice*, 18(1): 18–33.

Hampson, K.S. (2023) 'Cementing "Child First" in practice', in S. Case and N. Hazel (eds) *Child First: Developing a New Youth Justice System*, London: Palgrave Macmillan, pp 301–32.

Healy, D. (2012) 'Advise, assist and befriend: can probation supervision support desistance?', *Social Policy & Administration*, 46(4): 377–94.

HM Inspectorate of Probation (2016) 'Desistance and young people: an inspection by HM Inspectorate of Probation', HM Inspectorate of Probation, Available from: https://www.justiceinspectorates.gov.uk/hmiprobation/ wp-content/uploads/sites/5/2016/05/Desistance_and_young_people.pdf

HM Inspectorate of Probation (2021) 'Inspection standards for youth offending services', London: HM Inspectorate of Probation, Available from: https:// www.justiceinspectorates.gov.uk/hmiprobation/wp-content/uploads/ sites/5/2023/11/Standards-for-inspection-youth-offending-services-English.pdf

HM Inspectorate of Probation (2022) 'Youth offending services inspections: rules and guidance', London: HM Inspectorate of Probation, Available from: https:// www.justiceinspectorates.gov.uk/hmiprobation/about-hmi-probation/ about-our-work/documentation-area/youth-offending-services-inspection/

Holmes, J. and Slade, A. (2018) *Attachment in Therapeutic Practice*, London: Sage.

Houston, S. (2010) 'Building resilience in a children's home: results in an action research project', *Child and Family Social Work*, 15(3): 357–68.

Johns, D., Williams, K. and Haines, K. (2017) 'Ecological youth justice: understanding the social ecology of young people's prolific offending', *Youth Justice*, 17(1): 3–21.

Johnson, K. and Maruna, S. (2020) 'Doing justice to desistance narratives', in P. Ugwudike, H. Graham, F. McNeill, P. Raynor, F.S. Taxman and C. Trotter (eds) *The Routledge Companion to Rehabilitative Work in Youth Justice*, Abingdon: Routledge, pp 116–24.

Kazemian, L. (2007) 'Desistance from crime: theoretical, empirical, methodological and policy considerations', *Journal of Contemporary Criminal Justice*, 23(2): 5–27.

Laub, J.H. and Sampson, R.J. (2003) *Shared Beginnings, Divergent Lives: Delinquent Boys to Age 70*, Cambridge, MA: Harvard University Press.

Leibrich, J. (1994) 'What do offenders say about supervision and going straight?', *Federal Probation*, 58(2): 41–6.

Luthar, S., Chichetti, D. and Becker, B. (2000) 'The construct of resilience: a critical evaluation and guidelines for future work', *Child Development*, 7(3): 543–62.

Maruna, S. (1997) 'Going straight: desistance from crime and life narratives of reform', in A. Lieblich and R. Josselson (eds) *The Narrative Study of Lives: Volume 5*, Thousand Oaks, CA: Sage, pp 59–93.

Maruna, S. (2001) *Making Good: How Ex-convicts Reform and Rebuild Their Lives*, Washington, DC: American Psychological Association.

Maruna, S. and Farrall, S. (2004) 'Desistance from crime: a theoretical reformulation', *Kvlner Zeitschrift fur Soziologie und Sozialpsychologie*, 43: 171–94.

Maruna, S. and Mann, R. (2019) *Reconciling 'Desistance' and 'What Works'*, Manchester: HM Inspectorate of Probation, Available from: https://www.justiceinspectorates.gov.uk/hmiprobation/wp-content/uploads/sites/5/2019/02/Academic-Insights-Maruna-and-Mann-Feb-19-final.pdf

McAra, L. and McVie, S. (2017) 'Developmental and life-course criminology', in A. Liebling, S. Maruna and L. McAra (eds) *The Oxford Handbook of Criminology* (6th edn), Oxford: Oxford University Press, pp 607–38.

McAra, L. and McVie, S. (2022) 'Causes and impacts of criminal justice pathways: follow-up of the Edinburgh Study cohort at age 35', University of Edinburgh, Edinburgh Law School, Available from: https://www.law.ed.ac.uk/sites/default/files/2022-03/ESYTC%20Report%20%28March%202022%29%20-%20Acc.pdf

McIvor, G., Murray, C. and Jamieson, J. (2004) 'Desistance from crime? Is it different for women and girls?', in S. Maruna and R. Immarigeon (eds) *After Crime and Punishment: Pathways to Offender Reintegration*, Cullompton: Willan Publishing, pp 181–200.

McMahon, G. and Jump, D. (2018) 'Starting to stop: young offenders' desistance from crime', *Youth Justice*, 18(1): 3–17.

McNeill, F. (2006) 'Community supervision: context and relationships matter', in B. Goldson and J. Muncie (eds) *Youth Crime and Justice*, London: Sage, pp 125– 38.

McNeill, F. (2009) 'What works and what's just?', *European Journal of Probation*, 1(1): 21–40.

McNeill, F. (2014) *Desistance, Rehabilitation and Reintegration*, Glasgow: University of Glasgow, Available from: https://www.gla.ac.uk/schools/socialpolitical/research/sociology/blogresearch/criminology/headline_666048_en.html

McNeill, F. and Graham, H. (2020) 'Conceptualising rehabilitation: four forms, two models, one process and a plethora of challenges', in P. Ugwudike, H. Graham, F. McNeill, P. Raynor, F.S. Taxman and C. Trotter (eds) *The Routledge Companion to Rehabilitative Work in Youth Justice*, Abingdon: Routledge, pp 10–19.

McNeill, F., Batchelor, S., Burnett, R. and Knox, J. (2005) *21st Century Social Work: Reducing Re-Offending: Key Practice Skills*, Edinburgh: Scottish Executive.

McNeill, F., Farrall, S., Lightowler, C. and Maruna, S. (2012) 'How and why people stop offending: discovering desistance', Institute for Research and Innovation in Social Sciences, Available from: https://www.iriss.org.uk/sites/default/files/iriss-insight-15.pdf

Ministry of Justice (2016) 'The government's response to Charlie Taylor's review of the youth justice system', London: Ministry of Justice, Available from: https://assets.publishing.service.gov.uk/media/5a817a1ae5274a2e87dbdd72/youth-justice-review-government-response-print.pdf

Ministry of Justice/Youth Justice Board (2019) 'Standards for children in the youth justice system', London: Ministry of Justice.

Moffitt, T (1993) 'Adolescence-limited and life-course-persistent antisocial behavior: a developmental taxonomy', *Psychological Review*, 100(4): 674–701.

Mulvey, E.P. and Schubert, C.A. (2016) 'Issues to consider in future work on desistance from adolescence to early adulthood: observations from the Pathways to Desistance Study', in J. Shapland, S. Farrall and A. Bottoms (eds) *Global Perspectives on Desistance: Reviewing What We Know and Looking to the Future*, Abingdon: Routledge, pp 126–44.

Murray, C. (2009) 'Typologies of young resisters and desisters', *Youth Justice*, 9(2): 115–29.

National Association for Youth Justice (2019) 'Manifesto 2019/2020', London: NAYJ, Available from: https://thenayj.org.uk/cmsAdmin/uploads/state-of-youth-justice-2020-final-sep20.pdf

Nugent, B. (2015) 'Reaching the hardest to reach', *Youth Justice*, 15(3): 271–85.

Nugent, B. and McNeill, F. (2016) 'Young people and desistance', in A. Furlong (ed) *Routledge Handbook of Youth and Young Adulthood* (2nd edn), Abingdon: Routledge, 411–20.

Nugent, B. and Schinkel, M. (2016) 'The pains of desistance', *Criminology and Criminal Justice*, 16(5): 568–84.

Panuccio, E.A., Christian, J., Martinez, D.J. and Sullivan, M.L. (2012) 'Social support, motivation and the process of juvenile re-entry: an exploratory analysis of desistance', *Journal of Offender Rehabilitation*, 51(3): 135–60.

Paternoster, R. and Bushway, S. (2009) 'Desistance and the feared self: toward an identity theory of criminal desistance', *Criminal Law and Criminology*, 99(4): 1103–56.

Paterson-Young, C., Hazenberg, R. and Bajwa-Patel. M (2019) *The Social Impact of Custody on Young People in the Criminal Justice System*. Cham: Palgrave MacMillan.

Paterson-Young, C., Bajwa-Patel, M. and Hazenburg, R. (2022) '"I ain't stupid, I just don't like school": a "needs" based argument for children's educational provision in custody', *Journal of Youth Studies*, 25(4): 452–69.

Patterson, J.L. and Kelleher, P. (2005) *Resilient School Leaders: Strategies for Turning Adversity into Achievement*, Alexandria: Association for Supervision and Curriculum Development.

Phoenix, J. and Kelly, L. (2013) '"You have to do it for yourself": responsibilization in youth justice and young people's situated knowledge of youth justice practice', *British Journal of Criminology*, 53(3): 419–37.

Rex, S. (1999) 'Desistance from offending: experiences of probation', *The Howard Journal of Crime and Justice*, 38(4): 366–83.

Robinson, A. (2016) 'The resilience motif: implications for youth justice', *Youth Justice*, 16(1): 18–33.

Rutherford, A. (1992) *Growing Out of Crime: The New Era*, Winchester: Waterside Press.

Rutter, M. (2012) 'Resilience as a dynamic concept', *Development and Psychopathology*, 24(2): 335–44.

Sampson, R.J. and Laub, J. (1992) 'Crime and deviance in the life course', *Annual Review of Sociology*, 18: 63–84.

Shapland, J., Farrall, S. and Bottoms, A. (2016) 'Introduction', in J. Shapland, S. Farrall and A. Bottoms (eds) *Global Perspectives on Desistance: Reviewing What We Know and Looking to the Future*, Abingdon: Routledge, pp 1–8.

Sharp, G. (2012) *Offending Girls: Young Women and Youth Justice*. Abingdon: Routledge.

Sharpe, G. (2015) 'Precarious identities: 'young' motherhood, desistance and stigma', *Criminology and Criminal Justice*, 15(4): 407–22.

Smith, R. and Gray, P. (2019) 'The changing shape of youth justice: models of practice', *Criminology and Criminal Justice*, 19(5): 554–71.

Sroufe, L.A (2005) 'Attachment and development: a prospective, longitudinal study from birth to adulthood', *Attachment and Human Development*, 7(4): 349–67.

Taylor, C. (2006) *Young People in Care and Criminal Behaviour*, London: Jessica Kingsley.

Taylor, C. (2016) 'Review of the youth justice system in England and Wales', London: Ministry of Justice, Available from: https://assets.publishing.service.gov.uk/media/5a7ffc81ed915d74e622bcdb/youth-justice-review-final-report-print.pdf

Trotter, C. (2020) 'Effective supervision of young offenders', in P. Ugwudike, P. Raynor, F. McNeill, F. Taxman, C. Trotter and H. Graham (eds) *The Routledge Companion to Rehabilitative Work in Criminal Justice*, Abingdon: Routledge, pp 755–65.

Weaver, B. (2016) *Offending and Desistance: The Importance of Social Relations*, London: Routledge.

Wigzell, A. (2021) 'Explaining desistance: looking forward, not backwards', London: NAYJ, Available from: https://thenayj.org.uk/cmsAdmin/uploads/explaining-desistance-briefing-feb-2021-final.pdf

Wigzell, A. and Bateman, T. (2024, forthcoming) 'A question of age? Applying desistance with children', *Youth Justice*.

Williams, K.S. and Daniel, H. (2021) 'Applying Sen's capabilities approach to the delivery of positive youth justice', *Youth Justice*, 21(1): 90–106.

Williams, R. (1997) *Marxism and Literature*, Oxford: Oxford University Press.

Youth Justice Board (2002) 'Corporate plan 2002–3 to 2004–5 and business plan 2002–3', London: Youth Justice Board.

Youth Justice Board (2010) 'Youth justice: the scaled approach; a framework for assessment and intervention', London: Youth Justice Board, Available from: https://assets.publishing.service.gov.uk/media/5a8c01db40f0b6230269dc85/Youth_Justice_the_Scaled_Approach_-_A_framework_for_assessment_and_interventions.pdf

Youth Justice Board (2018) *Youth Justice Board for England and Wales Strategic Plan 2018–21*. London: Youth Justice Board.

Youth Justice Board (2021) 'Strategic plan 2021–2024', London: Youth Justice Board, Available from: https://assets.publishing.service.gov.uk/media/603f6d268fa8f577c44d65a8/YJB_Strategic_Plan_2021_-_2024.pdf

Youth Justice Board/Ministry of Justice (2023) 'Youth justice annual statistics 2021/22', London: Youth Justice Board.

PART I

Theoretical and conceptual perspectives on desistance and children

2

'Child First' and desistance

Neal Hazel and Stephen Case

Introduction: there's 'desistance' and there's 'desistance'

Neoliberalist jurisdictions globally have fixated on directly addressing offending children's behaviour and bringing about 'desistance' from that offending. In England and Wales, for instance, the principal aim of the youth justice system (YJS) is 'preventing offending'. Introduced in the Crime and Disorder Act 1998 (Section 37), it is the statutory duty for all people and agencies working within the system to have regard to preventing offending. Having this aim for a YJS is, of course, a specific political choice and not inevitable. Nor is it universal around the world. For instance, an established principal aim in other jurisdictions is for the system to act in whatever is the best interests of the child (Hazel, 2008), reflecting a primary principle in the UN Convention on the Rights of the Child (UNCRC) (Article 3). That aim is similar to the 'consideration' also present in England and Wales that courts 'shall have regard to the welfare of the child' (Children and Young Persons Act 1933, Section 44).

Nevertheless, the focus of the system's principal aim of preventing offending is clearly on crime reduction. There is no sense that there is any political will or intention to change this in the foreseeable future. While we may argue its shortcomings, this is the context within which policy and practice bodies in the system, and academics and other commentators outside of it, must try to drive improvement. For children who have not been in the criminal justice system, 'preventing offending' means ensuring policies and practice support children to not start offending. For those children who have already offended, it means ensuring policies and practice that stop the offending behaviour and any recidivism. The latter is 'desistance' in its broadest criminological sense.

In the 21st century, the dominant approach to pursuing desistance from offending by children has been the neo-correctionalist targeting of the 'risk factors' allegedly predictive of youth offending. However, this dominant 'risk management' approach is fundamentally flawed, lacks a theory of change and has negative consequences, including stigma in defining and treating the child as 'risky'. The criminogenic effect of stigma has long been recognised since early 'labelling theory' in youth delinquency research (Becker, 1963), but we also recognise it running contrary to more recent messages from adult-focused 'desistance theory' (see Chapter 1) around the need to allow progress from an 'offender' status. Accordingly, a broad consensus has developed among contemporary youth justice academics around the need for non-stigmatising youth justice that sees children as 'children first and offenders second' (Haines and Drakeford, 1998). Key messages from contemporary research advocate for youth justice that fundamentally emphasises the importance of promoting positive child outcomes, for example the Positive Youth Justice (PYJ) model (Haines and Case, 2015). However, we recognise in this chapter that this evidence-based model has similarly lacked a 'theory of change' in linking positive outcomes with the broad sense of desistance, which has limited its policy and practice traction. We argue that an appropriate theory of change can be recognised in research on the resettlement of children from custody, translated into the Constructive Working (CW) practice framework (Hazel et al, 2020), which recognises the central importance of facilitating children's 'pro-social identity'. Although derived from empirical research with younger people, this theory of change again reflects a central aspect of adult 'desistance' theory, that sustainable desistance requires an individual to 'shift' to a pro-social identity. To be appropriate across the YJS, however, it is necessary to recognise that the development of a pro-social identity does not need to assume the existence of an embedded pro-offending identity from which to shift.

The problems of pursuing desistance through risk management

The statutory duty of having 'regard to' desistance has, in effect, been interpreted as practitioners being able and expected to change children's behaviour directly. At the very least, youth justice agencies are expected to impact on children's attitudes and circumstances that are considered to determine their offending behaviour. As such, policy makers' and practitioners' attention has been on factors that are specifically understood to directly lower the 'risk' of reoffending as a vehicle for pursuing the primary aim of preventing negative outcomes (offending and reoffending, for example), as evidenced by desistance. This dominant risk management approach is fundamentally flawed, as is the research and its interpretation that has determined the 'factors' on which interventions have been based.

Risk management and its underpinning evidence base derived from the 'Risk Factor Prevention Paradigm' (RFPP) foster individualised and responsibilising explanations of offending by framing risk factors as personal 'deficits' (flaws, weaknesses) in psycho-social domains of children's lives (psychological, family, education, peer group, neighbourhood) that children somehow fail or refuse to resist or negotiate (Case and Haines, 2009). The

RFPP rests on an evidence-based central preventative premise to 'identify the risk factors for offending and implement prevention methods designed to counteract them' (Farrington, 2007, p 606). The evidence base has proven very attractive to youth justice stakeholders, who have readily and uncritically accepted the deterministic and decontextualised explanations of reductionism when seeking to prevent offending directly (Case, 2021). Explaining children's criminality on the basis of risk and the alleged deterministic, criminogenic influence of risk factors also treats children as objects whose fate is largely determined by the risks they embody, rather than regarding them as active individuals with a capacity to make choices, albeit that their options may be constrained by their socio-economic position (Case and Haines, 2009, p 20). Interventions in the United States have been criticised precisely because they ignore personal agency and individuals' interpretation of the immediate context (see Barton, 2006). To compound matters, the research and 'evidence-based' risk assessment tools erroneously reconstruct macro-level influences such as socio-economic deprivation and social marginalisation as individualised risk factors (see Harcourt, 2007; Tonry, 2019).

In England and Wales particularly, a neo-correctionalist punitiveness mobilised by risk-based crime-prevention (risk management) priorities has come to dominate policy and practice, mirroring the new penology in adult criminal justice (Feeley and Simon, 1992). It seeks to correct the perceived deficits of children who offend and to punish non-compliance and non-engagement with ameliorative, controlling interventions focused primarily on managing the risk of offending (see Hazel, 2008; Dunkel, 2014; Smith and Gray, 2019). Following the Crime and Disorder Act 1998, the newly created Youth Justice Board (YJB) commissioned academics to produce a series of Key Elements of Effective Practice (KEEP) based on systematic reviews that were inherently reductionist due to their elevation of quasi-experimental methodologies (Randomised Controlled Trials, for example) as a gold standard, which privileged studies that focused directly on RFPP studies of 'what works' to address offending and bring desistance directly. This predominance of quasi-experimental, risk-based studies focusing on desistance outcomes (themselves privileged by the 'what works' evaluation framework – Case et al, 2022) directly rendered 'certain research questions … "unaskable" because they cannot be addressed using experimental methods' (Prior and Mason, 2010, p 219), typically omitting theory of change questions of 'how' interventions may work, 'with whom' they work best and 'why' they may work with some children in some situations but not others.

The KEEP documents underpinned the use of 'Asset' as a standardised assessment framework for use across the YJS. Asset generated an evidence base through practice that was overwhelmingly populated by the 'risk factors associated with offending behaviour' (YJB, 2003, p 27) that had been widely replicated in artefactual RFPP and which were all situated within or interpreted as psycho-social risk categories/domains (living arrangements, family and personal relationships, education/training/employment, neighbourhood, lifestyle, substance use, physical health, emotional/mental health, perception of self and others, thinking and behaviour, attitudes to offending, motivation to change). Associated planning, judgements and decisions were framed almost entirely and inevitably by risk evidence and associated explanations. Practitioners were instructed to assess exposure to risk factors as a binary measure (yes/no) and to quantify their perceptions of the extent to which exposure to risks aggregated across each domain were associated with 'the likelihood of further offending': from 0 (no association) to 4 (very strong, clear, direct association). These were then added together to produce an overall one- or two-digit score for how 'risky' the child is for future offending. Quantitative judgements were supplemented with qualitative, narrative explanations in a small, summative 'evidence box' at the end of each section (Case and Haines, 2009).

Asset therefore embodied a staged process of reductionism when trying to bring about desistance directly that has rendered risk a decontextualised and dehumanised artefact and hindered the possibility of understanding children's individual lived realities and how these might be influenced (O'Mahony, 2009; Phoenix, 2009; Cox, 2020). Application of RFPP peaked in November 2009 with the inception of the 'Scaled Approach' assessment and intervention framework, which dictated that formal youth justice intervention must be proportionate to the child's assessed risk of offending (YJB, 2010; see Sutherland, 2009), formally extending processes of risk-based reductionism and invalidity into the sphere of intervention but justified by an under-theorised, partial and inconsistent evidence base for the 'effectiveness' of risk assessment and risk-based interventions (Case et al, 2022).

The fatal explanatory flaw with risk management for desistance: no theory of change

Risk management approaches deliberately eschew articulating a theory of change, even though this could provide an overarching understanding of the process within which individual strands of activity might cohere to achieve desistance (Hazel et al, 2017). The absence of an explicit 'theory of change' within the risk paradigm is a limitation that its proponents have nevertheless attempted to construct as a benefit: '[R]isk factors and interventions are based on empirical research rather than theories. The paradigm avoids difficult theoretical questions about which risk factors have causal effects' (Farrington, 2000, p 7). However, without a cogent theory of change, it is difficult to see how critical, reflective practice can be employed in order to rationalise, evaluate, improve and even replace contemporary (risk-based) youth justice interventions to benefit children. Research examining custody and re-entry, for example, has found that the decontextualised nature of the risk-focused practice messages has hindered practice (Hazel and Bateman, 2021). Any possible theory of change that could be discerned from the risk paradigm evidence base would inevitably reflect the reductionist nature of the model, constructing children who offend as laden with deficits (risk factors) that they cannot negotiate without the support of adult practitioners and enforced intervention.

Moreover, in focusing interventions directly on the offending behaviour and desistance from it, risk-based youth justice brings 'negative', punitive features. These include the (inadvertent) labelling and stigmatisation of children, excessive intervention, 'net-widening', doing justice 'to', not with children, and over-emphasising the prevention of negative outcomes (exposure to risk factors, reoffending, for example) (Case and Haines, 2009). This negative consequence of RFPP research and practice is now recognised by the YJB: 'Since the YJB was created, our understanding of how to prevent offending, has moved beyond a focus on managing the risk posed by children who offend. We now understand the criminogenic effects of children's involvement in the justice system and the damage that this can cause' (YJB, 2019, p 7). Such a concern is founded in long-established recognition of the criminogenic effects of 'labelling' through children's participation in the criminal justice system, where the deeper the contact (controlling for other factors) the more likely is further serious offending (see, for example, Huizinga et al, 2003; Petrosino et al, 2010; McAra and McVie, 2015; Smith, 2017). However, it would be amiss not to recognise that these arguments also relate to concepts and evidence in 'desistance theory' in the adult-based literature, which recognises the need to move on from criminogenic labels (Maruna, 2001). This is a more specific criminological understanding of what prevents offending in adults, which, among other principles, emphasises the need for those who offend to be allowed and facilitated to move beyond that status (see, for example, Maruna and Roy, 2007). In order to facilitate that, we contend that youth justice needs a paradigm shift and a new conceptual framework to understand its role in relation to the broad criminological understanding of desistance (preventing reoffending), informed by a cogent theory of change. In particular, this would need to counter the persistent weaknesses identified above in RFPP, by reconceptualising youth justice and desistance in a way that allows a strengths-based approach that is relevant to the child and integrated with the rest of their support towards positive outcomes, such as desistance and reduced recidivism.

Positive Youth Justice: a consensus of contemporary research understanding

Building on the academic understanding that these aims are best achieved when the system sees and treats children as 'children first and offenders second'

(Haines and Drakeford, 1998), this chapter's second author has summarised the principles that have emerged in this consensus in a model termed Positive Youth Justice (PYJ) (Haines and Case, 2015; Case, 2023; also Butts, 2014). Through this model, all youth justice practice should be child-friendly, child-appropriate and focused on the whole child, examining the full complexity of their lives, experiences, perspectives, needs, wishes and multi-faceted, context-specific interactions. Its adoption reasserts the position of the whole child, rather than an offending risk factor, as the primary focus of concern and intervention. The primary aim of PYJ is to promote positive behaviours and outcomes rather than prioritising the prevention or risk management of negative outcomes (which occur as by-products of poor child outcomes – Haines and Case, 2015). It is an engaging and positive child-friendly approach that radically re-orientates traditional offence/offender-focused and deficit-facing youth justice by emphasising that all provision should prioritise the central principle of 'children first, offenders second'. PYJ conceives of offending as only one element of the child's broader social status (see Drakeford, 2010) rather than as their defining master status. Positive Youth Justice practice should ensure that work with children at all stages of the YJS is developmentally appropriate and acknowledges their inherent 'child' status and capacity rather than 'adulterising' children (treating them like they were adults) in relation to their offending behaviour and desistance.

Fundamentally, we argue that this model points to the need for the YJS to focus primarily on achieving positive child outcomes. The aim of 'desistance' is best considered as a secondary outcome, which reduces the negative consequences of it being a direct focus. Professionals working within juvenile justice systems should prioritise the *promotion of positive behaviours/outcomes*: focusing prospectively on facilitating positive behaviours (engagement in pro-social activities, for example) and positive outcomes (such as educational attainment, employment) rather than primarily focusing retrospectively on the prevention of negative behaviours (such as offending) and outcomes (exposure to risk, for example) (Haines and Case, 2015; see also Case and Haines, 2018).

Youth justice should prioritise the facilitation of children's meaningful *engagement* (belief in, commitment to) across youth justice processes and decision-making that affects them rather than doing justice 'to' them in 'adult-centric' and non-inclusive ways. Crucially, youth justice practice should be perceived as *legitimate* (Tyler, 2011, 2007), enabling children in the YJS to feel that their treatment by official agencies is 'legitimate' in the sense of fair, moral and just (rather than unfair, unjust, punitive), which can increase the likelihood of their engagement and of intervention success, as well as children building positive relationships with the police and youth justice agencies. Finally, juvenile justice systems must focus more on *responsibilising adult professionals*, holding them primarily responsible for enabling children who offend to achieve their full potential and to gain access to support services, guidance and opportunities, rather than holding the relatively powerless and immature child primarily responsible (after Haines and Case, 2015).

Accordingly, a Child First conceptual framework that draws on the Positive Youth Justice model would prioritise the following overarching principles in relation to desistance in the broad criminological sense of preventing offending:

- *Positive primary foci*: practitioners should be diverted from the deficit-focused primary concern with desistance towards a positive, child-appropriate approach in which children are rewarded for their achievements, encouraged to maximise their strengths and provided with structural support that helps achieve positive child outcomes. Desistance is the secondary outcome but not the direct focus.
- *Children as part of the solution*: practitioners and policy makers should work in partnership with children to hold their interests, needs, rights and views as paramount throughout the youth justice process. The child is in a unique position to inform and engage with solutions that are relevant to their own strengths, aspirations and outcomes, which will then inform desistance.
- *Child-focused adults*: adult professionals must view themselves as working for the children rather than as representatives of other (often adult-focused) interest groups (for example the YJS, community, victims). The starting point for planning and delivery is the individual aims, motivations and lived context of the child (Brazier et al, 2010). The broader concerns with a crime-reductionist framework will be met in consequence of positive child outcomes.
- *Children's rights*: the priority for adult youth justice professionals must be to facilitate the expression of the child's views on issues that affect them (see UNCRC Article 12), enable equitable participation in decision-making regarding their crime-free futures (Taylor, 2016) and promote access to universal entitlements as set out in progressive policy statements and international conventions.
- *Engagement-based relationship building*: youth justice should emphasise positive and trusting relationships through which constructive interactions can be facilitated, rather than formal interventions per se. Positive relationships have been recognised as key in managing behaviour (Elwick et al, 2013) and role modelling (Knight, 2014) and are also vital for fostering engagement (Taylor, 2016). Engagement is conceptualised here not just as participation but as feeling a commitment based on the child's perceived relevance of that participation to their lives and positive futures (Bateman and Hazel, 2013).

Constructive Working: 'developing pro-social identity' as the theory of change for youth justice

Akin to the RFPP that it challenges, however, PYJ has also lacked an explicit 'theory of change' to understand how working with children in line with its constituent principles can facilitate its primary goal of promoting positive outcomes and its secondary goal of preventing offending (evidenced by desistance, for example). The rationale has been that youth justice specialist organisations or professionals are not needed to support development as children (Haines and Case, 2015). However, the consequent lack of a narrative, that is, a theory of change, to explain how interventions targeting positive child outcomes lead to desistance inevitably restricts the defensible decision-making of agents operating within a system with a crime-reductionist aim. Similarly, without such a theory of change, it is difficult for policy makers and governance agencies to justify progressive policy reform within the deficit-focused crime-reductionist political discourse, which has limited its policy and practice traction.

Therefore, we contend that the relationship between Positive Youth Justice, positive child outcomes and desistance is best understood through a theory of change developed from research on the resettlement (also known as re-entry) of children and young adults after periods in custody (Hazel et al, 2017; Hazel and Bateman, 2021). The 'Beyond Youth Custody' (BYC) research programme concluded that successful re-entry of children after custody can be understood as a personal journey involving a shift in identity (Hazel et al, 2017). Where the resettlement process is successful, it involved children being enabled to change the way they see themselves and their place in the world from one that is pro-offending to one that is pro-social. This theme dominated narratives, although it was sometimes uncomfortable for some children who were specifically involved with resettlement projects (BYC, 2017) to reconcile their own comments about a change from 'the old me' with a sense of continuous agency. As such, resettlement should not be seen as a single transition point from custody to community, nor even as following a sentence path, but as a desistance journey from an identity conducive to offending to one that promotes a crime-free life and social inclusion:

> 'I'd always had intelligence and vocabulary to talk to people in a different way and portray myself in a different way, but before, I was "street" and using slang. But it doesn't get me far in life. ... If you conduct yourself in a good way ... and portray myself in a good way, people will warm to me more. ... Everybody I know says I seem like a man now – I can't go round talking like a child in a hoody.' (23-year-old ex-offender, now construction worker; cited in Hazel et al, 2017, p 8)

As the journey in the quotation suggests, this understanding of identity is social and interactional (Jenkins, 2008), seeing the more positive narrative as fostered and reinforced through involvement in constructive activities and interactions and in the adoption of roles that promote it (Bateman and Hazel, 2013). This is a social interactionist view of identity (Jenkins, 2008), understanding that a sense of self and place in the world is co-constructed through relations with sociocultural contexts and others (Cote, 2006; Roeser et al, 2006). It becomes apparent that such facilitation is not primarily about intervening to address identified risks – or facilitate desistance – in a linear fashion but consists of providing support to the child to become agents of their own development towards positive outcomes and desistance.

This research has been translated into a practice model called Constructive Working (CW) (see, for example, YJB, 2018; Hazel et al, 2020). Fundamentally, the theory of change recognised in the research was that children and young adults who successfully resettled and desisted experienced a 'shift' to a more pro-social identity. Consequently, support should be reconceptualised not as addressing decontextualised risk factors solely as a means of reducing negative outcomes but as facilitating the child's pro-social identity development to encourage the promotion of positive outcomes (Hazel and Bateman, 2021). Within the proposed model, such constructive activities can be reframed as offering opportunities for children to enjoy positive interactions with others, develop skills for the future and provide them with confidence and an opportunity to take up roles that can help develop a pro-social identity. The model argues that youth justice practitioners are responsible for presenting children with the fresh 'AIR' of activities, interactions and roles that are the building blocks for exploring and developing pro-social identity for children in trouble (Hazel et al, 2020). It is, in other words, not a question of trying to manage the risk – or ensure desistance from offending – directly but of providing future-oriented structural support that can assist the child to achieve a pro-social identity. Within the crime-reductionist discourse, this leads to both prevention of, and desistance from, offending within the sense of the system's statutory principal aim.

Although a child's identity is deeply personal, and so requires their engagement, this does not mean that the development of a pro-social identity is the responsibility of the child. Nor does it mean that the solutions to facilitating identity development towards desistance are not structurally based. However, it does mean that forms of structural support (such as education and training) are not just 'ends in themselves' (HMIP, 2015, p 22). The maximum benefits from constructive activities are, however, only likely to be derived where they are clearly designed in the context of, and contribute to, the child's identified route in developing a pro-social identity. The evidence points to two distinct but reciprocal forms that are fundamental to enhancing the prospects that children will make the necessary shift: (1) personal support to guide their identity shift, and (2) structural support to enable it (Hazel et al, 2017).

The BYC/CW model highlighted five principles for support (the 5Cs) that were found by reinterpreting messages from existing research in light of contemporary understanding of the importance of identity development (Hazel et al, 2017; Hazel and Bateman, 2021):

1. *Constructive*: provision centred on a pro-social identity must necessarily be future-focused, strengths-based, empowering and motivating. Interventions that replay the negativity of past behaviour can be counterproductive (Bateman and Hazel, 2014).
2. *Co-created*: identity development is a personal journey taken by the child themselves, dependent on their agency, so their being and feeling engaged is a prerequisite of effective work (Bateman and Hazel, 2013; Bateman et al, 2013; Wright et al, 2015).
3. *Customised*: each child's identity, and route for developing pro-social identity, is unique, so the package of support – personal and structural – will need to be unique. In developing tailored interventions, particular attention should be paid to issues of diversity which are fundamentally relevant to identity and the framing of future aspirations. Children from particularly disadvantaged groups or those facing discrimination, girls and those from minority ethnic backgrounds may face additional obstacles in exercising agency, which, in turn, may require higher levels of support that takes explicit account of those barriers (Bateman and Hazel, 2014; Wright et al, 2015).
4. *Consistent*: the focus on developing a pro-social identity needs to be maintained throughout contact with the system and beyond (Hazel et al, 2012). Stable relationships and positive, consistent messages from practitioners should facilitate, rather than undermine, the child's identity development.
5. *Co-ordinated*: brokering support from a range of different agencies (Hazel et al, 2012) is needed to enable the child's route to pro-social identity. A coordinated response can build a network of trusted supporters, both formal and informal (Hazel et al, 2016), to ensure that the child is supported through any period of relapse, discrimination or labelling that challenges their identity development (Wright et al, 2015).

While grounded and developed empirically from research with children and young adults, it is recognised that this theory of change both mirrors and elaborates key conclusions within the adult-based 'desistance theory' literature. Criminologically, this is a more specific understanding of 'desistance', or what brings it about (discussed in more detail in this book's opening chapter). In particular, a shift to pro-social identity in adult offenders is considered within the literature to be central to sustained or 'secondary desistance' (see Maruna and Farrall, 2004).

We argue that fundamentally, CW's emphasis on pro-social identity development is also the converse of the dangers recognised in criminogenic stigma, which reflects our understanding of labelling theory, established largely with children and young adults (see, for example, Becker, 1963) and still very evident in youth justice research today (see, for example, Deakin et al, 2020; Day et al, 2023). In addition, the BYC study is certainly not isolated in pointing to the importance of children's changing identities in relation to their behaviour and status. It can be positioned within an established and growing literature that places the guiding and enabling of the child's development of their sense of self within youth justice and wider practice contexts, generally 'upstream' from custody. For example, empirical studies have pointed to the importance of allowing children in the YJS to 'reconceptualise' themselves and to 're-imagine their own capabilities' (Drake et al, 2014, p 33). Others have highlighted the importance of a sense of 'self-development' and 'self-hope' in the construction of a positive future identity (see, for example, Wainwright and Nee, 2013). Others have noted the importance of children's changing narratives about their situation in the world to their desistance from crime (Haigh, 2009). Other empirical research with children more explicitly uses adult-derived desistance theory discourse to point to the need for children to find a 'hook for change' to increase the chances of 'identity change' and 'confidence' in desistance (Mcmahon and Jump, 2018). Accordingly, the BYC research and CW model articulate a vital *theory of change* for how PYJ can influence children's behaviour and development, simultaneously addressing the restricted evidence base regarding the nature of the relationship between positive outcomes for children and desistance (Hazel and Bateman, 2021).

However, it should be noted that in order to ensure that this 'theory of change' is understandable and applicable beyond the context of resettlement to all youth justice, it is necessary to recognise a development in our interpretation of its central conceptual messaging. Although the central importance of pro-social identity for desistance clearly remains, we should be careful not to imply that children have an embedded 'pro-offending identity' from which to 'shift' (Hazel and Williams, 2023). We instead advocate for an emphasis on pro-social identity *development*. This emphasis is also a clear distinction from a dominance of 'redemption' within the adult-based 'desistance theory' literature (although it is sometimes noted that there may not always be evidence of 'an established criminal identity' in adults [McNeill and Weaver, 2010, p 3]). We acknowledge children's relative lack of development and maturity compared to adults – physically, cognitively, emotionally and in terms of social status and power. Likewise, children's identities are evolving, and adolescence has long been conceptualised as a key period of flux or development for identity – starting to 'find oneself' as an adult (since Erickson, 1968). We also recognise that children upstream in the YJS are less likely to have their identity tarnished by pro-offending stigma. Also, having transitory elements of an identity that are conducive to offending may not be uncommon or 'abnormal' for children (fighting as a schoolchild, for example). Furthermore, a child may have a pro-social identity generally but offend in response to its disruption (temporary or longer term) from an interruption to their status, roles or constructive relationships (for example, from being taken into care) (Hazel et al, 2020; Day et al, 2023). For these reasons, we advocate for the role of agencies in building positive child outcomes to be understood as encouraging and enabling the positive *development of resilient pro-social identity*, irrespective of the child's starting point.

Child First: an evidence-informed principle with accompanying theory of change

The central features of the PYJ model and CW have been amalgamated into 'Child First' – a four-tenet framework that acts as a decision making guide for evidence-based youth justice policy and practice. An operationalised version of this framework was first presented in a YJB information paper (YJB, 2018), in a development led by this chapter's first author, with an accompanying evidence report later developed by the second author (Case and Browning, 2021). Child First as the guiding principle for and animator of youth justice *practice* in England was first officially articulated in the 'Standards for children in the justice system' document (MoJ/YJB, 2019), which provided a 'framework for youth justice practice' and the 'minimum expectations for all agencies' to ensure that positive outcomes for children align with the new Child First principle (YJB, 2019, p 4). These revised 'national standards' for practitioners were, therefore, 'indicative of a clear distinction between the philosophy now espoused by the YJB [Child First] and that which informed the previous iteration of the standards [risk management]' (Bateman, 2020, p 4).

Revised somewhat in the YJB's 2021 Strategic Plan, the operationalised Child First read as four interrelated 'tenets' (YJB, 2021, pp 10–11):

1. Prioritise the best interests of children, recognising their particular needs, capacities, rights and potential. All work is child-focused, developmentally informed, acknowledges structural barriers and meets responsibilities towards children.
2. Promote children's individual strengths and capacities to develop their pro-social identity for sustainable desistance, leading to safer communities

and fewer victims. All work is constructive and future-focused, built on supportive relationships that empower children to fulfil their potential and make positive contributions to society.

3. Encourage children's active participation, engagement and wider social inclusion. All work is a meaningful collaboration with children and their carers.

4. Promote a childhood removed from the justice system, using pre-emptive prevention, diversion and minimal intervention. All work minimises criminogenic stigma from contact with the system.

It is in the second tenet that the theory of change for youth justice is most clearly stated. It presents the development of pro-social identity as the conduit by which working with children in the system in a strengths-based way will result in 'sustainable desistance'. Reflecting the interactionist definition developed in the BYC research, 'identity' has been defined in the policy and practice literature as 'how a child sees themselves and their place in the world' (YJB, 2022: Definitions). Pro-social identity specifically is defined as:

> Children see themselves as someone who will benefit other people or society as a whole and are less likely to get involved in negative or criminal activity. ... If a child has a pro-social identity then they feel empowered to make the right choices in their behaviour and with wider life decisions, including relationships. (YJB, 2022: Definitions)

No longer is it expected that practitioners will work in a decontextualised way, addressing a 'risk factor' that is assumed will result in desistance, regardless of individual circumstances or relevance. Indeed, no work should be undertaken like that – 'all work is constructive ... and positive', with that wording deliberately chosen here and in related documents to reference PYJ and the CW models (Hazel and Williamson, 2023). Relatedly, it is notable that this tenet, which focuses on what work should be done with children, omits any mention of sending them to any formal 'addressing offending' programmes, like 'knife crime awareness' courses (see, for example, MOPAC, 2021). In fact, by not including it in 'all work', this was intended as a signal to the sector that ideas of 'what works' had changed, and sending children to programmes underlining their offences was no longer seen as good practice (Hazel and Williamson, 2023).

Perhaps more importantly, the presence of this conduit of developing pro-social identity as the theory of change means that it is not expected that those working in the system should be focused on achieving a child's desistance directly. Unlike the RFPP, or indeed much of the adult 'desistance theory' literature, preventing offending does not need to be the primary goal – that will be a consequence of the goal of having helped the child to develop their pro-social identity. This shift in primary goal, and to see prevention of offending as the consequential or longer-term goal, is made even more explicit in the YJB's 'Vision' statement for how it sees a 'Child First' YJS: 'A youth justice system that sees children as children, treats them fairly and helps them to build on their strengths so they can make a constructive contribution to society. This will prevent offending, and create safer communities with fewer victims' (YJB, 2021). In this vision, the primary and secondary goals are delimitated even more, into separate sentences. In a Child First YJS, the sector is responsible for achieving the 'constructive' process of building positive child outcomes through treating them fairly and appropriate to their age, and by engaging them in positive 'activities, interactions and roles' (the fresh AIR) in society. Here, it is presented as not being within the gift (or perhaps role) of the YJS to directly prevent offending. However, desistance 'will' happen as a separate secondary consequence of working on the whole child and achieving positive child outcomes, in turn ensuring the safer communities and fewer victims that are the concern of a crime-reductionist political discourse.

Again, we understand the criticism from progressive academics that a Child First framework should see children's positive outcomes as a goal in itself, rather than leading to desistance and less offending (see Wigzell, 2021). However, the current context for Child First to be implemented is within a YJS that has an overall statutory aim of 'preventing offending' (Crime and Disorder Act 1998) under the overall governance of a justice ministry. To omit the positive effect of this way of working on reducing offending would clearly have been to turn a strength of Child First into a weakness and render it irrelevant to ministerial and civil service constituencies and their concerns. Nevertheless, both the second tenet and the mission statement, in quite a revolutionary move within the justice system, present the child's positive inclusion in society as the fulfilment of their potential as children as the primary goal.

Conclusion: promoting children first within a crime reduction discourse

In this chapter, we have argued that the neoliberal focus on crime reduction has meant that youth justice systems, in seeing 'desistance' in its broadest criminological sense as their primary goal, have tried to address children's offending behaviour too directly and literally. This has promoted a reductionist, negative-facing and flawed 'evidence-based' approach that has been partial (biased and incomplete) in its privileging of RFPP evidence, understandings of how interventions work (lacking theory of change), its chosen, static outcome measures (preventing negative outcomes) and its limited operationalisation of desistance. This has fostered youth justice interventions that are decontextualised, without a 'theory of change' to understand how they might work, and dangerous in their stigmatising deficit-focus, always treating children as risky potential offenders.

Partly in response to recognition of these flaws, a broad consensus in contemporary research in youth justice has emerged that emphasises the importance of promoting positive child outcomes, collated into a model of Positive Youth Justice. However, we recognise that lacking a coherent and explicit theory of change explaining how the promotion of positive child outcomes prevents offending has limited its traction in policy and practice within a crime-reductionist political discourse. An appropriate theory of change was drawn from the BYC/Constructive Working framework, which developed a set of practice principles that highlighted the central importance of facilitating children's 'pro-social identity' for effective resettlement after custody (and found to be useful more broadly in youth justice). Although developed from empirical research with children, and positioned here within a growing body of research highlighting the importance of how children see themselves to their outcomes within and beyond youth justice, it is recognised that this theory of change mirrors the concept of 'secondary desistance', through shifting from a criminal identity to a pro-social one, that has emerged in the adult 'desistance theory' literature. To be appropriate across the YJS, however, it is necessary not to assume that the child has an established criminal or pro-offending identity from which to shift but instead to emphasise the role for all agencies in 'developing' each child's pro-social identity. Crucially, the approach advocated here is more expansionist and holistic than the RFPP/risk-based desistance approach that it challenges – drawing on a broader (child-friendly) evidence base, an explicit (theory of change) understanding about how interventions may work, dynamic, process-led positive outcome measures and, thus, a more child-centric and appropriate operationalisation of desistance in a youth justice context.

The thrust of our arguments is illustrated by the amalgamation of two evidenced-based models to form the four-tenet principle of Child First, which has been adopted as the guiding principle for the YJS in England and Wales. In Child First, prevention of offending is recognised as a secondary consequence of developing pro-social identity; this allows practitioners to move away from the stigmatising deficit-focus of treating desistance from crime as a primary goal that they could directly achieve. This reframing enables policy and practice to focus on the whole child and on achieving positive child outcomes while also being compatible with the aims of a crime-reductionist discourse (but without the criminogenic stigma).

Indeed, the Child First guiding principle has already shown that it has benefitted from the theory of change to gain acceptance in policy and practice in England and Wales, and specifically in navigating the concerns of stakeholders with clear crime-reductionist mandates and priorities. For example, the Youth Custody Service has Child First underpinning its new policies (such as early and late release), and has adopted the development of children's pro-social identity as its theory of change (Hazel and Case, 2023). Similarly, the current HM Chief Inspector of Probation, while having some concerns about the fourth tenet around diversion, has publicly supported Child First, "believing that there should be a focus on developing each child's strengths and pro-social identity" (HMIP, 2022, p 5). Notably, more recently, HM Inspectorate of Probation praised as 'Outstanding' a youth offending team that has introduced an operating model that explicitly focuses on identity development, which 'ensures a Child First approach to desistance and positive outcomes for children' (HMIP, 2023, p 7). This is a reassuring message and model for practitioners who have been concerned about how to navigate perceived tensions between Child First and inspection criteria[1] that have been felt to be based on the narrow RFPP rather than the broader evidence base incorporated into the principle's four tenets (Day, 2022).

In conclusion, while arguing that the integration of a theory of change for desistance has allowed traction for progressive, evidence-informed, youth justice practice within the present political discourse, we further contend that it also provides a guiding principle that will inevitably raise challenging questions about assumptions within that discourse (Hazel and Case, 2023). Ultimately, this may lead policy makers to question whether a 'justice' system with a principal aim of preventing children's (re)offending is the most conducive environment to achieve that desistance.

Note

[1] In referencing inspection criteria, however, we are conscious that it is imperative that Child First's move from a deficit-based model to one that is focused on positive child outcomes requires an accompanying change in performance indicators by which the system can measure success (Case and Browning, 2021). Crucially, given its place as a theory of change, there is no current child-focused measure of pro-social identity in practice use (although a new scale has recently been found to be reliable in tests [Hazel and Birkbeck, forthcoming]).

References

Barton, W.H. (2006) 'Incorporating the strengths perspective into intensive juvenile aftercare', *Western Criminology Review*, 7(2): 48–61.

Bateman, T. (2020) 'The state of youth justice 2020', London: NAYJ.

Bateman, T. and Hazel, N. (2013) 'Engaging young people in resettlement: research report', London: Beyond Youth Custody/Nacro.

Bateman, T. and Hazel, N. (2014) 'The resettlement of girls and young women: evidence from research', London: Beyond Youth Custody/Nacro.

Bateman, T., Hazel, N. and Wright, S. (2013) 'Resettlement of young people leaving custody: lessons from the literature', London: Beyond Youth Custody/Nacro.

Becker, H. (1963) *Outsiders: Studies in the Sociology of Deviance*, New York: Free Press.

Beyond Youth Custody (2017) 'Lessons from youth in focus: research report', London: Beyond Youth Custody.

Brazier, L., Hurry, J. and Wilson, A. (2010) 'Post-16 education and training provision for young people involved in crime', London: Institute of Education.

Butts, J. (2014) 'Strengthening youth justice practices with developmental knowledge and principles', Baltimore: Annie E. Casey Foundation.

Case, S.P. (2021) 'Challenging the reductionism of "evidence-based" youth justice', *Sustainability*, 13(4): 1735 (online first).

Case, S.P. (2023) 'Challenging the risk paradigm: children first, positive youth justice', in S.P. Case and N. Hazel (eds) *Child First: Developing a New Youth Justice System*, London: Palgrave Macmillan, pp 51–82.

Case, S. and Browning, A. (2021) 'Child First justice: the research evidence-base', Loughborough University, Available from: https://repository.lboro.ac.uk/articles/report/Child_First_Justice_the_research_evidence-base_Full_report_/14152040

Case, S.P. and Haines, K.R. (2009) *Understanding Youth Offending: Risk Factor Research, Policy and Practice*, Cullompton: Willan Publishing.

Case, S.P. and Haines, K.R. (2018) 'Transatlantic "positive youth justice": coherent movement or disparate critique? *Crime Prevention and Community Safety*, 20(3): 208–22.

Case, S.P., Sutton, C., Monaghan, M., Greenhalgh, J. and Wright, J. (2022) 'Contextualising evaluations of interventions to prevent youth offending: "what works" and EMMIE', *Safer Communities*, 21(4): 272–89.

Cote, J.E. (2006) 'Identity studies: how close are we to developing a social science of identity? An appraisal of the field', *Identity*, 6: 3–25.

Cox, A. (2020) 'The new economy and youth justice', *Youth Justice*, 21(1): 107–126.

Day, A.-M. (2022) '"It's a hard balance to find": the perspectives of youth justice practitioners in England on the place of "risk" in an emerging "Child First" world', *Youth Justice*, 23(1): 58–75, Available from: https://doi.org/10.1177%2F14732254221075205

Day, A.-M., Clark, A. and Hazel, N. (2023) 'Hearing from justice-involved, care experienced children: what are their experiences of residential care environments and regimes?', *Journal of Children's Services*, 18(1): 47–60, Available from: https://doi.org/10.1108/JCS-02-2022-0011

Deakin, J., Fox, C. and Matos, R. (2020) 'Labelled as "risky" in an era of control: how young people experience and respond to the stigma of criminalized identities', *European Journal of Criminology*, 19(4): 653–73.

Drake, D.H., Ferguson, R. and Briggs, D.B. (2014) 'Hearing new voices: reviewing youth justice policy through practitioners' relationships with young people', *Youth Justice*, 14(1): 22–39.

Drakeford, M. (2010) 'Devolution and youth justice in Wales', *Criminology & Criminal Justice*, 10(2): 137–54.

Dunkel, F. (2014) 'Juvenile justice systems in Europe: reform developments between justice, welfare and "new punitiveness"', *Kriminologiljos Studijos*, 1(1): 31–76.

Elwick, A., Davis, M., Crehan, L. and Clay, B. (2013) 'Improving outcomes for young offenders: an international perspective', CfBT Education Trust.

Erikson, E.H. (1968) *Identity, Youth and Crisis*, New York: W.W. Norton.

Farrington, D.P. (2000) 'Explaining and preventing crime: the globalization of knowledge', *Criminology*, 38(1): 1–24.

Farrington, D.P. (2007) 'Childhood risk factors and risk-focused prevention', in M. Maguire, R. Morgan and R. Rainer (eds) *The Oxford Handbook of Criminology*, Oxford: Oxford University Press, pp 602–40.

Feeley, M. and Simon, J. (1992) 'The new penology: notes on the emerging strategy of corrections and its implications', *Criminology*, 30(4): 449–74.

Haigh, Y. (2009) 'Desistance from crime: reflections on the transitional experiences of young people with a history of reoffending', *Journal of Youth Studies*, 12(3): 307–22.

Haines, K. and Case, S. (2015) *Positive Youth Justice: Children First, Offenders Second*, Bristol: Policy Press.

Haines, K. and Case, S. (2018) 'The future of youth justice', *Youth Justice*, 18(2): 131–48.

Haines, K. and Drakeford, M. (1998) *Young People and Youth Justice*, London: Bloomsbury.

Harcourt, B. (2007) *Against Prediction*, Chicago: University of Chicago Press.

Hazel, N. (2008) 'Cross-national comparison of youth justice', London: Youth Justice Board.

Hazel, N. and Bateman, T. (2021) 'Supporting children's resettlement ("reentry") after custody: beyond the risk paradigm', *Youth Justice*, 21(1): 71–89.

Hazel, N. and Birkbeck, C. (forthcoming) 'A pro-social identity scale for children', University of Salford.

Hazel, N. and Case, S. (2023) 'Postscript: progress and challenges for progressing progressive Child First youth justice', in S.P. Case and N. Hazel (eds) *Child First: Developing a New Youth Justice System*, London: Palgrave Macmillan, pp 367–85.

Hazel, N. and Williams, P. (2023) 'Developing Child First as the guiding principle for youth justice', in S.P. Case and N. Hazel (eds) *Child First: Developing a New Youth Justice System*, London: Palgrave Macmillan, pp 169–201.

Hazel, N., Wright, S., Liddle, M., Renshaw, J. and Gray, P. (2012) 'Evaluation of the North West Resettlement Consortium: final report', London: Youth Justice Board.

Hazel, N., Wright, S., Lockwood, K., McAteer, L., Francis, V. and Goodfellow, P. (2016) 'The role of the family in resettlement', London: Beyond Youth Custody/Nacro.

Hazel, N., Goodfellow, P., Liddle, M., Bateman, T. and Pitts, J. (2017) '"Now all I care about is my future": supporting the shift; framework for the resettlement of young people leaving custody', London: Nacro.

Hazel, N., Drummond, C., Welsh, M. and Joseph, K. (2020) 'Using an identity lens: constructive working with children in the criminal justice system', London: Nacro.

HMIP (2015) 'Joint thematic inspection of resettlement services to children by Youth Offending Teams and partner agencies', London: HM Inspectorate of Probation.

HMIP (2022) '2021 annual report: inspections of youth offending services', HM Inspectorate of Probation.

HMIP (2023) 'An inspection of youth offending services in Swindon', HM Inspectorate of Probation.

Huizinga, D., Schumann, K., Ehret, B. and Elliot, A. (2003) 'The effects of juvenile justice processing on subsequent delinquent and criminal behavior: a cross-national study', Washington, DC: Final Report to the National Institute of Justice.

Jenkins, R. (2008) *Social Identity* (3rd edn), Abingdon: Routledge.

Knight, V. (2014) 'Framing education and learning in youth justice in England and Wales: some outcomes for young offender interventions', *British Journal of Community Justice*, 12(1): 49.

Maruna, S. (2001) *Making Good: How Ex-convicts Reform and Rebuild Their Lives*, Washington, DC: American Psychological Association.

Maruna, S. and Farrall, S. (2004) 'Desistance from crime: a theoretical reformulation', *Kolner Zeitschrift für Soziologie und Sozialpsychologie*, 43: 171–94.

Maruna, S. and Roy, K. (2007) 'Amputation or reconstruction? Notes on the concept of "knifing off" and desistance from crime', *Journal of Contemporary Criminal Justice*, 23(1): 104–24.

McAra, L. and McVie, S. (2015) 'The case for diversion and minimum necessary intervention', in B. Goldson and J. Muncie (eds) *Youth Crime and Justice*, London: Sage, pp 119–35.

McMahon, G. and Jump, D. (2018) 'Starting to stop: young offenders' desistance from crime', *Youth Justice*, 18(1): 3–17.

McNeill, F. and Weaver, B. (2010) 'Changing lives? Desistance research and offender management', SCCJR Project Report 03/2010.

MoJ/YJB (2019) 'Standards for children in the youth justice system 2019', London: Ministry of Justice.

MOPAC (2021) 'Brave space knife crime toolkit', London Mayor's Office.

O'Mahony, P. (2009) 'The Risk Factors Prevention Paradigm and the causes of youth crime: a deceptively useful analysis?', *Youth Justice*, 9(2): 99–114.

Petrosino, A., Turpin-Petrosino, C. and Guckenburg, S. (2010) 'Formal system processing of juveniles: effects on delinquency', *Campbell Systematic Reviews*, 1: 3–8

Prior, D. and Mason, P. (2010) 'A different kind of evidence: looking for "what works" in engaging young offenders', *Youth Justice*, 10(3): 211–26.

Roeser, R.W., Peck, S.C. and Nasir, N.S. (2006) 'Self and identity processes in school motivation, learning and achievement', in P.A. Alexander and P.H. Winne (eds) *Handbook of Educational Psychology*, Mahwah, NJ: Erlbaum.

Smith, R. (2017) *Diversion in Youth Justice: What Can We Learn from Historical and Contemporary Practices?*, London: Routledge.

Smith, R. and Gray, P. (2019) 'The changing shape of youth justice: models of practice', *Criminology and Criminal Justice*, 19(5): 554–71.

Sutherland, A. (2009) 'The "Scaled Approach" in youth justice: fools rush in', *Youth Justice*, 9(1): 44–60.

Taylor, C. (2016) 'Great expectations: towards better learning outcomes for young people and young adults in custody', London: Prisoners' Education Trust.

Tonry, M. (2019) 'Predictions of dangerousness in sentencing: déjà vu all over again', *Crime and Justice*, 48: 439–82.

Tyler, T. (ed) (2007) *Legitimacy and Criminal Justice: International Perspectives*, New York: Russell Sage Foundation.

Tyler, T. (2011) *Why People Cooperate: The Role of Social Motivation*, Princeton: Princeton University Press.

Wainwight, L. and Nee, C. (2013) 'The Good Lives Model: new directions for preventative practice with children?', *Psychology, Crime & Law*, 20(2): 166–82.

Wigzell, A. (2021) 'Explaining desistance: looking forward, not backwards', London: NAYJ.

Wright, S., Francis, V., McAteer, L. and Goodfellow, P. (2015) 'Ethnicity, faith and culture in resettlement: a practitioner's guide', London: Beyond Youth Custody/Nacro.

YJB (Youth Justice Board) (2003) 'Key Elements for Effective Practice/ KEEPS', London: Youth Justice Board.

YJB (2010) 'Youth justice: the Scaled Approach: a framework for assessment and interventions', London: Youth Justice Board.

YJB (2018) 'How to make resettlement constructive', London: Youth Justice Board.

YJB (2019) 'Youth Justice Board for England and Wales strategic plan 2019–2022', London: Youth Justice Board.

YJB (2021) 'Youth Justice Board for England and Wales strategic plan 2021–2024', London: Youth Justice Board.

YJB (2022) 'Case management guidance', London: Youth Justice Board, Available from: https://www.gov.uk/guidance/case-management-guidance

3

Child time, adult time, fugitivity and desistance

Diana Johns

Introduction

Criminologies of youth and childhood are remarkably adult-focused. There is a mountain of research evidence about young people's offending, and the reasons for it, yet criminology is largely bereft of child-focused perspectives. *Where is the child's voice? Where are the viewpoints of children?* Perhaps this lacuna is unsurprising given the focus of criminology on *crime*, which is an adult construct, and the way its social constructedness is frequently forgotten, ignored or belied by an emphasis on statistical data that tend to generate their own 'objective' reality. When we gather statistics about who is arrested, who appears before courts, who is imprisoned, for instance, we can easily slide into assumptions about these data having a self-evident existence. But these data do not exist in isolation. Rather, they are very often manifestations of policing practices and everyday decision-making that are inevitably infused with colonial histories, power relations and prejudices. Take the concept of *over-representation*, for example, which makes us think that it is the 'over-represented' themselves who are the problem rather than the deeply racialised systems and processes through which Black and Brown children are policed and criminalised. The way racialised children's lives can be both 'masked' and 'marked' by youth justice risk assessments (Cunneen, 2020) suggests that *over-criminalisation* is a more accurate term. Such blind spots in criminology explain, in part, how adult concepts and scales come to dominate responses to children who 'offend'. *Desistance* is one such concept: an adult notion increasingly applied uncritically, undifferentiated and unmodified, to non-adults.

In this chapter, I examine this problem through the lens of *time*. My rationale is that children and adults experience time differently. In *The Revolution of Everyday Life*, Vaneigem (2001 [1968], p 97) hints at this when he writes: 'The child's days escape adult time; their time is swollen by subjectivity, passion, dreams haunted by reality. Outside, the educators look on, waiting, watch in hand, till the child joins and fits the cycle of the hours. It's they who *have time*.' In describing how *the child's days escape adult time*,

57

Vaneigem introduces threads and imagery that can help us think about the differences between child time and adult time, and how these temporalities coexist, coincide, coalesce, diverge and collide. Youth and childhood are transitional stages of human development, inherently fleeting, marked by suppleness, malleability and growth. When we impose adult concepts on children's lives and experiences, however, we act as if this is not the case. Rarely factored in is the child's perspective. Least of all, children's experience of time. In this chapter, therefore, using Bronfenbrenner's social ecological *chronosystem* as a starting point, and the notion of *fugitivity*, I explore different conceptions of time – and how it is experienced by children – to show how desistance is always oriented beyond the child, outside the child's time. I argue that a deeper understanding and acknowledgement of child and youth temporalities is important for shaping – indeed limiting – youth justice intervention in children's lives. As McAra and McVie (2007) insist, after all, the key to reducing children's harmful behaviours is a *minimal intervention, maximum diversion* approach.

Desistance is a temporal concept, yet its temporality is largely taken for granted. Indeed, despite *change over time* being inherent to the idea of offending cessation, the conceptualisation of time is underdeveloped in desistance theory, youth justice scholarship and criminology more broadly. Desistance theory brings together theories of narrative and identity, social bonds and maturation and the life course (Maruna, 2001). Arguably, in the context of childhood, the most influential of these is the developmental life-course perspective. Developmental life-course criminology (see, for example, Farrington et al, 2019) conceives adolescent development in bio-psycho-social terms, focusing on cognitive, behavioural and environmental risk factors for so-called 'delinquency'. Developmental discourse thus tends to cast 'abnormal' child or adolescent behaviour in terms of pathology, risk and deficit. The problem, as others in this volume have made clear, is that children's ongoing neurodevelopment and *normal* adolescent rebellion, boundary-testing and risk-taking become risk factors (or areas of *criminogenic need*) to be addressed in youth justice intervention rather than reasons to rethink that intervention entirely. The harmful impacts of institutional involvement are scarcely considered, despite evidence that youth justice contact is associated with '*inhibited* desistance from offending' (McAra and McVie, 2007, p 319), and relationships with adults are shown to be critical in shaping children's outcomes, both positive and negative (Smith, 2006; Gopnik, 2022).

Desistance as a framework for working with children (as with adults) similarly risks casting them as the problem, by focusing on children's 'offending' behaviour as the starting point rather than the relationships and contexts within which children's experiences are embedded. Of course, desistance-based practice *can* be entirely contextual and relationship-oriented.

However, when desistance thinking falls into this risk-thinking trap – failing to problematise the processes through which children are criminalised and instead problematising children in ways that can limit their flourishing, growth and becoming – I would argue, it needs rethinking.

From this perspective, the desistance problem is not one of bringing children's 'bad' behaviour to an end. The problem rests with adults: as the architects, engineers and agents of the so-called *justice* system, it is beholden upon adults to uphold the principles the system is supposed to enshrine – that is, to do no harm and act justly. Criminalising children causes harm and rarely leads to just outcomes.[1] A desistance framework thus not only applies an adult concept with little relevance to young people's lives (as Barry [2010] suggests) but risks reproducing and thus perpetuating that harm. Before delving into the temporal complexities of children's lives, I briefly consider the rights of the child to be treated as a child.

Child rights

International human rights agreements[2] have sought to recognise and enshrine children's rights to childhood. The widely ratified United Nations Convention on the Rights of the Child (UNCRC, 1989), for instance, opens with the Universal Declaration of Human Rights' assertion that 'childhood is entitled to special care and assistance' (UNCRC preamble, p 3). In this spirit, the UNCRC emphasises *listening* to children, granting every child 'the right to express [their] views freely in all matters affecting [them], the views of the child being given due weight in accordance with the age and maturity of the child' (Article 12). Children are promised, specifically, 'the opportunity to be heard in any judicial and administrative proceedings affecting [them]' (Article 12). The UNCRC (Article 37) further guarantees that, in signatory states:

a. No child shall be subjected to … *cruel, inhuman or degrading* treatment or punishment …
b. … detention or imprisonment of a child shall be in conformity with the law and shall be used only as a measure of last resort and *for the shortest appropriate period of time*;
c. Every child deprived of liberty shall be treated with humanity and *respect for the inherent dignity* of the human person, and in a manner which takes into account *the needs of persons of his or her age*. (UNCRC, Article 37, emphasis added)

Laudable ideals and cherished values, undeniably. However, rights talk has limitations in that, first, it is 'thin' (Blattberg, 2009, p 45). Secondly, it tends to normalise a binary view of humans (adult/child, offenders/non-offenders) that can reduce complexity in unhelpful ways. The notion of 'offences committed by persons below eighteen years of age' (Article 37[a]), for instance, rests on the assumption that children *can* commit offences, as a natural 'fact', and ignores the fact that 'offences' are a construct, a product of social norms and legal definition. The 'child as offender' is abstracted, stripped of meaning, decontextualised through the process of abstraction.[3] As Blattberg (2009, p 45) notes, 'the root of "abstraction" denotes a "drawing away from" ... [whereas] the root of its opposite, "contextual," means "woven together"'. The danger is that in accepting a thin, one-dimensional rendering of the rights-bearing child 'offender', we focus on separateness rather than interrelatedness; we distance ourselves from real-life children and our obligations to attend to the thick, messy context of their lives. We may even responsibilise individual children for their actions, instead of taking collective responsibility for their circumstances. Abstraction, therefore, is dangerous – 'it detracts from a value's ability to motivate people to uphold it. This happens because ... the move from thick to thin language makes things less of a concern to us' (Blattberg, 2009, p 46); we *care less*.

Similarly, the child/adult binary blinds us to its conceptual instability: if childhood means being-not-yet-adult, and adulthood is being-no-longer-child, then the categories blur into each other, they are not fixed. Growing up is a process: fuzzy, complex, characterised by in-betweenness, emergence and transformation. Adolescent development exceeds adult rates of change yet is constrained within adult-imposed and adult-structured timeframes, implying the coexistence of multiple temporalities.

Temporal ecologies

Understanding how young people become involved in 'offending', how they negotiate criminalising processes and how they can be best supported towards positive change requires deep acknowledgement of and engagement with such complexities. Bronfenbrenner's bioecological framework (1995; Bronfenbrenner and Morris, 1998, 2006) affords a view of complexity, of how children's lives proceed simultaneously 'in the moment' (Haines et al, 2021) and across time. It provides a window into interrelatedness, multiplicity and contingency in ways that loosen and complicate binary constructs such as child/offender, good/bad. And though a social ecological framework is familiar to many, it is often misused (Tudge et al, 2009) or used in limited ways that tend to reinforce rather than dislodge simplistic conceptions. This is a problem when it limits our view of children's lives in terms of their possibilities and potential for growth, learning and change.

Bronfenbrenner sees human development as unfolding within five nested ecologies: the microsystem, mesosystem, exosystem, macrosystem and the chronosystem. In many ways, given youth and childhood are transitional stages that are time-bound and temporary, the *chrono*system is most relevant – *chronos* representing the early Greek personification of time – yet it is the least considered in practice, perhaps because some systems – those that are more easily identifiable – provide a practical map for relational work with children and families. For example, the *micro*system describes the individual child in their immediate context; the *meso-* and *exo*systems refer to ever-expanding circles of relationship between kin networks, friendship, school, work and neighbourhood settings.[4] And the *macro*system, which describes larger sociocultural, economic, political and structural conditions and circumstances, can be useful for locating sites of advocacy and intervention at a policy level. The *chrono*system, however, is less tangible, more abstract and therefore harder to know *what to do with* in practice. For this reason – or perhaps because Bronfenbrenner (1979) initially described four nested systems and added the chronosystem later (1986a, 1986b) – Bronfenbrenner's approach is often narrowly conceived as a two-dimensional schema used to model social relationships in a way that simplifies complexity (Tudge et al, 2009). Often the *chrono*system, and the critical element of *time*, is left out.

Time is central to Bronfenbrenner's understanding of human development. As his (1995) Process–Person–Context–Time model suggests, time is an intrinsic and 'defining property of the bioecological paradigm' (Bronfenbrenner and Morris, 2006, p 820). The model centres the importance of progressively more complex reciprocal social interactions, or *proximal processes*, which occur over time. And time is implied in his definition of development as 'continuity and change in the biopsychological characteristics of human beings, both as individuals and as groups. The phenomenon extends over the life course, across successive generations, and through historical time, both past and future' (Bronfenbrenner and Morris, 2006, p 793).

The chronosystem thus accounts for time at different scales. The chronosystem of children's lives encompasses wide-ranging and overlapping timescales: moment-to-moment feelings, everyday experiences, rhythms and routines; periods of hecticness and stability; annual events, seasonal rituals, life-course markers, milestones and turning-points; human eras, historical periods and cultural movements (such as #BlackLivesMatter). A chronosystemic perspective thus highlights how everyday experiences sit inside and are shaped by larger timescales and temporalities, and how 'historical events can alter the course of human development, in either direction, not only for individuals, but for large segments of the population' (Bronfenbrenner, 1995, p 643). Stern et al (2022), for example, have adapted Bronfenbrenner's bioecological model to focus on Black youth development and attachment processes in context. By showing the interrelatedness of 'systemic racism in its multiple forms (including environmental and medical racism), colorism, and historical trauma' (Stern et al, 2022, p 403), they illustrate how histories seep into families and communities, filter through generations, shaping children's lives in invisible yet material ways. In settler colonies, like Australia, this ecological context includes the ongoing impacts of colonisation.

Taking a *chronosystemic* perspective can thus help deepen our understanding of child and youth temporalities and how they sit inside, alongside *and* outside adult time; how children experience both 'the "ordinary magic" of cultural strengths, joy, and family resilience' (Stern et al, 2022, p 393) and the invisible currents of historical pain or shame. A deep embodied understanding of these complexities requires thick context rather than thin accounts drained of life by abstraction. One way to thicken and complexify the abstract gaze is through storytelling, as story awakens imagination. This matters because, in the first instance, supporting criminalised children to transcend a criminalised identity[5] requires *imagining them differently*. Imagination offers 'both the possibility of history and of a tomorrow' (Andrews, 2014, p 3), and through narrative imagination we become time travellers: listening in the present yet propelled into the 'not yet' of possible futures (Andrews, 2014, pp 2–5). Time travel is a useful metaphor for engaging with children, who tend to live and act 'in the moment' (Haines et al, 2021), as it invites us to engage with the scale and nonlinearity of child time. The quote at the beginning of this chapter – *The child's days escape adult time; their time is swollen by subjectivity, passion, dreams haunted by reality* – gives a glimpse into this temporality. How moments penetrate each other, projecting the past into the future, where nostalgia, yearning and remembering are intertwined and time is fragmented, punctuated by sensation and memory. Adult time is imposed over and encircles child time: 'Outside, the educators look on, waiting, watch in hand, till the child joins and fits the cycle of the hours. It's they who *have time*' (Vaneigem, 2001 [1968], p 97). These words are brought into sharp relief by a personal story about a bright 13-year-old I know. One day, he is called to the school principal's office with his mother (who shared the story with me), following repeated incidents of behaviour contravening school policy. The principal wants to convey the seriousness of the situation:

School Principal:	I've been here a long time …
13-year-old:	I've been here my whole life!

In this brief exchange, temporal worlds collide. For the child, 'my whole life' consists of his living memory; for the adult, this lifetime is merely a fragment of their own. It raises the question: *What is the meaning of a concept such as 'desistance' for a child whose 'whole life' fits into a fragment of an adult's career?*

Desistance projects a past into a future beyond the scale of a child's life. It assumes an ability to look back and forward, *from an adult perspective*, through a different temporality, beyond the horizon of the child's experience. This is an example of how adult concepts are frequently applied to children without thinking critically about that concept from a child's perspective. Our 'whole life' comprises the range of our experiences, everything we've ever done and everything that has happened to us. From a child's perspective, if desistance means a process of cessation over a timeframe that exceeds the extent of their 'whole life', what meaning can that possibly hold for them? Some argue, as Maruna et al (2015) point out, that tertiary or long-term desistance can only be measured at the end of life, in death. Desistance in the context of childhood, therefore, becomes empty, irrelevant, meaningless; bereft of life before it's even been conceived. My point here, to reiterate, is that desistance is an adult concept. My argument is that adults working within a desistance framework need to think critically about the history, the genealogy, the lines of descent of such concepts and to be aware of the assumptions built into them.

Time, for instance, is taken for granted. Yet how might we think differently if we think in terms of a teenager's temporality, where the gaps between things are as important as the events themselves? The paradox of 'the gap' (Johns et al, 2018) is highlighted by 'Elis' (not his real name), a young adult reflecting on his years of 'prolific offending' as a teenager, about what adults need to do to help young people move away from offending: "That's what they need to do, they need to give you a gap, to see if you're gonna do crime, or otherwise how are they gonna know if it's working or not?" For him, these gaps were critical: every opportunity to 'slip up' became an opportunity for progress and potential 'success'. Elis talked about this in terms of 'pushing the gaps':

> 'The first time I went to jail I went for four months, but there was like a gap of say eleven months, then I went back to jail for like eight months, then there'd be another gap for like a year, so every time I was making progress, even though I was going back to jail, and I was getting longer sentences ... the gaps was pushing.' ('Elis' in Johns et al, 2018, p 99)

To avoid the trap of seeing children as miniature adults, we need to be attuned to children's temporalities, to allow memory of what it means to be a child to surface. Rather than focusing on *not offending*, or desistance, perhaps concentrating on 'pushing' or stretching *the gaps in between* is more meaningful to a child. This involves turning towards the child, and their experiences, rather than orienting the child towards adult time. I explore these ideas in the following section.

Fugitivity

Paradoxically, while childhood and youth are short-lived – all too brief in retrospect – they are frequently experienced *in the moment* as a sense of immortality, invincibility, ongoing-ness. The notion of *fugitivity* captures this paradox, illuminating not only the ephemerality of youth and childhood but also the impetuosity and spontaneity that teenagers typically embody, recalling how *the child's days escape adult time*. Tracing the poetics and rhythms of fugitivity, Macharia (2013) muses:

> Fugitivity is time-distorting, multiplying and erasing, making legion and invisible: the time of growing and harvesting, the time of gathering and watching, the time of rescue and hibernation. ... Breaking temporal bounds with out-of-season memories and stories, the precise way to collect wild herbs. And the smell of ready ... the feeling of jump.

Macharia's lyrical language and opaque imagery is useful for thinking about fugitivity as *hard to pin down* – as a concept *and* a way of being young (including its sensory aspects – 'the smell of ready ... the feeling of jump') – how it might *feel*, for instance, to be a child: 'To sneak in and around, about and away, to crevice and burrow: to jump under fences (the world-making of fugitivity: this-then-that-this)' (Macharia, 2013).

Giroux (1996, pp 10–11) describes youth cultures as *fugitive cultures*, 'not because they are inherently oppositional ... but because they often do not conform to the imperatives of adults and mainstream culture'. Adult and mainstream cultural imperatives tend to emphasise conformity and compliance with norms that reflect histories and traditions about what is *right* and *proper*, whereas fugitivity means 'breaking from propriety, on the run from ownership' in Moten's terms (2018, p 130), as he elaborates: 'Fugitivity ... is a desire for and a spirit of escape and transgression of the proper and the proposed. It's a desire for the outside, for a playing or being outside, an outlaw edge ... it moves outside ... adherence to the law and to propriety' (Moten, 2018, p 131).

Youth itself is the escapee, perpetually policed, chased, on the run. This can mean being trapped in adult categories, 'ontologically incarcerated'[6] (Akomolafe, 2021; Du Cann and Akomolafe, 2021), by Moten's 'the proper and the proposed'. One way of fleeing this captivity is by producing 'fugitive knowledge ... forms that often exist either outside of the mainstream curriculum or are seen as unworthy of serious attention' (Giroux, 1996, pp 19–20). Thus, the fugitivity of youth, as Virno (2004, p 70) observes, is not passive but active, creative, adaptive, unruly: 'Nothing is less passive than the act of fleeing, of exiting. ... [And] exit consists of unrestrained invention which alters the rules of the game and throws the adversary completely off balance ... exit hinges on a latent kind of wealth, on an exuberance of possibilities.'

This knowledge, these stories, this 'exuberance of possibilities' is what we (adults) must pay attention to – listen to – in our efforts to understand young people's experiences of and perspectives on the world. Rather than being criminalised or punished, children need time to gather, in 'the bent school or marginal church ... to *be* in the name of *being otherwise*' (Moten, 2018, p 160, emphasis added). Children and young people need time to grow and learn in places of safety, time for what Akomolafe (Du Cann & Akomolafe, 2021) calls "making sanctuary", which means "gathering those who have been disarticulated by cracks in the environment to work with those cracks, rather than patching them up and returning to normal" (p 7).

Making sanctuary, working with cracks, takes time. It's adults who *have time*.

Escaping adult time

We might think of child time as *kairo*logical time, as opposed to the *chrono*logical time of adults and institutions and machines that reflect the prevailing linear way of understanding time. From the Greek, *chronos* is quantitative time – 'time as measure, the quantity of duration, the length of periodicity, the age of an object or artifact and the rate of acceleration of bodies' – whereas *kairos* may be understood as qualitative time – the 'right time' – the times of moments, tides, seasons, callings, events, the time to act (Smith, 1986, p 4). These different conceptualisations reflect differences within Western traditions (for example see Canales, 2016), and between Indigenous and non-Indigenous ways of being (for example see Iparraguirre, 2015), which are important for showing how time is not singular or linear but *multiple* and operating at different scales *simultaneously*. Vaneigem (2001 [1968], p 100), for instance, distinguishes different experiences of time. *Subjective* time is 'the space-time of moments, of creativity, pleasure and orgasm ... subjective life concentrated in the space of a point. ... It is lived experience without dead time'. On the other hand, *objective* time is

> time that flows away, in linear time, the time of things ... negative time ... dead time ... the time of the role, the time within life itself which encourages it to lose its character and renounce authentically lived space, to hold back and prefer appearances and the spectacular function. (1968, p 100)

By way of a story to illustrate these different space–time experiences, in her book *Bad Boys*, Ann Ferguson (2020) reflects on her 'exhausting journey through space and time' with a 12-year-old boy, Horace, on the afternoon she 'crossed over, if ever so briefly' (p 27) into his temporality. Horace had a reputation as 'a boy who was difficult and out of control' (p 14) – 'volatile' and 'insubordinate' – 'he tested, resisted, and defied the authority of certain adults' (p 15). She describes a field trip with Horace when he 'dragged me by the hand into his world one Saturday afternoon at the movies':

I was never aware of the exact moment when I stopped being an adult. But somewhere between *My Girl* and *Hook*, I began to have a good time. … That was when the whole experience began to be transformed from the planned linear motion from beginning to end to a kaleidoscopic back-and-forth of sights, sounds, and tastes. (Ferguson, 2020, pp 26–7)

Through spending time with Horace, Ferguson learnt 'to see kids not as humans-in-the-making but as resourceful social actors who took an active role in shaping their daily experiences … within structures of power' (2020, p 15). This story opens a window into the child's world, time-travelling and fugitivity, and how *the child's days escape adult time.*

Multiple, complex temporalities

For the Yolngu of north-east Arnhem Land, Australia, as for other Indigenous peoples, time is spiral, nonlinear, affective and plural. Past/present/future are not static, singular states that exist in a linear sense; rather they are circular, multiple, collective. From this perspective, a person 'does not simply exist as a lone individual, acting in a single time' (Bawaka Country et al, 2020, p 297). Time is multiple, abundant, swollen, full of possibility:

Human perception cannot even start to comprehend many of the complex temporalities at work here. … This is the seasonal time of clouds gathering. It is also the time of hydrological cycles, of water moving through aquifers for thousands of years, of transpiration and growth. And short spirals, of the flash of lightning, claps of thunder, of traveling sound and light. There is neither a single weather, nor a single time, nor an inherent difference between time and matter and embodied experience. (Bawaka Country et al, 2020, p 300)

From this perspective, we might consider 'the past, present and future as nested and folded together, encircling linear goal-centred dissected "clock" time through rhythmic, cyclical, spiral sensing' (Paradies, 2020, p 2). Moreton (2006) similarly differentiates Indigenous understandings of time – 'in this moment, the ever-present now' (p 318) – from Western time, characterised by *deferral* – 'temporality that is future bound rather than in this moment, the ever-present now' (p 318) – 'the present is suspended, and the temporal deferment displaces the moment' (p 200). This fits with emerging understandings in Western science, distinguishing 'time's arrow and time's cycle' (Gould, 1987), for instance, or *things* from *events*:

The difference between things and events is that things persist over time; events have a limited duration. A stone is a prototypical 'thing': we can ask ourselves where it will be tomorrow. Conversely, a kiss is an 'event'. It makes no sense to ask where the kiss will be tomorrow. *The world is made up of networks of kisses, not stones.* (Rovelli, 2018, p 98, emphasis added)

Thinking about the multiple temporalities of childhood, we might distinguish moments, events and experiences that each have their own timeframe and duration, unbounded and inestimable. Moments of *discovery*, for example, unfold over a series of moments threaded together by curiosity and wonder: seeing, for example, a silver coin reflected in a puddle of water as an object to be picked up, grasped in the fingers; discovering in that moment both the possibility and impossibility of holding the moon in the palm of your hand. *Play* likewise has its own duration, rhythm and *now-ness* that does not fit within linear time (think of Ferguson's day with Horace at the movies). Kisses of *joy* – the moments we live for and live by – are equally effervescent and fleeting. Other aspects of childhood have different tempos: how long it takes to build trust, for instance; the fluctuating, undulating, unpredictable rate of physical growth and development; the time it takes for traumatic events or experiences to percolate, settle or surface. These processes can work at geological scales.

Killing time

Why does any of this matter? What are the implications of thinking with the temporalities and fugitivity of youth and childhood? First, it is agreed that childhood is a special state of being, different from adulthood: '[C]hildhood is entitled to special care and assistance' (UNCRC preamble). But as adults we steal time – we kill children's time – 'siphoning off' life in ways that are unjustifiable from a rights perspective,[7] which values children's voices and experiences and their *inherent dignity*. Secondly, childhood is limited, short-lived. By taking time from a child – starving them of embodied, emotional, psychological, cultural, spiritual life – we are killing time and thereby killing the future. Time is used to regulate, order, control, punish, contain children's lives and behaviour every day: 'time out' – whether a chair in the corner of a room, an after-school detention or a custodial sentence – is time-theft used for punishment and control. Time is stolen from children whenever we impose adult time.

Youth justice intervention is always based on adult time, institutional time. Some consequences are benign; others may be irreparable, even fatal. Consider the period a child may spend remanded to custody: *one day in a child's life* is significant; weeks or months cause deep psychological and physical harm (Gooch, 2016). There may be serious and multiple harms, such as secure schools causing *spirit murder* (Love, 2016), a form of racial violence that steals and kills the spirits and humanity of people of colour (Williams, 1987).

Education scholar Bettina Love defines spirit murdering as the 'denial of inclusion, protection, safety, nurturance, and acceptance' (2016, p 2); it is 'a slow death, a death of the spirit, a death that is built on racism intended to reduce, humiliate and destroy people of colour' (Love, 2019, np). In Australia, for example, where children can be criminalised at the age of ten, where hundreds of children are incarcerated on an average day, mostly unsentenced, where *more than half* of all imprisoned young people are Aboriginal or Torres Strait Islander (despite First Nations children comprising only 5.8 per cent of Australian ten- to 17-year-olds) (AIHW, 2022, p 20), justice intervention harms children. From a human perspective, this is unsustainable.

Justice demands *care* and *caring*. We, adults, have time to care. We must spend time, listening. ... If we listen, we will understand that children live and act *in the moment* and that 'the long-term consequences of their behaviour (i.e. anything subsequent to the act itself) are strangers to children' (Haines et al, 2020, p 2). What happens in the distant future is unfamiliar territory, an unknown land to children, when they have no prior experience within which to frame their current experiences. How can a person foresee or make sense of what they are yet to experience? And if they cannot make sense of it – cannot imagine its weight, depth or length – if it is beyond the scale of their life, what's the point of it? This notion of *scale* becomes critical when we are thinking about children and how they are different from adults. As Rodriguez[8] (1997, p 19) writes: 'When lawmakers say a child is "unredeemable" at age 16 or 13 or even 10, they are setting in concrete the mental and emotional state of a person that is, in reality, always in flux.' They are imposing an adult temporal scale over a child's days – by nature short, ephemeral, yet experienced as long, slow, never-ending.

Child time is fugitive. It flees, but only through the lens of adulthood. Only when we look back, down, through our past experiences, including those lodged in memory and those lost in forgotten time. Child time is slow-moving (think of summers that last forever, school hours that drag). Adult time, in contrast, speeds up. It thickens, becomes denser, full of memory and experience. Like stew, it *reduces* the longer it simmers. We sense we are running out of time as death nears.

Conclusion

Fugitive time, swollen time, stolen time: 'The child's days escape adult time; their time is swollen by subjectivity, passion.' Adults intervene in children's lives every day in ways that isolate, humiliate, exclude, responsibilise, criminalise and punish. Youth justice intervention, instance by instance, by imposing adult time over the child's days, steals time from children's lives. By criminalising children, we siphon off life, we starve childhood of embodied, emotional, psychological, cultural and spiritual life. By stealing time, we smother hope, stifle subjectivity, dowse passions, and snuff out dreams ... 'dreams haunted by reality'. We build realities that box in, puncture, corrode and confine time swollen with possibility and potential. We bring death to the future. Thinking in this way pushes us to reckon with our ideas and practices of so-called *justice*; to consider that children's rights to childhood are not rescinded when they make mistakes; to admit that, as adults, we relinquish the right to claim we are acting 'justly' when stealing time from a child; to acknowledge that stealing a child's time is stealing life. We must desist. Desistance means the cessation of offending, the act of not acting, *doing no harm*.

Desistance is a negation, a non-action (recalling McAra and McVie's [2007] insistence on *minimal intervention*, maximum diversion, which implies less offending-focused work and more time spent in positive, life-giving activities with children). From this perspective, we might think of *doing less* in terms of how we apply adult concepts, timeframes, definitions and categories to children's lives. We might do more in terms of spending time with children, inhabiting children's worlds, according to children's timeframes. Taking Ferguson's (2020) lead, we might cross over into children's temporalities and thereby learn 'to see kids not as humans-in-the-making but as resourceful social actors' (p 15). And we might recall the words of Vaneigem: 'Outside, the educators look on, waiting, watch in hand. ... It's they who *have time*.' We adults, educators, parents, professionals, rule-makers, rule-enforcers – with our watches in hand – we *have time* to spare, to spend, to invest in every child.

Notes

[1] For the purposes of this discussion, a 'just' outcome is one that addresses the harm caused by someone's action/s and meets the needs of those harmed to feel safe and reassured that the harm will not recur. This is a restorative, reintegrative understanding of doing 'justice' that sees retributive approaches as too often adding harm to the original offence and thereby increasing the quantum of harm overall.

[2] Including the Universal Declaration of Human Rights (1948); the International Covenant on Economic, Social and Cultural Rights (ICESCR, 1966a); and the International Covenant on Civil and Political Rights (ICCPR, 1966b).

[3] I acknowledge the collaborative thinking of colleagues Professors Steve Case, Tim Goddard and Kevin Haines, with whom I have been engaging critically with the process of *decontextualisation* of youth justice and youth offending.

[4] See Johns *et al.* (2017) for further explanation of Bronfenbrenner's five nested systems.

[5] That is, a social identity imposed on a child by virtue of their criminalisation, notwithstanding that children may not themselves develop a criminalised *self*-identity, as others note in this volume.

[6] As Du Cann (Du Cann and Akomolafe 2021) describes, 'Bayo [Akomolafe] works in intense metaphor, using metaphysical infrastructure to enable us to perceive how we are kept trapped by civilisation and how we might liberate ourselves from its invisible manacles. The building blocks of his lexicon include the *slave ship* (with three decks of colonisers, slaves, and Earth resources); the *plantation*, where we are set to work; and the *fugitive* who escapes the capture of both'.

[7] Kelly Hayes used the expression 'siphoning off' life in her conversation with Ruth Wilson Gilmore on Abolition, the Climate Crisis and What Must Be Done, *Movement Memos* podcast, 14 April 2022.

[8] Chicano poet, novelist, children's book author and journalist Luis J. Rodriguez tells the story of his childhood as a gang member in his book *Always Running: La Vida Loca; Gang Days in LA.*

References

Andrews, M. (2014) *Narrative Imagination and Everyday Life*, Oxford: Oxford University Press.

Australian Institute of Health and Welfare (2022) 'Youth justice in Australia 2020–21', Cat no JUV 138, Canberra: AIHW.

Barry, M. (2010) 'Youth transitions: from offending to desistance', *Journal of Youth Studies*, 13(1): 121–36.

Bawaka Country, including Wright, S., Suchet-Pearson, S., Lloyd, K., Burarrwanga, L., Ganambar, R., Ganambarr-Stubbs, M. et al (2020) 'Gathering of the clouds: attending to Indigenous understandings of time and climate through songspirals', *Geoforum*, 108: 295–304.

Blattberg, C. (2009) 'The ironic tragedy of human rights', in *Patriotic Elaborations: Essays in Practical Philosophy*, Montreal: McGill–Queen's University Press, pp 43–59.

Bronfenbrenner, U. (1979) *The Ecology of Human Development: Experiments by Nature and Design*, Cambridge, MA: Harvard University Press.

Bronfenbrenner, U. (1986a) 'Recent advances in research on the ecology of human development', in R.K. Silbereisen, K. Eyferth and G. Rudinger (eds) *Development as Action in Context: Problem Behavior and Normal Youth Development*, New York: Springer-Verlag, pp 286–309.

Bronfenbrenner, U. (1986b) 'The ecology of the family as a context for human development: research perspectives', *Developmental Psychology*, 22(6): 723–42.

Bronfenbrenner, U. (1995) 'Developmental ecology through space and time: a future perspective', in P. Moen, G.H. Elder and K. Lüscher (eds) *Examining Lives in Context: Perspectives on the Ecology of Human Development*, Washington, DC: American Psychological Association, pp 619–47.

Bronfenbrenner, U. and Morris, P.A. (1998) 'The ecology of developmental processes', in W. Damon and R.M. Lerner (eds) *Handbook of Child Psychology: Theoretical Models of Human Development*, Hoboken: John Wiley & Sons, pp 993–1028.

Bronfenbrenner, U. and Morris, P.A. (2006) 'The bioecological model of human development', in W. Damon and R.M. Lerner (eds) *Handbook of Child Psychology* (6th edn, vol 1), Hoboken: John Wiley & Sons, pp 793–828.

Canales, J. (2016) *The Physicist and the Philosopher: Einstein, Bergson, and the Debate That Changed Our Understanding of Time*, Princeton: Princeton University Press.

Cunneen, C. (2020) 'Youth justice and racialization: comparative reflections', *Theoretical Criminology*, 24(3): 521–39.

Du Cann, C. and Akomolafe, B. (2021) 'When the bones of our ancestors speak to us: a fugitive conversation with Bayo Akomolafe', *Resilience*, 28 October, Available from: https://www.resilience.org/stories/2021-10-28/when-the-bones-of-our-ancestors-speak-to-us-a-fugitive-conversation-with-bayo-akomolafe

Farrington, D., Kazemian, L. and Piquero, A.R. (eds) (2019) *The Oxford Handbook of Developmental and Life-Course Criminology*, Oxford: Oxford University Press.

Ferguson, A.A. (2020) *Bad Boys: Public Schools in the Making of Black Masculinity* (revised edn), Ann Arbor: University of Michigan Press.

Giroux, H.A. (1996) *Fugitive Cultures: Race, Violence, and Youth*, New York: Routledge.

Gooch, K. (2016) 'A childhood cut short: child deaths in penal custody and the pains of child imprisonment', *The Howard Journal of Crime and Justice*, 55(3): 278–94.

Gopnik, A. (2022) 'Love lets us learn: psychological science makes the case for policies that help children', *Observer*, 35(5): 1–9, Available from: https://www.psychologicalscience.org/issue/sept-oct22

Gould, S.J. (1987) *Time's Arrow, Time's Cycle: Myth and Metaphor in the Discovery of Geological Time*, Cambridge, MA: Harvard University Press.

Haines, K.R., Case, S.P., Smith, R., Laidler, K.J., Hughes, N., Webster, C. et al (2021) 'Children and crime: in the moment', *Youth Justice*, 21(3): 275–98.

Iparraguirre, G. (2015) 'Time, temporality and cultural rhythmics: an anthropological case study', *Time & Society*, 24(3): 613–33.

Johns, D., Williams, K. and Haines, K. (2017) 'Ecological youth justice: understanding the social ecology of young people's prolific offending', *Youth Justice*, 17(1): 3–21.

Johns, D., Williams, K. and Haines, K. (2018) 'A study of "prolific" offending by young people in Wales, 2009–2015', Report to the Youth Justice Board, Cymru, and Welsh Centre for Crime and Social Justice.

Love, B. (2016) 'Anti-Black state violence, classroom edition: the spirit murdering of Black children', *Journal of Curriculum and Pedagogy*, 13(1): 22–5.

Love, B. (2019) 'How schools are "spirit murdering" Black and Brown students', *Education Week*, 23 May, Available from: https://www.edweek.org/leadership/opinion-how-schools-are-spirit-murdering-black-and-brown-students/2019/05

Macharia, K. (2013) 'Fugitivity', Gukira With(out) Predicates [blogpost], 2 July, Available from: https://gukira.wordpress.com/2013/07/02/fugitivity

Maruna, S. (2001) *Making Good: How Ex-convicts Reform and Rebuild Their Lives*, Washington, DC: American Psychological Association.

Maruna, S., Coyle, B. and Marsh, B. (2015) 'Desistance from crime in the transition to adulthood', in B. Goldson and J. Muncie (eds) *Youth Crime and Justice* (2nd edn), Los Angeles: Sage, pp 157–69.

McAra, S. and McVie, L. (2007) 'Youth justice? The impact of system contact on patterns of desistance from offending', *European Journal of Criminology*, 4(3): 315–45.

Moreton, R. (2006) 'The right to dream', unpublished PhD thesis, University of Sydney.

Moten, F. (2018) 'Uplift and criminality', in *Stolen Life*, London: Duke University Press, pp 115–39.

Paradies, Y. (2020) 'Unsettling truths: modernity, (de-)coloniality and Indigenous futures', *Postcolonial Studies*, 4: 438–56.

Rodriguez, L.J. (1997) 'Hearts and hands: a new paradigm for work with youth and violence', *Social Justice*, 24(4): 7–20.

Rovelli, C. (2018) *The Order of Time* , New York: Penguin.

Smith, D.J. (2006) 'Social inclusion and early desistance from crime', Edinburgh Study of Youth Transitions and Crime, Research Digest no 12.

Smith, J.E. (1986) 'Time and qualitative time', *Review of Metaphysics*, 40(1): 3–16.

Stern, J., Barbarin, O. and Cassidy, J. (2022) 'Working toward anti-racist perspectives in attachment theory, research, and practice', *Attachment & Human Development*, 24(3): 392–422.

Tudge, J., Mokrova, I., Hatfield, B. and Karnik, R. (2009) 'Uses and misuses of Bronfenbrenner's bioecological theory of human development', *Journal of Family Theory & Review*, 1(4): 198–210.

UN General Assembly (1948) *Universal Declaration of Human Rights* (UDHR), 10 December 1948, United Nations, 217 A (III).

UN General Assembly (1966a) *International Covenant on Economic, Social and Cultural Rights* (ICESCR), 16 December 1966, United Nations, Treaty Series, vol. 993, p. 3.

UN General Assembly (1966b) *International Covenant on Civil and Political Rights* (ICCPR), 16 December 1966, United Nations, Treaty Series, vol. 999, p. 171.

UN General Assembly (1989) *Convention on the Rights of the Child* (UNCRC), 20 November 1989, United Nations, Treaty Series, vol. 1577, p. 3.

Vaneigem, R. (2001 [1968]) *The Revolution of Everyday Life* (2nd edn), London: Rebel Press.

Virno, P. (2004) *A Grammar of the Multitude*, Los Angeles: Semiotext(e).

Williams, P. (1987) 'Spirit-murdering the messenger: the discourse of fingerpointing as the law's response to racism', *University of Miami Law Review*, 42(1): 127–57.

4

Should desistance thinking be applied to children in the criminal justice system?

Ross Little and Kevin Haines

Introduction

This chapter advances debate about key theoretical and methodological issues associated with research that claims to be affiliated with 'desistance thinking', the 'desistance paradigm' or 'desistance theory'. We question how meaningful or helpful it is to use such terms when discussing the behaviour and lives of children. Over the past century or so, the focus of the big criminological questions – predominantly focused on adults – has evolved, shifting over time from those asking why people commit crime to why people do *not* commit crime, through to how people move away from engaging in criminal behaviour or criminal lifestyles (Canton, 2016). The concept of desistance, which focuses on the latter, has emerged in recent decades to apparently challenge the Risk Factor Prevention Paradigm (RFPP) as a dominant way of understanding the journeys of adults through the criminal justice system.

This is an opportunity for pause to ask pertinent questions about the extent to which desistance *should* be adopted from the adult system and applied, without much evidence, to the youth justice system. The chapter is organised around three key questions, which we address in turn. First, what is desistance, and is it a theory? Secondly, does desistance theory sustain the weight of explanatory power that has been vested in it? Thirdly, what are the benefits for children?

The responses to these questions inform our concluding argument that, at best, it is too early to adopt desistance thinking when engaging with children who have committed an offence, or even multiple offences. Despite the transplanting of desistance thinking into youth justice policy, inspection and practice in recent years, Wigzell (2021) points out that there are good reasons to question its relevance and applicability to children. We endorse Wigzell's analysis and seek here to extend her questioning, first considering its theoretical underpinnings.

What is desistance, and is it a theory?

Desistance is a contested term that broadly considers 'the *process* of abstaining from crime by those with a previous pattern of offending' (HMIP, 2022, emphasis added). Weaver and McNeill (2010, p 37) note that 'there is no agreed theoretical or operational definition of desistance', and thus care needs to be taken when interpreting research findings. As a process, therefore, for example, Phillips (2017) has argued for a 'rhizomatic', less linear, understanding of 'the desistance journey' than hitherto, emphasising that it may take considerable time with many wrong-turns and dead-ends. This is consistent with empirical research with young adults (Johns et al, 2017), which finds that positive relationships with adult workers, akin to youth work relationships, founded on trustworthy and consistent relationships built over time, can help young people navigate developments in their lives. Whereas desistance focuses on offending/non-offending, "a social-ecological perspective decentres the young person as the source of the offending problem, seeing them in terms of the relationships, interactions and processes that define and influence their everyday lives and experience" (2017, p 7).

Desistance is often presented as if it were a theory, with 'desistance theory' in common parlance across the criminal justice sector among practitioners, policy makers and academics. However, we question whether desistance theory is actually a theory. Instead, it is rather descriptive of a process that might in principle look to a range of different theories. Use of the terms 'process' and 'journey', common within the mainstream desistance literature, coupled with repeated counter-predicted events (that is, reoffending), all point towards the conclusion that desistance refers to a mechanism used for convenience purposes to rescue probation from the vicissitudes of risk.

Looking deeper, we can see that a desistance process requires both the agency of the person committing offences and appropriate social support to allow and maintain desistance (Weaver and McNeill, 2010; Bottoms and Shapland, 2011; Carlsson, 2016; Shapland, 2022). A basic premise of desistance thinking, and practice, is that an individual has developed a self-identity based on that of 'an offender', and that the change process involves that individual changing their identity and desisting from crime (see, for example, Maruna, 2001). This pre-condition, of an established self-identity as an offender, is what, to a considerable extent, explains why desistance theory and research has focused on adults and why so little desistance research has been conducted with children. As a theoretical standpoint, however, it does not hold water as a universal approach to promoting positive lifestyle choices – rather it would apply *only* to those who had developed, and who could convincingly be shown to have developed, an offending identity (whatever that is).

Wigzell (2021) too cautions against assumptions that all children in the youth justice system have pro-criminal identities that need to be changed, since they risk doing more harm than good: they are deficit-focused and stigmatising. Such approaches make an implicit concession to risk-based thinking and assume that a child's offending is indicative of 'pro-criminal' thinking or attitudes. There is no evidence to support this. A danger is that supervision – and wider criminal justice contact – may even destabilise children's self-identity or reinforce doubts about self-worth, particularly given evidence that adolescence is a period of malleability (Nugent and McNeill, 2017), and they may accordingly be more susceptible to the potential labelling effects of the criminal justice system (McAra and McVie, 2007; Robinson, 2016). This is particularly true when such labels are applied uncritically and unthinkingly.

There is precedent for such behaviour. The RFPP has been rightly criticised for unfairly placing the responsibility for criminal behaviour more heavily on the individual child in a way that does not match children's lived realities, particularly in those neighbourhoods with access to the fewest resources (Johns et al, 2017). Applying such an apparently 'neutral' term as 'risk' without recognising the context and manner in which it is deployed is at best naïve and at worst ensures the perverse outcome that those children with access to the fewest resources are more likely to become subject to the criminal gaze of the state (Haines and Case, 2008). However, it is not particularly clear how the 'desistance paradigm' is different, as the focus remains on the individual child and their (re)offending.

Indeed, desistance discourse tends to quickly veer back to 'risks' presented by children (Wigzell, 2021). One of the problems here is how the vulnerabilities of children have been re-cast as risks to the rest of society (Phoenix, 2013). What these mean in the lives of children can change considerably over time and across different contexts: they are dynamic – if they exist at all for the vast majority of children who come to the attention of police and youth offending teams. When the system intervenes, or fails to intervene, it can be to exacerbate children's pre-existing vulnerabilities to harm, such as in the case of 'Child C' and their move from one local authority area to another, which became the subject of a Serious Case Review following his subsequent death (Bernard and Harris, 2019; Waltham Forest, 2020; Bernard, 2020).[1] This recognises that state agencies play a considerable part in determining the extent to which an individual is deemed to be on a 'desistance pathway', relative to an 'offending pathway'.

For desistance theory to be considered a theory, it has to stand alone and have distinctive qualities. It is our position that desistance theory fails the theory test on this ground. We suggested earlier that desistance has been adopted by some criminologists and the probation service as a more humane alternative to the RFPP that infused probation practice in the 2000s. We further suggest that desistance theory is an extension of the risk paradigm and does not represent a clear break from it. Which brings us to the question of whether it sustains the weight of explanatory power vested in it.

Does desistance thinking sustain the weight of explanatory power that has been vested in it?

In this section, we consider three good reasons to question the weight afforded to desistance-related explanations, particularly in relation to children. First, the requirement for a pre-formed 'offender' identity, mentioned earlier. Secondly, the way in which children are individualised and made responsible for decisions often outside their control, assuming adult-like agency; and thirdly, the possibility for desistance owes at least as much to decisions and processes within the agencies of the (youth) justice system as it does to decisions made by individual children.

The requirement of a pre-formed offender identity

Desistance-related research has typically not focused on children. In fact, for quite some time, research only considered children to the extent to which becoming a parent constituted part of the 'desistance journey' (Giordano et al, 2002; Blokland and Nieuwbeerta, 2005; Houchin, 2005; Kreager et al, 2010; Healy, 2012; Monsbakken et al, 2013; Craig, 2015; Robison and Hughes-Miller, 2016; Abell, 2018). Wigzell (2021) identifies three types of desistance-related research. First, research focusing on desistance at the individual level (maturational theories focusing on the process of ageing, and rational choice theories); second, research on the 'structural' level, correlated with life-course events such as changes in family roles, relationships and employment; and, third, and more recently, research which emphasises the importance of a *dynamic interaction* between an individual's social context and their beliefs, values and attitudes in relation to offending (King, 2014). Types of desistance have been identified at the primary (individuals ceasing offending), secondary (adopting a non-offending identity) (Maruna, 2012) and tertiary levels (others recognising the non-offending identity [McNeill, 2015]).

Primary-level desistance would then involve an individual child making a conscious decision to 'give-up' offending. As noted earlier, however, it is unclear whether they have, or are likely to have, an imagination of themselves as 'an offender' in the way pre-supposed. In fact, prior research on this issue tends to suggest that children and young people do not tend to define themselves as 'offenders' in this way (Matza, 1964). Even children found to be committing high numbers of offences are not committing them constantly but drift in and out of periods of offending depending on their social ecological contexts (Matza, 1964; Johns et al, 2017). Making an early step on the desistance journey the shedding of an identity that may not exist is, at the very least, problematic. This is before one questions the extent to which some children understand their behaviour to be unlawful, let alone appreciating its legal consequences.

Individualisation and responsibilisation: children are not mini-adults

Desistance research and its interpretation in both policy and practice remain individualistic in focus – often disconnected from specific analyses of the cultural and structural contexts in which forms of offending and desistance take place (Weaver, 2019). There is a problem in using research with adults to guide criminal justice theory, policy and practice with children. As Johns et al's (2017) research with young adults in a Welsh town reflecting back on the exploits of their mid-teens highlights, there are typically a number of socio-economic and cultural constraints that limit the life choices and modes of expression available to children convicted of high numbers of offences.

In emphasising the role of agency and individual choices, there is a risk that desistance thinking makes children responsible for decisions influenced by factors well beyond their control. They are thus unfairly made responsible for changing their own lives without access to the means or support to realistically do this (Phoenix and Kelly, 2013). Significant interest has been paid to 'turning points' in desistance-related literature, building on Sampson and Laub's (2003) description of marriage, employment and entering military service as developments that could provide the impetus for desistance, also recognising that such changes do not affect everyone the same way. Relatedly, Rocque and Posick (2021) report that perhaps the most consistent research finding is that for adults who have been engaged in criminal acts, a strong marriage or access to gainful employment can facilitate desistance, options that are far less available to children. Therefore, given that desistance research has focused to a large extent on adults, many of the findings will not be applicable to children unless they continue to offend into adulthood. Options available to adults that have been shown to be associated with reduced offending, such as getting a job or accessing benefits, are not open to children.

In recognising children's constrained agency, Haines and Case (2015, pp 76–9) argue that the responsibility rests with adults and the organisations they represent, not children. If children are not given the full social responsibilities of adulthood, it is wrong to invoke this responsibility when and if they come into conflict with the law and the youth justice system (2015, p 76). We note here the current disconnect between the minimum age of criminal responsibility (ten years in England and Wales) and the arrival of other civic entitlements and responsibilities, which typically emerge between the ages of 16 and 18 years (Bateman, 2012a).

The work of Johns et al (2017) found that the multiple structural obstacles faced by children in the youth justice system also present challenges for its practitioners. It suggests that the primary responsibility for 'supporting desistance' should be shared between wider society and agencies of the state. More fundamentally, these actors, who have the resources and hold decision-making power, should be held responsible for ensuring that every child has access to 'somewhere to go, something to do and someone to talk to', previously recognised as a fundamentally important governmental aspiration for children and young people (DFES, 2005). The 'Child First' paradigm in theory and practice is based on the premise that children are not simply mini-adults: childhood constitutes a distinct phase in human development and, consequently, children should be understood and treated differently from adults.

Desistance is at least as much determined by the behaviour of decision-makers within the youth justice system as the individual

Often overlooked is that individuals being recognised as being on 'a desistance journey' is contingent upon action, or inaction, by the agencies comprising the youth justice system. For example, in the decade between March 2008 and March 2018, the number of proven offences recorded for children decreased by a remarkable 72 per cent from 277,986 to 77,349 (Bateman, 2020a). While there is good evidence to suggest that levels of criminal offending have generally decreased across all offence types (but particularly less serious offences) in England and Wales over the first two decades of the 21st century (Bateman, 2020a), these figures are more considerably a product of changing system responses, not children's behaviour. Therefore, a child aged 16 in 2008 was more likely to be arrested and processed as part of the criminal justice system than a child of the same age 12 or so years later. The former was much more likely to be (re)arrested and much less likely to be able to evince a desistance narrative.

Likewise, the use of stop and search by police in England and Wales under the Police and Criminal Evidence Act 1984, and associated legislation, has fluctuated considerably over the previous 20 years (Home Office, 2022). So, desistance describes the process of moving away from crime or a criminal identity. Importantly, it may also describe moving away from the criminal justice *system*; this is much more difficult during periods of increased police enforcement activity. If police numbers increase, street policing activity intensifies or forms of public surveillance increase, it is likely that children would experience the consequences more acutely. A central government target, introduced in 2002, for the police to bring more detected offences through the criminal justice system resulted in a far higher increase in children entering the justice system for the first time between 2003 and 2007 (22 per cent), relative to adults (1 per cent) (Bateman, 2020b).

Distancing oneself from crime, and from the criminal justice system, may superficially appear to be the same thing, but they are not, and this pragmatic point has implications for one's likelihood for being recognised as 'rehabilitated' or a 'desister'. Indeed, we need only be aware of the consequences of court closures and backlogs in recent years (Harris and Goodfellow, 2021) to consider how unfinished court decisions and processes impact on children involved in them. A two- or three-year delay to proceedings has a disproportionate impact on the life of a child compared with a more mature adult with many more years' experience behind them. Since involvement with the criminal justice system is contingent on wider societal factors but impacts considerably on how children are perceived and how they see themselves, this poses a problem for desistance-oriented perspectives.

Desistance and 'rehabilitation'

The points in the preceding paragraph are pragmatic, but they also have implications for theoretical and policy-oriented discussions. For with desistance there is little agreement about when it has been achieved (Shapland, 2022), if at all. It thus remains a somewhat subjective decision as to when it might have occurred and whom the desistance narrative is available to. In such ambiguous terrain, the power to decide on such matters does not sit with a child but rests on the judgement of adult professionals. Desistance is thus an *indeterminate* project, with little shared understanding about when it has taken place. Research may inform such decisions but is quite some way from resolving this fundamental issue. For example, studies of recidivism typically use a one-year follow-up period of reconviction. Others have suggested much longer periods, decades, before desistance can be considered to have been achieved (see Shapland, 2022). There is a further issue here: recent research has brought attention to the harms associated with indeterminate custodial sentences (Straub and Annison, 2020). Here, we have a situation that we might understand as something of its community-based equivalent: the indeterminate community sentence.

The indeterminacy of desistance and the uncertainty around whether it can be seen to have been attained or achieved is one of its associated 'pains' (Nugent and Schinkel, 2016). There is an inherent assumption here too that a child shares similar understandings with adults in relation to certain behaviours, the extent to which they are criminal(ised) and the (legal) consequences of engaging in such behaviour. There has been convincing questioning of such an assumption, both as a matter of principle (Bateman,

2012a) and practice, for example in relation to 'joint enterprise' legislation (Just for Kids Law, 2015, 2016). One of the fundamental principles of joint enterprise is that an individual foresaw that an associate of theirs was likely to commit an offence (Crewe et al, 2015). In 2015, Just for Kids Law intervened in the Supreme Court case R v Jogee, successfully arguing that children and adolescents do not have the same ability to predict events or understand the consequences of theirs and other people's actions in the way that an adult would. Research by Hulley and Young (2022) highlights the role of the law, and its agents, in generating silence among young suspects, whose primary concern is the legal risks of talking. These young people face a precarious trap, as their silence is interpreted as guilt by the police, propelling them towards charge. They conclude that to avoid over-charging and to encourage young people with knowledge of serious violence to talk, structural systemic change is needed.

Reconviction is a commonly used, yet blunt, indicator of what some might call 'failed desistance' or desistance that has yet to begin. In this space, desistance risks becoming confounded with the language of rehabilitation. It thus potentially becomes a new proxy indicator for rehabilitation, or the lack of rehabilitation. In the absence of alternative markers and milestones, it becomes the dominant indicator of a child's progress in relation to the criminal justice system. In such a process, observations and knowledge about desistance can become twisted to become *compulsory* elements of the performance of rehabilitation. Indeed, the way the criminal justice system discusses desistance is rather different from the more nuanced academic accounts. Desistance is now something to be performed on the pathway to 'rehabilitation'. Being seen to be 'rehabilitated' is more accessible to some people than others, particularly Black men serving long sentences (Warr, 2022), some of which will have begun in childhood.

Associating cessation, or reduction, of offending with rehabilitation (whatever that means) assumes too much, for our understandings of offending behaviour are changing as society evolves, together with how we understand the harms associated with certain crimes. The nature of expanding drugs markets and associated 'county lines' operations is changing what it means to be understood as a victim or offender, particularly as a child (Stone, 2018). Emerging understandings of the complexity and impact of child criminal exploitation in contemporary society (Robinson et al, 2019) also impact on how the limits of children's agency are understood and appreciated.

To some extent, a desistance theorist might seek to swerve criticisms by pointing out how some methodologies (such as narrative) focus on the whole person and listen to their stories as a way of mitigating the role of 'risk thinking' associated with RFPP (see, for example, Graebsch and Maruna, 2022). However, there is a lack of clarity about whether such research is focusing on how people move away from *criminal behaviour* – playing into the normative assumptions of 'administrative criminologists' – or how they move away from the criminal justice *system*. And how these transitions are substantially similar or different. This seems to be at the heart of a criticism by German critical criminologists that find their work incompatible with desistance research (Peters, 20228). McNeill (2017), in responding to critiques of desistance as too individualistic, acknowledges that desistance thinking, especially as understood and practised by criminal justice agencies in the UK, is guilty of making 'the offence' the main issue, when the consequences of social inequalities, abuse and trauma are the matters that really need greater collective focus. Criminologists, he argues, should be contributing to imagining the "architecture of a just social order" (2017). Indeed, this is particularly necessary when considering the treatment of children in our society. We also agree that there is merit in focusing greater attention on how some of the country's largest and most powerful organisations might cease criminal, or at least harmful, behaviour. But this is not the focus of desistance research to date. Desistance research has focused on how individual adults move away from criminal behaviour, and we argue there is little merit in repeating the exercise for children: it is largely meaningless and inevitably focuses on the worst things they have done, encouraging further contact with a criminogenic system (McAra and McVie, 2010). Governmental interpretations of desistance have adopted crude quantitative shortcuts which further ensure a focus on recorded criminal offences in an apparent, and paradoxical, effort to 'reduce reoffending'.

Desistance and reducing reoffending

As noted, the approach to desistance as adopted by government continues to privilege and prioritise 'reducing reoffending' and recorded offence data associated with it. Short-term reconviction rates are the measure of success (Bateman and Wigzell, 2020). This runs counter to 'Child First' theory and practice: it is also emblematic of a Ministry of Justice approach fixated with offending and has little to offer society, the individual or, indeed, the probation service as a set of ambitions worthy of motivation. The absence of something does not automatically mean it has been replaced by something positive, and there is little interest in understanding this.

Re-offending data are privileged by government administrators because they are relatively simple to collect and measure. By contrast, children's lives, and the support needed to help them make the best of them, are more complex and time-consuming. Information and data on the harm done to others may be legitimate but is selective in understanding underlying causes (it's essentially uninterested in causes). Instead, we need to understand what is important in children's lives, not simply the easiest thing to measure. As Warner has argued in relation to adult education, a key guiding principle is to "make that which is important measurable, rather than that which is measurable important" (Warner, 2018, p 34). The reverse has happened during decades of managerialist influences (Feeley and Simon, 1992). In considering teaching practice in an age of accountability, Mockler and Stacey (2021) have argued for 'intelligent accountability' over 'performative accountability', and there may be something transferable here in relation to agents of youth justice.

Privileging offending data skews the assessment of children's circumstances. These assessments are retrospective, looking backwards, but not necessarily at the causes or the things that really matter. Youth justice assessments frame the intensity, depth and frequency of intervention. And yet children's lives are not static; they are dynamic. This can be contrasted with the information privileged by an 'ecological youth justice' approach, or a 'contextual safeguarding approach' (Firmin et al, 2019; Firmin, 2020) which seeks to understand the context for a child and how they experience the different layers of the social world around them. Qualitative accounts depict a more complex picture of relationships and social connections, particularly for young adults (Johns et al, 2017). Even if some children stop, or decrease, offending as they age, this does not mean it can be explained by desistance theory, as implied by proponents. Indeed, this becomes a circular argument. Here, because 'desistance' is a description of the process, there is an absence of evidence as to its effect. It provokes a question about the impacts on practice with children, and what's in it for them anyway?

What are the benefits for children?

In this section, we develop our discussion thus far and consider the implications of applying 'desistance'-related thinking with practitioners who work with children. Most importantly, we ask what the benefits for children are. What does it mean to work in a desistance-oriented way? Do agencies, such as HM Inspectorate of Probation (HMIP), for example (a proponent of desistance thinking), take a Child First, or child-friendly approach? Are desistance narratives available equally to all?

What does it mean to work in a desistance-oriented manner?

The prior discussion provokes the question of what it means for practitioners to work in a desistance-oriented manner. As Maruna and Mann (2019, p 4) have observed, desistance has become 'a near ubiquitous buzzword' in criminal justice policy and practice. Organisations refer to their work as being 'desistance-focused', and inspectorates proclaim support for desistance in practice. And yet, how would we really know if practice is 'desistance informed', and what would this mean?

The distance between the lives of salaried professionals and the lives of vulnerable children with little control over their lives creates questions about the implications for youth justice supervisory practices (Bernard, 2020). The 'cultural blindness' of supervisory practice to some extent echoes that of research practices. For example, only very recently has the significance of "trap life" for children and young adults, discussed subsequently, been recognised in academic literature (Reid, 2023). How well is this understood in policy-making circles and among those working in supervisory roles? This is difficult to answer, but the available evidence strongly suggests that this is, at least, a work in progress (Bernard, 2020).

A role for inspection?

HMIP have championed the application of desistance thinking to desistance practice (HMIP, 2016), although they have not hitherto taken a Child First approach to their work. While there have been more references to desistance in recent inspection reports, 'risk' remains the watchword, outnumbering 'desistance' by an average of two to one (Wigzell, 2021, p 13). However, desistance often appears to be used as a synonym for 'reducing offending' (a typical phrase being 'the implementation and delivery of services to support desistance were done well'). Notably this was a criticism HMIP made of practitioners in its thematic inspection (2016, p 37). What youth offending teams (YOTs) are actually doing to support desistance is anyone's guess; we are just supposed to trust they are doing it. Moreover, there continue to be relatively few references to desistance-inspired approaches. For example, both 'relationships' with young people and 'strengths' are mentioned an average of just six times in recent inspection reports. As Hampson (2018, p 30) asks: '[H]ow can they pursue a desistance-based agenda if the criteria upon which they will be judged by the inspectorate is still (for general inspections) firmly risk-focused?' This is a good question. Furthermore, we ask what this means, and why should they focus on a desistance-based agenda if it merely replaces 'reducing re-offending', and the risk-laden assumptions that accompany it.

Day's (2022) research considers how youth justice practitioners navigate risk in a Child First world. She notes that there is indeed an absence of information and evidence about implementation in practice, despite official bodies such as HMIP stating that it is 'happening'. Day notes that, like us, these should be primarily considered to be children, not offenders. Rather, there is frequently evidence they have been victims of poverty, abuse and trauma in early life. Desistance thinking asks how children move away from criminal behaviour and seems less concerned with considering how they move away from the criminal justice *system*. This is particularly relevant for the children caught up in the Metropolitan Police's 'gangs matrix', for example (Amnesty International, 2018).

Indeed, as Day notes, the principles for desistance focused practice (McNeill et al, 2012) are a long way from the practical reality. What does it mean for children to be engaged in relationships that matter, that build their social capital and support them to form 'healthy' identities? As recent research has shown, context makes a considerable difference to how children make sense of their environment, the options available to them and the extent to which others perceive they are moving away, or desisting from, crime. In relation to child sexual exploitation, Brown argues that in order to respond effectively we need to move beyond discussion of 'risk factors' and denial of agency towards an understanding of 'intersectional inequalities, social marginality, "critical moments" and how these shape the investments and actions of vulnerable young people' (2019, p 622). The idea of desistance is notable for its absence. This also connects with a question about what it would take for a child to be able to achieve 'tertiary desistance', to effectively 'perform' a desistance narrative to the satisfaction of adult supervisors making decisions about such things. Is such a status available to children? Is it available to all children equally regardless of background?

Are desistance narratives equally available to all children?

Despite continued awareness of discrimination and disproportionality in the criminal justice system, there are significant knowledge gaps, most notably on young Black men's experiences with court processes and associated with prison and probation services processes and practices (Robertson and Wainwright, 2020). As Brown (2019) notes, limited typographies of abuse and victimhood have also created service blindness to children who do not 'fit' our expectations of victimhood because of their gender, race, (dis)ability or social class. Indeed, there is evidence that Black young people are over-identified as perpetrators of harm and under-represented as victims (Berelowitz et al, 2013), and others have spoken to the 'adultification' (Davis and Marsh, 2020) of Black children that accelerates such disproportional treatment. This is not a new phenomenon, nor is it confined to the criminal justice system. For example, exclusion from mainstream schooling has been recognised as a problem disproportionally affecting African Caribbean boys (Joseph Rowntree Foundation, 2005).

However, there has been a 'strategic silence' on the issue of race, 'gangs' and the treatment of Black boys and men by the criminal justice system and partner agencies, where data are not recorded or analysed, and racial disproportionality is minimised and left unquestioned (Williams and Clarke, 2016). A greater consideration of how routine policies and practices in multi-agency systems, and the national context they operate within, might create this over-representation is thus long overdue. McAra and McVie's (2010) research on youth transitions and the criminogenic nature of (criminal justice) systems suggests the criminalisation of children leads to further harm. Relying on concepts such as 'desistance' distracts from the real issues that matter for children and the people that work closely with them. It contributes to the skewing of questions, such that they become focused on 'what is it about Black boys that means they are over-represented in multi-agency "county lines" cohorts?' rather than 'what is it about multi-agency "county lines" processes that result in a disproportionate representation of young Black people?' (Wroe, 2021, p 48). Pertinent here is what it means for children caught in the 'trap life' of the drug economy and the associated struggles of growing up poor, with family trauma and limited educational and employment opportunities. Wider than the 'gang' concept, Reid (2023) explains that the trap contextualises criminal motivation within material struggle and emotional pain. Overlooked by mainstream criminology until very recently, life for these children can be consumed by daily struggles experienced away from the traditions, certainties and safety fostered by legitimate activities and institutions. Reid argues convincingly that trap life is experienced as a psycho-social crisis, usually experienced during adolescence. Importantly, the consequences of trap life for children have not yet been considered in relation to the process of desistance. Indeed, further understanding of urban engagement in violence and criminality that accounts for social structures and individual psyche is needed before this would be possible or helpful.

Reid's ethnographic research on a London housing estate generated a typology of three different 'trapper' types (the Glutton, the Predatory and the Humble). Space does not permit a detailed consideration here, but we note that the first two trapper identities in particular are formed partly in childhood. Criminal behaviour of glutton trappers was heavily informed by "harrowing feelings of contempt at the poverty and abuse they experienced in their formative years and these memories of impoverishment and powerlessness weighed heavily" (Reid, 2023, p 174). Later, as men, they were prone to take their stress out by way of acting out their core wounds, for example feeling unwanted, weak and helpless. Reid notes that the process of becoming a glutton trapper is not pre-determined and is thus a complex one, influenced and/or moulded also by a wider sociocultural environment which equates self-worth with one's ability to demonstrate publicly and, at least within the peer group, that you can defend yourself and meet the expectations of 'road masculinity'.

Predatory trappers in the research tended to 'exhibit unaddressed toxic shame acquired in and/or left over from childhood' (Reid, 2023, p 177). They were significantly more likely than other trappers to recall incidents from their childhoods that provoked feelings of shame (for example, having to beg for food, being embarrassed by a parent's criminal lifestyle, being teased about their appearance and thus being assigned the label of 'tramp'), which became imprinted in their memories, strongly influencing their lives as adults, and especially their commitment to trap life. Motivations for predatory trappers to attack and rob 'lower-status', humble, trappers seemed 'expressive of their emotional fragility and their childhood shame colliding with their current anxieties' (Reid, 2023, p 177). Their emotional and volatile behaviour left them ill-equipped to participate effectively in a socio-economic life that demands the performance of social niceties. With the number of children estimated to live in poverty increasing to almost 4 million (Joseph Rowntree Foundation, 2023), the unwanted effects of it are likely to continue for such children, and wider society, for some time to come. It is not clear how a pre-occupation with 'desisting' from a fickle criminal justice system is particularly helpful here. Periods of more heavily resourced criminal justice infrastructure will simply see more of these children criminalised. Individual trajectories are complex and do not fit with binary measures of criminal behaviour.

Conclusion

On one level, it is not difficult to see the attraction of desistance-oriented thinking. Except that directing policy and practice in this way, without appreciating the complexities of some children's lives, is partial, misleading and unhelpful. Research with children on desistance is thin, and there is little justification for focusing on this term as things stand.

This chapter has considered three interrelated questions associated with desistance. In relation to the first, *What is desistance, and is it a theory?*, we argue that desistance theory is not a theory but rather a mechanism used for convenience purposes to rescue probation from the vicissitudes of risk. The basic premise of desistance theory, and practice, is that an individual has developed a self-identity based on that of 'an offender', and that the change process involves that individual changing their identity and thus desisting from crime. This pre-condition, of an established self-identity as an offender, is what, to a considerable extent, explains why desistance theory and research has been focused on adults and why so little desistance research has been conducted with children. As a theoretical standpoint, however, it does not hold water as a universal approach to promoting positive lifestyle choices – rather it would apply only to those who had developed and who could convincingly be shown to have developed an offending identity (whatever that is).

In response to the second question, about whether desistance thinking sustains the weight of explanatory power that has been vested in it, we consider three good reasons to question the weight afforded to desistance-related explanations, particularly in relation to children. First, the requirement for a pre-formed 'offender' identity, mentioned earlier. Secondly, the way in which children are individualised and made responsible for decisions often outside their control, assuming adult–like agency; and thirdly, the possibility for desistance owes at least as much to decisions and processes within the agencies of the (youth) justice system as it does to decisions made by individual children. The size and scope of this system can vary considerably over time, and with it, children's chances of desistance, or being seen to desist, fluctuate too.

Furthermore, there is a lack of agreement and clarity about what desistance is and when it may be achieved. The focus has tended to be on what it is *not* and the supposed presence of risk factors. But it is closer to this way of thinking than has hitherto been recognised. The practice of risk-based thinking continues, even if the language does not. It seems to us that desistance has served to provide an extension to the RFPP, rather than an alternative to it. While there are some differences between desistance thinking and the RFPP, we see the former as having been subsumed into the latter. There are indications that the use of 'desistance' in policy and practice is already shifting away from understandings being tentatively progressed by academic researchers. (For example, is desistance becoming a compulsory performative element of an individual's demonstrable – lack of – 'rehabilitation', rather than the more nuanced process being empirically observed by researchers?) Ultimately, 'desistance thinking' is being subsumed into policy and practice already profoundly shaped by risk narratives.

There has been very little research to date on desistance in relation to children, and no convincing evidence that supports the idea of adopting it now. If there is uncertainty about if and when adults have achieved desistance, then this uncertainty multiplies in relation to the shorter timescales of child lives. It is worth considering what child-focused desistance research would look like in practice, particularly as there is no agreement on what desistance actually is, or when it has been achieved.

In considering the third question, about the benefits of adopting desistance thinking in relation to children, we question whether there are any. Beyond limited measures of reoffending over the course of one year, children cannot effectively be seen to have desisted: they are unlikely to be able to perform desistance in any way that is meaningful. Tertiary desistance relies on the perspectives of others. From what we know from recent relevant research, it seems that some children, particularly those from Black and ethnically minoritised backgrounds, are less likely to be recognised as being on a desistance pathway, which contributes to potential future ethnic disproportionality in the criminal justice system. This can be because their contexts growing up have not been typically well understood or recognised, or because of systemic processes that mitigate against such understanding. We recognise that some of the practices associated with desistance thinking may overlap with those implied by a Child First philosophy. However, the latter offers a more appropriate philosophical base for adopting these practices.

Relatedly, recognising the principles and practice associated with informal learning, or youth work, is more likely to offer a more positive conceptual and linguistic framework.

This chapter has considered theoretical, methodological, policy-oriented and practical issues associated with desistance thinking. We consider that the alignment of childhood law-breaking to the framework of 'desistance' risks stifling advancements in our understanding of children's development in all its richness and complexity. A more appropriate approach may well be a more oblique one (Canton, 2013) that seeks to understand the relevance of interconnected experiences associated with poverty, mattering and belonging (Billingham and Irwin-Rogers, 2021) in a late capitalist society saturated with inequality and associated images of that inequality that permeate social media. We need a trained and trustworthy workforce tasked with understanding and connecting with children and young people (Brierley, 2021), with a focus on children first and foremost, and universal positive outcomes.

Note

[1] Child C was 14 years old and had been living in Waltham Forest for nine months before his murder in January 2019. He was deliberately knocked off a moped and then stabbed repeatedly. He had previously lived in Nottinghamshire and had started being home educated, but this arrangement broke down. He then had a lot of time unsupervised and was getting into trouble in the community. His mother moved him to Waltham Forest because she was concerned he was falling under bad influences. Before Child C's murder, there were issues of criminal exploitation, weapon-related incidents and exclusion from school.

References

Abell, L. (2018) 'Exploring the transition to parenthood as a pathway to desistance', *Journal of Developmental and Life-Course Criminology*, 4(4): 395–426.

Amnesty International (2018) 'Trapped in the matrix: secrecy, stigma and bias in the Met's gangs database', Available from: https://www.amnesty.org.uk/files/reports/Trapped%20in%20the%20Matrix%20Amnesty%20report.pdf

Bateman, T. (2012) *Children in Conflict with the Law 2012: An Overview of Trends and Developments*, London: The National Association for Youth Justice, Available from https://thenayj.org.uk/wp-content/uploads/2015/06/2012-NAYJ_briefing_Children_in_conflict_with_the_law.pdf

Bateman, T. (2020a) 'Youth justice news', *Youth Justice*, 20(1–2): 170–80, Available from: https://journals.sagepub.com/doi/pdf/10.1177/1473225419895404

Bateman, T. (2020b) 'The state of youth justice 2020: an overview of trends and developments', National Association for Youth Justice, Available from: https://thenayj.org.uk/cmsAdmin/uploads/state-of-youth-justice-2020-final-sep20.pdf

Bateman, T. and Wigzell, A. (2020) 'Exploring recent trends in youth justice reconvictions: a challenge to the complexity thesis', *Youth Justice*, 20(3): 252–71.

Berelowitz, S., Clifton, J., Firmin, C., Gulyurtlu, S. and Edwards, G. (2013) '"If only someone had listened": Office of the Children's Commissioner's inquiry into child sexual exploitation in gangs and groups', London: Office of the Children's Commissioner.

Bernard, C. (2020) 'Understanding the lived experiences of Black and ethnic minority children and families', Totnes: Research in Practice.

Bernard, C.A. and Harris, P. (2019) 'Serious Case Reviews: the lived experience of Black children', *Child and Family Social Work*, 24(2): 256–63.

Beyond Youth Custody (2017) 'Lessons from youth in focus: research report', London: Beyond Youth Custody, Available from: http://www.beyondyouthcustody.net/wp-content/uploads/Lessons-from-Youth-in-Focus-Research-Report.pdf

Billingham, L. and Irwin-Rogers, K. (2021) 'The terrifying abyss of insignificance: marginalisation, mattering and violence between young people', *Oñati Socio-Legal Series*, 11(5): 1222–49, Available from: https://doi.org/10.35295/osls.iisl/0000-0000-0000-1178

Blokland, A.A. and Nieuwbeerta, P. (2005) 'The effects of life circumstances on longitudinal trajectories of offending', *Criminology*, 43(4): 1203–40.

Bottoms, A. and Shapland, J. (2011) 'Steps towards desistance among male young adult recidivists', *Escape Routes: Contemporary Perspectives on Life after Punishment*, 43–80.

Brierley, A. (2021) *Connecting with Young People in Trouble: Risk, Relationships and Lived Experience*, Hook: Waterside Press.

Brown, K. (2019) 'Vulnerability and child sexual exploitation: towards an approach grounded in life experiences', *Critical Social Policy*, 39(4): 622–42.

Canton, R. (2013) 'The point of probation: on effectiveness, human rights and the virtues of obliquity', *Criminology & Criminal Justice*, 13(5): 577–93, Available from: https://doi.org/10.1177/1748895812462596

Canton, R. (2016) 'Why do people commit crimes?', in F. McNeill, I. Durnescu and R. Butter (eds) *Probation*, London: Palgrave Macmillan, pp 9–34, Available from: https://doi.org/10.1057/978-1-137-51982-5_2

Carlsson, C. (2016) 'Human agency, criminal careers and desistance', *Global Perspectives on Desistance: Reviewing What We Know and Looking to the Future*, 28–49.

Craig, J.M. (2015) 'The effects of marriage and parenthood on offending levels over time among juvenile offenders across race and ethnicity', *Journal of Crime and Justice*, 15(2): 163–82.

Crewe, B., Liebling, A., Padfield, N. and Virgo, G. (2015) 'Joint enterprise: the implications of an unfair and unclear law', *Criminal Law Review*, 4: 252–69.

Davis, J. and Marsh, N. (2020) 'Boys to men: the cost of adultification in safeguarding responses to Black boys', *Critical and Radical Social Work*, 8(2): 255–9.

Day, A.-M. (2022) '"It's a hard balance to find": the perspectives of youth justice practitioners in England on the place of "risk" in an emerging "Child-First" world', *Youth Justice*, 23(1): 58–75, Available from: https://doi.org/10.1177/14732254221075205

DfES (2005) 'Youth matters', Nottingham: DfES Publications.

Evans, J., Kennedy, D., Skuse, T. and Matthew, J. (2020) 'Trauma-informed practice and desistance theories: competing or complementary approaches to working with children in conflict with the law?', *Salus Journal*, 8(2): 55–76, Available from: https://search.informit.org/doi/10.3316/informit.399118262977096

Farrall, S., Hunter, B., Sharpe, G. and Calverley, A. (2014) *Criminal Careers in Transition: The Social Context of Desistance from Crime*, Oxford: Oxford University Press.

Feeley, M.M. and Simon, J. (1992) 'The new penology: notes on the emerging strategy of corrections and its implications', *Criminology*, 30(4): 449–74.

Firmin, C. (2020) *Contextual Safeguarding and Child Protection: Rewriting the Rules*, London: Routledge.

Firmin, C.E., Wroe, L. and Lloyd, J. (2019) *Safeguarding and Exploitation – Complex, Contextual and Holistic Approaches: Strategic Briefing*, London: Research in Practice.

Fitzpatrick, E., McGuire, J. and Dickson, J. (2015) 'Personal goals of adolescents in a youth offending service in the United Kingdom', *Youth Justice*, 15(2): 166–81.

Giordano, P.C., Cernkovich, S.A. and Rudolph, J.L. (2002) 'Gender, crime, and desistance: toward a theory of cognitive transformation', *American Journal of Sociology*, 107(4): 990–1064.

Graebsch, C. and Maruna, S. (2022) 'Desistance research and critical criminology: a conversation', *Kriminologisches Journal*, 3: 244–52, Available from: https://www.beltz.de/fachmedien/erziehungswissenschaft/zeitschriften/kriminologisches_journal/artikel/49410-desistance-research-and-critical-criminology-a-conversation.html

Gray, P. and Smith, R. (2019) 'Governance through diversion in neoliberal times and the possibilities for transformative social justice', *Critical Criminology*, 27: 575–80.

Haines, K. and Case, S. (2015) *Positive Youth Justice: Children First, Offenders Second*, Bristol: Policy Press.

Hampson, S.K. (2018) 'Desistance approaches in youth justice: the next passing fad or a sea-change for the positive?', *Youth Justice*, 18(1): 18–33.

Harris, M. and Goodfellow, P. (2021) 'The youth justice system's response to the COVID-19 pandemic: literature review', Alliance for Youth Justice, Available from: https://static1.squarespace.com/static/5f75bfbbfb67fc5ab 41154d6/t/618bdf2a6166520207116da5/1636556588695/Impact+of+ COVID+-+Literature+Review+FINAL+Updated+Oct+21.pdf

Healy, D. (2012) *The Dynamics of Desistance: Charting Pathways through Change*, Cullompton: Willan Publishing.

HM Inspectorate of Probation (2016) 'Desistance and young people', Manchester: HM Inspectorate of Probation, Available from: https://www. justiceinspectorates.gov.uk/hmiprobation/wp-content/uploads/sites/5/ 2016/05/Desistance_and_young_people.pdf

HM Inspectorate of Probation (2022) 'Desistance: general practice principles', Manchester: HM Inspectorate of Probation, Available from: https://www. justiceinspectorates.gov.uk/hmiprobation/research/the-evidence-base-probation/models-and-principles/desistance

Home Office (2022) 'Police powers and procedures: stop and search arrests, England and Wales, year ending 31 March 2022', Available from: https:// www.gov.uk/government/statistics/police-powers-and-procedures-stop-and-search-and-arrests-england-and-wales-year-ending-31-march-2022/ police-powers-and-procedures-stop-and-search-and-arrests-england-and-wales-year-ending-31-march-2022

Houchin, R. (2005) 'Social exclusion and imprisonment in Scotland: a report', Report to the Scottish Prison Service, Available from: https:// www.scotpho.org.uk/media/1847/social-exclusion-and-imprisonment-in-scotland-2005.pdf

Hulley, S. and Young, T. (2022) 'Silence, joint enterprise and the legal trap', *Criminology & Criminal Justice*, 22(5): 714–32, Available from: https://doi. org/10.1177/1748895821991622

Johns, D., Williams, K. and Haines, K. (2017) 'Ecological youth justice: understanding the social ecology of young people's prolific offending', *Youth Justice*, 17(1): 3–21.

Joseph Rowntree Foundation (2005) 'School exclusion and transition into adulthood in African-Caribbean communities (summary)', Available from: https://www.jrf.org.uk/sites/default/files/migrated/migrated/files/ 1859353509.pdf

Joseph Rowntree Foundation (2023) 'UK poverty 2023: the essential guide to understanding poverty in the UK', Available from: https://www.jrf.org. uk/work/uk-poverty-2023-the-essential-guide-to-understanding-pove rty-in-the-uk

Just for Kids Law (2015) Joint Enterprise, Available from: https://www.jus
tforkidslaw.org/what-we-do/fighting-change/strategic-litigation/past-
cases/joint-enterprise#:~:text=Joint%20enterprise%20is%20a%20com
mon%20law%20doctrine%20where,other%20party%20was%20likely%20
to%20commit%20that%20crime

Just for Kids Law (2016) Statement from Just for Kids Law, following
Supreme Court judgement in Jogee, Available from: justforkidslaw.org/
news/statement-just-kids-law-following-supreme-court-judgment-jogee

King, S. (2014) *Desistance Transitions and the Impact of Probation*, Abingdon:
Routledge.

Kreager, D.A., Matsueda, R.L. and Erosheva, E.A. (2010) 'Motherhood and
criminal desistance in disadvantaged neighborhoods', *Criminology*, 48(1): 221–57.

Maruna, S. (2001) *Making Good: How Ex-convicts Reform and Rebuild Their
Lives*, Washington, DC: American Psychological Association.

Maruna, S. (2012) 'Elements of successful desistance signaling', *Criminology
& Public Policy*, 11(1): 73–86.

Maruna, S. and Mann, R. (2019) 'Reconciling "desistance" and "what
works"', *Academic Insights*, 1: 3–10.

Matza, D. (1964) *Delinquency and Drift*, New York: John Wiley.

McAra, L., & McVie, S. (2007) Youth justice? The impact of system
contact on patterns of desistance from offending. *European Journal of
Criminology*, 4(3), 315–345.

McAra, L. and McVie, S. (2010) 'Youth crime and justice: key messages
from the Edinburgh Study of Youth Transitions and Crime. *Criminology
& Criminal Justice*, 10(2): 179–209.

McIvor, G., Murray, C. and Jamieson, J. (2004) 'Desistance from crime?
Is it different for women and girls?', in S. Maruna and R. Immarigeon
(eds) *After Crime and Punishment: Pathways to Offender Reintegration*,
Cullompton: Willan Publishing, pp 181–200.

McMahon, G. and Jump, D. (2018) 'Starting to stop: young offenders'
desistance from crime', *Youth Justice*, 18(1): 3–17.

McNeill, F. (2015) 'Desistance and criminal justice in Scotland', in H.
Croall, G. Mooney and M. Munro (eds) *Crime, Justice and Society in Scotland*,
London: Routledge, pp 212–28.

McNeill, F. (2017) 'A dialogue about desistance by Fergus McNeill', CEP
Probation, Available from: https://www.cep-probation.org/a-dialogue-
about-desistance-by-fergus-mcneill/

McNeill, F. and Weaver, B. (2010) 'Changing lives', *Desistance Research and
Offender Management*, SCCJR No. 3/2010.

McNeill, F., Farrall, S., Lightowler, C. and Maruna, S. (2012) 'How and why
people stop offending: discovering desistance', Insights evidence summary to
support social services in Scotland, Available from: https://www.iriss.org.uk/
resources/insights/how-why-people-stop-offending-discovering-desistance

Mockler, N. and Stacey, M. (2021) 'Evidence of teaching practice in an age of accountability: when what can be counted isn't all that counts', *Oxford Review of Education*, 47(2): 170–88.

Monsbakken, C.W., Lyngstad, T.H. and Skardhamar, T. (2013) 'Crime and the transition to parenthood: the role of sex and relationship context', *British Journal of Criminology*, 53: 129–48.

Nugent, B. and Barnes, P. (2013) 'Desistance and young people', *Scottish Justice Matters*, 1(2): 21–3.

Nugent, B. and McNeill, F. (2017) 'Young people and desistance', in A. Furlong (ed) *Routledge Handbook of Youth and Young Adulthood* (2nd edn), Abingdon: Routledge, pp 427–36.

Nugent, B. and Schinkel, M. (2016) 'The pains of desistance', *Criminology & Criminal Justice*, 16(5): 568–84.

Peters, H. (2022) 'Incompatibility resolution', *Criminological Journal* (3): 235–43, https://doi.org/10.3262/KJ2203235.

Phillips, J. (2017) 'Towards a rhizomatic understanding of the desistance journey', *The Howard Journal of Crime and Justice*, 56(1): 92–104.

Phoenix, J. (2013) *Out of Place: The Policing and Criminalization of Sexually Exploited Girls and Young Women*, London: The Howard League for Penal Reform, Available from: https://howardleague.org/wp-content/uploads/2016/04/Out-of-place.pdf

Phoenix, J. and Kelly, L. (2013) '"You have to do it for yourself": responsibilization in youth justice and young people's situated knowledge of youth justice practice', *British Journal of Criminology*, 53(3): 419–37.

Prior, D. and Mason, P. (2010) 'A different kind of evidence? Looking for "what works" in engaging young offenders', *Youth Justice*, 10(3): 211–26.

Reid, E. (2023) '"Trap life": the psychosocial underpinnings of street crime in inner-city London', *The British Journal of Criminology*, 63(1): 168–83, Available from: https://doi.org/10.1093/bjc/azac004

Robertson, L. and Wainwright, J.P. (2020) 'Black boys' and young men's experiences with criminal justice and desistance in England and Wales: a literature review', *Genealogy*, 4(2): 50, Available from: https://doi.org/10.3390/genealogy4020050

Robinson, G., McLean, R. and Densley, J. (2019) 'Working county lines: child criminal exploitation and illicit drug dealing in Glasgow and Merseyside', *International Journal of Offender Therapy and Comparative Criminology*, 63(5): 694–711.

Robison, K.J. and Hughes-Miller, M.H. (2016) 'Decentering motherhood: reentry strategies for women on parole and probation', *Women & Criminal Justice*, 26: 319–39.

Rocque, M. and Posick, C. (2021) 'Research on desistance', in J.C. Barnes and D.R. Forde (eds) *The Encyclopedia of Research Methods in Criminology and Criminal Justice, 2 Volume Set*, Hoboken: Wiley, pp 716–23.

Sampson, R.J. and Laub, J.H. (2003) 'Life-course desisters? Trajectories of crime among delinquent boys followed to age 70', *Criminology*, 41(3): 555–92.

Schinkel, M. (2019) 'Rethinking turning points: trajectories of parenthood and desistance', *Journal of Developmental and Life-Course Criminology* 5: 366–86, Available from: https://doi.org/10.1007/s40865-019-00121-8

Shapland, J. (2022) 'Once convicted? The long-term pathways to desistance', *The Howard Journal of Crime and Justice*, 61: 271–88, Available from: https://onlinelibrary.wiley.com/doi/full/10.1111/hojo.12473

Stone, N. (2018) 'Child criminal exploitation: "county lines", trafficking and cuckooing', *Youth Justice*, 18(3): 285–93.

Straub, C. and Annison, H. (2020) 'The mental health impact of parole on families of indeterminate-sentenced prisoners in England and Wales', *Criminal Behaviour and Mental Health*, 30(6): 341–9.

Waltham Forest Safeguarding Children Board (2020) 'Serious Case Review: Child C; a 14 year old boy; final version, May 2020', WFSCB, Available from: https://www.walthamforest.gov.uk/sites/default/files/2021-11/WFSCB%20-%20SCR%20Child%20C%20May%20final_.pdf

Warner, K. (2018) 'Every possible learning opportunity: the capacity of education in prison to challenge dehumanisation and liberate "the whole person"', *Advancing Corrections Journal*, (6): 32–45.

Warr, J. (2023) 'Whitening Black Men: narrative labour and the scriptural economics of risk and rehabilitation', *The British Journal of Criminology*, 63(5): 1091–107.

Weaver, B. (2016) *Offending and Desistance: The Importance of Social Relations*, London: Routledge.

Weaver, B. (2019) 'Understanding desistance: a critical review of theories of desistance', *Psychology, Crime & Law*, 25(6): 641–5.

Wigzell, A. (2021) 'Explaining desistance: looking forward, not backwards', London: National Association of Youth Justice.

Williams, P. and Clarke, B. (2016) 'Dangerous associations: joint enterprise, gangs and racism; an analysis of the process of criminalisation of Black, Asian and minority ethnic individuals', London: Centre for Crime and Justice Studies.

Wroe, L.E. (2021) 'Young people and "county lines": a contextual and social account', *Journal of Children's Services*, 16(1): 39–55, Available from: https://doi.org/10.1108/JCS-10-2020-0063

Youth Matters (2005) 'Green Paper on services for youth, Secretary of State for Education and Skills', Available from: https://dera.ioe.ac.uk/5387/7/youth%20mattters%20pdf_Redacted.pdf

PART II

The socio-structural dimensions of desistance

Young women and punishment within and beyond the penal system

Gilly Sharpe

Introduction

Feminist research on troublesome girls has revealed a close relationship between welfare and punishment, extending to the de facto punishment of girls through welfare mechanisms (for example Chesney-Lind, 1989; Carrington, 1993; O'Neill, 2001). Despite these scholarly insights, limited attention has been paid to similarities and continuities in young women's experiences of punishment and punitiveness across penal and welfare settings, and youth justice and penal practices have tended to be considered in isolation from other institutional arrangements. Such compartmentalisation serves to fragment experiences which are overlapping and interwoven, and which may have cumulative and enduring effects on individuals over time. This chapter, through a focus on the structural and cultural contexts which shape both lawbreaking and desistance (Weaver, 2019), examines the treatment and punishment of marginalised young women across three domains: education, criminal labelling and the benefits system. Following Carvalho et al (2020, pp 265–6), I conceptualise young women's experience of punitiveness as multi-faceted and 'a central feature of a range of intersecting experiences and practices'. I argue that schools, formal and informal youthful criminal labels and the welfare benefits system constitute intersecting and sometimes mutually constitutive sites of punishment which, in combination, are likely to have a toxic impact on marginalised young women's sense of self as well as on their economic and social prospects.

Trans-institutional inaction and punishment

Research evidence on the backgrounds of young women in the youth justice system attests to their frequent experience of family violence, abuse and exploitation, as well as histories of state care (Batchelor, 2005; Douglas and Plugge, 2006; Sharpe, 2012; Chesney-Lind and Shelden, 2014; Vaswani, 2018). Care experience itself constitutes a significant and gendered pathway into the justice system, particularly youth custody (Carlen, 1988; Jacobson et al, 2010; Goodfellow, 2017; MoJ/YJB, 2017; Fitzpatrick et al, 2023). For example, two thirds of girls aged ten to 17 who entered penal custody in England and Wales between 2014 and 2016 were, or had previously been, 'looked after' by the state, and almost half (46 per cent) had been subject to a Child Protection Plan (MoJ/YJB, 2017).[1] Marginalised girls who experience childhood maltreatment are frequently responded to with indifference and disbelief, rather than sympathy and support, by statutory services (Allnock and Miller, 2013; Jay, 2014; Sharpe, 2016; Ofsted, 2021). A substantial body of scholarship has demonstrated that statutory children's social care services and interventions may be experienced by young women as no less punitive than penal sanctions, particularly when they involve secure care (O'Neill, 2001; Ellis, 2018). Several of the 52 youth justice system-involved women interviewed by Sharpe (2012, p 132), for example, explained that social workers had 'abandoned' them or 'closed the case', leaving them bereft of adult support. Moreover, statutory 'gender-neutral' services are often inaccessible to girls with multiple or complex needs who do not meet eligibility thresholds for support by statutory services because they are deemed too low risk, or, conversely, too high risk, or else too young or too old, to be offered support. This can leave young women feeling 'pushed out and left out', sometimes developing their own coping strategies which lead to them becoming the 'problem' rather than the victim (Agenda, 2022).

In addition to welfare inaction, marginalised girls experience overtly punitive responses within a range of state institutions on account of their class position and social background (Sharpe, 2024). Many of the 52 girls and young women interviewed by Sharpe (2012) disclosed bullying at school,[2] and others believed they had been treated unfairly or with intolerance by teachers, resulting in a lack of attachment to education and learning. There is a close association between school-based punishment and childhood criminalisation. Almost three quarters (71 per cent) of children with a criminal record, compared with 15 per cent of the general school population, have been suspended from school, and one tenth (versus 1 per cent of all pupils) have been permanently excluded (Department for Education, 2022). Marginalised girls and boys who are subject to disciplinary punishment in the classroom may be labelled as troublemakers from an early age (Reay, 2017), with 'recycling' or re-labelling effects if and when they subsequently come into contact with law enforcement agencies (McAra and McVie, 2005).

At a slightly older age as they transition into adulthood, many criminalised young women will be required to navigate both discriminatory criminal records disclosure requirements and a misogynistic and anti-youth welfare benefits system, in which claimants are represented as 'scroungers' and 'skivers' (Jensen and Tyler, 2015) and treated with hostility and a lack of compassion (O'Hara, 2020; Tyler, 2020). The possession of a criminal record, particularly among those with childcare responsibilities, impedes women's ability to work, leaving them reliant on the welfare benefits system, where they may find themselves negatively judged and further punished. The following section explores school-based disciplinary punishment and exclusion, experiences which frequently foreshadow, as well as overdetermine, girls' subsequent encounters with the youth justice system.

Punishment at school

There is a raft of evidence that children in the youth justice system have experienced school exclusion and disruption, as well as disengagement from education, and these experiences do not seem to differ markedly by gender, unlike among the general population (Jacobson et al, 2010; Department for Education, 2022). However, the relationship between disadvantage and exclusion from school does appear to be somewhat gendered. A notable finding of the major UK government-commissioned Timpson review of school exclusions (Department for Education, 2019) was that girls supported by social care – namely girls considered to be children 'in need', looked after by the state or subject to a Child Protection Plan – were significantly more likely than other girls to experience exclusion from school, a differential that was much less pronounced among boys.

Osler (2006) has contended that school exclusion is a social justice issue, and substantial evidence supports this position. Schools are a central site of social and civic participation for children, and exclusion from school can stem from, as well as worsen, existing social exclusion and disadvantage. Exclusion from school can have an enduring impact on individuals' future opportunities (Partridge et al, 2020). Exclusion is disproportionately experienced by children of colour, individuals with disabilities and marginalised children, identities which frequently intersect (Gillborn, 2015). Children with special educational needs and disabilities (SEND) are six times more likely to be excluded from school than pupils without SEND, and in England children eligible for free school meals – an indicator of poverty – are four times as likely to be permanently excluded (Partridge et al, 2020). Educational failure is also more prevalent in more unequal societies (Wilkinson and Pickett, 2010), where school attainment has been demonstrated to depend largely on one's parents' economic, cultural and social capital rather than on individual ability or motivation (Reay, 2017). Reay (2017) contends that working-class children experience little sense of belonging at school, such that schools may impede, rather than enable, social mobility.

School exclusion broadly mirrors youth justice system involvement in terms of gender: boys are twice as likely as girls to be suspended from school and four times as likely to be permanently excluded (Department for Education, 2019), resulting in exclusion being seen as a boys' problem. McAra and McVie (2012), drawing on longitudinal data from the Edinburgh Study of Youth Transitions, a cohort of around 4,300 mainly White individuals in Scotland, found that badly behaved girls were more likely than their male counterparts to evade school exclusion. By contrast, one New Zealand-based longitudinal examination of the relationship between school exclusion and subsequent justice system involvement among 593 individuals concluded that there was a lower threshold of tolerance for girls' misbehaviour at school than for boys' (Sanders et al, 2020). It is important to note here that recorded statistics are limited in describing and explaining school disciplinary practices and classroom responses to 'challenging' behaviour. Girls may be excluded in less visible and more informal ways than their male counterparts: for example, through the use of 'off-rolling', self-exclusion and unofficial school moves (Osler et al, 2002; Social Finance, 2020; Agenda, 2021).[3] Official data which record gender alone also mask intersectional differences relating to race, class and sexuality. Gypsy Roma girls (and boys) are excluded from school at the highest rate of all groups (Roma Support Group, 2017), and Black Caribbean girls are excluded at twice the rate of White British girls, with mixed White and Black Caribbean young women three times as likely to experience school exclusion (Partridge et al, 2020; Agenda, 2021). White middle-class norms and expectations of docility and quiet unassertiveness may lead to the punishment of girls who infringe gender norms, particularly if they employ physical violence (Jackson, 2006; Osler, 2006; Carlile, 2009).

Exclusion from school can relate indirectly to maltreatment outside school. Most of the young women in one recent consultation with previously excluded individuals explained their exclusion from school with reference to having to cope with abuse, violence and trauma (Agenda, 2021). As indicated earlier, girls' needs may go unnoticed and unmet at school and elsewhere. Non-verbal signs of maltreatment or neglect, such as a lack of personal care, bruises, excessive tiredness or emotional withdrawal, may be overlooked or ignored. Allnock and Miller (2013) conducted retrospective interviews with 60 young adults – 53 women and seven men – who had experienced sexual abuse and family violence during childhood. Four fifths of the respondents had attempted to disclose their abuse to a professional before turning 18, the majority while the abuse was still ongoing. However, as other studies have also found (Radford et al, 2011; Ofsted, 2021), most had not felt able to make a verbal disclosure but instead attempted to communicate in other less direct ways, such as through clues in their actions or by using indirect words. Forty-two per cent of those attempting to make disclosures had not been 'heard', and no action had been taken. It is extremely difficult for young people who are suffering abuse to make sense of what is happening to them: they may blame themselves, as well as fear the consequences of disclosure. This signals a need for increased awareness among professionals who work with children and highlights the importance of asking sensitive direct questions in a safe environment, as well as providing information to children about help-seeking processes and support mechanisms (Allnock and Miller, 2013).

Schools' failure to respond to non-physical or superficially 'non-serious' bullying can also lead to exclusion of the 'victim'. All of the 81 girls interviewed for one study of girls and exclusion (Osler, 2006) were of the opinion that there is a direct relationship between bullying and school exclusion. Verbal bullying and taunting between girls may be normalised and attract no response from teachers, even when it is persistent and emotionally damaging (Sharpe, 2024). Physical violence perpetrated by young women, by contrast, may be seen as particularly serious and shocking. A girl who is the victim of persistent verbal abuse and psychological violence may therefore find herself without support from education professionals; yet she may be excluded if she subsequently 'explodes' in retaliation.

Inaction and a lack of concern by teachers can have a lasting impact on young women's sense of self. Sharpe (2024) analysed the retrospective accounts of 36 women in their 20s of their teenage experiences of school. The majority of respondents believed that their teachers had low expectations of them and that their school had little interest in their wellbeing, resulting in them feeling devalued and unimportant. Several of the women had also been excluded from school immediately prior to sitting external GCSE exams, perhaps in an attempt to avoid harming the schools' exam results and attainment rankings. Being prevented from obtaining qualifications is an acutely punitive act with potentially lifelong consequences.

Criminal records and media representations: gendered marks of shame

Lawbreakers are widely stigmatised, with effects that can endure long after crime has been left behind. Criminal women in particular are subject to negative appraisals on account of being seen as failed women, failed citizens and, in some cases, failed mothers (Schur, 1984; Sharpe, 2015; Gålnander, 2020; Rutter and Barr, 2021). The possession of a criminal record is a formal mark of shame with specific generational and gendered impacts. Criminal records imposed on children have been likened to 'life sentences' (Stacey, 2018). Disclosure requirements pertaining to childhood criminal records were until recently far more permissive in England and Wales than in many other jurisdictions (Sands, 2016), despite the purpose and effectiveness of disclosing childhood misdemeanours, in some cases decades after their occurrence, being questionable. In November 2020, existing criminal records disclosure filtering rules in England and Wales were changed, and youth pre-court disposals (cautions, reprimands and final warnings) were no longer to be subject to automatic disclosure through an enhanced Disclosure and Barring Service certificate, as was previously the case (Beard, 2021). Several years before this welcome change, the House of Commons Justice Committee (2017, para 65) commented that the (then) existing disclosure regime discriminated against children from Black, Asian and other minoritised backgrounds, young asylum seekers, children in the care system and young women forced into prostitution. In addition to these groups, marginalised young women more broadly are disproportionately affected – and punished – by criminal records disclosure requirements. Women have been estimated to be around twice as likely as men to have their criminal records disclosed when applying for work (Unlock, 2021). Marginalised young women with few qualifications are disproportionately represented in work in the public-facing service and care sectors (McDowell, 2016), where enhanced disclosure of one's previous lawbreaking is usually required. Unlock's (2021) research, which drew on survey data from 511 women with criminal records in England and Wales, revealed substantial post-conviction problems, with most respondents (86 per cent) citing employment as the biggest problem in their lives.

In addition to formal criminal records checks, information technology and data-sharing systems, as well as the social media gossip machinery, make it more difficult to conceal one's criminal past (Lageson and Maruna, 2018). Furthermore, young women who have committed serious and/or violent offences are at high risk of trial by media, since their lawbreaking is frequently presented as particularly shocking or salacious and thus more newsworthy than that of young men (Chesney-Lind and Irwin, 2008; Sharpe, 2012). The court of public opinion, ever more vitriolic in the age of social media, is frequently swayed by cultural representations of female lawbreakers. Women defendants – as well as victims, in cases of sexual violence – are routinely demonised and vilified, as well as masculinised (Chesney-Lind and Eliason, 2006), or depicted as more depraved than their male counterparts. These often-distorted representations frequently invoke class: offending girls are constructed both as disreputable and immoral subjects and as objects of disgust. Such depictions arguably constitute a generalised punitiveness towards criminal girls and women. They may also influence decision-making by criminal justice and other professionals (Chesney-Lind and Irwin, 2008; Sharpe, 2009). While some professionals will be critical about media portrayals of women and intermittent moral panics that girls' and women's behaviour is getting worse or that they are becoming more violent, it is quite feasible that professional assessment practices and judgements affecting marginalised and criminalised women will be influenced by media (mis)representations of an apparently rising tide of girlhood alcohol consumption or violence (Sharpe, 2009).

Female defendants' less frequent appearance in court may also render individual girls and women more visible and memorable. While there are legal restrictions on the press reporting of criminal cases involving child defendants in order to protect their privacy and avoid unnecessary stigma, there are indications that judges have become progressively more willing to lift these restrictions and allow the public exposure of child defendants (Stone, 2015). This more permissive approach appears to be underpinned by an incorrect and unsupported belief that 'naming and shaming' has the potential to deter others. As Stone (2015, p 100) has persuasively argued, this indicates a failure on the part of sentencers to distinguish between public interest imperatives and 'the gratuitous appeasement of public curiosity'.

Disclosing one's criminal past is a risky undertaking for women (Gålnander, 2020): in addition to compromising one's employment prospects, the shame of declaring oneself an offending woman, as well as fear of the consequences of so doing, is likely to be considerable. In some cases, this may cause individuals to shun contact with support services and avoid applying for jobs for which they are suitably qualified and experienced (Sharpe, 2024). This leaves many criminalised British young women at the mercy of a harsh and punitive welfare benefits system.

The punitive political economy of welfare in austerity Britain

The political economy is a central consideration in women's pathways into and out of crime, and the impact of economic policies, particularly in relation to state welfare, is likely to be enduring as well as multi-generational, affecting any dependent children as much as, if not more than, their mothers. Most female lawbreakers experience financial hardship (Corston, 2007), and, while precise data are not available, many criminalised mothers (Epstein, 2014), and probably the majority of criminalised *young* mothers (Sharpe, 2015), are lone parents. Beginning with the Thatcher administration of the 1980s, successive governments' pursuance of a neoliberal agenda involving the rolling back of the state has led to the dismantling of the welfare settlement and social rights that had been in place since the post-war period. A plethora of 'welfare reforms' introduced by UK governments since the 1980s have progressively lessened the financial security and economic position of already-marginalised groups, disproportionately impacting migrants, minority ethnic groups, people with disabilities, and women and children and contributing to increased inequality between citizens (Taylor-Gooby, 2013). Indeed, the contemporary UK welfare system was described by Philip Alston, human rights lawyer and former-UN special rapporteur on extreme poverty and human rights, as so sexist that it could have been drawn up by "a group of misogynists in a room" (Ward, 2018). Meanwhile, citizenship has been redefined around the dual axes of paid work/worklessness and inclusion/exclusion (Tyler, 2013, p 161), with the consequence that poor people, including those engaged in unpaid care work, must be coerced into work in order to fulfil the obligations of citizenship. Contemporaneous with waged labour becoming more central as a marker of citizenship, employment in the UK and elsewhere has become increasingly precarious, particularly for young people (McDowell, 2016). Young people with criminal records are thus required to navigate an economic system which demands their inclusion in the labour market yet simultaneously excludes them on account of their past misdeeds.

Criminalised young women are less likely than their male counterparts to be supported, either financially or practically, by their families of origin, and they are more likely to experience homelessness (Sharpe, 2012; Prison Reform Trust/Women in Prison, 2018). Women in general tend to leave the family home earlier than men,[4] and family violence, discord and childhood maltreatment may propel marginalised young women out of the family home at a young age (Blaauboer and Mulder, 2010; Sharpe, 2012). The male respondents in one British longitudinal study examining young men's desistance from crime remained at 'home', in most cases, well into their 20s (Bottoms and Shapland, 2016), which is likely to have mitigated financial strain while providing some degree of practical and personal support, in turn aiding desistance efforts. Conversely, living alone – without, and especially with, dependent children – is more expensive, particularly for younger people who are poorly supported through social policy. Adults aged under 25 are entitled to lower rates of welfare benefits, due in part to a middle-class assumption that they will either remain in the family home or live in shared accommodation with friends. For those in employment, the national minimum wage is lower for workers under 23. When paid work is made difficult or impossible due to lone motherhood and the possession of a criminal record, financial strain is likely to be very considerable for women living independently.

Social security retrenchment in the UK during austerity has resulted in a punitive benefits system with increasingly stringent conditions of entitlement and harsh sanctions if these are not met. While welfare conditionality is not new, having been introduced in 1996, its reach was extended significantly under the Coalition and subsequent Conservative governments' austerity policies, during which time conditions first imposed by the earlier Labour administration on formerly exempt groups, including lone parents and people with disabilities, became more stringent (Whitworth and Griggs, 2013). 'Work conditions' for individuals in receipt of welfare assistance have become even tougher under Universal Credit, which, since its phased introduction between 2013 and 2018, has led to a reduction in income for most claimants (Tiratelli et al, 2023),[5] with particularly negative consequences for women, lone parents and their children (Andersen, 2020; Carey and Bell, 2022). A new rule introduced in January 2023 requires Universal Credit claimants who work part time to increase their working hours (to at least 15, rather than 12, as was previously the case), or to increase their earnings by at least 25 per cent, in order to remain eligible for the benefit. This change will, again, affect women unequally, as well as their children and others they care for, not least due to the high cost and inaccessibility of childcare provision in Britain.[6]

As indicated, conditions attached to welfare eligibility have been found to disproportionately affect already-vulnerable groups, including disabled people and lone parents, who are also more likely to be sanctioned (their benefit payments stopped or reduced) (Rabindrakumar, 2017; Reeves and Loopstra, 2017). Sanctions, it has been claimed, push lone parents further from work while adding to their financial and emotional burden.[7] They also propel dependent children further into poverty. Half (49 per cent) of children in lone-parent families were in relative poverty in 2019, double the already-high rate (25 per cent) for children in two-parent families (Cribb et al, 2022). Young people under 25, too, are disproportionately sanctioned, with young people aged 20–24 the most likely group to receive a sanction (Harrison, 2023: 10). Welfare assessors have the power to act as 'accuser, judge and jury' (Standing, 2016, p 194) and to control access to financial support. They may exercise discretion regarding the imposition of a benefits sanction if work conditions have not been met, and there is potential for such decisions to be influenced by cultural stereotypes or character judgements based on a woman's criminal past and/or social class position. Working-class women are routinely judged to be unrespectable, feckless and aggressive – 'the [type of] women who tell their kids to fuck off in the social' (McKenzie, 2015, p 51). Already deviant by virtue of their (former) lawbreaking and their possession of a criminal record, criminalised young women may be viewed as untruthful and undeserving in their interactions with welfare assessors. This has potentially serious consequences for their financial circumstances and in turn may constrain their opportunities to leave crime behind.

Conclusion

This chapter has examined young women's experiences of gendered and generational punishment within three domains that are normally considered in isolation from one another: school, the imposition of criminal records and labels and the welfare benefits system. Research on young women's – and indeed young men's – lawbreaking and their desistance from crime has paid insufficient attention to the ways in which institutions and practices beyond the penal system punish and exclude marginalised and criminalised individuals. This is an important omission, since the punishment of young women extends far beyond the penal system. Moreover, criminalised and disadvantaged young women's experiences of discipline and punishment within a range of state institutions are likely to intersect and overlap, and their treatment in one setting or context may influence their reception in others, either contemporaneously or at a later point in time.

Punishment can be structural in origin – for example, criminal records disclosure requirements or welfare benefits eligibility conditions. It also operates at the micro level through individuals' everyday interactions with teachers, judges and welfare assessors. At both levels, punitive and exclusionary policies and practices ultimately communicate to girls and young women that their lives are of little value. They also have the potential to limit women's opportunities well into the future. The reduction of punitiveness towards young women and the promotion of social (re-)inclusion thus requires change at multiple levels.

As discussed earlier, research evidence suggests that girls' exclusion from school is frequently related to, or precipitated by, verbal bullying. Bullying may in turn be associated with family distress and structural disadvantage, both of which may affect girls' appearance, demeanour, behaviour and attendance at school. The availability within schools of mainstreamed and well-resourced emotional support that is available to all at the point of need and for as long as required would increase the possibility of girls' welfare needs being recognised and met before problems escalate. Such provision is currently scarce (Agenda, 2022). Over a quarter of young women aged 16–24 have experienced symptoms of mental illness, and one in eight are likely to experience posttraumatic stress disorder (McManus et al, 2016). This suggests that in-school wellbeing support would benefit a substantial proportion of female students.

In relation to criminal records disclosure, while there has been welcome legislative change restricting the disclosure of one's criminal past, the minimum age of criminal responsibility in England and Wales remains, at ten, extremely low. Raising this age would significantly reduce the number of criminalised children, and it would improve girls' and boys' future employment prospects. Furthermore, convictions received as a juvenile remain eligible for disclosure for five and a half years, with particular implications for young women and men who live independently and must support themselves financially.

Finally, poverty and structural marginalisation over-determine women's crime and narrow their law-abiding options (Carlen, 1988). The UK's current highly punitive welfare benefits system discriminates against women 'by design' (Garnham, 2018). Yet women with a criminalised past, few or no qualifications and childcare responsibilities may be forced to rely on it. Without changes to the welfare system focused on supporting women and their children, rather than sanctioning them and pushing them further into poverty, marginalised women with a criminal past will continue to be punished, potentially long after they have left crime behind.

Notes

[1] A Child Protection Plan is made when a child is judged to be at risk of significant harm.

[2] The interviewees in this study were aged 13–19 years. Six individuals were aged 18 or 19 years old.

[3] 'Off-rolling' is where a pupil is removed from a school roll without the formal exclusion process – for which there are accountability mechanisms – having been followed, or by encouraging a parent to take their child out of school. Importantly, off-rolling does not lead to the identification of a new educational placement (Partridge et al, 2020), thereby undermining the child's right to education.

[4] This is around two years earlier in the UK. See https://www.ons.gov.uk/peoplepopulat ionandcommunity/birthsdeathsandmarriages/families/datasets/youngadultslivingwitht heirparents

[5] See 'Childcare responsibilities' on the Understanding Universal Credit website, Available from: https://www.understandinguniversalcredit.gov.uk/new-to-universal-credit/your-responsibilities

[6] The average net UK childcare cost, when state funding was taken into account, was the sixth highest of all Organisation for Economic Co-operation and Development countries in 2022. See https://data.oecd.org/benwage/net-childcare-costs.htm

[7] See 'How benefit sanctions push single parents further from work', LSE Blog, 18 April 2018, Available from: https://blogs.lse.ac.uk/politicsandpolicy/how-benefit-sanctions-push-single-parents-further-from-work

References

Agenda (2021) 'Girls at risk of exclusion: Girls Speak briefing', Available from: https://weareagenda.org/wp-content/uploads/2021/09/Girls-at-risk-of-exclusion-Agenda-briefing-September-2021.pdf

Agenda (2022) 'Pushed out, left out', Girls Speak final report, London: Agenda Alliance.

Allnock, D. and Miller, P. (2013) 'No one noticed, no one heard: a study of disclosures of childhood abuse', London: NSPCC.

Andersen, K. (2020) 'Universal credit, gender and unpaid childcare: mothers' accounts of the New Welfare Conditionality Regime', *Critical Social Policy*, 40(3): 430–49.

Batchelor, S. (2005) '"Prove me the bam!" Victimisation and agency in the lives of young women who commit violent offences', *Probation Journal*, 52(4): 358–75.

Beard, J. (2021) 'The retention and disclosure of criminal records', Briefing paper CBP6441, 10 February, London: House of Commons.

Blaauboer, M. and Mulder, C.H. (2010) 'Gender differences in the impact of family background on leaving the parental home', *Journal of Housing and the Built Environment*, 25(1): 53–71.

Bottoms, A.E. and Shapland, J. (2016) 'Learning to desist in early adulthood: the Sheffield Desistance Study', in J. Shapland, S. Farrall and A.E. Bottoms (eds) *Global Perspectives on Desistance: Reviewing What We Know, Looking to the Future*, Abingdon: Routledge, pp 99–125.

Carey, M. and Bell, S. (2022) 'Universal credit, lone mothers and poverty: some ethical challenges for social work with children and families', *Ethics and Social Welfare*, 16(1): 3–18.

Carlen, P. (1998) *Women, Crime and Poverty*, Milton Keynes: Open University Press.

Carlile, A. (2009) '"Bitchy girls and silly boys": gender and exclusion from school', *International Journal on School Disaffection*, 6(2): 30–6.

Carrington, K. (1993) *Offending Girls: Sex, Youth and Justice*, St Leonards, New South Wales: Allen & Unwin.

Carvalho, H., Chamberlen, A. and Lewis, R. (2020) 'Punitiveness beyond criminal justice: punishable and punitive subjects in an era of prevention, anti-migration and austerity', *British Journal of Criminology*, 60(2): 265–84.

Chesney-Lind, M. (1989) 'Girls' crime and women's place: toward a feminist model of female delinquency', *Crime & Delinquency*, 35: 5–30.

Chesney-Lind, M. and Eliason, M. (2006) 'From invisible to incorrigible: the demonization of marginalized women and girls', *Crime, Media, Culture*, 2: 29–47.

Chesney-Lind, M. and Irwin, K. (2008) *Beyond Bad Girls: Gender, Violence and Hype*, New York: Routledge.

Chesney-Lind, M. and Shelden, R.G. (2014) *Girls, Delinquency and Juvenile Justice* (4th edn), Hoboken: Wiley-Blackwell.

Corston, J. (2007) 'The Corston report: a report by Baroness Jean Corston of a review of women with particular vulnerabilities in the criminal justice system', London: Home Office.

Cribb, J., Wernham, T. and Xu, X. (2022) 'Pre-pandemic relative poverty rate for children of lone parents almost double that for children living with two parents', London: Institute for Fiscal Studies, Available from: https://ifs.org.uk/articles/pre-pandemic-relative-poverty-rate-children-lone-parents-almost-double-children-living-two

Department for Education (2019) 'Timpson review of school exclusion', DfE-00090–2019, Available from: https://assets.publishing.service.gov.uk/government/uploads/system/uploads/attachment_data/file/807862/Timpson_review.pdf

Department for Education (2022) 'Education, children's social care and offending', London: Department for Education/Ministry of Justice.

Douglas, N. and Plugge, E. (2006) 'Female health needs in young offender institutions', London: Youth Justice Board.

Ellis, K. (2018) 'Contested vulnerability: a case study of girls in secure care', *Children & Youth Services Review*, 88: 156–63.

Epstein, R. (2014) 'Mothers in prison: the sentencing of mothers and the rights of the child', Howard League, *What is Justice?* Working paper 3/2014, London: Howard League.

Fitzpatrick, C., Hunter, K., Shaw, J. and Staines, J. (2023) 'Painful lives: understanding self-harm amongst care-experienced women in prison', *Criminology and Criminal Justice*, 23(3): 348–65.

Gålnander, R. (2020) '"Shark in the fish tank": secrets and stigma in relational desistance from crime', *British Journal of Criminology*, 60(5): 1302–19.

Garnham, A. (2018) 'Universal credit discriminates against women by design. Here's how', *New Statesmen*, 17 January 2018.

Gillborn, D. (2015) 'Intersectionality, critical race theory, and the primacy of racism: race, class, gender, and disability in education', *Qualitative Inquiry*, 21(3): 277–87.

Goodfellow, P. (2017) 'Outnumbered, locked up and overlooked? The use of penal custody for girls in England and Wales', London: Griffins Society.

Harrison, K. (2023) *The Sanctions Spiral: The Unequal Impact and Hardship Caused by Sanctions in Universal Credit*, Citizens Advice.

House of Commons Justice Committee (2017) 'Disclosure of youth criminal records: first report of session 2017–19', London: House of Commons.

Jackson, C. (2006) '"Wild" girls? An exploration of "ladette" cultures in secondary schools', *Gender and Education*, 18(4): 339–60.

Jacobson, J., Bhardwa, B., Gyateng, T., Hunter, G. and Hough, M. (2010) 'Punishing disadvantage: a profile of children in custody', London: Prison Reform Trust.

Jay, A. (2014) 'Independent inquiry into child sexual exploitation in Rotherham, 1997–2013', Report for Rotherham Metropolitan Borough Council.

Jensen, T. and Tyler, I. (2015) '"Benefits broods": the cultural and political crafting of anti-welfare commonsense', *Critical Social Policy*, 35(4): 470–91.

Lageson, S.E. and Maruna, S. (2018) 'Digital degradation: stigma management in the internet age', *Punishment & Society*, 20(1): 113–33.

McAra, L. and McVie, S. (2005) 'The usual suspects? Street-life, young people and the police', *Criminal Justice*, 5(1): 5–36.

McAra, L., and McVie, S. (2012) 'Negotiated order: the groundwork for a theory of offending pathways', *Criminology & Criminal Justice*, 12(4): 347–75.

McDowell, L. (2016) 'Post-crisis: youth, identity, class and gender', in A. Furlong (ed) *Routledge Handbook of Youth and Young Adulthood*, Abingdon: Routledge, pp 50–7.

McKenzie, L. (2015) *Getting By: Estates, Class and Culture in Austerity Britain*, Bristol: Policy Press.

McManus, S., Bebbington, P., Jenkins, R. and Brugha, T. (eds) (2016) *Mental Health and Wellbeing in England: Adult Psychiatric Morbidity Survey 2014*, Leeds: NHS Digital.

Ministry of Justice/Youth Justice Board (2017) 'Key characteristics of admissions to youth custody, April 2014 to March 2016: England and Wales', London: Ministry of Justice/Youth Justice Board.

O'Hara, M. (2020) *The Shame Game: Overturning the Toxic Poverty Narrative*, Bristol: Policy Press.

O'Neill, T. (2001) *Children in Secure Accommodation: A Gendered Exploration of Locked Institutional Care for Children in Trouble*, London: Jessica Kingsley.

Ofsted (2021) 'Review of sexual abuse in schools and colleges', Available from: https://www.gov.uk/government/publications/review-of-sexual-abuse-in-schools-and-colleges/review-of-sexual-abuse-in-schools-and-colleges

Osler, A. (2006) 'Excluded girls: interpersonal, institutional and structural violence in schooling', *Gender and Education*, 18(6): 571–89.

Osler, A., Street, C., Lall, M. and Vincent, K. (2002) 'Not a problem? Girls and exclusion from school', Leicester: New Policy Institute & Centre for Citizenship Studies in Education.

Partridge, L., Strong, F.L., Lobley, E. and Mason, D. (2020) 'Pinball kids: preventing school exclusions', London: Royal Society of the Arts.

Prison Reform Trust/Women in Prison (2018) 'Home truths: housing for women in the criminal justice system', Available from: https://prisonreformtrust.org.uk/wp-content/uploads/2018/02/home-truths-june-2018.pdf

Rabindrakumar, S. (2017) 'On the rise: single parent sanctions in numbers', London: Gingerbread.

Radford, L., Corral, S., Bradley, C., Fisher, H., Bassett, C., Howat, N. et al (2011) 'Child abuse and neglect in the UK today', London: NSPCC.

Reay, D. (2017) *Miseducation: Inequality, Education and the Working Classes*, Bristol: Policy Press.

Reeves, A. and Loopstra, R. (2017) '"Set up to fail"? How welfare conditionality undermines citizenship for vulnerable groups', *Social Policy & Society*, 16(2): 327–38.

Roma Support Group (2017) 'Fulfilling their potential? Exclusion of Roma pupils in the English educational system', Roma Support Group, Available from: https://drive.google.com/file/d/0B2lw1_Krq5gnell0TmdtUWcyTFE/view?resourcekey=0-usa4l14NZrBKn5Q9fkhQSA

Rutter, N. & Barr, U. (2021) 'Being a "Good Woman": stigma, relationships and desistance', *Probation Journal*, 68(2): 166–85.

Sanders, J., Liebenberg, L. and Munford, R. (2020) 'The impact of school exclusion on later justice system involvement: investigating the experiences of male and female students', *Educational Review*, 72(3): 386–403.

Sands, C. (2016) 'Growing up, moving on: the international treatment of childhood criminal records', Standing Committee for Youth Justice.

Schur, E. (1984) *Labeling Women Deviant: Gender, Stigma, and Social Control*, New York: Random House.

Sharpe, G. (2009) 'The trouble with girls today: professional perspectives on young women's offending', *Youth Justice*, 9(3): 254–69.

Sharpe, G. (2012) *Offending Girls: Young Women and Youth Justice*, Abingdon: Routledge.

Sharpe, G. (2015) 'Precarious identities: "young" motherhood, desistance and stigma', *Criminology & Criminal Justice*, 15(4): 407–22.

Sharpe, G. (2016) 'Re-imagining justice for girls: a new agenda for research', *Youth Justice*, 16(1): 3–17.

Sharpe, G. (2024) *Women, Stigma and Desistance from Crime: Precarious Identities in the Transition to Adulthood*, Abingdon: Routledge.

Social Finance (2020) 'Maximising access to education: who's at risk of exclusion? An analysis in Cheshire West and Chester', London: Social Finance.

Stacey, C. (2018) 'A life sentence for young people', Maidstone: Unlock.

Standing, G. (2016) *The Precariat: The New Dangerous Class*. London: Bloomsbury Academic.

Stone, N. (2015) 'Naming child defendants: in the public interest?', *Youth Justice*, 15(1): 93–103.

Taylor-Gooby, P. (2013) *The Double Crisis of the Welfare State and What We Can Do about It*, Basingstoke: Palgrave Macmillan.

Tiratelli, M., Bradford, B. and Yesberg, J. (2023) 'The political economy of crime: did universal credit increase crime rates?' *British Journal of Criminology*, 63(3): 570–87.

Tyler, I. (2013) *Revolting Subjects: Social Abjection and Resistance in Neoliberal Britain*. London: Zed.

Tyler, I. (2020) *Stigma: The Machinery of Inequality*, London: Zed.

Unlock (2021) '"Angels or witches": the impact of criminal records on women', Maidstone: Unlock.

Vaswani, N. (2018) 'Adverse childhood experiences in children at high risk of harm to others: a gendered perspective', Glasgow: Children and Young People's Centre for Justice.

Ward, V. (2018) 'UK's welfare system is cruel and misogynistic, says UN expert after damning report on poverty', *The Telegraph*, Available from: https://www.telegraph.co.uk/news/2018/11/16/welfare-system-cruel-misogynistic-un-expert-warns-damning-report

Weaver, B. (2019) 'Understanding desistance: a critical review of theories of desistance', *Psychology, Crime & Law*, 25(6): 641–58.

Whitworth, A. and Griggs, J. (2013) 'Lone parents and welfare-to-work conditionality: necessary, just, effective?', *Ethics and Social Welfare*, 7(2): 124–40.

Wilkinson, R. and Pickett, K. (2010) *The Spirit Level: Why Equality Is Better for Everyone*, London: Penguin.

6

Supporting girls in care to desist from offending behaviour

Jo Staines, Julie Shaw, Katie Hunter and Claire Fitzpatrick

Introduction

The over-representation of care-experienced individuals in the criminal justice system has been widely documented (see Staines, 2016 for an overview) yet, despite recent changes to policy and practice, remains problematic. For example, recent Department for Education and Ministry of Justice (MoJ) (2022) data revealed that, while 5 per cent of all school children sampled had received a caution or sentence, 11 per cent of those with experience of the care system had done so. This disproportionality continues throughout the justice system, with over half (52 per cent) of the children in custody having previous experience of the care system (Her Majesty's Inspectorate of Prisons, 2021). Such over-representation particularly affects girls and women – previous research has found that around a third of adult women in custody are care-experienced compared with a quarter of men (MoJ, 2012).

Explanations for the disproportionate involvement of care-experienced people in justice systems contend that a complex interaction exists between experiences of early trauma, experiences during care and structural factors within and around care and justice systems (Shaw, 2014; Staines, 2016). Care-experienced individuals share overlapping biographies with those involved in criminal justice systems and often have similar experiences of inter-familial harm, family instability, disadvantage and deprivation, low educational attainment, mental health problems and difficulties with drugs and alcohol (see Staines, 2016). Becoming 'looked after' can both reduce and increase the likelihood of criminal justice involvement – the former through the provision of high-quality, stable placements that enable and facilitate desistance, the latter through processes of labelling and criminalisation (Darker et al, 2008; Schofield et al, 2014). The experience of care itself – relationships with staff/carers, behaviour management strategies, interactions with peers and so forth – influences the likelihood of involvement in the justice system, which is further affected by statutory and professional responses to children in care (Shaw, 2014). Moreover, children in care are at particular risk of child criminal and/or sexual exploitation (Calouri et al, 2020), which can exacerbate their criminalisation.

The experiences of both care and justice systems may be affected by gender, yet developing an understanding of girls' experiences and needs within justice systems primarily designed for boys has been somewhat neglected (Goodfellow, 2019). Similarly, studies of care-experience have often focused on generic experiences of those in care rather than specifically on the distinctive experiences of boys and/or girls. Correspondingly, there is only a nascent understanding of the specific experiences of care-experienced girls who are also involved with the youth justice system (McFarlane, 2010; Humphery, 2019; Fitzpatrick, 2022; Fitzpatrick et al, 2022). Taking a gendered perspective can help to explain why care-experienced girls may be accelerated through justice systems more rapidly than boys and provide insights into how their involvement in offending behaviour can be reduced. For example, girls in care may have experienced higher levels of adversity and difficulties prior to placement than boys (O'Neill, 2001; Lipscombe, 2006; Henriksen, 2018), which can contribute to increased youth justice involvement. Girls may also experience differential treatment within the care and justice systems, partly due to preconceived stigma and professional reluctance to work with girls, a greater reliance on police involvement when girls present 'challenging behaviour', increased risk of sexual exploitation and subsequent criminalisation and a lack of recognition of gender differences within care provision (O'Neill, 2001; Bateman and Hazel, 2014; Humphery, 2019).

Care-experienced girls who do become involved in the youth justice system may experience a 'triple whammy' of negative stereotyping based on their gender, care status and alleged offending behaviour, with ethnicity potentially adding another layer of discrimination for some (Hunter, 2022). As well as influencing their routes into offending behaviour, these factors may also affect their ability to desist. There is neither space nor need here to rehearse wider theories of desistance, other than to state that the authors of this chapter adopt McNeill's (2017) stance that desistance is neither individualistic nor reductionist but needs to be situated within society and state agencies. Further, in line with the Youth Justice Board's Child First approach, child-first desistance needs to focus not on individual deficits but on the structural constraints and barriers that children face (Wigzell, 2021). As the causes of offending behaviour often lie beyond the individual, so do the solutions to criminalisation, yet – again following McNeill (2017) – the process of desistance can only be fully understood by centring lived experiences.

While desistance research generally has not focused on care-experienced individuals, it is feasible to assume desistance may be harder for care-experienced children whose situations and experiences differ from those living with their family. In their review of the literature on desistance, Bevan (2015) highlights a range of factors that are known to be correlated with desistance yet which may be less commonly experienced by those in the care system, often because of institutional policies and practices within care. Furthermore, although the transitional factors that influence desistance are thought to be similar for males and females, the process of desistance is not gender-neutral (Uggen and Kruttschnitt, 1998; McIvor et al, 2004), yet many current approaches to desistance may either be deemed 'gender-neutral' or primarily aimed towards the male majority. Drawing on findings from a recent research project, the discussion here thus explores why the actions of statutory agencies and professionals may make desistance more difficult for care-experienced individuals, particularly care-experienced girls and young women.

The research

Interviews were undertaken with 40 professionals working with girls and young women across the care and justice systems: four police officers, eight youth offending team (YOT) staff, six children's services workers, four probation officers, seven prison officers and 11 members of the judiciary. The interviews were part of a study funded by the Nuffield Foundation, which explored the disproportionate involvement of care-experienced girls and women in the youth and criminal justice system, and which also included interviews with 54 girls and women. The research was approved by the Lancaster University Ethics Committee and Her Majesty's Prisons and Probation Service's National Research Committee. Adherence to stringent ethical standards was maintained throughout, notwithstanding the impact of the COVID-19 pandemic (see Fitzpatrick et al, 2022 for full details of the research and participants).

The research identified a range of ways that professionals can support care-experienced girls to desist from offending behaviour, despite the structural disadvantages they may face. In particular, professionals highlighted the importance of changing state responses to girls' behaviour, prioritising diversion and restorative approaches over prosecution; challenging judgemental and stereotypical assumptions held by professionals about girls in care; providing positive relationships that also model alternative identities for girls in care and raise aspirations for them; and supporting girls in care through key transitions in their lives, such as the move to independent living. Furthermore, professionals emphasised the need to recognise and address the impact of trauma and victimisation on care-experienced girls' behaviour.

Reducing criminalisation through diversion and restorative justice

Fundamentally, care-experienced children face criminalisation via the care and justice systems and so have to counter the impact of structural criminalisation – a focus on desistance as the 'correction' of individual deficits is thus particularly inappropriate given that the systems themselves are 'creating' offending. As McNeill (2017) argues, there is an 'irremediable problem' in approaches to desistance that forget issues of who and what gets criminalised, and how social inequality and injustice are amplified through criminalisation. The care and justice systems, and related professionals and practices, play a significant role in criminalising children in care and equally are critical in supporting or frustrating desistance.

Throughout many of the interviews, it was recognised that reducing such criminalisation, through the use of diversionary and/or restorative practices, was essential in enabling desistance and reducing the number of children recorded as having committed offences. Many of the interviewees reflected on recent changes that had reduced the amount of reoffending by children in care:

'Diversion away from court and doing restorative work with the children's home … that's been major … now we've got more flexibility to say "hang on a minute, can we do some restorative work in the children's home or can we do some work in relation to this?", and then you know we're seeing that some of those young people aren't coming back.' (YOT 2)

Some participants believed that there was now more understanding of the need for the police and care providers to divert children from the youth justice system, including through the use of restorative justice. However, it was also acknowledged that the use of diversion was "variable" and inconsistent, with some police forces or care homes being "much less tolerant" (Children's Services 5) than others.

The level of tolerance demonstrated could also vary on understandings of how 'serious' an incident was, with some professionals stating that diversionary or restorative approaches are not suitable for all incidents:

'Obviously if somebody's in fear or in danger of course we would expect them to call the police, if it's really, really serious, we did have one boy who held his social worker up against the wall with a knife to his throat. Obviously in that situation you call the police.' (YOT 7)

Sexual assaults were seen as particularly difficult to manage through restorative processes:

'The example they'll give is like someone stole the eggs and threw them at somebody's bedroom door the other week, so they sit down and explain to them like "because you did that we have no eggs, that meant somebody couldn't do their baking" and they explain all the consequences of it ... but it's like what do you do when it's a sexual assault?' (Children's Services 6)

Furthermore, Hodgson (2022) cautions that girls' experiences of restorative approaches may not always be positive and that they may feel disempowered, with their own victimisation side-lined and their needs neglected throughout the process. In particular, Toor (2009) notes that understanding the role of honour (*izzat*) and shame (*sharam*) in the lives of British Asian girls highlights the limits of using restorative justice with this group. It is important to ensure that restorative practices do not add to girls' pre-existing vulnerabilities, and that there is recognition of how girls' lives are shaped by experiences of social injustice, oppression and inequality, which is arguably even more important where girls may have a mistrust of professionals and/or feel they have previously not been listened to (Hodgson, 2022).

Interviewees emphasised the need for sufficient "resources and training"(YOT 3) to ensure that all relevant professionals, including foster carers, are able to identify when and how to implement diversionary or restorative approaches. Addressing issues of poor alignment or communication between different justice agencies was also raised:

'I don't understand why the police ... and the CPS have such a poor relationship. Why the youth offending team aren't involved at an earlier stage by the police ... I know there's a national programme at the moment to try and encourage the police to think diversion but a lot of the time they're just not thinking about it, and the CPS need a specialist unit ... so in every level there is delay and not smart working.' (Judiciary 2)

Recognising and challenging stigma

Children in care and care-experienced adults may be affected by stigma and negative labelling, which need to be actively countered to support desistance (Maruna, 2001). Professionals, and adults in the wider community, may have low aspirations for children in care, which are perpetuated by repeated narratives of low academic achievement (Ellis and Johnston, 2019) and involvement in offending (the irony of writing this chapter is not lost here – although the aim is to challenge such stigma and illuminate structural disadvantage). Girls may also feel more judged, and experience greater 'reputational damage', than boys, with their care status adding another layer of vulnerability to arrest (Uggen and Kruttschnitt, 1998; McIvor et al, 2004; Sharpe, 2015).

The professionals interviewed discussed the importance of challenging and reducing the impact of labelling and the stigmatisation of being in care, which for some care-experienced girls is compounded by their gender, and for others their gender and ethnicity. They reiterated the belief that girls and women in general face more punitive sanctions due to perceived 'double deviancy' and gendered judgements (Heidensohn, 1985; Gelsthorpe and Worrall, 2009), with one interviewee stating that "girls can be treated a little bit more harshly" and that offending behaviour is "expected of bad lads but bad girls should be punished" (Children's Services 4). These stigmatising attitudes were recognised at different levels throughout the care and justice systems, including within the criminal courts:

'In terms of government, I think it's kind of looking at the way courts sentence young females because you know like research shows, females are dealt with very punitively in the court system, and it's about you know maybe educating magistrates. ... You know why is this happening and bringing this to their attention, you know is it like the old stereotype that girls should be more nurturing, they shouldn't be aggressive in their behaviours, you know some of them stereotypes need to be challenged.' (YOT4)

Stigmatisation and labelling can make it more difficult for care-experienced girls to desist from offending, partly because they may internalise such beliefs and partly because the attitudes held affect others' responses to them (Moore et al, 2018), which can subsequently have an impact on girls' access to the labour market.

Trauma, victimisation and mental health support

From the outset, the professionals interviewed acknowledged that girls in care had typically experienced a wide range of trauma and victimisation, including harms potentially committed by their family, which were then compounded by the state's (lack of) actions. One participant said that a care-experienced girl they were supporting "felt so totally alone, she'd been abandoned by her family originally, gone into care and then been abandoned by the system" (Children's Services 3). As discussed elsewhere (Staines et al, 2023), feelings of isolation, abandonment and not belonging can contribute to the onset of offending behaviour, whereas feeling a sense of belonging can contribute to desistance (Brierley, 2021).

Furthermore, the interviewees recognised the need to provide mental health services, including counselling, to girls in care to ensure that they do not "end up basically going down the criminal route" (YOT3) as a result of unaddressed or unresolved trauma (including the impact of prior sexual abuse, which was prevalent among the girls and women in this study). Mental health problems are correlated with continued involvement in criminal justice systems; again, children in care are more likely to experience mental health problems than children in the general population (Wijedasa et al, 2022) yet often find it difficult, if not impossible, to access timely and effective mental health support. The state's failure to provide appropriate mental health support and/or other trauma-informed support for children within its care can thus significantly affect their pathways to desistance.

More positively, there were clear indications that some organisations are paying heed to research and good practice on trauma-informed responses – for example, one police officer discussed how being trauma-informed means they "understand the context of their life and the impact that that may have had on the behaviour" (Police 4). Nonetheless, such awareness was not universal, and there were also calls for greater training and provision of trauma-based support and care "across the whole of the country" (Children's Services 5). Indeed, the widespread provision of appropriate mental health support/trauma-informed responses could in turn serve to alleviate the tendency to draw women and girls inappropriately into the justice system for welfare reasons (Children's Commissioner, 2019), thus reducing unnecessary and potentially damaging criminalisation.

Positive relationships and role models

Consistent, positive family, social and professional relationships are widely recognised as being important in supporting desistance (Graham and Bowling, 1995; France and Homel, 2006), perhaps particularly for girls (McIvor et al, 2004) – but the development and maintenance of such relationships may be harder for children in care, given the frequency with which some children have to move (often with concomitant changes of school and teachers) and the high levels of social worker turnover. Family relationships are also less likely to be positive where children have experienced abuse and/or neglect, a common experience for many children in care. Moreover, many care-experienced children have limited networks of social support, particularly when they have experienced multiple placement moves and/or been placed 'out of area' – again, situations for which the state has responsibility but that may exacerbate criminalisation and hinder desistance. Being able to disassociate with peers involved in offending behaviour and establish more pro-social friendships can help some children move away from offending behaviour (Maruna and Roy, 2007) – yet children in care (particularly those living in residential care) may have less agency over their peer relationships and the activities they are involved in because of state control and interventions. Many children in care have very limited, if any, choice about where and with whom they live: they may have restrictions placed on how and where they can spend their free time and may find it harder to avoid associating with others involved in offending behaviour.

The interview participants reiterated the importance of stable, supportive relationships in aiding desistance but also recognised the impact of staff turnover, particularly of social workers, for children in care and how employment conditions need to be improved to reduce staff changes:

'Relationships may have started to form but that staff member may then leave, and there's only so many times … a child or a young adult can invest in a professional without just thinking "well I know how this is going to end". … Goes back then to resources … not so much how much we pay, it's not about the money, it's about how we invest in those professionals as human beings. The space for reflection on learning, so if you go to a training session … how is that then implemented into your practice, how can you reflect on that rather than just ticking the box that you went?' (Children's Services 3)

The professionals emphasised the need to provide long-term, consistent, unwavering support, recognising that "you don't build trusted relationships overnight" (Police 2) but also that the girls may not appear to welcome support when it is offered:

'Girls' feedback will always be "yes, I know I was really hard work and I told you to F off left, right and centre, yes I was abusive with you … but you stuck at it and you come back to the care home … you kept with me". That consistency with an individual, showing that you listened, showing that you genuinely cared.' (Police 2)

Working practices need to be developed that enable professionals to provide support as and when required and appropriate for the young person, rather than in accordance with set timeframes:

'Young people have told us … "don't give up on me just because I'm in a bad place right now" … it means that everything should hold them for a little bit and be with them through the bad times to then be able to do the work with them when they come out the other side.' (Children's Services 4)

A particular challenge for professionals supporting care-experienced girls was the balance between being available as and when needed and not encouraging dependence. For example, one children's services professional said:

'They need to know that somebody's there but they don't need them to be there all the time, so they need the ability to be able to drop in for that ad hoc. … What they don't necessarily need is somebody calling in every Tuesday to make sure they're okay, 'cos they might be okay on Tuesday but then by Thursday they're really not.' (Children's Services 4)

However, another highlighted that they had experienced "young people becoming so dependent that they think they're going to be moving in with you" (Children's Services 5).

Many of the girls and young women interviewed described the impact and importance of their relationship with a YOT worker, which was often the main source of consistent support (see Staines et al, 2023). However, contact with the youth justice system itself can be criminogenic, impeding natural processes of desistance (McAra and McVie, 2011), and it is not acceptable for care-experienced girls to only receive support once they are already in contact with the youth justice system. Although the focus of this chapter is on desistance, given the early trauma that many girls have faced it is also important to note that support needs to be provided much earlier and from outside the youth justice system. Furthermore, the professionals interviewed emphasised how support had to be provided on a multi-agency basis, acknowledging that "it's not one agency can solve it" (Police 1) and that "everyone in that [support] network needs to communicate and be really strong and confident in who they are in their role" (Children's Services 2).

Children in care who are also involved in offending behaviour may have limited access to role models who provide a 'script' by which to enact a conventional, pro-social role (Rumgay, 2004). Such new social identities take time to establish, which may be harder for care-experienced children whose lives are disrupted by placement moves and who may experience more challenges that test their ability to 'stick to the script' and maintain a non-offending persona. Some of the professionals discussed the lack of suitable role models for girls in care, including those from minoritised ethnic backgrounds and those who may identify as LBGT+. One YOT practitioner described themselves as being "a bit of an alternative role model for girls … offer[ing] the girls in the criminal justice system something slightly different" (YOT 4). Others talked about the need to build girls' confidence and to encourage them to have positive aspirations and hope for the future, which can help sustain desistance (McMahon and Jump, 2018): "It's about having an opportunity to build that [confidence] … 'cos a lot of them have, in my experience a lot of lack of self-worth, self-esteem, kind of goal aspirations and I guess it's about motivating them and finding those strengths that they would want to develop" (Probation 1). There are interesting parallels here between the professionals' comments on supporting girls to build their confidence and the recognition that practitioner networks also need to be confident in who they are and what they can achieve.

Transition to independence

Transitional events between adolescence and adulthood, such as leaving home, forming intimate partnerships and having children, can be key turning points in offending trajectories and are particularly associated with desistance for girls (Graham and Bowling, 1995). However, although leaving home may be a critical juncture for those actively choosing to move away, many care-experienced individuals have no choice over 'leaving' home, having been removed from home by the state, and have little control over when they move to unsupported accommodation. Often there is a lack of preparation for independent living from the care system, which can compound the negative impact of such transitions. Moreover, the transition to independence can coincide with transitions from youth services to adult services, including the youth to criminal justice system, Child and Adolescent Mental Health Services to adult mental health services and so forth, presenting multiple cliff edges that may threaten to derail any attempts to desist from offending (Agenda and AYJ, 2021). Further, most children leaving home will be able to rely on ongoing support from their families, including being able to return home should they need – options that are not available to many children leaving care:

> 'Care leavers do not have that safety net around them. ... [Moving on] is a massive ask of anyone and then if you take a young person who had been though the criminal justice system and has potentially to a certain degree maybe been institutionalised and then ... "see you later, this is how you're expected to cope now".' (Children's Services 4)

Many of the interviewees discussed the difficulties in ensuring suitable accommodation was available for girls leaving care, particularly those moving to independence from custody, with the acknowledgement that "placements aren't plentiful and most of our young people that end up with us don't read well on paper, so it's a challenge" (Children's Service 1; see also Sharpe, 2015). Conversely, one interviewee discussed a more positive outcome for a care-experienced girl leaving custody, highlighting the benefits of longer-term planning for resettlement:

> 'Six weeks prior to her release I started to ask social services for an address and I wasn't being given an address and some professionals would think "there's a lack of resources, a lack of housing", but I actually felt really strongly about this. ... What hope has this girl got of resettlement if she doesn't even know where she's going to be living the day up to her release? ... After battling and challenging they came up with an address ... then I arranged for her to get early release for

the day to go and visit her property, view where it was, get her head round where her sofa was going to be, all the little things like you should be planning, and that was really positive ... she started to get really excited about her release because she knew the area, she could visualise being there.' (YOT 4)

Further, while desistance may be related to parenthood for some young mothers (Sharpe, 2015), and although some care-experienced people become parents at a relatively early age, they are likely to face intensive and intrusive scrutiny and are more likely to have their own children taken into care (Roberts, 2021), which again may counter attempts to desist from offending behaviour. Care-experienced girls who become mothers may have less family and social support on which to draw, such that motherhood may become another source of strain rather than positively influencing desistance (Sharpe, 2015). Moreover, the additional stigma and scrutiny they are subject to may negate the beneficial impacts of parenthood:

'I do think they're [pregnant care-experienced girls] more scrutinised like and ... it becomes very hard to work with that young person because they just feel like you're all just social workers and you're trying to take their child off them. So any work that you would have done to like build up a working relationship with them as their social worker, I can imagine that relationship becomes very strained very quickly. ... You're dealing with a lot of stigma and a lot of difficulties in sort of gaining that person's trust back then.' (Children's Services 6)

Conclusions

Overall, it is possible to see how state and institutional responses to girls in care may make it much harder for them to desist from offending behaviour but equally how pockets of good practice exist that highlight how care-experienced girls can be supported to desist from offending – and, indeed, how criminalisation can be avoided in the first place. Adequate support, training and information need to be provided within both the care and justice systems to ensure that such good practice is shared and sustained nationally. The professionals interviewed recognised desistance as a process that could be supported or hindered by the actions of others and emphasised that responsibility for supporting desistance needs to be shared across all relevant agencies and across all levels of policy and practice, with clear leadership from government:

'We've got a Department for Education, Ministry of Justice, a Home Office, etc, none of whom collaborate or cooperate. [If] they can't do it there's immediate barriers in the way of us all doing it. ... [We] are trying to challenge this on a county-wide level, even a national level, but it's got to come from them and there's got to be some better cross-communication between government departments in order to set the tone really.' (Police 4)

The application of Child First principles to both the care *and* youth justice systems would help to ensure that both systems respond in a non-stigmatising and non-criminogenic way to the 'challenging' behaviours of those in care. Continuing to counter the 'triple whammy' of stigma that care-experienced girls who offend may experience, both within the wider community and at all levels of the justice system, is crucial, including raising aspirations for girls in care and enabling them to achieve their hopes and ambitions. The impact of social structures and institutional practices needs to be addressed, within a whole-child approach that also recognises care-experienced girls' agency (see also France and Homel, 2006; Wigzel, 2021).

Strategies and interventions designed to support desistance, including diversion and restorative justice, need to be implemented in gender-appropriate ways that recognise the particular needs and experiences of girls, many of whom will have experienced significant levels of abuse, victimisation and exploitation. There were positive examples of trauma-informed responses to care-experienced girls within different agencies, but these were not widespread and need to be supported by timely and accessible mental health provision. The importance of consistent relationships in facilitating desistance, and supporting care-experienced girls more broadly, is undeniable: professionals need to be enabled to provide flexible and ongoing support – by creating sufficient time and space for them to attend and implement training, but also by reducing the instability and movement within the care system that regularly fractures the formal and informal support systems that girls in care are able to establish.

When support does need to be withdrawn, for financial and/or resource issues or when a child becomes 'adult', the ending of support should be proactively managed so that it tapers off and/or smoothly transfers to alternative services, avoiding the 'cliff edges' that care-experienced girls so often experience. The transition to independent living for care-experienced girls needs to be properly planned, supported and resourced to ensure progress made in desisting from offending can be maintained. The particular needs of care-experienced girls leaving custody and those who are or who become parents must be carefully managed, as they may require additional support – yet may feel subject to unwarranted surveillance and fear further judgement. Again, there were examples of proactive and effective planning and support for transitions, but this should be routine practice rather than being exceptional or resulting from 'a battle', reliant on the confidence and tenacity of the professionals involved.

An overarching message from the research was that many of the girls and young women had become involved in offending behaviour due to early experiences and the failure of the state to provide timely support or intervention. This behaviour was then exacerbated by institutional policies and practices that created instability and conflict, which drew girls further into the justice system. Often, girls were only able to access appropriate support and interventions once they were involved with the youth justice system, which is clearly problematic – girls should not have to get into trouble to access the support they need. However, enabling care-experienced girls to desist from offending should not just focus on individual trajectories and the failure to provide early support but should acknowledge and address how the structures of care and justice can create and sustain offending behaviour. Addressing wider issues of instability – in both placements and professional relationships – labelling and stigma, gendered judgements and accelerated transitions to adulthood is essential if desistance is to be achieved.

References

Agenda and Alliance for Youth Justice (2021) 'Falling through the gaps: young women transitioning to the adult justice system', Available from: https://weareagenda.org/wp-content/uploads/2021/04/Falling-through-thegaps-YWJP-transitions-briefing-paper.pdf

Bateman, T. and Hazel, N. (2014) 'The resettlement of girls and young women: Research Report', Beyond Youth Custody, Available from: http://www.beyondyouthcustody.net/resources/publications/resettlement-girls-young-women-research-report/

Bevan, M. (2015) 'Desistance from crime: a review of the literature', *Practice: The New Zealand Corrections Journal*, 3(1): 5–9.

Brierley, A. (2021) *Connecting with Young People in Trouble: Risk, Relationships and Lived Experience*, Hook: Waterside Press.

Calouri, J., Corlett, M. and Stott, J. (2020) 'County lines and looked after children', London: Crest Advisory, Available from: https://b9cf6cd4-6aad-4419-a368-724e7d1352b9.usrfiles.com/ugd/b9cf6c_83c53411e21d4d40a79a6e0966ad7ea5.pdf

Children's Commissioner (2019) 'Who are they? Where are they? Children locked up', London: Office of the Children's Commissioner.

Darker, I., Ward, H. and Caulfield, L. (2008) 'An analysis of offending by young people looked after by local authorities', *Youth Justice*, 8(2): 134–48.

Department for Education and Ministry of Justice (2022) 'Education, children's social care and offending: descriptive statistics', Available from: https://www.gov.uk/government/publications/education-childrens-social-care-and-offending

Ellis, K. and Johnston, C. (2019) 'Pathways to university: the journey through care; findings report one', University of Sheffield, Available from: https://figshare.shef.ac.uk/articles/report/Pathways_to_University_from_Care_Recommendations_for_Universities/9578930

Fitzpatrick, C. (2022) 'Challenging perceptions of care experienced girls and women', *Prison Service Journal*, 258: 19–24, Available from: https://www.crimeandjustice.org.uk/sites/crimeandjustice.org.uk/files/PSJ%20258%20January%202022.pdf

Fitzpatrick, C., Hunter, K., Shaw, J. and Staines, J. (2022) 'Disrupting the routes between care and custody for girls and women: final report', Available from: https://wp.lancs.ac.uk/care-custody/resources

France, A. and Homel, R. (2006) 'Societal access routes and developmental pathways: putting social structure and young people's voice into the analysis of pathways into and out of crime', *The Australian and New Zealand Journal of Criminology*, 39(3): 295–309.

Gelsthorpe, L. and Worrall, A. (2009) 'Looking for trouble: a recent history of girls, young women and youth justice', *Youth Justice*, 9(3): 209–23.

Goodfellow, P. (2019) 'Outnumbered, locked up and over-looked? The use of penal custody for girls in England and Wales', The Griffin Society, Available from: https://www.thegriffinssociety.org/outnumbered-locked-and-overlooked-use-penal-custody-girls-england-wales

Graham, J. and Bowling, B. (1995) 'Young people and crime', London: Home Office.

Heidensohn, F. (1985) *Women and Crime*, London: Macmillan Press.

Henriksen, A.-K. (2018) 'Vulnerable girls and dangerous boys: gendered practices of discipline in secure care', *Young*, 26(5): 427–43.

Her Majesty's Inspectorate of Prisons (2021) 'Children in custody 2019–20: an analysis of 12–18-year-olds' perceptions of their experiences in secure training centres and young offender institutions', London: HMIP.

Hodgson, J. (2022) 'Offending girls and restorative justice: a critical analysis', *Youth Justice*, 22(2): 166–88.

Humphery, D. (2019) 'Working with female offenders in care: the perspectives of professionals from youth offending teams', unpublished PhD thesis, University of East Anglia.

Hunter, K. (2022) '"Out of place": the criminalisation of Black and minority ethnic looked after children in England and Wales', *Prison Service Journal*, 258: 13–18, Available from: https://www.crimeandjustice.org.uk/sites/crimeandjustice.org.uk/files/PSJ%20258%20January%202022.pdf

Lipscombe, J. (2006) 'Care or control? Foster care for young people on remand', London: BAAF.

Maruna, S. (2001) *Making Good: How Ex-convicts Reform and Rebuild Their Lives*, Washington, DC: American Psychological Association.

Maruna, S. and Roy, K. (2007) 'Amputation or reconstruction? Notes on the concept of "knifing off" and desistance from crime', *Journal of Contemporary Criminal Justice*, 23(1): 104–24.

McAra, L. and McVie, S. (2011) 'Youth justice? The impact of system contact on patterns of desistance', in S. Farrall, M. Hough, S. Maruna and R. Sparks (eds) *Escape Routes: Contemporary Perspectives on Life after Punishment*, Abingdon: Routledge, pp 81–106.

McFarlane, K. (2010) 'From care to custody: young women in out-of-home care in the criminal justice system', *Current Issues in Criminal Justice*, 22(2): 345–53.

McIvor, G., Murray, C. and Jamieson, J. (2004) 'Desistance from crime: is it different for women and girls?', in S. Maruna and R. Immarigeon (eds) *After Crime and Punishment: Pathways to Offender Reintegration*, Cullompton: Willan Publishing, pp 181–98.

McMahon, G. and Jump, D. (2018) 'Starting to stop: young offenders' desistance from crime', *Youth Justice*, 18(1): 3–17.

McNeill, F. (2017) 'A dialogue about desistance', Plenary address at the British Criminology Conference at Sheffield Hallam University, Available from: https://www.cep-probation.org/a-dialogue-about-desistance-by-fergus-mcneill

Ministry of Justice (2012) 'Prisoners' childhood and family backgrounds', London: Ministry of Justice.

Moore, K.E., Milam, K.C., Folk, J.B. and Tangney, J.P. (2018) 'Self-stigma among criminal offenders: risk and protective factors', *Stigma and Health*, 3(3): 241–52.

O'Neill, T. (2001) *Children in Secure Accommodation: A Gendered Exploration of Locked Institutional Care for Children in Trouble*, London: Jessica Kingsley.

Roberts, L. (2021) *The Children of Looked After Children*, Bristol: Policy Press.

Rumgay, J. (2004) 'Scripts for safer survival: pathways out of female crime', *The Howard Journal of Crime and Justice*, 43(4): 405–19.

Schofield, J., Biggart, L., Ward, E., Scaife, V., Dodsworth, J., Haynes, A. et al (2014) 'Looked after children: reducing risk and promoting resilience', London: BAAF.

Sharpe, G. (2015) 'Precarious identities: "young" motherhood, desistance and stigma', *Criminology and Criminal Justice*, 14(4): 407–22.

Shaw, J. (2014) *Residential Children's Homes and the Youth Justice System: Identity, Power and Perception*, Basingstoke: Palgrave Macmillan.

Staines, J. (2016) 'Risk, adverse influence and criminalisation: understanding the over-representation of looked after children in the youth justice system', London: Prison Reform Trust.

Staines, J., Fitzpatrick, C., Shaw, J. and Hunter, K. (2023) 'We need to tackle their wellbeing first: understanding and supporting care-experienced girls in the youth justice system', *Youth Justice*, Available from: https://doi.org/10.1177/14732254231191977

Stanley, E. (2016) *The Road to Hell: State Violence against Children in Postwar New Zealand*, Auckland: Auckland University Press.

Toor, S. (2009) 'British Asian girls, crime and youth justice', *Youth Justice*, 9(3): 239–53.

Uggen, C. and Kruttschnitt, C. (1998) 'Crime in the breaking: gender differences in desistance', *Law and Society Review*, 32(2): 339–66.

Wigzell, A. (2021) 'Explaining desistance: looking forward, not backwards', London: National Association of Youth Justice.

Wijedasa, D.N., Yoon, Y., Schmits, F., Harding, S. and Hahn, R. (2022) 'A survey of the mental health of children and young people in care in England in 2020 and 2021', Bristol: University of Bristol, Available from: https://mhcat.blogs.bristol.ac.uk/publications

7

Black and mixed-heritage boys: desistance through a co-creative Critical Race and postcolonial lens

John Wainwright

Introduction

This chapter explores the everyday lives of Black and mixed-heritage boys in England and Wales, in their families, communities and their experiences of the criminal justice system (Lammy, 2017; HMIP, 2021a, b). Black and mixed-heritage children are disproportionality represented throughout the criminal (youth) justice system in contrast to being only 4% of the general population, the proportion of those children with initial contact with the police is 16%, 35% of those remanded or sentenced to custody and 41% of the child custodial population (Mullen et al, 2014; Taylor, 2016; Lammy, 2017; Robertson and Wainwright, 2020; HMIP, 2021a; YJB/MOJ, 2021 The focus of this chapter is on Black boys, rather than girls, because the experience of rac(ism) and disproportionality in the system is particularly pronounced for boys. Likewise, there are a particular set of circumstances and experiences of racism that Black boys endure inside and outside of the criminal justice system that are different from the form that boys of (South) Asian heritage experience. For this reason, boys of (South) Asian heritage are not discussed in the chapter. Although there are intersecting experiences of commonality for both Black and mixed-heritage girls and (South) Asian boys that resonate with those of Black boys, there is also a particularity for girls and South Asian boys that focuses on differences based on gender and/ or faith and culture respectively (Mullen et al, 2014; Lammy, 2017). Taking this as an acknowledged point of departure, Critical Race Theory (CRT) will be used to discuss understandings of Black and mixed-heritage boys' experiences in the criminal justice system and possible strategies of desistance (Crosby, 2016; Delgado and Stefancic, 2017; Dutil, 2020). Likewise, an awareness of the postcolonial *Other* will inform an understanding of Black and mixed-heritage boys' experience within society (Fanon, 1967; Glynn, 2014). A focus on the family, the Black community, contested spaces, the education and the criminal justice system(s) can provide much to inform how practice and policy can develop effective strategies of desistance (McHugh, 2018; Wainwright, et al, 2020; Wainwright, 2021).

Black and mixed-heritage boys' experiences of racism

The everyday experience of Black and mixed-heritage boys in England and Wales is very different from their White peers (Harries 2012, 2014). This difference reflects their experience of racism, where individual physical appearance and cultural differences evoke responses from society and its institutions that *Other* them, alienating individuals and constructing them into a despised and denigrated threat and danger (Miles and Brown, 2004; Apena, 2007; Sims-Schouten and Gilbert, 2022) as potential offenders and rarely, if ever, as victims (Wainwright et al, 2020; Wainwright, 2021). In this way, Black and mixed-heritage boys are marked out by a racism that accentuates somatic and phenotypic identifiers that characterise body shape and facial characteristics, respectively, sorting and separating individuals from White society (Roland-Dow, 2011; Walker, 2020). This demonisation of difference identifies them as the Other, insidiously affecting how they feel about themselves and experience the world around them (Walker, 2020; Wainwright, 2021). Black and mixed-heritage boys understand from a very early age that, outside of their family environment, and sometimes within it, the expectations of them from White British society are extremely low and quite often pathologising and criminalising (Byfield and Talbot, 2020; Eddo-Lodge, 2020). Hence, Black and mixed-heritage boys experience a psycho-social world that defines them as inherently of little worth which means that their behaviour is often managed by the state, in particular, the education and the criminal justice system (IRR, 2020).

It is important to explain some of the terms used in this chapter and to contextualise them in relation to Black and mixed-heritage boys and the criminal justice system. Black boys are described in this chapter as those of African and/or Caribbean heritage. Black, here, is capitalised to emphasise a recognition of Blackness as an identity and experience, in a positive cultural and political sense (Wainwright, 2009, 2019). This identification also recognises the persistent experience of individual micro aggressions and structural racism, which, acknowledged by Black boys or not, has a detrimental and debilitating effect on their everyday experiences, curtailing opportunities and limiting their horizons (Harries, 2012, 2014). Likewise, when considering boys of mixed heritage, where one birth parent is of African/Caribbean and one is of White British or European heritage, there is a particular identity and signifier regarding how they experience and where they see themselves in the world (Barn and Harman, 2006, 2013). For this chapter, the term mixed heritage is used, but certain semantic problematics of this are acknowledged: mixed-ness might assume that ethnicities or heritages are fixed, ossified and that mixing them is something that is less than human, almost mixing two species or, indeed, 'races' (Miles and Brown, 2004; Song and Aspinall, 2012; Caballero and Aspinall, 2018). The terminology does, however, admit consideration of the combination of cultural, social and political perspectives that inform mixed-heritage individuals' identity and experience (Harman, 2010; Barn and Harman, 2013). This is of particular importance when considering their experiences, their cultural and political identification in their world, their familial experiences and their everyday interactions with their peers in their local neighbourhood and community (Song and Aspinall, 2012; Caballero and Aspinall, 2018). Additionally, this also enables insight into how wider society views and responds to such individuals (Barn and Harman, 2013).

Many boys of mixed heritage, brought up in a family with a Black parent and/or living within a Black or multi-ethnic community, identify as Black. They identify with their predominantly Black peers and may share a cultural, psycho-social and political worldview (Wainwright et al, 2020, 2021). Mixed-heritage boys may also identify with their peers' everyday experience of racism and institutionally ingrained exclusions from education, employment and other opportunities (Taylor, 2016; Lammy, 2017). Boys of mixed heritage experience the same institutional racism in the criminal justice system that leads to disproportionally anomalous treatment and outcomes. In other words, they are similarly pathologised by many aspects of Whiteness and White society (Gilbourne, 2008; James, 2014).

Conversely, it must be acknowledged that some boys of mixed heritage do not identify as culturally, politically and psycho-socially Black, may have White peers and predominantly reside in a White neighbourhood or community (Barn and Harman, 2006). This may or may not inform whether they experience the education and criminal justice system in such a pathologising way. Many mixed-heritage boys have both Black and White peers, and social class and location play a powerful role in their experiences of family education and the criminal justice systems (Wainwright et al, 2020). Thus, Black and mixed-heritage boys in different temporal and spatial zones negotiate a fluid identity, because of their 'mixedness' (Song, 2021). While they present as being Black and of African/Caribbean heritage, with cultural and identity associations with Black peers, many mixed-heritage boys have formative experiences and an ongoing understanding and identification with White peers (Caballero, 2014; Song, 2021).

Black boys and adultification

Black and mixed-heritage boys are also subject to the process of adultification where they are assumed to be older than they are and consequently treated more punitively in the education and criminal justice system (Davis and Marsh, 2020; HMIP, 2021a). Yet, Black and mixed-heritage boys are undeniably children, defined in terms of their emotional, psycho-social and cultural development (Case and Haines, 2015, 2021; YJB, 2021). They will respond to adverse situations as children, even though they are perceived by authorities as otherwise (Case and Haines, 2021; HMIP, 2021a). For Black and mixed-heritage boys, however, the racist trope of being big, Black and threatening and/or violent prevails in school and when encountering the police and the wider criminal justice system and when in conflict with their peers or persons of authority (Williams and Clarke, 2018; Wainwright and Larkins, 2020; Wainwright, 2021). In other words, Black boys are not perceived, responded to or *treated as children* but often as violent threats (Williams and Clarke, 2018). Although it needs to be acknowledged that children are not treated as children once they offend (Case and Haines, 2015), and within this context the adultification of Black children who do offend is particularly problematic, exacerbating punitive responses (HMIP, 2021a). Such institutionalised racism informs the everyday experiences of adultification for Black and mixed-heritage boys, further exacerbating their alienation from White society (Calverley, 2013; Glynn, 2013, 2016). Moreover, Black boys may not be perceived as vulnerable and/or responding to trauma in their lives but as angry, physical and threatening (Williams and Clarke, 2016; Davis and Marsh, 2020). They are rarely sympathetically understood as victims of violent or other offences. This is despite increasing interest in trauma-informed approaches across public services (Crosby, 2016; Dutil, 2020).

Blackness: racialisation and CRT

CRT starts with the premise that society is institutionally and structurally racist, that racism has a structural impact on Black people's lives and that White people and Whiteness are net beneficiaries of this (Gilbourne, 2008, 2015). This perspective presents key principles to provide a prism through which to understand and hear the experiences of Black people in society (Dixson, 2018). CRT acknowledges that race and the racialisation of Black people is socially constructed, as is demonstrated by the adultification of Black and mixed-heritage boys. Further, CRT opens up the possibility of a postmodern/intersectional analysis, which provides an opportunity for exploring the multi-dimensional and fluid spaces of Black and mixed-heritage people's experience of rac(ism) and identity (Glynn, 2014, 2016). Importantly, it privileges the (counter-)narratives of the Black community, and in this context those of Black and mixed-heritage boys (Delgado and Stefancic, 2017). Thus, CRT provides a theoretical framework to understand the experiences of Black and mixed-heritage boys before, during and after they enter the criminal justice system to inform strategies for desistance (Glynn, 2014, 2016; Wainwright et al, 2020).

CRT and the postcolonial *Other* provide a lens that enables a critical understanding of the racialising of Black and mixed-heritage boys. The Other is particularly relevant to postcolonialism as it identifies communities and individuals who are Black (of African heritage) or of South Asian heritage to be perceived as inferior, of less worth, both from their continents and countries of origin and within communities in the UK, the United States and Europe. Black and mixed-heritage boys (and communities) are viewed through a prism of being intellectually, culturally and socially estranged, less civilised and outside White society (Fanon, 1967). This provides an opportunity to contextualise how Black and mixed-heritage boys are perceived in everyday society as the Other, a threat and demonised. This Othering is particularly, but not exclusively, experienced by Black and mixed-heritage boys who are from socio-economically deprived backgrounds and contested spaces in their everyday lives (Glynn, 2016; Williams and Clarke, 2016; McKeown and Wainwright, 2020). The postcolonial Other provides a lens on the world that positions Black and mixed-heritage boys' experience of their everyday existence as that of estrangements and exclusions from the White world that surrounds them (Fanon, 1967; Glynn, 2016; Wainwright et al, 2019; McKeown and Wainwright, 2020; Wainwright et al, 2020; Wainwright, 2021).

Importantly, when considering Black and mixed-heritage boys' experience of living in marginalised places and contested spaces of multiple deprivation, an acknowledgement of the structural racism and everyday Othering provides an opportunity to consider how there *are* possibilities for some to consider desistance from offending behaviour, and these examples merit closer scrutiny (McHugh, 2018; Wainwright, 2021; Wainwright et al, 2024).

Contested spaces and communities

The experiences of Black and mixed-heritage boys reflect urban geographies of structural and economic patterns of disadvantage afflicting contemporary cities and their historical development. Thus, the places and spaces that Black and mixed-heritage boys negotiate are in communities that are economically, socially and culturally marginalised from large parts of their city (Palmer, 2009; Calverley, 2013). Their marginalisation is evidenced by multiple deprivations in terms of familial trauma and an inadequate lack of social service response, an education system that fails Black boys and an absence of youth activities and interventions and inadequate housing (HMIP, 2021a). This is compounded for Black and mixed-heritage boys as they are exposed to the everyday experience of many forms of racism and the subsequent trauma (Hall et al, 2023). Importantly, there is often limited or no mainstream employment or economic opportunities for Black and mixed-heritage boys to access (EHRC, 2016). This is further compounded by a lack of opportunity to develop social capital skills that are critical to enter and engage in formal and rewarding employment opportunities (McNeil and Maruna, 2008; McNeil, 2018). In this way, Black and mixed-heritage boys are provided with limited or no opportunities for other activities except offending behaviour to enhance their status and/or economic circumstances (Palmer, 2009). This is not to excuse behaviour that may involve selling drugs, or at times the use of serious violence, including guns, as victims and perpetrators, that often accompanies it. Instead, it is to contextualise how they experience their precarious cultural and psycho-social environment and the lack of tangible alternative social, cultural, educational and employment opportunities available for Black and mixed-heritage boys (Calverley, 2013; Glynn, 2014; McNeil, 2018).

For some Black and mixed-heritage boys, along with White boys, their everyday experience and interactions with other children and adults are, at times, precarious and dangerous (Pitts, 2020). Many Black boys describe their local communities as like a "war zone" (HMIP, 2021a). Spaces must be entered and negotiated with an element of trepidation due to an awareness that they always have the possibility of escalating into violence, with the possibility of the use of knives or guns (Pitts, 2020). Black and mixed-heritage boys have described how in some places the spaces they frequent with their peers are only negotiated in groups, or gangs (Palmer and Pitts, 2006; McHugh, 2018). In some metropolitan cities, carrying knives is a necessity for self-defence in these contested spaces, with the potential for violent encounters with other Black, mixed-heritage and/or White groups of boys (Wainwright et al, 2020; Hall et al, 2023). Such contestation involves individuals or groups of boys moving into other boys' spaces and this being perceived as a threat and/or insult to their pride by other groups of boys (Palmer and Pitts, 2006; Palmer, 2009). In other metropolitan cities, Black and mixed-heritage boys are pulled into activities that involve drugs, by their peers and/or adults who use them for doing the running, buying and selling (Disley and Liddle, 2016; Whittaker et al, 2017). In such circumstances, Black and mixed-heritage boys are far more likely to be drawn into acts of violence, often as victims: either coerced into this offending behaviour or in self-defence, because of competition for a drug market with other groups of boys/young men (Goldson, 2011; Pitts, 2020; Hall et al, 2023).

Further, much has been written about whether Black and mixed-heritage boys and older Black young men are involved in informal social and group networks, or 'gang' activity (Palmer, 2009; Pitts, 2020). Williams and Clarke suggest that there is no formal pattern of offending activity by Black and mixed-heritage boys in local communities, any more than their White peers, just fluid networks that focus on opportunities that emerge in streets and communities, including profiteering from drugs (Williams and Clarke, 2016, 2018). Williams and Clarke argue that 'gang' is an appropriated and racialised name that the state imposes on Black and mixed-heritage boys to justify their criminalisation through specific workings of the criminal justice system. A narrative of gangs, for example, can serve to legitimate excessive stop and searching by the police and disproportionately punitive treatment and sentencing in the courts and custodial settings (Williams and Clarke, 2016, 2018). In contrast, others argue there is significant evidence, particularly, in London, of groups of Black and mixed-heritage boys having formal networks of operations, some with clear lines of command and management, that are organised as gangs to ensure an effective and protected drugs operation and/or protection of their specific places and space (Palmer, 2009; Whittaker et al, 2017; Pitts, 2020). Either way, in London boroughs particularly, groups of Black and mixed-heritage boys are engaged in informal networks that involve serious violence towards other Black (and White) children over contested spaces for drugs and their [profits from selling drugs] (Whittaker et al, 2017; Pitts, 2020). This offending behaviour can involve Black and mixed-heritage boys being key protagonists in county lines drug dealing, where the expansion of their drug markets is extended to rural towns (Hall et al, 2023). Often this involves Black and mixed-heritage boys being in various levels of authority in the drug-selling network (Whittaker et al, 2017; Pitts, 2020).

Desistance

Desistance is a term used to describe the processes by which individuals work their way towards a crime-free life and ultimately to a non-criminal identity. It is centrally important, therefore, to how children, young people and adults understand and develop strategies and resources to avoid repeating offending behaviour (Robertson and Wainwright, 2020; Burke, et al, 2023). In many ways, the challenges and difficulties that Black and mixed-heritage boys experience in considering moving away from offending behaviour are like those experienced by their White peers (Wainwright and Larkins, 2020; Wainwright et al, 2020). Yet, the possible role of race, ethnicity and structural racism and their potential effect on the capacity to desist from crime have been neglected in many studies of desistance (Calverley, 2013; Durrance et al, 2013). These include the intersectional challenges of class, multiple deprivation, alienated neighbourhoods and communities, community and family trauma, the psycho-social impact on children and the violence that may follow (Glynn, 2016) and the navigation of everyday experiences of racism, being *Othered* and pathologised by the education, welfare and criminal justice system (Fanon, 1967; Calverley, 2013). Much of the available work on desistance focuses on the intersectional challenges that children experience (Glynn, 2014, 2016), but because of the significant variance in this experience at a community, individual and familial level, it is naïve to assume there is a generic strategy or intervention that can encourage Black boys to stop offending (Calverley, 2013; Glynn, 2016). There is also an understanding that if Black and mixed-heritage boys do desist from offending, there need not be a linear process of achievement, and often they may relapse back into offending behaviour (Glyn, 2013).

Thus, the desistance process is likely to involve relapses, and generic and homogenised interventions are unlikely to be effective and should instead be replaced by individual, holistic services (Farrall, 2002, cited in Moffatt, 2014). In a similar way, cognitive behavioural programmes, used within *what works* initiatives, do not accommodate the specific challenges experienced by Black and mixed-heritage boys involved in offending behaviour (Calverley, 2013). Indeed, many desistance theorists question the efficacy of the *what works* approach on the basis that it is far too instrumental and detached from the complex structural and individual challenges children and adults experience when trying to desist from offending (McNeil and Maruna, 2008; Burke et al, 2023).

Additionally, attention should be focused on the 'complex individual identities' of Black and mixed-heritage boys (Durrance et al, 2013, p 146). Consideration must also be given to differences in patterns of desistance between different ethnicities (for example, Somali, Jamaican and Nigerian) that constitute Black and mixed-heritage boys' heritage (Calverley, 2013). Further, while also considering an assessment of risk of offending behaviour, there is a need to explore the Black and mixed-heritage boys' values, goals and strengths. A key element of working towards these individual goals is through exploring positive and negative influences of family and social networks within relevant spaces (Durrance et al, 2013).

Arguably, Black and mixed-heritage boys may not develop the same kind of social capital or resources from their families as some white children, which may hinder their ability to desist. For example, resettlement after a prison sentence may be particularly difficult as Black boys are often not able to return to their family home (Calverley, 2013). A lack of post-prison resettlement support is also connected with the racialised and structural barriers that Black and mixed-heritage boys experience. For Black boys who are 16 years or older, this includes a paucity of training and education opportunities after leaving prison (Glynn, 2013, 2014). There is a dearth of studies acknowledging the identity of Black and mixed-heritage boys while they are in the criminal justice system and in prison, with the Lammy review a notable exception (Jacobson et al, 2010; Glynn, 2013; Lammy, 2017). Further, their intersectional needs regarding masculinity, class, poverty and at times chaotic social networks formed in contested places and spaces are often not addressed within the criminal justice system (Glynn, 2014, 2016).

Some suggest desistance needs to be predicated on human and social relationships and strategies that develop social capital among people (McNeil and Maruna, 2008; Mullen et al, 2014; Burke et al, 2023). For Black and mixed-heritage boys to desist, social capital is particularly important in developing resilience in their local communities. Yet, much work on desistance is focused on generic offending and not Black and mixed-heritage boys, and there needs to be much more of a focus on their complex and multifaceted identities (Calverley, 2013; Glynn, 2014). There is also significant evidence that the education, criminal justice and wider welfare systems have not been able to provide adequate and sustainable pathways for Black and mixed-heritage boys to be able to move away from offending behaviour (HMIP, 2021a, b). This includes a lack of alternative education that provides motivation and genuine opportunity for Black and mixed-heritage boys (Calverley, 2013; Glynn, 2016). These alternative pathways can often be located within the Black community, led by authentic and credible Black role models in the voluntary sector, or community spaces where discussions of possibilities for a future of hope for Black boys can take place. These discussions can focus on education and training that is co-created and acknowledges and explores racism, poverty, familial difficulties and contested spaces. Importantly, though, these community spaces can enable an affirmation and celebration of Blackness, of being of African heritage and how this can be galvanised as a catalyst to focus on achievable strategies to engage in learning that enables a pathway to active employment and citizenship (Larkins and Wainwright, 2020 Wainwright et al, 2020).

There is also inadequate social/children's services provision to acknowledge and address the trauma that Black and mixed-heritage families experience in their everyday lives (Crosby, 2016; Glynn, 2016; Dutil, 2020). There are very few or no alternative housing opportunities to move Black boys away from peers that are involved in offending, nor the opportunity to find decent training or employment opportunities that can be successfully accessed and maintained (Calverley, 2013). In other words, for many Black and mixed-heritage boys, the contested spaces, the violent places, provide an environment where there is little alternative but for them to continue offending behaviours with their peers, and there is no incentive to change and take responsibility for their actions and no coherent strategy from those agencies that should support them in this process (Glynn, 2016; McHugh, 2018; Pitts, 2020; HMIP, 2021a). For many Black and mixed-heritage boys, there is little hope and no opportunity to change, or pathways to achieve it.

Co-creating desistance through CRT

This chapter has suggested that there needs to be a recognition of some key principles when working with Black and mixed-heritage boys to support individual desistance journeys for Black youngsters. These encompass the reality that racism, along with multiple deprivations, is an everyday experience for Black and mixed-heritage boys (Glynn, 2014, 2016; Delgado and Stefancic, 2017). Acknowledging this and an identity of Blackness and the *Othering* they experience is central to an understanding of developing strategies for them to desist (Fanon, 1967; Apena, 2007). Further, strategies for desistance with Black and mixed-heritage boys can only have any real effect when their voices, their (counter-)story telling is at the centre of this process (Crosby, 2016; Delgado and Stefancic, 2017; Dutil, 2020). By listening to their voices and placing their experiences and perspectives at the centre of strategies to inform practice and policy, there is an opportunity to develop multi-dimensional, flexible and bespoke interventions that address the intersectional needs of Black and mixed-heritage boys (Freire, 1973; Glynn, 2016). The risk of violence, serious at times, that Black and mixed-heritage boys face as perpetrators and victims is an everyday reality in many contested places and spaces for Black and mixed-heritage boys. When co-working with them, there needs to be a realistic acknowledgement of the trauma experienced that has led to and is a consequence of this behaviour (Palmer and Pitt, 2006; Whittaker et al, 2017). The places and spaces in their local communities that Black and mixed-heritage boys inhabit are often contested by other Black and White boys and young adults (Wainwright et al, 2020). Further, it is important to acknowledge the psycho-social, emotional and multi-faceted deprivation that many Black and mixed-heritage boys' experience in their communities which provide traumatic challenges for them negotiate in their childhood

Desistance narratives must be underpinned for all boys, Black, mixed heritage and White, by the authenticity of their experiences and reality and not downplayed or ignored when racism is a clear factor. In other words, working with Black and mixed-heritage boys involves anti-racist practice, and this is good practice.

First, the (counter-)voices of Black and mixed-heritage boys need to be at the centre of any meaningful desistance strategy. This means that to enable Black and mixed-heritage boys to develop a way of moving away from offending their perspectives, their stories, challenges and aspirations need to be heard and placed at the centre of any transformational plans for change in their lives (Dixson, 2018; Wainwright and Larkins, 2020; Wainwright et al, 2020). This will acknowledge their experience of racism, of *Othering*, of everyday threats of violence from peers and adults, and harassment by the police. But, it will also acknowledge the individuality and intersectionality of their identities and aspirations (Apena, 2007; Glynn, 2016). Importantly, the world, their world, will inform any co-created solutions for desistance.

Secondly, developed spaces for Black and mixed-heritage boys can provide an opportunity in the context of the Black Lives Matter (BLM) movement, which offers alternative, positive narratives for Blackness and boys of African heritage. BLM provides a prism that radiates a positive message with an alternative worldview where to be Black is to be proud and loud, listened to and heard. The ideas of BLM are presented as assertive, strong, potent and possibly life changing in their liberatory messages for Black boys, young people and Black communities. The BLM messages also provide a means to develop alternative masculinities that need not feel emasculating but nevertheless are more pro-social, collectivist and community focused. These are physical spaces of difference where masculinities can be developed and co-created with Black and mixed-heritage boys that have the resilience to resist psycho-social and physical pressure by their peers and adults to join groups or gangs of boys and young men who are involved in offending behaviour. These liberatory messages, this movement, could provide a counter-space to the narrative of pathological stereotypes and violence (Dixson, 2018; Kelly et al, 2020; Wainwright, 2021). In contrast, a creative, cultural, assertive Black masculinity can be encouraged to flourish where it is acceptable to be a Black or mixed-heritage boy, to be male, but to eschew violence and gangs for a more proactive, positive and empowering Black identity; a Black identity with a future of optimism, not of anger and alienation (Dixon, 2018; Kelly et al, 2020).

Thirdly, Black and mixed-heritage boys' worlds are often shaped by the trauma their parents experienced in their own lives, through economic, political and cultural exclusion from society (Gilbourne, 2015). This trauma, in part, is manifested through racism in their everyday experience of poverty, alienation from mainstream society that has a psycho-social impact on Black and mixed-heritage parents, leaving them feeling diminished and worthless (Crosby, 2016; Whittaker et al, 2017; Dutil, 2020). In turn, this can place unbearable pressure on their relationships with their partners and undermine their resilience to parent their Black and mixed-heritage sons in a consistent and nurturing way (Calverley, 2013). Black and mixed-heritage parents often have multiple types of low-paid employment, which can mean they are often away from the family home for long periods (Davis and Marsh, 2020). With limited contact with their parents, Black and mixed-heritage boys can rely on their peers in their local neighbourhood as an alternative source of support, which provides a space to become involved in offending behaviour (Palmer, 2009). To encourage desistance and move Black and mixed-heritage boys away from engaging with groups of boys that offend, their needs to be a strategic response by the local state to fill this space left by parents who are, for many understandable reasons, not present (HMIP, 2021a, 2021b). This may involve more youth services, a supportive child welfare service to work with the trauma of Black families to support parenting, wider provision of kinship (in family) caring and a housing service that responds to crisis and the needs of Black and mixed-heritage boys (Glynn, 2014, 2016).

Fourth, the education system has consistently blamed, pathologised and disproportionately excluded Black and mixed-heritage boys from mainstream schooling and placed them in pupil referral units (PRUs) (Wainwright et al, 2020). Personal testimony from Black boys and His Majesty's Inspectorate of Probation (HMIP) studies have demonstrated that taking Black boys out of mainstream schooling is often the catalyst for their journey into mixing with peers who are involved in offending behaviour (Wainwright et al, 2020; HMIP, 2021a, b). Further, evidence suggests that removing them from mainstream schooling sends a direct message of failure and blame to Black boys that can push them towards alienation from formal education and closer to peers who provide an alternative source of opportunity and income through offending (Palmer, 2009; Dixson, 2018). Yet a postcolonial and CRT lens suggests that being *Othered* and alienated from society needs a response that acknowledges their (counter-)voice, their identity and their understanding of their experience of being Black (Gilbourne, 2015; Glynn, 2016). Thus, mainstream schooling, PRUs and Black community educational provision needs to develop a coherent strategy to focus on keeping Black and mixed-heritage boys in purposeful schooling. The teaching needs to be led by positive male Black role models able to provide an education that reflects a Black cultural heritage and has relevance to their everyday lives (Apena, 2007; Wainwright and Larkins, 2020). Further, the education provided should ensure a genuine pathway of opportunity for training and employment for Black and mixed-heritage boys (Wainwright et al, 2023). Exclusion is particularly problematic for Black children because 60 per cent of Black and mixed-heritage boys who are subject to court orders are seen as disruptive and are excluded from school, often permanently (HMIP, 2021a). Further, they are twice as likely to be excluded from school permanently compared to their white peers (HMIP, 2021a).

This process of school exclusion contributes significantly to Black and mixed-heritage boys becoming criminalised, being drawn into and disproportionately represented in the criminal justice system (DfE, 2019; IRR, 2020; HMIP, 2021a). In a recent report, the Institute of Race Relations suggests that PRUs are a *pipeline to prison* for Black children (IRR, 2020).

Black and mixed-heritage boys are often excluded from school, placed in PRUs and have to negotiate fractured family lives where the only space to spend more time with their peers is in their local space, or places some distance from where they live, where everyday life can be much more perilous.

Fifth, evidence suggests that Black and mixed-heritage boys listen and respect peer mentors who have had a similar experience to them and been excluded from school and involved in offending behaviour, including serious violence (Apena, 2007; Larkins and Wainwright, 2020; Wainwright et al, 2020). Importantly, this peer-led mentoring should challenge offending behaviour from a prism of Blackness that understands the everyday experiences of these boys in their local places and spaces in their communities (Wainwright et al, 2020). While it is acknowledged that there are many mitigating reasons for offending behaviour, it is important that peer mentors work with the boys to talk about the risks their offending poses to their local community, their peers and themselves (Larkins and Wainwright, 2020). For any change in behaviour to move away from offending to desistance, the peer mentors need to commit to a long-term working relationship with the Black and mixed-heritage boys (Wainwright et al, 2020). However, to provide the space for Black peer mentors to work with Black boys, potential barriers of institutional racism, because of exclusion for example, organisational criminal records checks on individuals that work with children and young people may need to be more flexible and accommodating of those who may who may have a record of criminal offences in the past to encourage and support members of the Black community committing to this role. Further, the role of Black peer mentors needs to be given the status and financial renumeration that is commensurate with engaging in affirmative life-changing work that may benefit Black and mixed-heritage boys and the wider (Black) community (Apena, 2007).

Sixth, the intersectional experiences and fluid individual identities of Black and mixed-heritage boys need to be acknowledged and addressed within work on desistance (Durrance et al, 2013). Resources need to be invested in the Black and mixed-heritage places and spaces that are often contested by individuals and groups of Black, mixed-heritage and (sometimes) White boys. A change of narrative needs to be initiated whereby there is a flexible package available for communities to work with Black and mixed-heritage boys using methods that are grounded in their realities, familial trauma, of contested spaces, the use of violence, overuse of stop and search by the police and disproportionality throughout the criminal justice system (Glynn, 2016). This could include a comprehensive, flexible and bespoke youth service package that is culturally relevant to the everyday lives of Black and mixed-heritage boys (Wainwright et al, 2019; Wainwright et al, 2020). For instance, establishing hubs that are centres of the many and ever-changing representations of Black culture, including music and conversations about racism, contested spaces and conflict over drugs, respect and dignity, guns, knives, family and peers. These hubs need to be in the most dangerous places, the most violent spaces, and to be relevant and authentically owned and led by peers in the Black community (Palmer, 2009; Wainwright et al, 2019)

Seventh, co-creative action research could be developed with Black and mixed-heritage boys to explore their world from their perspective to create solutions for offending behaviour, in particular the cultures, economy and psycho-social world that drives serious violence, guns and knives in contested spaces (Larkins and Wainwright, 2020; Wainwright and Larkins, 2020;

Wainwright et al, 2020). Black and mixed-heritage boys' worldviews need to be at the centre of desistance strategies, as it is only by understanding their experience, and co-creating alternative models of intervention that acknowledge the fluidity and ever-changing reality of their everyday lives, that there can be a genuine opportunity to bring about changes that can lead to desistance, in the short and medium term (Wainwright et al, 2020; Wainwright, 2021).

Eighth, in this chapter the idea of a contested space has been described in physical/material terms, specifically the violence that Black and mixed-heritage boys experience. However, there is also a possibility to explore the notion of a contestation which is about a collision of ideas. To develop this further, there could be open and honest discussion between Black peer mentors and the push of desistance in contrast to the pull of criminality. By definition, the physical contestation of these ideas will also coincide with physical conflict in a space where, quite literally, older Black peers physically coerce Black and mixed-heritage boys back into offending or otherwise manipulate, bully and entice them psycho-socially to do the same. This conflict of ideas is between those of liberation from the push of desistance and appreciative enquiry[1] (Cooperrider et al, 2008; Dixson, 2018; Kelly et al, 2020; Larkins and Wainwright, 2020) that focuses on the positive aspects of hope in Black and mixed-heritage boys' lives in contrast to the pull of offending they experience from the local drug market, violence and guns. These conversations could be articulated and argued in alternative, safe, community resources that are accessible and credible spaces to Black and mixed heritage boys (Cooperrider et al, 2008; Dixson, 2018).

This practice manifestation of psycho-social space could be designed to actively keep out offenders, protecting the space for active desisters (or those trying to desist), maximising, modelling and facilitating positive pro-social relationships. These resistant spaces could be designed practicably and include investing in and developing resources available to Black and mixed-heritage boys, for example: training, employment, pro-social modelling and the development of a liberatory Black network and safe and comfortable accommodation away from peers who may pressure them to offend (Cooperrider et al, 2008; Dixson, 2018; Larkins and Wainwright, 2020).

CRT and a postcolonial prism suggest opportunities to critically appreciate how Black and mixed-heritage boys' cultures are constantly changing depending on the spaces they are in, the ethnicity and intersectional identities of their peers, the fluidity of migrant identities and how this informs their understanding of Blackness, Othering and racism (Mullen et al, 2014; Pitts, 2020; Wainwright, 2021). Strategies to encourage desistance need to be sensitive to the constant movement and shifting identities of Black and mixed-heritage boys and how this is central to their sense of self and wellbeing (Apena, 2007; Wainwright et al, 2020).

In sum, CRT and a postcolonial lens through co-creation and inspiration from BLM provide opportunities for practicable, credible and durable strategies for Black and mixed-heritage boys to desist from offending. All these strategies need investment, in resources, from the state, Black communities, peer mentors and most importantly from Black and mixed-heritage boys at the centre of the milieu of contested places, spaces, racism, offending and too often, violence. Yet, surely, it is time for all involved to invest the necessary energy, resources to change the (counter-)narrative for Black and mixed-heritage boys. The (ongoing) alternative is too damning to contemplate.

Note

[1] Appreciative enquiry is a method of working with children that focuses on the positive aspects of their lives, for example familial relationships, peers and/or a particular skill or hobby they enjoy. Within the context of working with Black and mixed-heritage boys, it is suggested that co-creative work in spaces with appreciate enquiry can be a particularly positive and potentially liberating experience for them.

References

Apena, F. (2007) 'Being Black and in trouble: the role of self-perception in the offending behaviour of Black youth', *Youth Justice*, 7(3): 211–28.

Barn, R. and Harman, V. (2006) 'A contested identity: an exploration of the competing social and political discourse concerning the identification and positioning of young people of inter-racial parentage', *The British Journal of Social Work*, 36(8): 1309–24.

Barn, R. and Harman, V. (2013) 'Mothering across racialized boundaries: introduction to the special issue', *Ethnic and Racial Studies*, 26(8): 1265–72.

Burke, L., Carr, N., Cluley, E., Collett, S. and McNeill, F. (2023) 'Introduction: reforming, reimagining and moving forward; for what purpose?', in L. Burke, N. Carr, E. Cluley, S. Collett and F. McNeill (eds) *Re-imagining Probation Practice: Re-forming Rehabilitation in an Age of Penal Excess*, London: Routledge, pp 1–28.

Byfield, C. and Talburt, T. (2020), 'Targeted intervention in education and the empowerment and emotional well-being of Black boys', in R. Majors, K. Carberry and T.S. Ransaw (eds) *The International Handbook of Black Community Mental Health*, Bingley: Emerald Publishing, pp 293–306, Available from: https://doi.org/10.1108/978-1-83909-964-920201019

Caballero, C. (2014) 'Mixed emotions: reflections on researching racial mixing and mixedness', *Emotion, Space and Society*, 11: 79–88.

Caballero, C. and Aspinall, P. (2018) *Mixed Race Britain in the Twentieth Century*, London: Palgrave.

Calverley, A. (2013) *Cultures of Desistance: Rehabilitation, Reintegration and Ethnic Minorities*, Abingdon: Routledge

Case, S. and Haines, K. (2015) *Positive Youth Justice*, Bristol: Policy Press.

Case, S., and Haines, K. (2021) 'Abolishing youth justice systems: children first, offenders nowhere', *Youth Justice*, 21(1): 3–17, Available from: https://doi.org/10.1177/1473225419898754

Cooperrider, D.L., Whitney, D. and Stavros, J.M. (2008) *Appreciative Inquiry Handbook: For Leaders of Change*, San Francisco: Berrett-Koehler Publishers.

Crosby, D. (2016) 'Trauma-informed approaches to juvenile justice: a critical race perspective', *Juvenile and Family Court Journal*, 67(1): 5–18.

Davis, J. and Marsh, N. (2020) 'Boys to men: the cost of "adultification" in safeguarding responses to Black boys', *Critical and Radical Social Work*, 8(2): 255–9.

Delgado, R. and Stefancic, J. (2017) *Critical Race Theory: An Introduction* (3rd edn), New York: New York University Press.

Department for Education (2019) 'Timpson review of school exclusion', DFE.

Disley, E. and Liddle, M. (2016) 'Urban street gangs in ending gang and youth violence areas: local perceptions of the nature of gangs and whether they have changed in the last two years', London: Ministry of Justice.

Dixson, A.D. (2018) '"What's going on?": a critical race theory perspective on Black Lives Matter and activism in education', *Urban Education*, 53(2): 231–47.

Durrance, P., Dixon, L. and Bhui, H.S. (2013) 'Creative working with minority ethnic offenders', in J. Brayford, F. Cowe and J. Deering (eds) *What Else Works? Creative Work with Offenders*, Cullompton: Willan, pp 138–54.

Dutil, S. (2020) 'Dismantling the school-to-prison pipeline: a trauma-informed, critical race perspective on school discipline', *Children & Schools*, 42(3): 171–8.

Eddo-Lodge, R. (2020) *Why I Am No Longer Talking to White People about Race*, London: Bloomsbury.

Equality and Human Rights Commission (2016) 'Healing a divided Britain: the need for a comprehensive race equality strategy', Available from: http://hdl.handle.net/20.500.12389/22284

Fanon, F. (1967) *Black Skin, White Masks*, trans C. Markmann, New York: Grove Books.

Farrall, S. (2002) *Rethinking What Works with Offenders: Probation, Social Context and Desistance from Crime*, Cullompton: Willan Publishing.

Freire, P. (1973) *Pedagogy of the Oppressed*, New York: Seabury Press.

Gilbourne, D. (2008) 'Coincidence or conspiracy? Whiteness, policy and the persistence of the Black/White achievement gap', *Educational Review*, 60(3): 229–48, https://doi.org/10.1080/00131910802195745

Gilbourne, D. (2015) 'Intersectionality, critical race theory, and the primacy of racism: race, class, gender, and disability in education', *Qualitative Inquiry*, 21(3): 277–87.

Glynn, M. (2013) 'Impacts on the desistance process', unpublished PhD thesis, Birmingham City University.

Glynn, M. (2014) *Black Men, Invisibility and Crime: Towards a Critical Race Theory of Desistance*, Abingdon: Routledge.

Glynn, M. (2016) 'Towards an intersectional model of desistance for Black offenders', *Safer Communities*, 15: 24–32.

Goldson, B. (2011) 'Youth in crisis?', in B. Goldson (ed) *Youth in Crisis? Gangs, Territoriality and Violence*, London: Routledge, pp 1–19.

Hall, B., Khan, R. and Else, M. (2023) 'Criminalising Black trauma: grime and drill lyrics as a form of ethnographic data to understand "gangs" and serious youth violence', *Genealogy*, 7(1): 2. https://doi.org/10.3390/genealogy7010002

Harman, V. (2010) 'Experiences of racism and the changing nature of White privilege among lone White mothers of mixed race children in the UK', *Ethnic and Racial Studies*, 33(2): 176–94.

Harries, B. (2012) 'Talking race in everyday spaces of the city', unpublished PhD thesis, University of Manchester.

Harries, B. (2014) 'We need to talk about race', *Sociology*, 48: 1107–22.

HMIP (2021a) 'The experiences of black and mixed heritage boys in the youth justice system', Manchester: HMIP.

HMIP (2021b) 'Race equality in probation: the experiences of Black, Asian and minority ethnic probation service users and staff; a thematic inspection by HM Inspectorate of Probation', March, HMIP.

HM Inspectorate of Probation (2022) '2021 annual report: inspections of youth offending services', Manchester: HMIP.

Institute of Race Relations (IRR) (2020 'How Black working class youth are criminalised and excluded in the English school system: a London case study', London: IRR.

Jacobson, J., Phillips, C. and Edgar, K. (2010) '"Double trouble"? Black, Asian and minority ethnic offenders' experiences of resettlement', Available from: https://www.clinks.org/sites/default/files/2018-12/Double%20Trouble.pdf

James, M. (2014) 'Whiteness and loss in outer East London: tracing the collective memories of diaspora space', *Ethnic and Racial Studies*, 37(4): 652–67, https://doi.org/10.1080/01419870.2013.808761

Kelly, S., Jérémie-Brink, G., Chambers, A.L. and Smith-Bynum, M.A. (2020) 'The Black Lives Matter movement: a call to action for couple and family therapists', *Family Process*, 59(4): 1374–88.

Lammy, D. (2017) 'The Lammy review: an independent review into the treatment of, and outcomes for, Black, Asian and minority ethnic individuals in the criminal justice system', Available from: https://assets.publishing.service.gov.uk/government/uploads/system/uploads/attachment_data/file/643001/lammy-review-final-report.pdf

Larkins, C. and Wainwright, J. (2020) '"If rich people gave more money to poor people": young people's perspectives on reducing offending and implications for social citizenship', *Children and Youth Services Review*, 110: 1–8.

McHugh, R. (2018) 'Educating "gangsters": social space and becoming "gang" involved', unpublished PhD thesis, Sheffield Hallam University.

McKeown, M. and Wainwright, J. (2020) 'Echoes of Frantz Fanon in the place and space of an alternative Black mental health centre', *Critical and Radical Social Work*, 8(3): 323–38.

McNeill, F. (2018) 'Rehabilitation, corrections and society: the 2017 ICPA Distinguished Scholar Lecture', *Advancing Corrections Journal*, 5: 10–20.

McNeill, F. and Maruna, S. (2008) 'Giving up and giving back: desistance, generativity and social work with offenders', in G. McIvor and P. Raynor (eds) *Developments in Social Work with Offenders*, Research Highlights in Social Work 48, London: Jessica Kingsley, pp 224–339.

Miles, R. and Brown, M. (2004) *Racism*, London: Routledge.

Moffatt, S. (2014) 'Prospects for a desistance agenda', Criminal Justice Alliance, Available from: http://criminaljusticealliance.org/wp-content/uploads/2015/03/Prospects-for-a-Desistance-Agenda-Full-report.pdf

Mullen, J., Blake, M., Crook, J. and Martin, C. (2014) 'The Young review: improving outcomes for young Black and/or Muslim men in the criminal justice system', Final report, Available from: https://www.clinks.org/publication/young-reviewlt/files/clinks_youngreview_report

Palmer, S. (2009) 'The origins and emergence of youth "gangs" in a British inner-city neighbourhood', *Safer Communities*, 8(2): 17–26, Available from: https://doi.org/10.1108/17578043200900015

Palmer, S. and Pitts, J. (2006) '"Othering" the brothers: Black youth, racial solidarity and gun crime', *Youth & Policy*, 91: 5–22.

Pitts, J. (2020) 'Black young people and gang involvement in London', *Youth Justice*, 20(1–2): 146–58.

Robertson, L. and Wainwright, J. (2020) 'Black boys' and young men's experiences with criminal justice and desistance in England and Wales: a literature review', *Genealogy*, 4(2): 50.

Rolon-Dow, R. (2011) 'Race(ing) stories: digital storytelling as a tool for critical race scholarship', *Race, Ethnicity and Education*, 14(2): 159–73.

Sims-Schouten, W. and Gilbert, P. (2022) 'Revisiting "resilience" in light of racism, "othering" and resistance', *Race and Class*, 64(1): 84–94, Available from: https://journals.sagepub.com/doi/10.1177/03063968221093882

Song, M. (2021) 'Who counts as multiracial?', *Ethnic and Racial Studies*, 44(8): 1296–323.

Song, M. and Aspinall, P. (2012) 'Is racial mismatch a problem for young "mixed race" people in Britain? The findings of qualitative research', *Ethnicities*, 12(6): 730–53.

Taylor, C. (2016) 'Review of the youth justice system in England and Wales', Available from: https://assets.publishing.service.gov.uk/media/5a7ffc81e d915d74e622bcdb/youth-justice-review-final-report-print.pdf

Wainwright, J. (2009) 'Racism, anti-racist practice and social work: articulating the teaching and learning experiences of Black social workers', *Race Ethnicity and Education*, 12(4): 495–512.

Wainwright, J. (2021) 'Introducing the special issue on the experiences of Black, Asian and minority ethnic (BAME) children and families in the welfare context', *Genealogy*, 5(4): 89.

Wainwright, J. and Larkins, C. (2020) 'Race, ethnicity, young people and offending: the elephant in the room', *Social Identities*, 26: 128–44.

Wainwright, J., McKeown, M. and Kinney, M. (2019) '"In these streets": the saliency of place in an alternative Black mental health resource centre', *International Journal of Human Rights in Healthcare*, 13: 31–44.

Wainwright, J., Robertson, L., Larkins, C. and McKeown, M. (2020) 'Youth justice, Black children and young men in Liverpool: a story of rac(ism), identity and contested spaces', *Genealogy*, 4(2): e57.

Wainwright, J., Burke, L. and Collett, S. (2024) '"A lack of cultural understanding and sometimes interest": towards half a century of anti-racist policy, practice and strategy within probation', *Probation Journal*. Available from: https://doi.org/10.1177/02645505231213977

Walker, S. (2020) 'Systemic racism: big, Black, mad and dangerous in the criminal justice system', in R. Majors, K. Carberry and T.S. Ransaw (eds) *The International Handbook of Black Community Mental Health*, Bingley: Emerald Publishing, pp 41–60, Available from: https://doi.org/ 10.1108/978-1-83909-964-920201004

Whittaker, A., Cheston, L., Tyrell, T., Higgins, M., Felix-Baptiste, C. and Havard, T (2017) 'From postcodes to profits: how youth gangs have changed in Waltham Forest', London: South Bank University.

Williams, P. and Clarke, B. (2016) 'Dangerous associations: joint enterprise, gangs and racism: an analysis of the processes of criminalisation', Available from: https://www.crimeandjustice.org.uk/sites/crimeandjustice.org. uk/files/Dangerous%20assocations%20Joint%20Enterprise%20gangs%20 and%20racism.pdf

Williams, P. and Clarke, B. (2018) 'The Black criminal other as an object of social control', *Social Sciences*, 7(11): 234.

YJB (2021) 'Youth Justice Board strategic plan 2021–2024', Youth Justice Board for England and Wales.

YJB and MOJ (2021) 'Youth justice statistics 2019/20: England and Wales', Available from: https://www.gov.uk/government/statistics/youth-justice-statistics-2019-to-2020

8

Growing in maturity, growing in faith, growing out of crime: the role of children's and young people's faith in desistance

Tim Rosier

Introduction

Within public health, there has been a growing interest over many years in the benefits of faith, belief and spirituality on health and wellbeing outcomes (LeConte, 2017). The same is true within the field of criminal justice, particularly with the emergence of 'Spiritual Criminology', which recognises the spiritual dimension of human existence (Ronel and Yair, 2018; Amitay and Ronel, 2022), as well as research exploring the role of faith in desistance from crime (Maruna, 2001; Giordano et al, 2008). However, to date much of the existing desistance literature has focused on adult journeys of faith and their links to pathways from crime. This chapter will seek to redress this balance by drawing on research from a number of fields including criminology, youth studies, religious education, health and social care and human psychology. In doing so, the chapter will highlight new insights drawn from a range of literature that seeks to understand the faith journeys of children while identifying new opportunities for positive engagement with faith as a means of understanding and facilitating children's desistance from crime. As well as contributing to the emerging field of 'Child First youth justice' (Case and Browning, 2021), this chapter will also make recommendations for policy makers and practitioners as well as create new frames for future academic research.

Some key terminology

In seeking to truly understand the holistic nature of working with children in trouble with the law, it is important to understand the concepts and terminology of religious faith and spirituality. 'Faith', 'religiosity' and 'spirituality', often used interchangeably, are unique and distinct concepts (Newman, 2004). Newman's model of faith, spirituality and religion

Figure 8.1: Faith, Spirituality and Religion model

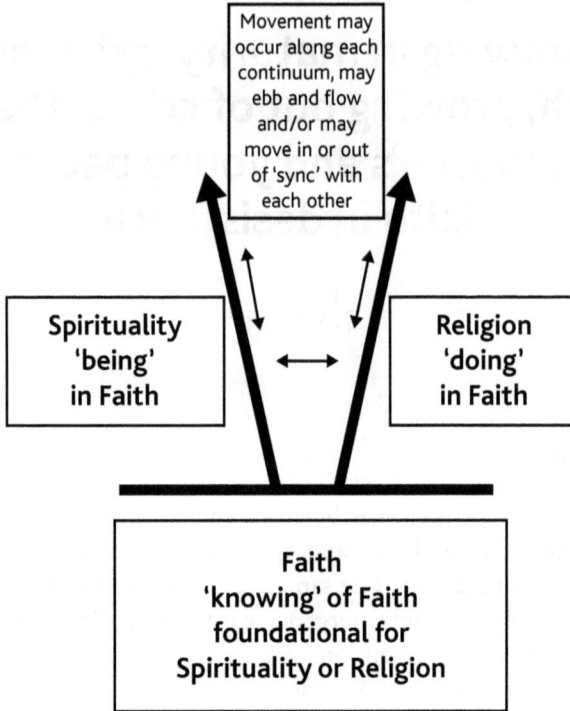

Source: Newman (2004)

(2004) can be used by practitioners to understand the distinctiveness and connectivity of each concept (see Figure 8.1).

'Faith' is notoriously difficult to define as it is intensely personal and private, meaning different things to different people. However, despite its definition being reliant on other associated terms and therefore circular, it is foundational for an individual's spirituality and religiosity and based on the process of 'making meaning' from knowledge, experiences and deeply held beliefs (Fowler, 1981; Hellwig, 1990). 'Spirituality' is often conceptualised as the *internal* expression of faith that engages the cerebral and emotional aspects of humanity (Moss, 2005; LeConte, 2017). 'Religiosity', on the other hand, is concerned more with the *external* expression of faith through engagement with religious institutions, practices and other adherents (Miller and Thoresen, 2003). Spirituality and religiosity are not mutually exclusive but feed off and develop each other, thereby deepening faith. Religiosity can be described as a structured set of beliefs and practices shared by a community related to spirituality (Canda, 1990), while spirituality 'propels the search for connectedness, meaning, purpose and ethical responsibility. It is experienced, formed, and shaped and expressed through a wide range of religious narratives, beliefs, and practices, and is shaped by many influences in family, community, society, culture, and nature' (Yust et al, 2006, p 8; Granqvist and Nkara, 2017). While some researchers use 'spirituality' as a catch-all term that bridges both religious and non-religious groupings, many spiritual commentators argue that spirituality cannot be understood in purely analytical and rational terms but necessarily with the additional lens of understanding the personal religious faith experiences and activity of the individual (Utsey et al, 2007; Green, 2008). It is the author of this chapter's view that 'spirituality' has to have some form of connection to a higher being or transcendental influence to differentiate it from the internal emotional and cerebral facets of human existence. Taken together, these three interconnected concepts form the foundation and framework for the 'spiritual' element of an individual's holistic identity. An understanding of the subtle but unique distinctives of these terms is helpful when applying them to matters of desistance.

Models and theories of desistance

As earlier chapters of this book have explored in more detail, desistance is a relatively recent paradigm for understanding abstinence from criminal behaviour among those individuals for whom offending has become a pattern of behaviour (McNeill et al, 2012). And yet it is something of an enigma with a lack of agreement around definitions, parameters or outcome measurements despite forming the bedrock of more recent youth justice penal policy and intervention philosophies, which have moved away from long-standing risk paradigms (YJB, 2019; Wigzell, 2021). In its most basic form, desistance can be described as a process concerned with the giving up of crime and sustained cessation of offending behaviour (Laub and Sampson, 2003; Maruna, 2001). It describes an individual's change of state from ongoing, regular offending to a permanent state of non-offending behaviour (Uggen and Kruttschnitt, 1998). The process is often likened to a journey; not a straightforward linear trajectory, but often a complex zig-zag path of overcoming challenges and change (Glaser, 1964). And yet the more nuanced dynamics and stages within the process of desistance have only recently become the focus of more academic study. The focus of desistance within children specifically is, as yet, very much under-researched and critiqued (Wigzell, 2021), hence the rationale for this book.

Early proponents of desistance in the 20th century took an ontogenetic view which viewed behaviour change within the context of an individual's lifespan. Such views asserted that there is a clear relationship between age and crime and that individuals simply grow out of crime as they mature (Glueck and Glueck, 1940, 1974). More recently, research has identified both biological and neurobiological factors as relevant aspects of the maturation process (Shulman et al, 2016), in some cases resulting in crime getting harder and harder to the point of a 'crystallisation of discontent' where an individual simply gets fed up with the criminal life and its effects and chooses to step away (Paternoster and Bushway, 2009).

Since the mid-1980s, however, other more complex theories of desistance have emerged which view the process within situational and sociogenic frameworks (Farrington, 1992; Sampson and Laub, 1993; Pezzin, 1995). Such theories look beyond immediate intrinsic biological and neurobiological factors linked to maturation and to extrinsic factors such as environmental and structural influences (Barry, 2011; Bottoms, 2014) as well as the situational contexts and social connections that impact on an individual's sense of identity and belonging (LeBel et al, 2008; Weaver, 2015). This has led to the emergence of theories that differentiate between behaviour on one hand and connectedness, identity formation and holistic development as part of the desistance process on the other (Maruna, 1999; Gardner, 2011). Maruna and Farrall (2004) propose that there are two types of desistance, namely 'primary desistance', which focuses on the behavioural by way of a crime-free gap, and 'secondary desistance', which focuses more on the role and identity of the individual over a longer period of time (Maruna and Farrall, 2004). However, McNeill (2016) broadened the concept further still, suggesting that 'tertiary desistance' describes the wider social change and sense of belonging experienced by the individual over the longer term. The sense of belonging derived from one's reformed identity and the recognition and acceptance of others was further reflected by Nugent and Schinkel (2016), who suggested that there are three types of desistance, namely 'act-desistance' (not actually committing an offence), 'identity-desistance' (the internalisation of non-offending identity) and 'relational-desistance' (the recognition of change by others and acceptance of their new ways). These sociogenic theories recognise that humans are fundamentally social beings that yearn for and thrive on interactions and connectedness that provide positive reference points for life and a sense of worth from being known and valued by others. This is in stark contrast to the destructive individualism that was increasingly evident in the penal policy of the late 1990s onwards, which motivated offenders by promising a contingent reward such as early release or increased privileges, rather than acting out of the intrinsic worth and positive social benefits of moral behaviour, a situation that could be referred to as 'rehabilitative hedonism' (Rosier, 2015). Narrative theories of desistance focus on the 're-storying' of one's life through the development of a 'redemption script' that leads to a new self-identity and prioritises renewed motivation, concern for others and a different future outlook (Maruna, 2001). In recognition of the complexity of all three theoretical positions within the desistance literature, McNeil (2003) believes true desistance is probably located within the interaction between all three dimensions.

The role and impact of spirituality on desistance from crime

One area of study linked to the sociogenic and narrative frameworks of desistance is that of the role and influence of spirituality or 'religiously motivated desistance' (Hallet and McCoy, 2014; DiPietro and Dickinson, 2021). As discussed earlier, the term 'spiritual' is often used to refer to the individual faith experience as well as the religious and spiritual outworking in someone's life. There is an increasing recognition that spirituality, in the fullest sense of the term, can facilitate a protective role against offending and reoffending by providing a framework for redemption narratives, personal sustenance and building hope from which a process of desistance can emerge (Smith, 2017). Furthermore, engagement in religious acts of corporate worship can offer a place for undermining reoffending through the availability and adoption of socially supportive bonds, a sense of renewed purpose and the common good, and the recognition of transcendental authority leading to a meaningful life (Lee et al, 2017; Smith, 2017; Holligan and McLean, 2018; Johnson, 2021). As such, spirituality can alter and shape an individual's renewed *identity* and provide a mechanism for *belonging* to a group of like-minded, pro-social individuals (Johnson and Siegel, 2006).

Identity

An individual's identity is influenced and shaped by several different factors including their biological make-up as well as psycho-social, emotional and spiritual influences. Spirituality and a commitment to a form of religion can offer a 'cognitive blueprint for how one is to proceed as a changed individual' (Giordano et al, 2008, p 102). A key concept within religious paradigms is that of 'conversion', which often describes a profound change of mind, direction and being that leads to a new identity. Maruna et al (2006) describe conversion as the process of 'reinterpreting one's autobiographical self', which can facilitate desistance in a number of ways. First, conversion can create a new personal and spiritual identity where the self-perception is affirmed by the acceptance of a higher being and promise of a new beginning. Second, it can give purpose and meaning to painful life experiences which may have preceded periods of offending as well as providing an ongoing means of coping (LaConte, 2017; Torraiba et al, 2021). Third, conversion can empower the powerless from being a prisoner to an agent of God with renewed importance. Fourthly, it can provide a helpful framework and language for forgiveness – either of themselves or of others who may have had a previous negative impact on their life experience and subsequent decisions leading to offending. Finally, conversion can provide a way of allowing control to lie elsewhere for future uncertainties, thereby removing the burden of fear of uncertainty which can sometimes stand in the way of desistance progress, and lead to hope.

While existing narrative theories of desistance research have focused on the re-storying of one's life that leads to a new 'true' self-identity (Maruna, 2001; Rocque, 2015), it is important for those working with children to differentiate between what constitutes a child simply growing up to become who they are and the significant departure from an old self caught up in offending to a completely new identity (Wigzell, 2021). As such, it is important to handle identity narratives with care when working with children.

Belonging

While the internal and personal elements of spirituality are important, it is the accompanying engagement with the socio-structural elements of religious institutions, corporate practices and other adherents that gives deeper meaning to an individual's faith experience, a concept known as 'transformative agency' (Miller and Thoresen, 2003; Newman, 2004; King, 2013). Fowler (1986) describes faith as an irreducibly relational phenomenon with trust a vital component. When engaging with issues of spirituality, it is important not only to focus on the beliefs and practices of a particular religion but also to understand the dynamic influence of trusting religious/faith communities often centred on places of worship such as churches, mosques, synagogues and temples (Armstrong, 2014). These relationships are often couched in the language of family or community, which underlines the depth of relationship, loving informality, selfless interactions and predisposition for serving others (Tee et al, 2017). Fowler argues that the "self is bound to others by trust and loyalty. But ties to others are mediated, formed, and deepened by a shared and common trust in, and loyalties to, centres of supra-ordinate value" (Fowler, 1986, p 12). There is also often a culture of forgiveness and forbearance within religious communities that fosters stronger relationships and a sense of belonging (Kidwell, 2009). The diversity of people that make up more formal types of religious community presents an interesting dynamic in itself that can serve as a positive influence towards desistance. Anything that reduces the amount of time an offender spends with people of the same age and sex is known to be a proven desistance factor by facilitating time with pro-social others (Warr, 2002; Giordano et al, 2008). This perspective is rooted in social control theory, which assumes that deviant or criminal behaviour is a natural, human tendency that is constrained by both internal controls (religious morals) and external controls such as social bonds and a level of trust and accountability to other like-minded people (Hirschi, 1969; Cox and Matthews, 2007). Locating or facilitating authentic links to religious/faith communities where children can belong is much more challenging, however, due to their age, the role of family in sharing religious views (Hough et al, 2018), gaining permissions for children to engage in appropriate activities and ensuring that the necessary safeguarding measures are in place, understood and followed (IICSA, 2022).

The promise of spirituality can act as a 'hook for change' through being a source of pro-social capital, with most religious teachings reinforcing pro-social behaviours while enhancing positive emotions and overall sense of wellbeing (Giordano et al, 2008). Therefore, the positive role and impact of spirituality on desistance from crime influences an individual's identity and belonging. However, like other life factors that potentially contribute to promoting positive change such as marriage or steady employment, research on the role and impact of spirituality is extremely sparse and potentially incomparable when applying it to children (Laub et al, 1998; Mulvey et al, 2004). It is, therefore, important to consider a wider body of research from different disciplines specific to the life experiences of children in order to build a fuller picture.

The faith journeys of children

While there is a growing body of compelling literature around the impact of spirituality on desistance, there is very little to no research that specifically focuses on the spirituality of children or desistance in childhood. Key theories from the 20th century around human development such as those concerned with cognitive development (Piaget, 1936), psycho-social development (Erikson, 1958) and moral development (Kohlberg, 1958) provide helpful frameworks in understanding an individual's journey from childhood, through adolescence and into adulthood and the thought processes and behaviours that are evident at each stage. However, these early human development theories lacked consideration of the spiritual dimension and the impact this has on identity formation, values and a sense of belonging – key features of sociogenic desistance. Although several models have been developed since then that seek to explain spiritual development (for example Jones, 2022 – a simplified process model of faith development), the seminal work of James W. Fowler (1981) provides much of the foundational basis for variations of these models today. Fowler suggests there are seven stages that shape an individual's faith development over the course of a lifespan. These stages have some correlation to Piaget and colleagues' theories and provide helpful links and comparisons when considering wider issues of faith and spirituality as part of an individual's holistic development from childhood to adulthood. Table 8.1 seeks to provide a comparative and integrative overview of these theories.

The faith of Generation Z

An important body of literature to consider is that of generation theory (Mannheim, 1952)), which describes a 'unique type of social location

Table 8.1: Fowler's Faith Development Model (1981) with additional insight about expected characteristics

Fowler's stage	Ages	Explanation	Link/similarity to other theory
0 – Primal undifferentiated faith	Birth–2 years	Here, the baby acquires experiences from the outer environment that either instil feelings of trust and assurance (from being comforted, living in a secure and stable environment and experiencing a sense of consistency and care from parents). These personalised experiences, according to Fowler, essentially translate into feelings of trust and assurance in the universe and harmony with the divine. Conversely, experiences of parental or environmental neglect and/or abuse at this stage of development can result in the formation of feelings of mistrust and fear with respect to the universe and the divine, sowing the seeds for later doubt and existential angst.	**Piaget** – reflexive behaviour linked to sensorimotor stage of cognitive development, where thinking takes place in and through the body. **Erikson** – first stage of 'trust versus mistrust; self is good, world is good'. **Kohlberg** – individual has no personal morality – does what pleases the child.
1 – 'Intuitive-projective' faith	3–7 years	Children at this stage have acquired language and the ability to work with symbols to express thoughts. Children at this stage don't develop formalised religious beliefs but are instead affected by the psyche's exposure to the unconscious, and by a relative fluidity of patterns of thought. Faith at this stage is experiential and develops through encounters with stories, images, the influence of others, a deeper intuitive sense of what is right and wrong, and innocent perceptions of how God causes the universe to function.	**Piaget** – pre-operational thinking stage (lacking consistent logical-mental structures) – egocentric, magical, perception dominated. **Erikson** – control of self/body, wilfulness. **Kohlberg** – learning rules, right, wrong and punishment, reciprocity.
2 – Mythical-literal faith	7–12 years	Children at this stage have a belief in justice and fairness in religious matters, a sense of reciprocity in the workings of the universe (for example doing good will result in a good result, doing bad will cause a bad thing to happen) and an anthropomorphic image of God (for example, a man with a long white beard who lives in the clouds). Religious metaphors are often taken literally, thus leading to misunderstandings.	**Piaget** – concrete operational stages of cognitive development, where true logical thinking begins to develop in the child's mind. **Erikson** – competence, master skills, work/play with peers. **Kohlberg** – morality – not disturb conscience; socially sensitive, show respect/duty, obeys rules.

Table 8.1: Fowler's Faith Development Model (1981) with additional insight about expected characteristics (continued)

Fowler's stage	Ages	Explanation	Link/similarity to other theory
3 – Synthetic-conventional faith	12 years–early adulthood	This stage is characterised by the identification of the adolescent/adult with a religious institution, belief system or authority, and the growth of a personal religious or spiritual identity. Conflicts that occur when one's beliefs are challenged are often ignored because they represent too much of a threat to one's faith-based identity.	This stage and all subsequent stages correspond to **Piaget's** stage of formal operational thinking, thus making it possible for the adolescent or adult to perceive the divine as an abstract or formless manifestation. **Erikson** – peers paramount, faith in self. **Kohlberg** – majority rules, exception if violate welfare of person, laws for mutual good, cooperation.
4 – Individuative-reflective faith	Mid-20s to late 30s	This stage is often characterised by angst and struggle as the individual takes personal responsibility for their beliefs or feelings. Religious or spiritual beliefs can take on greater complexity and shades of nuance, and there is a greater sense of open-mindedness, which can at the same time open up the individual to potential conflicts as different beliefs or traditions collide.	**Piaget** – abstract thinking, analytical. **Erikson** – characterised by love, mutuality. **Kohlberg** – conformity to rules of society, internal locus of control.
5 – Conjunctive faith	Mid-life crisis	A person at this stage acknowledges paradoxes and the mysteries attendant on transcendent values. This causes the person to move beyond the conventional religious traditions or beliefs they may have inherited from previous stages of development. A resolution of the conflicts of this stage occurs when the person is able to hold a multi-dimensional perspective that acknowledges 'truth' as something that cannot be articulated through any particular statement of faith.	
6 – Universalising faith (or 'enlightenment')	Later adulthood	This stage is only rarely achieved by individuals. A person at this stage is not hemmed in by differences in religious or spiritual beliefs among people in the world but regards all beings as worthy of compassion and deep understanding. Here, individuals 'walk the talk' of the great religious traditions.	

Source: Neuman (2011)

based on the dynamic interplay between being born in a particular year with the socio-political events that occur throughout the life course of the birth cohort, particularly when the cohort comes of age' (McMullin et al, 2007, p 299). Although there are legitimate criticisms of this theory, it does provide a helpful framework for understanding the external influences that shape people's beliefs and behaviours in their formative years (Perrin, 2020).

When considering children in trouble with the law, it is helpful to consider the hallmarks of 'Generation Z' (those born between 1996 and 2010) and how their spirituality is affected and shaped by the external factors experienced during their formative years. It is argued that the key defining characteristics of this generation are that they are 'recession marked, wi-fi enabled, multi-racial, sexually fluid, and post-Christian' (Emery-White, 2017, p 39). Studies reveal that while there is a strong suspicion and rejection of traditional institutions (such as the Church and its interaction with the state), Gen Z-ers in the West have bucked the trend in terms of their outright rejection of faith and spirituality (Apeland and Shuker, 2021). It seems that Gen Z-ers are not necessarily dependent on the religious views and practices of their Generation X or Y parents/grandparents but through the influence of being global citizens and digital natives in new constitutions of online community, and presented with existential global challenges through 24-hour news, have come to their own conclusions about matters of faith and belief. They have been described as less 'religious' but more 'spiritual', with deeper convictions and more energy than their parents or grandparents might have had (Perrin, 2020). Furthermore, they have a stronger sense of social responsibility and commitment to social action while being more socially conservative but ideologically progressive than their older counterparts (Emery-White, 2017; Perrin, 2020).

Considering this, other evidence highlights how Gen Z-ers are more likely to pray regularly and attend a variety of places of worship than their older counterparts (Perrin, 2020; Savanta Com Res, 2021, 2022). This was particularly true during the COVID-19 pandemic, when faith communities boomed with adolescents and young adults due to the availability of religious services online (Edelman et al, 2022). These latest studies continue to show that 'emerging adulthood' (ages 15–22) is still a pivotal life-stage in the defining life experiences and faith development journeys of individuals (Fowler, 2004; Arnett, 2006; Perrin, 2020).

Recommendations for policy makers and practitioners

Religious literacy training and development

Secular assumptions about the nature and relevance of religion have resulted in society losing the ability to talk well about religion and becoming ambivalent about the potential a person's faith may have in shaping positive life outcomes (Dinham, 2015, 2016, 2018). The result is what can be described as poor religious literacy, borrowed from the notion of 'cultural literacy' (Hirsch, 1988), which Dinham and Shaw (2017, p 1) describe as struggling to understand the 'grammars, rules, vocabularies and narratives underpinning religions and beliefs'. Individual assumptions can often lead to an 'institutional stance' which can further complicate or restrict the ability to respond to the diversity of religion and belief positively (Dinham and Jones, 2012). Religion and belief are often addressed by overarching frameworks such as 'anti-oppressive/discriminatory' practice, yet it is argued that these are often tokenistic and result in standards that aim only to establish what is the minimum required (Crisp and Dinham, 2019). There is a risk that this ambivalence is evident within those agencies working within the youth justice sector. This was highlighted by the All-Parliamentary Party Group (APPG) on Religious Education (2017), which undertook an inquiry into UK government departments regarding their level of, and plans for, religious literacy training. Various government departments responded, yet interestingly, neither the Ministry of Justice (responsible for prisons and probation) nor the Youth Justice Board (the non-departmental body responsible for the youth justice system) responded to the inquiry. However, a significant number of religious groups and faith organisations consistently highlighted a lack of understanding and trust across government, which often resulted in a heavy handedness or practices which eroded religious freedoms and trust. In response to these findings, the APPG made 24 recommendations, some of which are relevant to issues raised within this chapter and incumbent upon those in government departments working with children in trouble with the law. The APPG recommended that the government should ensure that training programmes covering both equality and diversity and religious literacy are provided for civil servants and others in the public sector; secondly, the government should commission an inquiry into the effectiveness of training currently offered by the civil service and other public services for the improvement of staff religious literacy; thirdly, public services and government departments should publish audits of the availability of training in religious literacy and religious matters, including statistical data on the number of staff completing this training and their levels of seniority. Levels of religious literacy within government departments and other public services should be scrutinised by Parliament and by external academic experts in this field; fourthly, the responsibility for faith and integration should be reinstated into a single cabinet position brief. A responsibility for promoting and facilitating religious literacy should be included within this ministerial brief. The minister should champion projects which seek to improve religious literacy and seek out opportunities through which government could encourage civil society to improve religious literacy in the school, the workplace or the local community (APPG for Religious Education, 2017). These recommendations clearly apply to a number of training routes into youth justice, including probation, youth work, social work and education. In response to this inquiry, the Civil Service Faith and Belief Toolkit (Cabinet Office, 2019) was designed and developed to foster better understanding and engagement between civil service colleagues. The toolkit provides a helpful blueprint for developing such ways of working between professionals and service users that could be disseminated out to other government departments.

As the evidence about the breadth of spirituality and religious adherence in 'Generation Z' discussed earlier shows, there has been a rapid change in the religious landscape of the UK since the 2010s, with young generations embracing less rigid forms of faith and spirituality than their older generational counterparts (Dinham and Francis, 2016; Emery-White, 2017; Perrin, 2020). This rapid change combined with a lack of religious literacy has resulted in broader society increasingly becoming ill-equipped to engage positively with the current reality of religion and belief and has left practitioners, particularly those working with children, on the back foot when it comes to engaging with those who profess some sort of faith. If religion is to be viewed alongside race, ethnicity, gender and class as a concept central to an understanding of society, there is a need for improved religious literacy among practitioners too, recognising this is a key life skill which is central to the effective, peaceful functioning of a plural democracy (Moore, 2007; Shaw, 2018). Robust religious literacy should not only be concerned with understanding the 'building blocks' of religious traditions (Prothero, 2007) but also the 'ability to discern and analyse the fundamental intersections of religion and social/political/cultural life through multiple lenses' too (Moore 2007, p 56; Parker, 2020).

Dinham (2016) seeks to address this need by presenting a Religious Literacy Framework which suggests the knowledge, skills and approaches required by professionals to engage with people more effectively around issues of religion and belief. The framework consists of four parts, namely categorisation, disposition, knowledge and skills. 'Categorisation' encourages critical thinking about the concept of religion and landscape in which religion and belief are framed. It explores how different people think of and categorise/ define religion and belief and considers what people and organisations need to know or what they think they mean and be able to articulate this clearly in order to enable discourse and debate. 'Disposition' promotes the questioning of one's own prejudices towards religion/non-religion/another's religion and challenges the unconscious emotional assumptions that people bring to discussions around religion and belief (Kanitz, 2005).

Being able to identify assumptions, emotions and potential prejudices is seen as a critical precursor to engagement with religious diversity. 'Knowledge' encourages greater capacity and openness to acquiring further knowledge beyond basic general knowledge and seeks to develop confidence and experience to ask questions and create a culture in which people can do this without fear and misunderstanding. This involves recognising and understanding religion and belief as fluid and manifested in evolving identity rather than static traditions. Evidence submitted to the APPG on Religious Education (2017) suggested that some public sector workers in particular lack the understanding and awareness of how people 'live out' their religious beliefs in a way that may be different from the formal positions of their traditions depending on the context. 'Skills' considers the religious literacy within professional practice and the ability to translate broad knowledge into an emotionally literate meaningful encounter with people.

The need for greater religious literacy development through effective training and practice is vital. The current extent of skills training and ability within the workforces is debateable and unclear but is dependent on the context, sector or setting as well as the length of professional training programmes and the resources available for training practitioners.

Knowledge and skills for working with children's faith in youth justice contexts

Much of the desistance literature talks about 'supporting change' with the right attitude from practitioners such as those within the youth justice system (McNeill, 2009). This means working 'with' rather than 'on' children in ways that are perceived to be legitimate by the child being engaged. To do this well around issues of spirituality, practitioners require a certain level of knowledge about multiple religions and belief systems as well as a unique toolbox of empathetic skills.

Key skills for any practitioner in this space must include strong reflective practice and reflexive thinking (Thomson and Pascal, 2012). It is vital for practitioners to reflect on their own positionality around issues of spirituality and identify potential biases borne out of age, 'generation', personal religious experiences (good and bad) and their own faith/lack of faith (Wahler, 2012; Case et al, 2020; Chafota, 2020). Alongside this, practitioners should develop reflexive thinking that challenges assumptions about certain religions as well as intersectionality issues of culture, race and gender (Glynn, 2015; Johnston, 2021). Examples include perceptions around children of Black heritage and the conflation of ethnic, cultural and religious identities and practices, and Muslim children whose faith identity has largely been viewed through the risk-factor lens of the Prevent agenda rather than any potential positive influence upon desistance (Al-Krenawi and Graham, 2000; Belton and Hamid, 2011; Robinson-Edwards and Pinkney, 2018; DiPietro and Dickinson, 2021; Johnston, 2021). Additionally, practitioners developing an awareness of where they might be on Fowler's model (1981) in terms of their own faith development compared to where the child might be is helpful in knowing how to approach in-depth discussions about spirituality and cultivate open, trusting relationships.

McGuire (2008) distinguishes between religion in the sense of the prescribed teachings of a particular faith tradition with institutionally defined beliefs and practices and religion as 'lived out' within a particular cultural context. It is, therefore, important for practitioners to recognise that beliefs and practices may not always be consonant in everyday embodied practice, and a level of informed discernment is required which comes from good religious literacy. Youth justice practitioners should not only take the time and effort to explore the basic foundations and tenets of the child's religion but also take an empathetic and asset-based approach to finding out what their faith means to them and how they can seek further connections and places to belong, to allow them to live out their faith experience more authentically (Guignon, 2004). Part of this requires the practitioner to recognise the difference between age-appropriate authenticity and religious maturity which comes with age. A child may still have quite concrete religious views borne out of rigid thinking but still be sincere and authentic in the way these are expressed.

It is also important for practitioners to consider the role of other professionals and volunteers, either within a particular agency or through inter-professional working, in supporting consistent engagement around spirituality. While spirituality plays an important role in desistance, this is often moderated by cognitive functioning and ability. For those with lower neurological functions, additional cognitive-behavioural treatments may be beneficial alongside supporting religious practices (Stansfield, 2017).

Approaches and frameworks

The lack of religious literacy within the public sector workforce is, in part, down to the absence or tokenistic inclusion of spirituality within professional development and training programmes. While professionals within the youth justice sector are drawn from a number of different training routes, the findings of the APPG on Religious Education (2017) clearly highlight a consistency of concern. The Youth Justice Effective Practice Certificate, which was launched in 2012 and is widely recognised as a good foundation for practice, explores the current state of theory, practice and evidence relating to working effectively with children in the youth justice system (Unitas, 2022). However, issues of religion are only briefly addressed in the Theoretical Approaches to Crime and Deviance and implicitly in the Assessment of the Child modules. There is no recognition of the spiritual element of the holistic person or of spirituality as a positive desistance factor. Greater recognition of the holistic nature of humanity including the spiritual paradigm is urgently needed (Fowler, 2001). As such, there is much to learn from other professional disciplines including those of youth work, social work, paediatric nursing and wider allied health and social care practices.

Within professional youth work, there is some recognition of spirituality within the National Occupational Standards (NOS), namely B1 – 'Facilitate the personal, social, spiritual and educational development of young people' (NYA, 2020). How this is applied in practice varies and is the focus of some debate. However, there is recognition that youth work training lacks the depth and clarity needed for youth workers to engage with this NOS well (Benson et al, 2008; Stanton, 2015; Thompson and Shuker, 2021). There are also blurred lines between the delivery of faith-based youth work and youth work that can facilitate conversations about faith and spirituality (Seal and Harris, 2016; Bright et al, 2018, cited in Alldred et al, 2018; Thompson, 2019; McFeeters et al, 2021).

Within social work, while there are encouraging signs of a broader appreciation of spirituality, research suggests that most social workers experience considerable difficulties in identifying and responding appropriately to the religious and spiritual needs of their service users (Gilligan and Furness, 2006; Crisp, 2008; Gray, 2008; Stirling et al, 2010). In response to this, Gilligan and Furness (2006) developed a framework to help social workers identify when religion and belief are significant in the lives of their service users and how to take account of this in practice. The framework consists of nine interconnected key principles that can also be reframed as questions to aid practitioners to reflect on and assess the relevance of their own religious beliefs and those of service users. This framework may be transferable to work within youth justice but is, as yet, untested (see Figure 8.2).

Figure 8.2: Principles for reflection on religion and belief framework

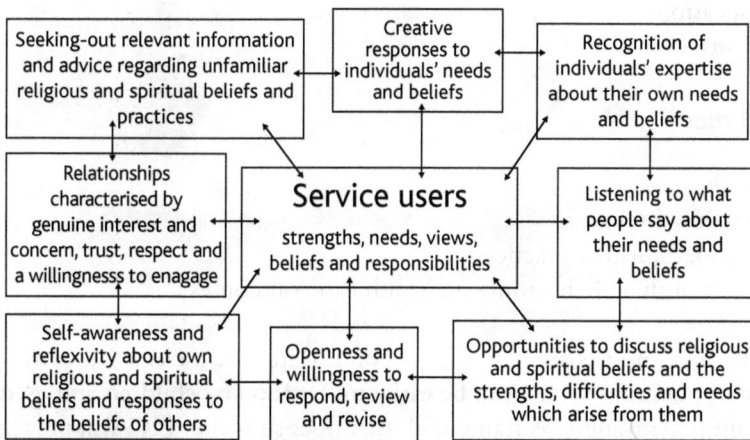

Source: Adapted from Gilligan and Furness (2006)

Within the health field, there are a range of quantitative tools that offer a structured and empirically robust approach to understanding an individual's religious beliefs with a view to responding strategically and appropriately to holistic treatment needs. Examples include Burgess's 20-item tool for assessing philosophy of life, sources of hope, trusting relationships and self-actualisation (Burgess, 1997); Ellison's spiritual wellbeing scale (Ellison, 1983); Elkins' spiritual orientation inventory (Elkins et al, 1998); Dossey's 45-question spiritual assessment tool (Dossey, 1998); the JAREL 21-question spiritual wellbeing scale (Hungelmann et al, 1996); and Leetun's spiritual wellness assessment tool for older adults (Leetun, 1996). However, these approaches are complex, in-depth and assume a level of comprehension in both the professional and the service user for them to be effective. When working with children, it is arguably more helpful to have a simpler approach which can be easily adapted by the professional depending on the age, circumstance and need of the child (Neuman, 2011). As such, acronymic models for assessing a patient's faith needs in health may provide a helpful framework in which professionals in other sectors, including youth justice, can explore relevant considerations and issues with the children with whom they engage (Maddox, 2001; Burns et al, 2004; Heilferty, 2004). These models can help professionals structure their thinking and understanding while also providing a helpful structure for including spiritual wellbeing within their written assessments. Such examples include:

BELIEF model

- Belief system
- Ethics or values
- Lifestyle
- Involvement in religious community
- Education
- Future events

HOPE model

- Hope
- Organised religion
- Personal spiritual practices
- Effect of these behaviours on health care/outcomes

While these models are helpful, they do not include a clear and consistent range of questions which can be easily understood by children and used by relevant practitioners. A framework that does so is the 'FICA' approach to a spiritual assessment in primary care (Matthews, 1998):

F: Faith
- Does religious faith or spirituality play an important part in your life?
- Do you consider yourself to be a religious or spiritual person?

I: Influence
- How does your religious faith or spirituality influence the way you think about the way you care for yourself?

C: Community
- Are you a part of any religious or spiritual community or congregation?

A: Address
- Would you like me to address any religious or spiritual issues and concerns with you?

A tool that focuses more on the levels of religious commitment rather than awareness is that of the Religious Commitment Inventory (RCI) 10 (Worthington et al, 2003). This is a ten-item measure of the extent to which people follow their religious values, beliefs, and practices measured on a scale from one (not at all true of me) to five (totally true of me). Although the RCI-10 is considered to be an excellent means of measuring the religious commitment of adults, it was untested and considered to be too complex for use with children. In response to this, Miller et al (2013) made modifications to the RCI-10 to make the scale suitable for use with adolescents by simplifying the language to be commensurate with a grade-six reading level and tweaking one of the questions by splitting it into two clearer questions (known as the Religious Commitment Inventory for Adolescents – RCI-A). While the early results of their study were positive in terms of its consistency and reliability in predicting behaviours over time, and notwithstanding the positive links highlighted between religious commitment and desistance (Hallett and McCoy, 2014; Robinson-Edwards and Pinkney, 2018; Jang, 2020), it remains unclear which face-to-face professional contexts this would be helpful, appropriate and easy to use in. Further research and application within a youth justice context may prove helpful.

Conclusion

This chapter has sought to redress the balance of research around spirituality and desistance being primarily focused on adults by engaging a wider body of research that considers the holistic development of children and adolescents, as well as approaches and insights from a wider range of professional disciplines that work with this cohort. In contributing to the emerging fields of 'Child First youth justice' (Case and Browning, 2021) and 'Spiritual Criminology' (Ronel and Yair, 2018; Amitay and Ronel, 2022), this chapter also makes clear recommendations for policy makers and practitioners around the need for improved religious literacy and understanding of the influences and spiritual outlook of the current generation of 'emerging adults' as well as greater self-reflection and reflexivity around the impact of personal experiences and biases around religion and belief. It is also clear that further research and academic study is specifically required that focuses on the unique needs of children compared to adults if the true potential of spirituality within the desistance paradigm is to be realised (Wigzell, 2021).

References

Alldred, P., Cullen, F., Edwards, K. and Fusco, D. (eds) (2018) *The SAGE Handbook of Youth Work Practice*, London: SAGE Publications.

Al-Krenawi, A. and Graham, J.R. (2000) 'Islamic theology and prayer: relevance for social work practice', *International Social Work*, 43(3): 289–304.

All-Party Parliamentary Group on Religious Education (2017) 'Improving religious literacy: a contribution to the debate', London: APPG on Religious Education.

Amitay, G. and Ronel, N. (2022) 'The practice of spiritual criminology: a non-doing companionship for crime desistance', *International Journal of Offender Therapy and Comparative Criminology*, 67(4): 420–41.

Apeland, G. and Shuker, L. (2021) 'Faith in young people', Luton: Youthscape Centre for Research.

Armstrong, R. (2014) 'Trusting the untrustworthy: the theology, practice and implications of faith-based volunteers' work with ex-prisoners', *Studies in Christian Ethics*, 27(3): 299–309.

Arnett, J. (2006) *Emerging Adulthood: The Winding Road from the Late Teens through the Twenties*, Oxford: Oxford University Press.

Barry, M. (2011) 'Youth justice policy and its influence on desistance from crime', in M. Barry and F. McNeill (eds) *Youth Offending and Youth Justice*, London: Jessica Kingsley, pp 78–94.

Belton, B. and Hamid, S. (2011) *Youth Work and Islam: A Leap of Faith for Young People*, Rotterdam: Sense Publishers.

Benson, P.L., Roehlkepartain, E.C. and Hong, K.L. (2008) *Spiritual Development: New Directions for Youth Development*, London: John Wiley & Sons.

Bottoms, A.E. (2014) 'Desistance from crime', in Z. Ashmore and R. Shuker (eds) *Forensic Practice in the Community*, Abingdon: Routledge, pp 251–73.

Bright, G., Thompson, N., Hart, P. and Hayden, B. (2018) 'Faith-based youth work: education engagement and ethics', in P. Alldred, F. Cullen, K. Edwards and D. Fusco (eds) *The SAGE Handbook of Youth Work Practice*, London: SAGE, pp 197–212.

Burgess, W.A. (1997) *Psychiatric Nursing*, Stamford: Appleton & Lange.

Burns, C.E., Dunn, A.M., Brady, M.A., Barber-Starr, N. and Blosser, C.G. (2004) *Paediatric Primary Care: A Handbook for Nurse Practitioners* (3rd edn), St Louis: Saunders.

Cabinet Office (2019) 'Faith and Belief Toolkit: a practical guide providing information about faith and belief in the civil service', available from: https://www.gov.uk/government/publications/faith-and-belief-toolkit

Canda, E. (1990) 'Afterword: spirituality re-examined', *Spirituality and Social Work Communicator*, 1(1): 13–14.

Case, S. and Browning, A. (2021) 'Child First justice: the research evidence-base', Loughborough University, available from https://yjresourcehub.uk/images/Evaluation%20Library/YOT_Talk_Full_Report_European_Journa l_of_Criminology_March_2021.pdf

Case, S., Drew, J., Hampson, K., Jones, G. and Kennedy, D (2020) 'Professional perspectives of youth justice policy implementation: contextual and coalface challenges', *The Howard Journal of Crime and Justice*, 59(2): 214–32.

Chafota, E. (2020) 'Unconscious bias: how might it affect social work', briefing to Gloucestershire County Council.

Cox, M. and Matthews, B. (2007) 'Faith-based approaches for controlling the delinquency of juvenile offenders', *Federal Probation*, 71(1): 31–7.

Crisp, B.R. (2008) 'Social work and spirituality in a secular society', *Journal of Social Work*, 8(4): 363–75.

Crisp, B.R. and Dinham, A. (2019) 'Are the profession's education standards promoting the religious literacy required for twenty-first century social work practice?', *British Journal of Social Work*, 49: 1544–62.

Dinham, A. (2015) 'Public religion in an age of ambivalence: recovering religious literacy after a century of secularism', in L. Beaman and L. van Arragon (eds) *Issues in Education and Religion: Whose Religion?*, Leiden: Brill, pp 19–33.

Dinham, A. (2016) 'Religious literacy: what is the future for religion and belief?', University of Sheffield, Available from: https://www.sheffield.ac.uk/news/nr/comment-religious-literacy-what-is-the-futurefor-religion-and-belief-1.570731

Dinham, A. (2018) 'Religion and belief in health and social care: the case for religious literacy', *International Journal of Human Rights in Healthcare*, 11(2): 83–90.

Dinham, A. and Jones, S. (2012) 'Religious literacy in higher education: brokering public faith in a context of ambivalence', *Journal of Contemporary Religion*, 27(2): 185–201.

Dinham, A. and Francis, M. (eds) (2016) *Religious Literacy in Policy and Practice*, Bristol: Policy Press.

Dinham, A. and Shaw, M. (2017) 'Religious literacy through religious education: the future of teaching and learning about religion and belief', *Religions*, 8(7): 119 (1–13).

DiPietro, S. and Dickinson, T (2021) '"God is real": narratives of religiously motivated desistance', *Criminology*, 59(4): 645–70.

Dossey, B. (1998) 'Holistic modalities and healing moments', *American Journal of Nursing*, 98(6): 44–7.

Edelman, J., Vincent, A., Kolata, P., O'Keeffe, E., Stuerzenhofecker, K., Minott, M.A. et al (2021) 'British ritual innovation under COVID-19: the final report of the project Social Distance, Digital Congregation (BRIC-19)', Manchester Metropolitan University and the University of Chester.

Elkins, D.N., Hedstrom, L.J., Hughes, L.L., Leaf, J.A. and Saunders, C. (1988) 'Toward a humanistic-phenomenological spirituality: definition, description, and measurement', *Journal of Humanistic Psychology*, 28: 5–18.

Ellison, C.W. (1983) 'Spiritual well-being: conceptualisation and measurement', *Journal of Psychology and Theology*, 11: 330–40.

Emery-White, J. (2017) *Meet Generation Z: Understanding and Reaching the New Post-Christian World*, Grand Rapids, MI: Baker Books.

Erickson, E.H. (1958) *Young Man Luther: A Study in Psychoanalysis and History*, New York: W.W. Norton.

Farrington, D. (1992) 'Explaining the beginning, progress, and ending of antisocial behaviour from birth to adulthood', in J. McCord (ed) *Facts, Frameworks, and Forecasts: Advances in Criminological Theory*, vol 3, New Brunswick: Transaction Publishers, pp 253–86.

Fowler, J.W. (1981) *Stages of Faith: The Psychology of Human Development and Quest for Meaning*, San Francisco: HarperCollins.

Fowler, J.W. (1986) *Faith Development and Pastoral Care*, Philadelphia: Augsburg Fortress Press.

Fowler, J.W. (2001) 'Faith development theory and the postmodern challenges', *The International Journal for the Psychology of Religion*, 11(3): 159–72.

Fowler, J.W. (2004) 'Faith development at 30: naming the challenges of faith in a new millennium', *Religious Education*, 99(4): 405–21.

Gardner, J. (2011) 'Keeping faith: faith-talk by and for incarcerated youth', *The Urban Review*, 43(1): 22–42.

Gilligan, P. and Furness, S. (2006) 'The role of religion and spirituality in social work practice: views and experiences of social workers and students', *British Journal of Social Work*, 36(4): 617–37.

Giordano, P.C., Longmore, M.A., Schroeder, R.D. and Seffrin, P.M. (2008) 'A life-course perspective on spirituality and desistance from crime', *Criminology*, 46(1): 99–132.

Glaser, D. (1964) *The Effectiveness of a Prison and Parole System*, Indianapolis: Bobbs-Merrill.

Glueck, S. and Glueck, E. (1940) *Juvenile Delinquents Grown Up*, New York: Commonwealth Fund.

Glueck, S. and Glueck, E. (1974) *Of Delinquency and Crime*, Springfield: C.C. Thomas.

Glynn, M. (2015) 'Towards an intersectional model of desistance for Black offenders', *Safer Communities*, 15(1): 24–32.

Granqvist, P. and Nkara, F. (2017) 'Nature meets nurture in religious and spiritual development', *British Journal of Developmental Psychology*, 35(1): 142–55.

Gray, M. (2008) 'Viewing spirituality in social work through the lens of contemporary social theory', *British Journal of Social Work*, 38(1): 175–96.

Green, M. (2008) 'Putting spiritual development of young people on the map: an English perspective', *New Directions for Youth Development* , 118: 59–72.

Guignon, C. (2004) *On Being Authentic*, London: Routledge.

Hallett, M. and McCoy, S. (2014) 'Religiously motivated desistance: an exploratory study', *The International Journal of Offender Therapy and Comparative Criminology*, 59(8): 855–72.

Heilferty, C.M. (2004) 'Spiritual development and the dying child: the pediatric nurse practitioner's role', *Journal of Pediatric Health Care*, 18: 271–5.

Hellwig, M.K. (1990) 'A history of the concept of faith', in M. Lee (ed) *Handbook of Faith*, Birmingham, AL: Religious Education Press, pp 3–23.

Hirsch, E. (1988) *Cultural Literacy: What Every American Needs to Know*, New York: Vintage.

Hirschi, T. (1969) *Causes of Delinquency*, Berkeley: University of California Press.

Holligan, C. and McLean, R. (2018) 'Criminal desistance narratives of young people in the west of Scotland: understanding spirituality and criminogenic constraints', *Religions*, 9(6): 1–13.

Hough, C., Abbott-Halpin, E., Mahmood, T. and Mohammed, H. (2018) 'Faith, family and crime: an exploration of Muslim families' involvement with the criminal justice system and its impact on their health and social needs', London: Barrow Cadbury Trust.

Hungelmann, J., Kenkel-Rossi, E., Klaasen, L. and Stollenwerk, R. (1996) 'Focus on spiritual well-being: harmonious interconnectedness of mind–body–spirit; use of the JAREL Spiritual Well-Being Scale; assessment of spiritual well-being is essential to the health of individuals', *Geriatric Nursing*, 17: 262–6.

Independent Inquiry into Child Sexual Abuse (2022) 'The report of the Independent Inquiry into Child Sexual Abuse', Available from: https://assets.publishing.service.gov.uk/government/uploads/system/uploads/attachment_data/file/1112123/the-report-independent-inquiry-into-child-sexual-abuse-october-2022.pdf

James, S.R., Ashwill, J.W. and Droske, S.C. (2002) *Nursing Care of Children: Principles & Practice* (2nd edn), Philadelphia: Saunders.

Jang, S.J. (2020) 'Religiosity, crime, and drug use among juvenile offenders, research outreach (Behavioural Sciences)', Available from: https://researcho utreach.org/wp-content/uploads/2020/10/Sung-Joon-Jang.pdf

Johnson, B.R. (2021) 'How religion contributes to the common good, positive criminology, and justice reform', *Religions*, 12(6): 402 (1–11).

Johnson, B.R. and Siegel, M. (2006) 'The role of African American churches in reducing crime among Black youth', Philadelphia: Baylor University.

Johnston, C. (2021) 'Girls of colour in the youth justice system: an intersectional exploration', unpublished PhD thesis, University of Sheffield.

Jones, B. (2022) 'Reimagining Fowler's Stages of Faith: shifting from a seven stage to a four-step framework for faith development', *Journal of Beliefs & Values*, 44(2): 159–72.

Kanitz, L. (2005) 'Improving Christian worldview pedagogy: going beyond mere Christianity', *Christian Higher Education*, 4(2): 99–108.

Kidwell, J. (2009) 'Exploring the relationship between religious commitment and forgiveness through quantitative and qualitative study', unpublished PhD thesis, Iowa State University.

King, S. (2013) 'Transformative agency and desistance from crime', *Criminology & Criminal Justice*, 13(3): 317–35.

Kohlberg, L. (1958) 'The development of modes of thinking and choices in years 10 to 16', unpublished PhD thesis, University of Chicago.

Laub, J.H. and Sampson, R.J. (2003) *Shared Beginnings, Divergent Lives: Delinquent Boys to Age 70*, Cambridge, MA: Harvard University Press.

Laub, J.H., Nagin, D.S. and Sampson, R.J. (1998) 'Trajectories of change in criminal offending: good marriages and the desistance process', *American Sociological Review*, 63: 225–38.

LeBel, T.P., Burnett, R., Maruna, S. and Bushway, S. (2008) 'The "chicken and egg" of subjective and social factors in desistance from crime', *European Journal of Criminology*, 5(2): 131–59.

Leconte, J. (2017) 'Wearing my spiritual jacket', *Health Education and Behaviour*, 44(5): 696–704.

Lee, M., Pagano, M., Johnson, B., Post, S. and Leibowitz, G. (2017) 'From defiance to reliance: spiritual virtue as a pathway towards desistance, humility and recovery among juvenile offenders', *Spirituality in Clinical Practice*, 4(3): 161–75.

Leetun, M. (1996) 'Wellness spirituality in the older adult', *Nurse Practitioner*, 21(8): 60–70.

Maddox, M. (2001) 'Teaching spirituality to nurse practitioner students: the importance of the interconnection of mind, body, and spirit', *Journal of the American Academy of Nurse Practitioners*, 13(3): 134–9.

Mannheim, K. (1952) 'The problem of generations', in P. Kecskemeti (ed), *Essays on the Sociology of Knowledge*, London: Routledge and Kegan Paul, pp 276–320.

Maruna, S. (1999) 'Desistance and development: the psychological process of "going straight"', The British Criminology Conferences: Selected Proceedings. Volume 2. Papers from the British Criminology Conference, Queens University, Belfast, 15–19 July 1997.

Maruna, S. (2001) Making Good: How Ex-convicts Reform and Rebuild Their Lives, Washington, DC: American Psychological Association.

Maruna, S., and Farrall, S. (2004) 'Desistance from crime: a theoretical reformulation', Kolner Zeitschrift für Soziologie und Sozialpsychologie, 43: 171–94.

Maruna, S., Wilson, L. and Curran, K. (2006) 'Why God is often found behind bars: prison conversions and the crisis of self-narrative', Research in Human Development, 3(2–3): 161–84.

Matthews, D. (1998) The Faith Factor: Proof of the Healing Power of Prayer, New York: Viking Press.

McFeeters, M., Hammond, M. and Taylor, B. (2021) 'Christian faith-based youth work: systematic narrative review', Journal of Beliefs & Values, 43(4): 448–60.

McGuire, M.B. (2008) Lived Religion: Faith and Practice in Everyday Life, Oxford: Oxford University Press.

McMullin, J., Comeau, T.D. and Jovic, E. (2007) 'Generational affinities and discourses on difference', British Journal of Sociology, 58(2): 297–316.

McNeill, F. (2003) 'Desistance-focused probation practice', in W.H. Chui and M. Nellis (eds) Moving Probation Forward: Evidence, Arguments and Practice, Harlow: Pearson, pp 146–62.

McNeill, F. (2009) 'What works and what's just?', European Journal of Probation, 1(1): 21–40.

McNeill, F. (2016) 'The fuel in the tank or the hole in the boat? Can sanctions support desistance?', in J. Shapland, S. Farrall and A. Bottoms (eds) Global Perspectives on Desistance: Reviewing What We Know and Looking to the Future, Abingdon: Routledge, pp 265–81.

McNeil, F., Farrall, S., Lightowler, C. and Maruna, S. (2012) 'How and why people stop offending: discovering desistance', Institute for Research and Innovation in Social Services, Available from: https://www.iriss.org.uk/sites/default/files/iriss-insight-15.pdf

Miller, W., Shepperd, J. and McCullough, M. (2013) 'Evaluating the Religious Commitment Inventory for Adolescents', Journal of Religion and Spirituality, 5(4): 242–51.

Miller, W.R. and Thoresen, C.E. (2003) 'Spirituality, religion, and health: an emerging research field', American Psychologist, 58(1): 24–35.

Moore, D. (2007) Overcoming Religious Illiteracy: A Cultural Studies Approach to The Study of Religion in Secondary Education, New York: Palgrave Macmillan.

Moss, B. (2005) Religion and Spirituality, Lyme Regis: Russell House Publishing.

Mulvey, E.P., Steinberg, L., Fagan, J., Cauffman, E., Piquero, A.R., Chassin, L. et al (2004) 'Theory and research on desistance from antisocial activity among serious adolescent offenders', *Youth Violence and Juvenile Justice*, 2(3): 213–36.

National Youth Agency (NYA) (2020) 'Youth work in England: policy, practice and the National Occupational Standards', Available from: https://unitas.uk.net/youth-justice/youth-justice-effective-practice-certificate-yjepc

Neuman, M. (2011) 'Addressing children's beliefs through Fowler's Stages of Faith', *Journal of Paediatric Nursing*, 26: 44–50.

Newman, L. (2004) 'Faith, spirituality, and religion: a model for understanding the differences', *The College of Student Affairs Journal*, 23(2): 102–10.

Nugent, B. and Schinkel, M. (2016) 'The pains of desistance', *Criminology & Criminal Justice*, 16(5): 568–84.

Parker, S. (2020) 'Religious literacy: spaces of teaching and learning about religion and belief', *Journal of Beliefs & Values*, 41(2): 129–31.

Paternoster, R. and Bushway, S. (2009) 'Desistance and the feared self: toward an identity theory of criminal desistance', *Criminal Law and Criminology*, 99(4): 1103–56.

Perrin, R. (2020) *Changing Shape: The Faith Lives of Millennials*, London: SCS Press.

Pezzin, L.E. (1995) 'Earnings prospects, matching effects, and the decision to terminate a criminal career', *Journal of Quantitative Criminology*, 11: 29–50.

Piaget, J. (1936) *Origins of Intelligence in the Child*, London: Routledge & Kegan Paul.

Prothero, S. (2007) *Religious Literacy: What every American needs to know – and doesn't*, New York: Harper Collins.

Robinson-Edwards, S. and Pinkney, C. (2018) 'Black men, religiosity, and desistance: exploring Islam, desistance and identity', *Safer Communities*, 17(1): 47–67.

Rocque, M. (2015) 'The lost concept: the (re)emerging link between maturation and desistance from crime', *Criminology & Criminal Justice*, 15(3): 340–60.

Ronel, N. and Yair, B. (2018) 'Spiritual criminology: the case for Jewish criminology', *International Journal of Offender Therapy and Comparative Criminology*, 62(7): 2081–102.

Rosier, T. (2015) 'What is the purpose of prison?', Contribution to a colloquium with Bishop James Langstaff at the Houses of Parliament, 20 November.

Sampson, R.J. and Laub, J. (1993) *Crime in the Making: Pathways and Turning Points through Life*, Cambridge, MA: Harvard University Press.

Savanta ComRes (2021) 'Prayer and church attendance survey', Available from: https://comresglobal.com/polls/prayer-and-church-attendance-survey

Savanta ComRes (2022) 'Survey of UK young adults on how often they have prayed and what they have prayed about', Available from: https://comresglobal.com/polls/church-of-england-polling-on-prayer

Seal, M. and Harris, P. (2016) *Responding to Youth Violence through Youth Work*, Bristol: Policy Press.

Shaw, M. (2018) 'New representations of religion and belief in schools', *Religions*, 9(11): 1–14.

Shulman, E.P., Smith, A.R., Silvia, K., Icenogle, G., Duell, N., Chein, J. et al (2016) 'The dual systems model: review, reappraisal, and reaffirmation', *Developmental Cognitive Neuroscience*, 17: 103–17.

Smith, E.E. (2017) *The Power of Meaning: Creating a Life That Matters*, New York: Crown.

Stansfield, R. (2017) 'Religion and desistance from substance use among adolescent offenders: the role of cognitive functioning', *Criminal Behaviour and Mental Health*, 28: 350–60.

Stanton, N. (ed) (2015) *Youth Work and Faith: Debates, Delights, and Dilemmas*, Lyme Regis: Russell House.

Stirling, B., Furman, L.D., Benson, P.W., Canda, E.R. and Grimwood, C. (2010) 'A comparative survey of Aotearoa New Zealand and UK social workers on the role of religion and spirituality in practice', *British Journal of Social Work*, 40(2): 602–21.

Tee, M., Pagano, M., Johnson, B., Post, G., Leibowitz, G. and Dudash, M (2017) 'From defiance to reliance: spiritual virtue as a pathway towards desistance', *Spirituality in Clinical Practice*, 4(3): 161–75.

Thompson, N. (2019) 'Where is faith-based youth work heading?', in G. Bright and C. Pugh (eds) *Youth Work: Global Futures*, Rotterdam: Sense Publishers, pp 166–83.

Thompson, N. and Pascal, J. (2012) 'Developing critically reflective practice', *Reflective Practice*, 13(2): 311–25.

Thompson, N. and Shuker, L. (2021) 'The "secular culture" of youth work training: are JNC-recognised programmes in English universities equipping youth workers to work with diverse religious communities?', Luton: Youthscape Centre for Research.

Torralba, J., Oviedo, L. and Cantera, M. (2021) 'Religious coping in adolescents: new evidence and relevance', *Humanities and Social Sciences Communications*, 8: 121.

Uggen, C. and Kruttschnitt, C. (1998) 'Crime in the breaking: gender differences in desistance', *Law & Society Review*, 32(2): 339–66.

Unitas (2022) 'Youth Justice Effective Practice Certificate (YJEPC)', Available from: https://unitas.uk.net/youth-justice/youth-justice-effective-practice-certificate-yjepc

Utsey, S.O., Bolden, M.A., Williams, O., Lee, A., Lanier, Y. and Newsome, C. (2007) 'Spiritual well-being as a mediator of the relation between culture-specific coping and quality of life in a community sample of African Americans', *Journal of Cross-cultural Psychology*, 38(2): 123–36.

Wahler, E (2012) 'Identifying and challenging social work students' biases', *Social Work Education*, 31(8): 1058–70.

Warr, M. (2002) *Companions in Crime: The Social Aspects of Criminal Conduct*, Cambridge: Cambridge University Press.

Weaver, B. (2015) *Offending and Desistance: The Importance of Social Relations*, London: Routledge.

Wigzell, A. (2021) 'Explaining desistance: looking forwards, not backwards', NAYJ briefing, London: National Association of Youth Justice.

Worthington, E., Wade, N., Hight, T., Riplet, J., McCullough, M., Berry, J. et al (2003) 'The Religious Commitment Inventory-10: development, refinement, and validation of a brief scale for research and counselling', *Journal of Counselling Psychology*, 50(10): 84–96.

Youth Justice Board (2019) 'Youth Justice Board for England and Wales: strategic plan 2019–2022', Available from: https://assets.publish ing.service.gov.uk/government/uploads/system/uploads/attachment_d ata/file/802702/YJB_Strategic_Plan_2019_to_2022.pdf

Yust, K.M., Johnson, A.N., Sasso, S.E. and Roehlkepartain, E.C. (eds) (2006) *Nurturing Child and Adolescent Spirituality: Perspectives from the World's Religious Traditions*, Lanham, MD: Rowman & Littlefield.

PART III

The application of desistance thinking to children

Desistance approaches in youth justice: conceptualisations, barriers and enablers

Kathy Hampson

Introduction

As a contested term with several different conceptualisations, 'desistance' (cessation of crime) has been accused of being 'hampered by definitional, measurement, and theoretical incoherence' (Sampson and Laub, 2001, p 1). This confusion has persisted into youth justice, further complicating the situation because it originated from research on adult offenders rather than children. Applying this contested adult concept to children is therefore not without additional complications, sometimes ignored (McMahon and Jump, 2018). This chapter will explore these complications to seek a more child-appropriate understanding of 'desistance' for youth justice before exploring barriers and enablers for practice. Discussions are informed throughout by views of youth justice practitioners[1] through training evaluation questionnaires (Hampson, 2018), interviews and a group forum, reflecting the 'coalface' experiences of those working directly with justice-involved children.

Development of the 'desistance' concept

Since the Crime and Disorder Act of 1998, the criminal justice system in England and Wales has been dominated by 'risk' (risk of reoffending, risk of harm to others), coalescing around why people *start* offending ('risk factors' predicting offending). Probation and youth justice work concentrated almost entirely on mitigation of risk, giving a strongly *deficit*-focus (what needs to be reduced/stopped) (Hampson, 2018). However, a parallel track was developing focusing on why people *stop* offending, emphasising strengths/ capacities rather than addressing deficits/risks. One notable development was the Good Lives Model, designed for adult sex offenders, which acknowledged that offenders' life goals (aspirational 'goods') were similar to non-offenders, with the model seeking to build these up rather than mitigate negatives (Ward, 2002).

Research examined differences between those successful in giving up crime (desisters) compared to those who were not (persisters), looking to desisters for ways to design successful interventions (Maruna, 2001). Sampson and Laub (2001) criticised research only looking at criminal onset, suggesting that criminological theory should account for onset, continuation *and* desistance from crime. If reasons for *desistance* are known, then developing these could be more effective in addressing criminal behaviour than addressing reasons for onset, as desistance mechanisms may be *different* (Sampson and Laub, 2001). However, the increasing dominance of 'risk' tended to recognise factors for desistance as merely the opposites of those leading to offending onset (LeBlanc and Loeber, 1993). This resulted in deficit-focused interventions in both adult and youth justice through the 1990s and start of the 21st century (Hampson, 2018).

Although much of adult probation practice is still risk-focused (based largely on 'Risk, Needs, Responsivity'; HMIP, 2020), it was first to recognise that positive, strengths-based approaches could be more likely to lead to 'desistance' from crime (see 'New Me' suite of courses,[2] Ministry of Justice, 2021; Good Lives Model, Wong and Horan, 2021). Yet youth justice remained steeped in risk-factor prevention. The Edinburgh Study of Youth Transitions and Crime challenged this by finding that mere involvement with the youth justice system was criminogenic (McAra and McVie, 2007), so increasing contact for children (cf. the Scaled Approach, 2009[3]) to provide a more comprehensive response could be counterproductive at best and actively damaging at worst.

Desistance within the adult sector has been categorised into stages (primary, secondary and tertiary, discussed earlier in this book; see Maruna and Farrall, 2004). Despite a paucity of research looking into the meaningful application of desistance principles to *children* (some had looked at young adults, who arguably share some similar characteristics with children; see Bottoms et al, 2004), such principles began to be applied into practice but initially with little critique. In fact, using adult-centric interventions with children has not been particularly successful: for example, using Good Lives with adolescents showed 'mixed results' (Mallion et al, 2020, p 5), possibly because drivers for offending in children did not equate with the same 'primary goods' as adults, adolescence being characterised (differently from adults) by 'impulsivity, emotional turmoil, and the development of relationships independent of parents' (Mallion et al, 2020, p 6). This highlights that children are not 'mini adults', and therefore what applies to adults cannot be transferred wholesale to children (Haines and Case, 2015).

Children's offending appears to differ significantly from adults', first because the life stage of childhood brings with it limitations in terms of the power and (allowed) ability to have agency over their own lives (Martin et al, 2018). Children are often dominated by adult decisions, leaving them little scope for making choices towards their own desistance (for example, not having the freedom of choice concerning education options, living space/location and legally limited agency, such as the power to vote or give sexual consent), and this is especially true in youth justice spaces (Daly and Rap, 2018; Smithson and Jones, 2021). Children are also likely to be offered less agency within organisations, for example what they might like to study at school or college, often being forced to fit in with what is available rather than what they would actually like to do (Case and Hazel, 2020). Adults could be seen as having much more agency – even though this is sometimes constrained – as they are more likely to be able to make their own choices, so children's agency, being compromised by adult-centric processes, cannot be seen as equivalent.

Children are rarely committed to an offending lifestyle (although it should be acknowledged that some children do self-identify as 'criminal', especially those who have experienced incarceration as a result of their offending, but nevertheless identify *positive* interventions as more effective in changing this than anything looking backwards at previous offending behaviour; see Day et al, 2020); rather, they have been characterised as drifting in and out of criminal activity as an adolescent, naturally desisting into adulthood (Matza, 1964; Moffitt, 1993), although more recent research has perhaps developed a more nuanced understanding of the place of 'drift' as also applying to those involved in more frequent offending, who still waver day to day in their offending behaviour (Barry, 2006). If adult desistance is characterised by transforming an established offender identity to a *new* non-offending personal narrative/identity (Maruna, 2001; Farrall, 2005), then the fact that children may not (and may *never*, according to life-course theory; Moffitt, 1993) have established 'offending identities' possibly means that this process may not necessarily apply to them. Children who offend (which, for many people, is a normal part of growing up) are much more likely to desist because of pro-social development and maturity. However, this apparently natural process is not simple, given that trauma affects brain development and maturation processes (as do developmental delays and disorders, all of which characterise justice-involved children) (ADCS/AYM/LGA, 2021). Natural maturation out of offending cannot therefore be assumed, either within specific age-ranges (desistance may not occur during childhood), or even sometimes at all. Youth justice practitioners therefore potentially have a role in promoting pro-social development *as a means towards desistance*. Research has identified that practitioners working positively with children's strengths, facilitating children in developing personal goals, all within the context of a supportive relationship, positively impact desistance from crime *as a by-product* of working towards pro-social aims, rather than the negative[4] focus of stopping offending (Fitzpatrick et al, 2015; Johns et al, 2017; Hampson, 2018; Deakin et al, 2022).

The principle of Child First justice, now adopted by the Youth Justice Board (YJB)[5] as its 'strategic approach and central guiding principle' (YJB, 2021, p 10), helpfully situates pro-social development within its four 'tenets',[6] seeing this resulting from a strengths-based *positive* approach to interventions, embedded in supportive relationships (Case and Browning, 2021). Although Good Lives did not translate well to children, its positive focus on sought-after goals is echoed here, now more appropriately applied, through Child First justice, to *children*. The stage has been set therefore for 'desistance' approaches – turning away from offending as a function of assisted pro-social development – to be applied to youth justice. However, as an approach, its adoption has not been smooth or linear, with confounding complications causing confusion for practitioners.

Confounders of youth justice 'desistance' approaches in practice

The development of 'desistance' approaches to youth justice has not been simple, clear or undisputed, beginning from adult-oriented research (identity/ personal narrative shift), slowly developing through critical commentaries into something more child-oriented. This conceptual journey has muddied the waters for practice, resulting in confusion (as later practitioner experiences will demonstrate). This section will explore sources of confusion originating from the YJB (conceptualisation, communication, systems, training) and the inspectorate (conceptualisation and inspection criteria, both within desistance-themed and ordinary inspections).

Communication, AssetPlus and training

To facilitate a shift from risk-focus towards a desistance-focused strengths-based approach (eventually encompassing pro-social development), the YJB developed a new assessment and planning framework – AssetPlus.[7] AssetPlus rejected previous actuarial approaches to assessing 'risk of reoffending' but ironically replaced this with an equivalent – YOGRS (youth version of the adult- and offender-focused Offender Group Reconviction Scale), which still predicted reoffending through quantification (YJB, nd), thus maintaining a risk focus (in both approach and language; Cattell and Aghajani, 2022).

AssetPlus adopted 'desistance' language, but its accompanying guidance used an adult-centric explanation – 'ceasing and refraining from offending or other antisocial behaviour among those for whom offending had become a pattern of behaviour' (YJB, 2014a, p 1), largely based on McNeill et al's (2012) opening definition, not originally specifically applied to children (and ignoring the finer aspects of conceptualisation discussed later). The inclusion of 'pattern of behaviour' is problematic for children in negating the idea of 'drift', discussed earlier. This immediately created conceptualisation issues for youth offending teams (YOTs).[8]

AssetPlus introduced a new section capturing 'factors for desistance' and 'factors against desistance'; however, this seems to have been a 'bolt-on' to what was still basically risk-dominated – at best incorporating positive factors, at worst contradictory to its core (Hampson, 2018). This possibly resulted either from lack of clarity (or questioning) around applying 'desistance' to children, or a reluctance to leave 'risk' behind; but it caused significant confusion for practitioners (Hampson, 2018). Illustrative of this is the negative phrasing of two of the five intervention plan areas ('not offending', 'not hurting others'; YJB, 2014b, p 18). This reverts systemic goals to the negative aim of stopping children offending, rather than seeing offending cessation as resulting from positive pro-social development, the setting and attainment of (positive) goals and strong relationship building – the latter being in keeping with Child First justice, the former a reversion to negative risk-based foci.

Adding to this confusion, training for AssetPlus was provided on a 'train the trainer' basis, where a couple of staff members received initial training and then cascaded learning to staff (Picken et al, 2019a). Not surprisingly, this approach to instigating an entirely new way of thinking – positive strengths-based as opposed to risk dominance – was limited in its success, potentially resulting in misunderstandings being perpetuated, with staff trainers ill-equipped to answer queries and questions. Only 29 per cent of those interviewed for the AssetPlus process evaluation were trained by someone outside their organisation on '[c]oncepts underlying AssetPlus (including desistance and the good lives model)' (Picken et al, 2019b, p 27), reflecting the lack of direct contact between practitioners and qualified trainers. As this figure also included additional online training materials, it is probably an *over*estimation of those receiving the initial training; but since all YOT workers were required to complete a desistance theory module on the Youth Justice Interactive Learning System,[9] this figure should have been 100 per cent. More than half of those interviewed for that evaluation deemed their initial AssetPlus training 'inadequate' (Picken et al, 2019a, p 43).

This was echoed in the desistance thematic inspection of YOTs, which criticised the training programme, citing the lack of understanding demonstrated by case managers (HMIP, 2016). It should be noted, however, that the process evaluation (possibly inadvertently) underlined the risk focus still evident within AssetPlus, with rating questions such as: 'AssetPlus helps me to make useful intervention plans for children who are at risk of offending' (Picken et al, 2019a, p 46). Conversely, 64 per cent of practitioners interviewed could see that AssetPlus helps them focus on 'strengths and other desistance factors' (Picken et al, 2019a, p 47) – some recognition of the changing emphasis, even if 'risk' still seems dominant.

It is unfortunate, and possibly a missed opportunity, that this process evaluation did not ascertain whether practitioners properly understood the underlying ... concepts (by asking them to define those concepts, which could have highlighted misconceptions) of underlying desistance and strengths-based concepts (as applicable to children); rather, it concentrated on technical issues like whether computer programs were 'pulling through' information and custody connectivity. Such issues are far more easily addressed than understanding of conceptual intricacies. However, the current author's own research into understanding of desistance (emphases on positive, strength-based approaches) showed this to be poorly reflected in AssetPlus assessments, as practitioners appeared to have used it similarly to Asset (the previous system, which did not facilitate desistance theory), resorting to what they know rather than developing different practice, due to insufficient retraining after more than 20 years of risk-focus (Hampson, 2018).

Inspectorate thematic inspection/s shaping practice?

The inspectorate in charge of youth justice-related inspections is HM Inspectorate of Probation (HMIP), which, alongside adult-focused functions in probation, covers routine periodic YOT inspections, alongside specific thematic ones (child custody sites[10] are mainly inspected by HM Inspectorate of Prisons). In 2016, HMIP published their first desistance thematic inspection report for justice-involved children, significant in both the gathering momentum of desistance approaches in youth justice and confusion over the concept's application to children. It begins with the same adult-centric definitional emphasis on movement from a 'sustained pattern of offending', again taken from an adult-centric source (Maruna, 2001), without questioning this for *children's* offending (HMIP, 2016, p 4). Ironically, it swiftly acknowledged the paucity of child-centric research on desistance, without appearing to apply this to the – sometimes adult-centric – research-backed desistance themes against which it then measured YOT performance, declaring it 'not sufficiently effective' (HMIP, 2016, p 4).

Helpfully, themes emphasised by HMIP (2016) included the importance of building good relationships, collaboration, addressing structural barriers, creation of opportunities and building self-worth. Unhelpfully, they also included restorative justice, which is contested in its use with children (see Suzuki and Wood, 2018); rational choice (as a source of desistance theory, but problematic in terms of whether children really have unfettered choice in the same way that – some – adults do); reference to 'cognitive transformation', which assumes an offending identity 'transformed' to a non-offending one; and lack of explicit emphasis on positive strengths-based working (HMIP, 2016). This therefore created confusion over what 'desistance' for children should look like, also not reflecting YJB communications, with their emphasis on positive strengths-based working (YJB, nd). It would have been helpful had the YJB and HMIP collaborated in conceptualising desistance, but this reflects a wider lack of congruence between these two agencies (with their different functions and origins, HMIP being an adult-oriented agency) which contributes to a more generalised divergence of approach.

While HMIP may have judged 'desistance' important enough for a thematic inspection, general practice did not seem impacted, as subsequent routine YOT inspections all remained risk-focused, barely mentioning desistance, surely perpetuating mixed messages (Hampson, 2018). HMIP changed inspection criteria to better reflect desistance (HMIP, 2018), but although this could have been an opportunity to completely turn away from risk thinking/practice, it became an awkward blend of both, sometimes resulting in YOTs otherwise praised for positive and supportive work with children being rated inadequate because of HMIP's emphasis on risk (see HMIP, 2019). Since then, HMIP has again reworked their inspection framework, inching towards better terminology (HMIP, 2021) but still clearly (and explicitly) based on risk–needs–responsivity (RNR)[11] through their 'ASPIRE' model[12] (HMIP, 2020a, p 46).

This was emphasised further within an HMIP 'academic insight' paper – 'Risk and desistance: a blended approach to risk management' (Kemshall, 2021). Although the disclaimer states that academic insights do not necessarily reflect inspectorate views, this chimes with their risk *and* desistance 'blended' approach and reads like a justification. The paper does not specifically focus on children, but some cited research is based on 'young offenders', which brings a heavy implication of application to justice-involved children (Kemshall, 2021). This approach is perhaps inevitable from an adult-focused inspectorate (HMIP is responsible for probation inspections, issues of which were clearly identified by one YOT practitioner in conversation with the researcher – "they came along with their probation hats on and saw it as risk taking with risky offenders, rather than being child friendly"), which questions whether this is appropriate, when perhaps a child-focused inspectorate might be better (like Ofsted/Estyn).

Indicating some optimism for potential change is a more recent joint statement issued by the HMIP and the YJB (HMIP, 2022). Although risk still dominates, being mentioned first ('advocate actions to reduce a risk of harm'), it concedes that language used in relation to children should change: 'better worded as ensuring safety and wellbeing of all'. If HMIP and the YJB are at last working together (as recommended by Peer Power; Peer Power/YJB, 2021), then incorporating *child-appropriate* desistance approaches into practice is more likely to succeed. However, there is a looming threat in the potentially negative repercussions of the Police, Crime, Sentencing and Courts Act 2022, which is not only a 'missed opportunity for youth justice' (YJLC, 2022) but also challenges current directions, with child custody predicted to 'more than double by September 2024'[13] (NAO, 2022, p 6). Nowhere within government rhetoric on youth justice can 'Child First' or strengths-based working be found, indicating the worrying possibility that current trajectories could radically change.

The development of appropriate desistance-based approaches for youth justice has clearly been nonlinear – confused, confusing, at times contradictory. The impact of this chequered transition (still underway) has been felt by practitioners in their experience and understanding, as will now be discussed.

Findings from desistance training discussions, feedback and evaluation

The process evaluation commented that several YOTs had brought in training to bolster original YJB AssetPlus training (Picken et al, 2019). The author of this chapter provided more in-depth training on the underlying concepts of applying 'desistance' to youth justice to most of the YOTs in Wales from 2015, and with additional top-ups since. Data from evaluations of that training (Hampson, 2018) as well as conversations held more recently with practitioners and practitioner group discussions (Hampson, 2023) provided insight into understandings of 'desistance' in youth justice practice and the barriers encountered in its development.

Practitioners generally welcome this change

The principle of building towards pro-social development through positive, strengths- and relationship-based approaches was almost universally celebrated by practitioners ("I was looking forward to this training as it sings from my hymn sheet"; "Very refreshing to hear that practitioners are now being taught this way"). Interestingly, potentially giving reason for optimism, recent training evaluations saw 'desistance' as fitting with other sector changes, indicating a general direction of travel, with one practitioner commenting: "It sits very well alongside other major training initiatives of the last couple of years ... where emphasis is on building high-quality relationships with young people and focusing more on the constructive qualities of their lives."

One practitioner, talking in 2021, articulated the benefits and importance of working in this way with children:

'I think we are moving towards a more strength-based way of practising which I firmly am an advocate for, that you find something the kid likes, you find the strengths ... they're good at woodwork, they're good at this, they're good at that – grab it and go, because actually a lot of the kids suffer from low self-esteem, anxiety and they don't want to be sitting there discussing all the things they've done wrong and all bad that's happened, because they get that from school, from parents … they want opportunity, they want positivity, so give it to them! That's how you build the relationship with them.'

As the quote illustrates, justice-involved children have disproportionately negative educational experiences and exposure to adversity. Positive working was seen as especially important, given levels of trauma in the children ("Healing the brain by doing positive activities so they're not in fight flight all the time"), recognising the need to consciously build children's confidence and self-esteem and create safe environments.

Practitioners noted (and welcomed) that this approach requires an entirely new way of thinking about, and working with, children, commenting: "change of looking at things from risk"; "different way of thinking"; "totally different approach"; but they could see difficulties in its outworking, both in terms of the children – "desistance is a journey and we may not see it within yp's [young person's] time at YOS" – and what the 'system' might allow: "The need to move away from negativity highlighted – we all know this but how to put this into practice to satisfy management levels/employers, courts not clear."

Practitioners felt poorly trained

Originally, after practitioners were assumed to have completed a Youth Justice Interactive Learning Space module on 'desistance', they received internal cascaded training from the centralised programme; almost half identified themselves as having a poor or fairly poor understanding, with one practitioner commenting that their knowledge was 'not good enough for me to work confidently enough'. The drawbacks of the initial training were not because the issues are necessarily difficult or even that they met with resistance – since evaluations from subsequent training (Hampson, 2023) showed improved generalised knowledge about desistance, with most attendees initially describing themselves as 'somewhat familiar' with the concept – but post-training saw all attendees describe their knowledge as very familiar, showing that there is still room for improvement.

Practitioners find AssetPlus challenging

A consistent theme, echoed within both the process evaluation (Piken et al, 2019aPiken et al, 2019a) and the later outcome evaluation of AssetPlus (Cattell and Aghajani, 2022), was that completing assessments is extremely time-consuming (AssetPlus was described by one practitioner as a "massive monster"), allowing little opportunity for practitioners, already pressed, to apply newly acquired 'desistance' understanding, as one fed back: "AssetPlus is such an energy sapping thing … to approach differently, some exhaustion with the task of AssetPlus has usually already set in."

Other practitioners saw the lengthiness of AssetPlus as directly impacting on the amount of face-to-face work which they could achieve with children: "It just means that the case holder's got more work beforehand and less time with the kids … you seem to be spending hours and hours and hours more at your computer, and you see half a dozen kids half an hour each a week"; "The amount of paperwork that needs to be done and the time it takes away from actually working with these kids is ridiculous." This perception of increased time spent on AssetPlus was also reflected in the outcome evaluation, which also noted that time taken to complete AssetPlus has increased rather than decreased as practitioners got used to the new format (Cattell and Aghajani, 2022).

Others also expressed the frustration that AssetPlus did not seem to naturally fit desistance approaches well: "Not got much desire to spend even more time grappling with AssetPlus and trying to get it to do something it's not very well set up to do"; "AssetPlus is a barrier rather than aid to working with children/young people."

AssetPlus includes a self-assessment for the child, but practitioners were very dismissive of this, finding it extremely difficult timewise ("we're supposed to get them in and have them inform the plan, but … you don't have time to involve them"), but also finding the design of the child's input into AssetPlus extremely un-child friendly:

> 'The self-assessment forms are just shocking. They're not child friendly are they? Yes … they're asking questions directly to the child, but they're not laid out in the most child friendly way … I asked a young person to complete one the other day, and I helped him to complete it and the look on his face when he realised it was front and back four pages.'

A defence for AssetPlus was offered by the then Head of YJB Cymru, who commented: 'People deliver outcomes, not systems. Aim is AssetPlus facilitates' (Kennedy, 2016, cited in Hampson, 2018). This might be true, but if the system actively confounds rather than facilitates, then it becomes a problem requiring a solution.

Practitioners worry about organisational and systemic barriers

Practitioners were keenly aware that they work within both internal YOT management systems and report gatekeeping, and wider systems including the police and courts. These could be seen as resisters or enablers to new 'desistance' practice.

There were concerns about the need for management to 'get' it ("it will take time and practice and good understanding/guidance from managers"; "Wholesale shift of YOT statutory practice, change of plans, needs to be passed up to managers"), but seeing its influence peter out up the management levels ("I would like to see this approach used more by higher management"). Some practitioners have experienced managerial blocking of these developments, being much more likely to remain risk-focused ("me and my boss clash on this because she is very risk, everything's addressed by risk"). This reluctance could be due to concerns about defensible decision-making and the fear they could be criticised for not adequately assessing risk, especially as the inspectorate appears to still privilege risk in their assessment of practice (HMIP, 2020a). However, others experienced management which has actively facilitated this: "[S]he [the manager] really does drive new practices and considering she's trained as a probation officer so would have been trained in a very different way. She really champions the approach." This approach will only be possible and sustainable if those in management positions truly understand it and therefore sympathetically gatekeep desistance-friendly reports and plans.

However, beyond YOT organisation, other agencies can also either facilitate or inhibit this development. Staff appear to have had mixed experiences of both courts and police. The police are possibly perceived as being naturally offence-focused ("I do find sometimes the police struggle with that, especially if they've been around a long, long time ... they are trained to deal with offenders and to ... stop them from committing offences. So sometimes there's a clash of culture"); in the practitioner discussion group, concerns were raised that the local inspector expected offence-focused work in community resolutions, indicating lack of understanding. However, others could see that the police are encompassing new ways of working ("I think the 'lock them up took away the key' mob is gone now"). Hopefully this will continue to develop, as the current national strategy ('Child centred policing') proposes as a 'key principle': 'Engagement should be positive and opportunities sought to enhance our relationship with them' (NPCC, 2015, p 8).

Some practitioners expressed concern over whether courts and magistrates were going to be similarly trained, seeing an issue with desistance-friendly court reports if not. One practitioner related a particularly difficult encounter:

'I would say back two years ago we had a young person come in, extremely low cognitive ability. He'd offended quite a few times. Major concerns about exploitation and when he was in court, he's got very low ability on communicating, so if somebody's speaking to him ...

he needed time to process before he'd come up with an answer ... I'd put all that in the report and yet they stood in front of him, he's got his hands in his pockets, head down ... "you should be ashamed, your parents are disgusted with you" and really gave him what-for ... I was thinking, what have I spent three weeks writing or two weeks writing? 17 pages of PSR [pre-sentence report]. Read it, please ... because he doesn't understand what you're saying ... and you've lost him ... and because he didn't respond properly they gave him a harsher order.'

However, the same practitioner also related the solution, as magistrate training was subsequently provided resulting in very positive responses to their desistance-focused court reports. Another practitioner also described good communicative relationships between the YOT and courts, recalling a joint working party (including magistrates) around making courts more child friendly:

'She's [YOT manager] really, really good at linking in with magistrates and making sure they're getting trained and being kept up to date ... you've still got your grey-haired men and women magistrates who still want to lock them up. I think, as DJs [district judges] retire that that would always say "I'm going to send you to prison if you turn up again in front of me"; they've sort of gone out to grass and I think things are progressing.'

This shows that while such concerns are real and can be detrimental to the treatment of justice-involved children, progress is being made, with training as key.

Practitioners are concerned about lack of time and funding

Child-appropriate desistance working pivots on staff being able to build strong, supportive relationships with children (Wigzell, 2021). However, *lack* of time to do this was almost universally highlighted by practitioners: "We usually have about a month or so to get the AssetPlus done before they go to the Referral Order Panel to start the work with him ... to build a relationship it's difficult to get to know anyone in the first month"; "Time is a barrier because if you've only got somebody for ... a three-month order, it takes a lot of time to build up that relationship."

Other time limitations were also identified ("we've got these young people coming through that need quite intensive support and we haven't got the time to give it to them"). This is compounded by the lengthy AssetPlus process.

Several practitioners identified lack of funding as problematic, especially since creative positive interventions might be more expensive than static meetings in an office. The practitioner discussion group noted that available activities were boring, where they used to be adventurous and fun. Another practitioner commented:

'There just aren't the resources out there to do the stuff. ... I want to take a kid out mountain biking ... we had the summer arts through the summer, we've got Activ8 where they go doing the climbing wall, mountain biking, all sorts of arty stuff. It's all just come to a grinding halt.'

What are the solutions going forwards?

Solutions to some of the issues, like funding and time, are simple – more money and emphasis on relationship building – but not easy to facilitate, especially in the current, post-COVID-19 financial crisis (exacerbated by the effects of the Ukrainian–Russian war and the cost-of-living crisis). Good-quality, on point training is needed for all involved with youth justice (every agency and at every level) to ensure that understanding coalesces around aspects of desistance appropriate for children (in line with Child First justice). Unitas, the YJB's preferred training provider, has given cause for concern since some of its training modules are not desistance-oriented, which could potentially cause further confusion through mixed messaging of older modules being much more risk-focused (Hampson, 2023). Practitioners who have accessed Unitas materials have detected a risk flavour in much of it ("there's a lot about the risks and the strengths came second I would probably say"; "a lot of it is to do with managerialism and the 'what works'"). However, one practitioner was able to say, having received Unitas training and reflected upon it:

'I was able to ... see that maybe I was focusing too much on risk, and maybe that was a barrier to engagement, where I'm just like focusing on negatives. But if I focus on the positives and build a relationship with the young person ... that can help improve engagement moving forward.'

It is worth noting, therefore, that while there is inconsistency in what Unitas have provided, some of their newer material is much more focused on desistance-friendly content, for example their modules on Child First justice, relationship-based working and one specifically on desistance (Youth Justice Institute, 2023).

AssetPlus appears to be causing practitioners difficulties in terms of its length and ability to facilitate child-appropriate desistance approaches. While this also should be reviewed, local action can mitigate some of the issues, as one practitioner described: "[T]he AssetPlus intervention plan wasn't particularly child friendly so ... all practitioners came together and we devised one that we could sit with the young person and they would put their bits on there, what they wanted, so it was very child friendly." Applying good-quality knowledge of what makes for child-appropriate desistance approaches also equips practitioners to be able to use AssetPlus to facilitate rather than hinder. This also requires good buy-in from well-trained managers (and management boards). However, YOT case management guidance has now been updated to better incorporate Child First principles, also reflecting the shift from risk-focused to strengths-based approaches with an emphasis on good relationship building, which should in time help managers make this shift themselves (YJB, 2022).

Conclusion

Applying 'desistance' and related terminology to youth justice is not without its pitfalls: definitional confusion has arisen from different conceptualisations (HMIP, YJB, YOTs, Unitas) and poorly designed training packages. This has led to confusion for practitioners and delays in building a system which truly encourages positive pro-social development through strength-based working and the building of strong and supportive relationships – seeing *desistance* (cessation of offending) as a natural outcome of these rather than an explicit (negative) goal (to 'prevent offending' having been the YJB's focus since its inception through the Crime and Disorder Act 1998). However, the trajectory appears to be *towards* a more positive relationship-based system, with developments within YJB case management guidance, HMIP inspection criteria and training on desistance (and related areas, like Child First justice and trauma-informed working) all reinforcing this. To truly cement this in practice, good-quality training based on a centrally agreed understanding of how desistance can be applied to children needs to be provided at all levels both within YOTs *and* partner agencies. Systems (HMIP inspection criteria and any YJB-mandated assessment and planning framework – currently AssetPlus) need to also be congruent with this shared understanding so *all* build together towards an understanding of desistance as being facilitated by encouraging positive pro-social development.

However, the YJB should be mindful of potential threats which might lead back towards an offender/offence-focus. Time will tell what effect the Police, Crime, Sentencing and Courts Act 2022 (indicative of an increasingly punitive approach to justice by the Conservative Government of the time, which has not acknowledged any of the Child First developments) will have and whether the current financial crisis will result in youth justice funding cuts, which are likely to create further bumps in the road towards a truly positive-facing youth justice system for England and Wales.

Notes

[1] Youth justice practitioners are professionals (from a variety of backgrounds, like social work, education, probation, health) working directly with children either in the youth justice system, or deemed potentially likely to be, providing one-to-one support.

[2] These courses for people on probation ask them to look at their 'new me' (non-offending) future, what that might look like and what the motivations might be, in order to understand the issues for their 'old me' (when they were offending) to strengthen desistance in the future.

[3] The Scaled Approach closely tethered the amount of contact a child had with the youth justice system to their assessed risk factors, so those with a higher level of assessed risk were required to attend more often (YJB, 2010).

[4] 'Desistance' could be argued to be an unhelpful term for children as it is essentially focusing on *stopping* something, rather than the positive approach of looking towards more pro-social development, relationships, activities and goals.

[5] The YJB is the non-departmental agency with overall responsibility for youth justice practice in England and Wales, put in place by the Crime and Disorder Act 1998.

[6] The four Child First tenets are: seeing children as children, developing pro-social identity for positive child outcomes, collaboration and promotion of diversion (Case and Browning, 2021).

[7] AssetPlus was piloted in 2014 (rolled out from 2015) to replace the previous case management system – Asset, which was entirely focused on risk (and to an extent, protective) factors, culminating in an additive number presenting the 'risk of reoffending', which in turn, with the Scaled Approach, dictated frequency of contact.

[8] YOTs work directly with justice-involved children to support them both statutorily (through court orders) and voluntarily (for example, when a child is given a Youth Caution).

[9] Youth Justice Interactive Learning System was the YJB's method of online training delivery to practitioners within the YOTs, now accessed through the Youth Justice Resource Hub. However, training has now generally been transferred to the YJB's preferred provider, Unitas, through its 'Youth Justice Institute' (https://youthjusticeinstitute.co.uk).

[10] There are three different types of child custody – Young Offender Institutions (YOI) for non-vulnerable boys aged 15–18, Secure Training Centres (STC) for younger/ somewhat more vulnerable boys and girls and Secure Children's Homes (SCH) for the most vulnerable/youngest children. YOIs and STCs are inspected by HMI Prisons, but SCHs (run by local authorities) are inspected by Ofsed/Estyn.

[11] RNR is an adult-centric model-base bringing more flexibility and consideration of the individual into probation work (HMIP, 2020b) but still ostensibly based on risk, so it can at best be seen as a modified version of the previous risk factor prevention paradigm.

[12] ASPIRE stands for Assessment, Sentence Planning, Implementation, Review and Evaluation (HMIP, 2020a, p 46).

[13] While some improvements are proposed under this Act, for instance a more rigorous process for custodial remand (which might reduce it), other aspects are likely to *increase* numbers of children in custody, for instance by allowing courts more freedom in amount of time given, changing automatic release for some offences from half-way to two thirds through the sentence, increases to custodial sentence lengths for weapons offences (despite the fact that most weapons offences for children are possession, not use).

References

ADCS/AYM/LGA (2021) 'A youth justice system that works for children', Available from: https://adcs.org.uk/assets/documentation/ADCS_AYM_ LGA_A_Youth_Justice_System_that_Works_for_Children_FINALx.pdf

Barry, M. (2006) *Youth Offending in Transition: The Search for Social Recognition*, Abingdon: Routledge.

Bottoms, A., Shapland, J., Costello, A., Holmes, D. and Muir, G. (2004) 'Towards desistance: theoretical underpinnings for an empirical study', *The Howard Journal of Crime and Justice*, 43(4): 368–89.

Case, S. and Hazel, N. (2020) 'Child First, offender second: a progressive model for education in custody', *International Journal of Educational Development*, 77: 102244.

Case, S. and Browning, A. (2021) 'Child First justice: the research evidence-base', Available from: https://repository.lboro.ac.uk/ndownloader/files/26748341/1

Cattell, J. and Aghajani, K. (2022) 'AssetPlus outcome evaluation', Youth Justice Board, Available from: https://assets.publishing.service.gov.uk/government/uploads/system/uploads/attachment_data/file/1079447/AssetPlus_Outcome_Evaluation.pdf

Daly, A. and Rap, S. (2018) 'Children's participation in youth justice and civil court proceedings', in U. Kilkelly and T. Liefaard (eds) *International Human Rights of Children*, Singapore: Springer, pp 299–320.

Day, A., Bateman, T. and Pitts, J. (2020) 'Surviving incarceration: the pathways of looked after and non-looked after children into, through and out of custody', Available from: https://uobrep.openrepository.com/bitstream/handle/10547/623926/Survivingincarcerationfinal.pdf?sequence=3&isAllowed=y

Deakin, J., Fox, C. and Harragan, A. (2022) 'Help or hindrance? Rethinking interventions with "troubled youth"', *International Journal of Law in Context*, 18(1): 100–15.

Farrall, S. (2005) 'On the existential aspects of desistance from crime', *Symbolic Interaction*, 28(3): 367–86.

Fitzpatrick, E., McGuire, J. and Dickson, J. (2015) 'Personal goals of adolescents in a youth offending service in the United Kingdom', *Youth Justice*, 15(2): 166–81.

Haines, K. and Case, S. (2015) 'An alternative model of positive youth justice', Centre for Crime and Justice Studies blog, Available from: https://www.crimeandjustice.org.uk/resources/alternative-model-positive-youth-justice

Hampson, K. (2018) 'Desistance approaches in youth justice: the next passing fad or a sea-change for the positive?', *Youth Justice*, 18(1): 18–33.

Hampson, K. (2023) 'Cementing Child First in practice', in S. Case and N. Hazel (eds) *Child First: Developing a New Youth Justice System*, New York: Springer, pp 301–31.

HMIP (2016) 'Desistance and young people', Available from: www.justiceinspectorates.gov.uk/hmiprobation/wp-content/uploads/sites/5/2016/05/Desistance_and_young_people.pdf

HMIP (2018) 'Standards for inspecting youth offending services', Available from: www.justiceinspectorates.gov.uk/hmiprobation/wp-content/uplo ads/sites/5/2018/04/Youth-offending-standards-March-18-final.pdf

HMIP (2019) 'An inspection of youth offending services in Leeds', Available from: https://www.justiceinspectorates.gov.uk/hmiprobation/inspecti ons/leeds/

HMIP (2020a) 'Annual report: inspection of youth offending services (2019–2020)', Available from: www.justiceinspectorates.gov.uk/hmiprobat ion/wp-content/uploads/sites/5/2020/11/HMI-Probation-Youth-Ann ual-Report-2020.pdf

HMIP (2020b) 'The risk–need–responsivity model', Available from: www. justiceinspectorates.gov.uk/hmiprobation/research/the-evidence-base- probation/models-and-principles/the-rnr-model

HMIP (2021) 'Youth offending inspection: external guidance manual', Available from: www.justiceinspectorates.gov.uk/hmiprobation/wp-cont ent/uploads/sites/5/2021/05/Youth-Guidance-Manual-External-v5.2- May-2021.pdf

HMIP (2022) 'Joint statement from HM Inspectorate of Probation and the Youth Justice Board', Available from: https://www.justiceinspectorates. gov.uk/hmiprobation/media/press-releases/2022/03/hmipyjbstatement/

Johns, D., Williams, K. and Haines, K. (2017) 'Ecological youth justice: understanding the social ecology of young people's prolific offending', *Youth Justice*, 17(1): 3–21.

Kemshall, H. (2021) 'Risk and desistance: a blended approach to risk management', HMIP academic insights 2021/07, Available from: www. justiceinspectorates.gov.uk/hmiprobation/wp-content/uploads/sites/5/ 2021/06/Academic-Insights-Kemshall.pdf

Kennedy, D. (2016) Twitter message, 1 July, Available at: https://twitter.com

Laub, J.H. and Sampson, R.J. (2001) 'Understanding desistance from crime', *Crime and Justice*, 28: 1–69.

LeBlanc, M., and Loeber R. (1993) 'Precursors, causes, and the development of criminal offending,' in D.F. Hay and A. Angold (eds) *Precursors and Causes in Development and Psychopathology*, New York: Wiley, pp 233–263.

Mallion J.S., Wood J.L. and Mallion A. (2020) 'Systematic review of "Good Lives" assumptions and interventions', *Aggression and Violent Behavior*, 55: 101510.

Martin, S., Forde, C., Horgan, D. and Mages, L. (2018) 'Decision-making by children and young people in the home: the nurture of trust, participation and independence', *Journal of Child and Family Studies*, 27(1): 198–210.

Maruna, S. (2001) *Making Good: How Ex-convicts Reform and Rebuild Their Lives*, Washington, DC: American Psychological Association.

Maruna, S. and Farrall, S. (2004) 'Desistance from crime: a theoretical reformulation', *Kolner Zeitschrift für Soziologie und Sozialpsychologie*, 43: 171–94.

Matza, D. (1964) *Delinquency and Drift*, New York: Wiley.

McAra, L. and McVie, S. (2007) 'Youth justice? The impact of system contact on patterns of desistance from offending', *European Journal of Criminology*, 4(3): 315–45.

McMahon, G. and Jump, D. (2018) 'Starting to stop: young offenders' desistance from crime', *Youth Justice*, 18(1): 3–17.

McNeill, F., Farrall, S., Lightowler, C. and Maruna, S. (2012) 'How and why people stop offending: discovering desistance', IRISS, Available from: www.iriss.org.uk/sites/default/files/iriss-insight-15.pdf

Ministry of Justice (2021) 'Correctional Services Accreditation and Advice Panel (CSAAP) currently accredited programmes', Available from: https://assets.publishing.service.gov.uk/government/uploads/system/uploads/atta chment_data/file/960097/Descriptions_of_Accredited_Programmes_-_Final_-_210209.pdf

Moffitt, T. (1993) 'Adolescence-limited and life-course-persistent antisocial behavior: a developmental taxonomy', *Psychological Review*, 100(4): 674–701.

NAO (2022) 'Children in custody: secure training centres and secure schools', Available from: www.nao.org.uk/wp-content/uploads/2022/04/Children-in-custody-secure-training-centres-and-secure-schools.pdf

NPCC (2015) 'Child centred policing', Available from: npcc.police.uk/documents/edhr/2015/CYP%20Strategy%202015%202017%20August%202015.pdf

Peer Power/YJB (2021) 'Co-creation and participation in practice project', London: Peer Power/YJB, Available from: www.peerpower.org.uk/wp-content/uploads/2021/09/Long-Report-YJB-Design-by-Lizzie-Reid-final-1.pdf

Picken, N., Baker, K., d'Angelo, C., Fays, C., Strang, L. and Sutherland A. (2019a) 'Process evaluation of AssetPlus', RAND, Available from: www.rand.org/content/dam/rand/pubs/research_reports/RR3100/RR3177/RAND_RR3177.pdf

Picken, N., Baker, K., d'Angelo, C., Fays, C. and Sutherland, A. (2019b) 'Process evaluation of AssetPlus: annexes', RAND, Available from: https://assets.publishing.service.gov.uk/government/uploads/system/uploads/atta chment_data/file/853175/AssetPlus_annexes.PDF

Smithson, H. and Jones, A. (2021) 'Co-creating youth justice practice with young people: tackling power dynamics and enabling transformative action', *Children & Society*, 35(3): 348–62.

Suzuki, M. and Wood, W.R. (2018) 'Is restorative justice conferencing appropriate for youth offenders?', *Criminology & Criminal Justice*, 18(4): 450–67.

Ward, T. (2002) 'The management of risk and the design of good lives', *Australian Psychologist*, 37(3): 172–9.

Wigzell, A. (2021) 'Explaining desistance: looking forward, not backwards', NAYJ briefing, Available from: https://thenayj.org.uk/cmsAdmin/uploads/explaining-desistance-briefing-feb-2021-final.pdf

Wong, K. and Horan, R. (2021) 'Needs assessment: risk, desistance and engagement', HMIP Academic Insights, Available from: www.justiceinspectorates.gov.uk/hmiprobation/wp-content/uploads/sites/5/2021/03/Academic-Insights-Needs-assessment-risk-desistance-and-engagement-Wong-and-Horan.pdf

YJB (nd) 'The use of the Youth Offender Group Reconviction Scale (YOGRS) in AssetPlus', Available from: www.whatdotheyknow.com/request/499216/response/1213139/attach/4/FR8445%20YOGRS%20and%20AssetPlus%20fact%20sheet.pdf?cookie_passthrough=1#:~:text=What%20is%20YOGRS%3F,release%20if%20sentenced%20to%20custody

YJB (2010) 'Youth justice: the Scaled Approach', Available from: https://assets.publishing.service.gov.uk/media/5a8c01db40f0b6230269dc85/Youth_Justice_the_Scaled_Approach_-_A_framework_for_assessment_and_interventions.pdf

YJB (2014a) 'Desistance table: supporting guidance', Available from: https://assets.publishing.service.gov.uk/government/uploads/system/uploads/attachment_data/file/381418/EPC6_Desistance_table_Supporting_Guidance_Nov_2014.pdf

YJB (2014b) 'AssetPlus model document', Available from: https://assets.publishing.service.gov.uk/government/uploads/system/uploads/attachment_data/file/364092/AssetPlus_Model_Document_1_1_October_2014.pdf

YJB (2021) 'Strategic plan 2021–2024', Available from: https://assets.publishing.service.gov.uk/government/uploads/system/uploads/attachment_data/file/966200/YJB_Strategic_Plan_2021_-_2024.pdf

YJB (2022) 'Case management guidance', Available from: https://www.gov.uk/guidance/case-management-guidance

YJLC (2022) 'Police, Crime, Sentencing and Courts Act: a missed opportunity for youth justice', Available from: https://yjlc.uk/resources/legal-updates/police-crime-sentencing-and-courts-act-missed-opportunity-youth-justice

Youth Justice Institute (2023) 'Courses', Available from: https://youthjusticeinstitute.co.uk/courses

10

Summer Arts Colleges: using the arts to promote educational engagement and desistance

Martin Stephenson

The belief in the moral and educative benefits of involvement in the arts is long-standing for those in the criminal justice system (Carey, 2005). Participation in the arts has wide-ranging benefits including enhanced educational attainment, increased employability, improved skills in planning and organising and reduced offending behaviour (Jermyn, 2004; Hughes, 2005). This research base, however, has shortcomings (Mowlah et al, 2014), including research with small sample sizes, lack of quantitative evidence and unsupported assumptions about the links between interventions and outcomes (Brice Heath, 2008). Much of the work has focused on custody and has been with adults (McNeill et al, 2011). Additionally, evidence on transferable skills from the arts to other areas of learning is not robust, and the mechanisms are unclear (Detterman, 1996; Winner et al, 2013). From experience, the arts are often viewed as a luxury item in youth justice, with managers and practitioners experiencing challenges in justifying these interventions in terms of fulfilling their statutory objective of preventing offending. This is partly the result of a lack of empirical evidence on positive outcomes and partly an absence of an accepted theory of change concerning desistance.

The Summer Arts College (SAC) programme was a partnership initiative between the Youth Justice Board and Arts Council England designed to increase the low levels of engagement in education by children in the community youth justice system (YJB, 2006). The accompanying research programme was designed in two phases to remedy some of the weaknesses in the arts–youth justice evidence base. The first examined the short- and longer-term educational outcomes and offending from 2007 to 2012 (Stephenson et al, 2014). The second was from 2014 to 2016 and had two important additional features, [which are detailed below].

This chapter considers the impact of arts interventions through the SAC programme on educational engagement, achievement and reoffending in both the short and longer term. After reviewing outcomes, it examines the various influences on desistance, such as the effects of incapacitation and increases in human and social capital. Next, self-efficacy is discussed as a potential mechanism whereby successful participation in this arts programme can positively affect other areas of children's lives. Finally, the chapter considers the implications for practice.

Education and desistance

Educational achievement is one of the most potent predictors of outcomes in adult life (Hobcraft, 2002; Strand, 2021). Success in education may indirectly influence desistance by contributing to high-quality employment but may be equally significant through developing social bonds and attachments to pro-social peer groups (Stevens et al, 2007). In addition, educational success is likely to engender self-confidence and hope, which are also important attributes for desistance (Day et al, 2010; Paterson-Young et al, 2019).

Negative educational experiences have always been and remain commonplace for children in the youth justice system (Stephenson, 2007; DfE and MoJ, 2016; Crosweller et al, 2022; DfE and MoJ, 2022). While a substantial body of evidence highlights the association between detachment from mainstream education and offending by children, there is little evidence demonstrating effective reintegration into education (Hurry et al, 2006; Stephenson, 2007). Despite the limited research, there is evidence that school attendance following custody is linked to a reduction in reoffending (Blomberg et al, 2011).

Accumulating both human and social capital may be particularly important for vulnerable children as a counterbalance to the significant structural barriers they face (Robertson, 2018). Vulnerable children are more likely to need to rely significantly on professional adults, and their abilities to form effective relationships with them will be important. In addition, socially marginalised children may seek to gain social capital by belonging to delinquent peer groups (Barry, 2006; Robertson, 2018).

Although the development of social capital in children in contact with the criminal justice system is under-researched, it appears to be important for healthy socio-psychological development and is predictive of later outcomes in life (Stevens et al, 2007; Klocke and Stadtmuller, 2019). School is a key area for accumulating both human and social capital (Stevens et al, 2007). For example, quantifiable educational outcomes such as gaining a qualification and improving literacy and numeracy are readily identifiable examples of human capital gained from engagement in education. Similarly, cultivating fruitful networks and relationships within schools with teachers and peers helps build social capital (Stevens et al, 2007), which is associated with educational success (Acar, 2011).

SACs

The SAC programme (2007–22) was one of the longest-running initiatives in recent youth justice history (Stephenson et al, 2014). Initial research findings led to significant revisions in the project model, and its implementation and outcomes stimulated further research. Initial findings suggested positive outcomes in terms of educational engagement and progression combined with short- and longer-term reductions in offending. This led to further research that concentrated on how and why such changes occurred in the participants (Stephenson et al, 2019).

SACs ran three-week, full-time, structured arts programmes for children in the community youth justice system during school holidays. They addressed the low level of engagement in education, training or employment (ETE) by offering new and interesting participatory arts and cultural activities. It was hoped these activities would provide unique opportunities to promote engagement in education and training and help children equip themselves with transferable attitudes and skills.

There were two critical aspects of SACs. First, they were intensive, structured, full-time and novel experiences with considerable emphasis on attendance and participation. The aim was to jumpstart a new approach to learning and acquire the necessary routines for future engagement in education. Secondly, the curriculum deliberately focused on participatory arts. The emphasis was not on aesthetic value and correct techniques but on the creative processes employed, completion and reflection.

The Arts Award assessment was based on providing good evidence of planning and reviewing artistic process rather than artistic quality. Art was to be about individual expression, novelty and participation, not passing or failing. The unique feature of participatory arts is their 'no fail' nature compared to, for example, sport. The rationale was that educational careers hitherto characterised by failure and non-completion might benefit from quasi-educational activities that the children could not get wrong and yet still receive formal recognition through an educational qualification and acclaim for success. The language used, however, echoed adult education rather than youth justice: for example, all communication referred to participants as *students* who were attending a *college*.

Theory of change

The SAC programme's theory of change relied heavily on several psychological theories such as the theory of planned behaviour (Ajzen, 2002), goal-setting theory (Locke and Latham, 2002) and social cognitive theory (Bandura, 1997). The programme objectives can be grouped into proximal (immediate intended outcomes directly related to the project experience) and distal (longer-term and more indirect intended outcomes). Re-engagement with ETE and desistance from offending were the distal objectives. It was proposed that these would be achieved via proximal objectives, including the impact on children's socio-cognitive skills, particularly self-efficacy and accompanying changes in attitudes, such as increased motivation for education. Within this causal chain, proximal influences were seen to include changes in literacy levels, numeracy and self-efficacy. The hypothesis was that these changes could lead to re-engagement with education, which would then increase human and social capital and conventional ties that would assist desistance. Figure 10.1 illustrates a theory of change for how participatory

Figure 10.1: Theory of Change

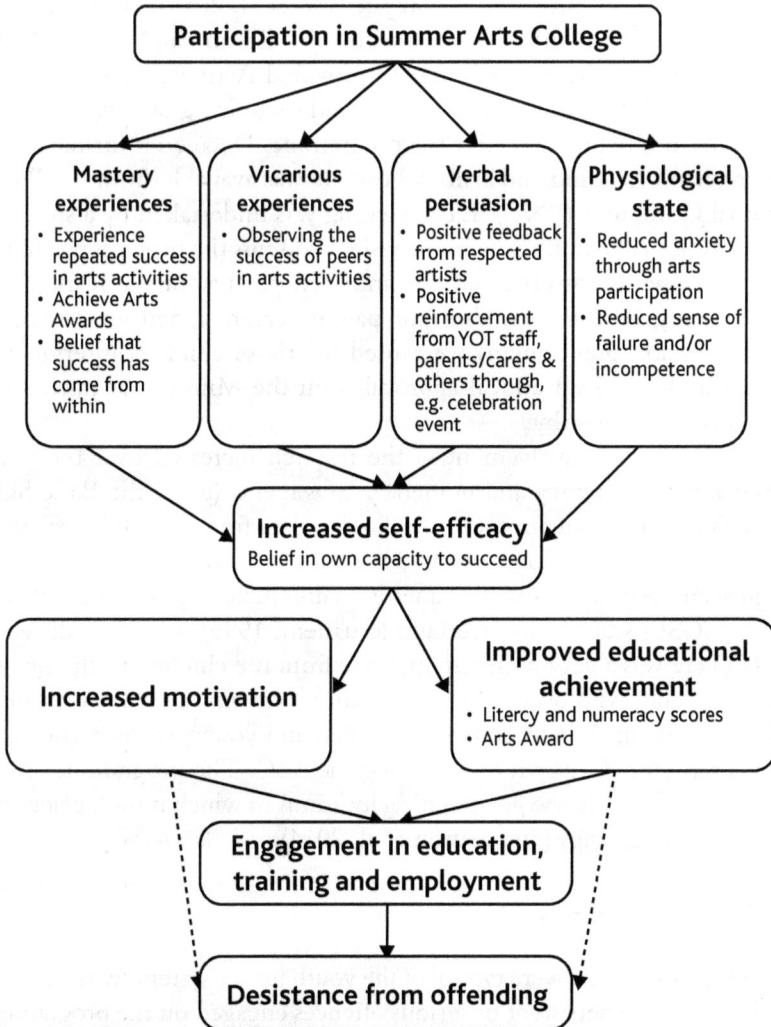

Source: Stephenson et al (2019)

arts via the mechanism of self-efficacy can raise educational achievement and engagement and subsequent desistance.

Research methodology

There were two phases to the research. The first examined the short- and longer-term educational outcomes and offending from 2007 to 2012 (Stephenson et al, 2014). The second was from 2014 to 2016 and had two important additional features. Children's educational engagement was tracked for the 12 months following the programme to parallel the 12-month reconviction analysis. And before and after surveys and questionnaires were introduced to gain insight into any change mechanisms associated with the programme (Stephenson et al, 2019). In total, 2,308 children across 85 youth offending teams (YOTs) in England and Wales were included in the research. YOTs provided Asset data and details of the children's ETE provision, offending and sentencing during the three-month periods before and after the programme. Detailed information on longer-term offending and criminal careers was available from the Police National Computer (PNC). ETE tracking was undertaken by a specialist organisation. YOT staff made home visits to discuss the programme and its research elements with the children and their parents/carers. If informed consent was given, then children and parents/carers signed agreements to participate, and pseudonyms were used for those children interviewed. The research received ethical approval from the Ministry of Justice and the University of Derby.

Children's direct involvement in the research increased over the years. Before and after literacy and numeracy assessments (using the Basic Skills Agency's initial assessment tool) were undertaken from the initiative's start. Exit surveys were used from 2011 to 2013. Pre- and post-programme surveys and pre- and post-psychometric questionnaires including the General Self-Efficacy (GSE) scale (Schwarzer and Jerusalem, 1995) were introduced in 2014. There was a very high response rate from the children to the surveys and assessments, with over 80 per cent of those who finished the programme completing them. In addition, 120 children and young adults participated in semi-structured interviews following the SAC. The programme's scale, longevity and the diverse geographical locations in which it took place lend weight to the findings (Stephenson et al, 2014).

Profile of participants

The SAC participants were typical of the youth justice system, with children involved in more persistent or serious offences engaged on the programme. Most were in their mid-teens and male. While participants' ages ranged from 12 to 19 years, the great majority were between 15 and 17 years old, with an average age of 16.3 years. Males comprised nearly 90 per cent of the children engaged on the programme, and nearly half of the children identified as being from Black and minority ethnic backgrounds.

Their educational disadvantages were high compared to their mainstream peers, with just over half having been in ETE in the three months before the SAC programme. Many experienced disruptions in education, with nearly a quarter having attended three or more primary schools and 41 per cent having attended three or more secondary schools. Exclusions also took their toll, with just over one third receiving multiple permanent exclusions.

Many missed out on an assessment for special educational needs (SEN) due to exclusion and non-attendance. Even so, at least 17 per cent possessed a statement of SEN compared to only 2.8 per cent of the general population (DfE, 2022). By the programme's start, only a quarter had achieved functional literacy (Level 1 – that expected of the average 11-year-old). Given their average age, the great majority were at least five years behind their peers. The situation was even worse for numeracy, where only 13 per cent were assessed at Level 1 at the beginning of the SAC programme. In addition, few qualifications had been achieved, even for older participants past the compulsory school attendance age. Instability and disruption also marred their home lives, with nearly one in three being care experienced, and one in six having experienced homelessness during their secondary school years.

Outcomes

The immediate programme outcomes monitored included programme attendance, programme completion rates, Arts Award achievement, changes in literacy and numeracy levels and short-term offending. This was complemented by the collection and measurement of softer outcomes, such as attitudinal shifts towards the arts and education and changes in self-belief. The longer-term outcomes of educational engagement and offending were also assessed.

Engagement

The SAC programme intended to encourage greater engagement in education from children who had previously experienced challenges in this area. The completion rates were high at 84 per cent compared to other ETE projects for children in the youth justice system, which tend to be between 30 and 50 per cent (Hurry and Moriarty, 2003; Moore et al, 2004). Research has shown that non-completion of programmes is damaging educationally and tends to be associated with increased offending (Palmer et al, 2007). Conversely, completion is an important act, particularly for children whose educational experience has been characterised by failure and non-completion, as the following interview response emphasised:

> 'Just finishing was my main thing. 'Cos sometimes I start summat like that and not finish it, because of bad behaviour or summat. But ... this time I thought, "Just don't say anything and just complete it". So yeah ... that was the best part of it – to me anyway.' (Noah, 14)

Academic achievement

The Arts Award was the keystone for the programme and its associated curriculum. It provided a focal point for both the YOT staff and the artists guiding the day-to-day work and culminated in the celebration event at the end of the SAC, where students received their certificate in front of parents/carers and local authority staff and elected members. The Arts Award was the first qualification 80 per cent of the children had achieved. Despite the shortness of the programme, statistically significant improvements in literacy occurred. Overall, 942 children (70 per cent) increased their literacy score. The numbers of children at Level 1 literacy increased from 283 to 525. The mean literacy score increased from 53.7 pre-programme to 57.5 post-programme (paired sample t-test; $p<0.001$). There were similar improvements in numeracy, with 926 children increasing their score. The mean numeracy score increased from 35.5 to 38.3 ($p<0.001$). The numbers of children at Level 1 numeracy increased from 228 to 416.

Post-programme ETE engagement

There was a significant reduction in the number of children not engaged in ETE in the three months following the programme compared to the three months before. Out of the total of 1,441 children with full ETE records, 772 had not been engaged in ETE in the three months prior to the SAC, and this fell by nearly a quarter to 586 in the three months after the programme ($p < 0.001$).

Offending

Offending was monitored in the short term by comparing offending in the three months prior to the SAC programme, during the programme and in the subsequent three months. There was a one-year reconviction study completed using the data on the PNC. The mean frequency of offending rate during the programme was statistically significantly lower than the frequency rate before the programme ($p < 0.01$; see Stephenson et al, 2014, pp 85–7 for detailed discussion of methodology). The rate after the programme rose but remained significantly lower than pre-programme (p < 0.01). While this decrease in the three-month post-programme period could be a result of regression to the mean (the random fluctuation in the number of offences committed from one time period to the next, for example an extreme number of offences in the first time tends to revert to a more average number subsequently), the significant slump in offending rates during the programme was more likely due to incapacitation effects.

There was a clear inverse relationship between educational engagement levels and offending rates in all periods examined. Those children who had not been engaged in ETE during the pre-programme period but did engage during and after the SAC programme showed significant reductions in reoffending (p < 0.01). Conversely, those whose educational engagement did not change between the pre- and post-periods saw a significant reduction during the programme, but reoffending rates rose in the post-period to rates slightly higher than in the pre-period (p < 0.01).

Examining reoffending rates in the year following the programme using matched demographic and offending data revealed that the participants from the SAC sample were significantly less likely to reoffend than their equivalents in the national cohort. Furthermore, regression analysis indicated that engagement in ETE at a high level in the three months following the SAC programme was the dynamic explanatory variable most highly associated with desistance after one year (n = 735, OR = 1.98, p < 0.001).

Attitudinal change

A key objective was to examine changes in attitudes towards the arts, with attitudinal changes noted for most children engaged in SACs. In addition to scaled questions on experience, skills and overall attitudes, there were a series of statements for completion on a five-point scale from strongly disagree to strongly agree. These statements were directly related to the notion that participatory arts might have intrinsic features that could boost self-efficacy, not only in the arts but in related domains. For example, by the end of the programme, the proportion of children who agreed with the statement 'There is no right or wrong way when it comes to art' had risen from 48 per cent at the start of the SAC to 73 per cent at the end (p < 0.001). Consequently, children particularly sensitive to recurrent failure could have mastery experiences crucial in developing self-efficacy (Bandura, 1997; Margolis, 2005). This is illustrated by the following interviewees:

> 'It's just a different way of doing things. You can't say because he's doing it this way and I'm doing it that way that my way is right and his is wrong. His way is right in his way and your way is right in your

way, but when it comes to it both your ways are right, just completely different.' (Manouk, 14)

'Like it gives you like that kind of freedom, because you know that you're not going to get it wrong, so you know that it's not going to remind you of a situation that you've been in before, so it's just going to be like "oh, well, that's good, that's excellent", you're not going to get the response, "well, this could be improved".' (Jamie, 16)

Notably, given their low literacy levels, there was a significant increase ($p < 0.001$) in belief in their ability to use different art forms to communicate ideas, experiences and emotions (measured by agreement with a before and after statement on this aspect of the arts). There were strong positive reactions from the children when their artwork was displayed at public exhibitions or, more importantly, left legacies through community artwork. Some children commented on their sense of pride when friends and family viewed such art but also saw it as a means of changing community opinion about them as offenders. As one interviewee, who had artwork displayed in a community zoo, explained: "[O]ther people can see. ... 'cos even though we're like criminals and that, still doesn't mean ... [w]e're bad. So ... everyone knew like it was like youth offenders that what did it all so, might have made people change their mind a bit" (Damien, 16).

Desistance processes

Leading desistance theories tend to differ according to their emphasis on structural or subjective factors and the interplay between them (see, for example, the discussion by McMahon and Jump, 2018). The exercise of agency is a significant subjective factor. The SAC theory of change proposes strong proximal effects on children's self-efficacy which is a vital part of agency (Bandura, 1997; Schwarzer and Luszczynska, 2006; Johnston et al, 2019). The SAC experience can be examined from four perspectives: incapacitation, changes in human capital, social capital and attitudes. These are helpful analytical categories, but the children's experiences often crossed these artificial boundaries. For instance, increasing their human capital by achieving an Arts Award as a first qualification caused accompanying changes in self-efficacy and increased their social capital via improved relationships with their parents/carers.

Incapacitation

Incapacitation appeared to work in two main ways: containment, whereby the sheer length of the day and its routines left children little time and energy for antisocial activities and diversion, in that they avoided people and places more likely to lead to offending. Short-term cessations in offending, even if caused primarily by containment and diversion, may be particularly beneficial in an adolescent's life, where a week is a long time. Keeping busy rather than identity change may be important. Keeping busy can be beneficial in preventing boredom and association with delinquent peers, help to deal with emotional problems and inculcate new habits and routines relevant to engagement with education (Goodwin, 2022). The different physical space of the SAC and its accompanying routines perhaps brought a spatial dynamic to desistance for some young people (Farrall, 2016). And many agreed with these sentiments:

'Actually, it did help keep me out of trouble. ... 'Cos I knew that if I was in there at certain times, I wouldn't mix with the people I meet. It was good that I was there. A few of them did [get picked up by the police] while I was there, so it was good.' (James, 17)

'It can ... change their daily routine if their routine is negative. If they're doing negative things daily, then it will give them alternative activities to do and it'll help them develop, well, it helped me develop an interest and a passion and something I can work towards and hopefully better my life and bring me out of whatever type of hardships I may be in.' (Leon, 18)

Increases in human capital

Educational qualifications and increases in academic skills are important measures of human capital for children (Stephenson et al, 2014). There were human capital gains for the children who completed the SAC, with over 90 per cent achieving an Arts Award and the majority improving their literacy and numeracy skills. There was greater positivity about future education. This included acknowledging the importance of self-discipline in studying for exams and a determination to do well:

'I'm just so proud of myself, for having the strength to do that [SAC] and the strength to meet new people. It's just that I've found this kind of new self-worth and self-confidence and it's just changed me for the better. ... Yeah, I'm a lot happier. I'm just, I'm more focused on me and my exams and what I need to do for myself. It gave me the confidence to think that I am worth it, I can do it and to think about what I want rather than what I need to do for everybody else.' (Amara, 15)

Increases in social capital

Children's testimonies emphasised how their stock of positive, active connections with other people increased on the SAC. There was improved trust, and mutual understanding with three networks: artists and YOT staff, parents and carers, and other students. Many artists connected well with the children as they were open about their backgrounds and life challenges. The children contrasted this with the approach they had experienced from teachers in formal education:

> 'I struggle to learn, and he broke it down and made me understand. ... I kind of relate to what he said. Like when he wasn't good in school, when he said he struggles in life and all that stuff, I could relate to him. And he was showing me, and the main thing it was all about the learning, so I got on really well with him.' (Jaxon, 14)

Relationships with YOT staff also developed positively due to the daily contact and were often much appreciated: "It wasn't kind of looking down on us. ... They weren't treating us like children – they were treating us like we were equals to them, which most professionals now, just don't do" (Amara, 16). Seeking approval from trusted professionals for increasing pro-social behaviour can be an important dynamic for change, specifically in the transition to adulthood, and may particularly apply to these children as they are likely to have experienced considerable disapproval for behaviour from professionals such as teachers (Rex, 1999; Maruna, 2001).

There was a positive impact on home relationships for some children. Gaining approval from a parent and/or carer and making them proud could motivate behavioural change, leading to positive engagement on the SAC. Children described how negative their relationships had been before coming to the SAC and how they had changed for the better. Having something constructive to do each day and their achievements and new experiences on the SAC gave the children something positive to talk about and share with their parents/carers at the end of each day. One interviewee described how this repaired her relationship with her mother:

> 'In [the past] she was "you are wasting the electric" and me screaming "shut up" and just stupid things like that, but when I went to the Summer College, I was able to go "I have some photos here, look at these". ... Like there was one point where we wouldn't ever talk really and that, but now if I have the slightest problem ... then we sit down and have a good proper chin wag and that, we have got a bond now.' (Kate, 15)

Peer relationships and approval are particularly important to children (Moreira et al, 2021).

Consequently, there were concerns in the design of the SAC project model about the adverse effects of forming potentially delinquent peer groups.

Nevertheless, one of the most striking features of the children's responses was their emphasis on developing a positive attachment to their group. Despite these undoubted risks, which may have provoked confrontations or exacerbated antisocial behaviour and possibly even led to offending on occasions, the development of a group identity appears to have provided some protective elements. The participatory and cooperative nature of arts activities promoted this generally positive group cohesion:

'Summer Arts it was like everyone helped each other, so. ... It was like a chain, obviously the links in a chain if they're loose, they break, but our chain, it was solid all the way around, like it wasn't a few links dropping out, it were just a full solid chain.' (Jamie, 16)

Attitudinal shifts

The exercise of personal agency to overcome structural barriers has been identified in both studies of desistance and educational engagement and attainment (Johnston et al, 2019; Schoon and Cook, 2021). Self-efficacy is a crucial mechanism of agency. Self-efficacy is a belief in personal competence which motivates a decision to act, the effort expended and persistence (Bandura, 1997). This important element of social cognitive theory was thought relevant to SACs for several reasons. First, self-efficacy is modifiable, and interventions appear to be more effective on those with the lowest self-efficacy, which was a reasonable supposition for children on an SAC. An arts-based programme was thought to be more likely to be effective in raising self-efficacy because of its novelty and lack of association with children's pre-existing beliefs about their attainment. Self-efficacy acts upon motivation and achievement across many behavioural areas, including health, offending and educational engagement (Schwarzer and Luszczynska, 2006; Seddon et al, 2013; Johnston et al, 2019). The empirical evidence base on a wide range of health interventions is impressive (Schwarzer and Luszczynska, 2006). And changes in specific and GSE have been found to be associated with reductions in offending and reintegrating Not in Education, Employment, or Training (NEET) young people (Seddon et al, 2013; Johnston et al, 2019).

Self-efficacy judgements are based on mastery (personal attainment), vicarious experience (others' attainment), persuasion and arousal (for example anxiety). It is plausible to assume that a participatory arts course with a quasi-educational framework of the Arts Award allows for a much greater scope for attainment for children whose educational history was usually characterised by failure. Similarly, there would be many opportunities for positive vicarious experiences in these no-fail activities. Exposure to artists and YOT staff could also result in persuasive support, particularly when compared with their experience of formal schooling and poor interaction with teachers. Self-efficacy is modified by feedback which, in the case of the SAC programme, could be through successive achievements in the arts activities and the formal acclaim of achieving an Arts Award and the celebration event. The novelty of the arts activities could potentially stimulate gains in self-efficacy, as it would not be based automatically on their past performance.

One critical question was the extent to which increases in specific self-efficacy, in this case, arts self-efficacy (a scale was devised to measure arts self-efficacy), would translate into an increased belief in overall competence, particularly regarding educational engagement and achievement. If so, this might be the transmission mechanism between participation in the arts and educational outcomes. Specific self-efficacy can clearly vary between domains for an individual: for example, a child could have high perceived self-efficacy for maths and a low self-efficacy for sport. Changes in one would be unlikely to affect the other. However, GSE is formed by aggregating previous experiences, successes and failures: 'Powerful mastery experiences that provide striking testimony to one's capacity to effect personal changes can also produce a transformational restructuring of efficacy beliefs that is manifested across diverse realms of functioning' (Bandura, 1997, p 53). Phase 2 of the SAC research therefore examined the proposition that greater GSE would be generated by success in the arts programme and would translate into increased specific educational self-efficacy and improved educational performance.

It was found that arts self-efficacy increased significantly by the end of the programme ($p < 0.001$), and this was associated with a significant increase in GSE. Furthermore, this increase (measured using Schwarzer and Jerusalem's scale [1995]) was associated with increases in literacy and numeracy self-efficacy and with the increases recorded in literacy and numeracy scores between the start and end of the programme.

Changes in GSE were also associated with the distal objectives of the programme. A small sample of children ($n = 27$) on Youth Rehabilitation Orders and where there was a full year of ETE tracking data and PNC records revealed some notable differences. Those children who desisted from offending in the year following the SAC programme had, on average, increased their GSE significantly during the SAC, whereas those who reoffended had not. The desisters also increased their engagement in ETE over the year following the programme and, on average, participated in 28 per cent more ETE than those who reoffended. While these are correlations rather than causation, they are all plausible and consistent with the theory of change outlined earlier.

Conclusions

The collaborative work of more than 500 youth justice practitioners, artists and nearly 3,000 children over the 16 years between 2007 and 2022 has yielded valuable results. There is now a clear theory of change linking arts interventions to educational engagement and achievement and potentially to desistance supported by empirical findings. This should facilitate future partnerships between youth justice and arts organisations. In addition, the impressive short-term outcomes, such as high engagement and completion accompanied by educational achievement, demonstrate the importance of participatory arts underpinned by relational practice. Longer-term outcomes emphasise just how significant a life-course development engagement in education is to a child.

The findings on self-efficacy are potentially valuable for practitioners. The mainstream education system has failed these children and is a significant structural impediment to their re-engagement. Yet brokering access to mainstream education remains largely beyond YOT control (HMIP, 2022). Moreover, even custodial establishments cannot guarantee suitable, full-time educational engagement, and custody exacerbates children's detachment from education on their release (Stephenson, 2007; Lanskey, 2015; Paterson-Young et al, 2019). While YOT practitioners struggle to have much effect on such structural problems, they can help some children develop their agency via the key mechanism of increased self-efficacy.

This is certainly not to claim that raising self-efficacy is a panacea. Children face greater constraints on exercising their agency than adults and are more dependent on the support and protection of others. Their social and situational contexts can overwhelm even high levels of self-efficacy. But promoting relationships and interventions that can help a child increase their perceived self-efficacy does have some significant benefits. It brings a focus on nurturing self-belief and encouraging strengths rather than an emphasis on reducing deficits and stressing personal responsibility.

While there are several dimensions to agency, a focus on self-efficacy could be beneficial within youth justice. It can be operationalised more effectively than some alternatives. For example, the notion of identity change may be irrelevant to many children in the youth justice system, is not straightforward to measure and difficult to influence in the duration of a typical youth justice intervention (Wigzell, 2021; Goodwin, 2022). The value of self-efficacy is that it is modifiable by various interventions, readily measurable through a short, robust questionnaire (Schwarzer and Jerusalem, 1995) and meaningful in its effects over several domains. The challenge to practitioners is how to replicate the intensity and nature of the learning experiences of SACs within their everyday practice.

References

Acar, E. (2011) 'Effects of social capital on academic success: a narrative synthesis', *Educational Research and Reviews*, 6(6): 456–61.

Ajzen, I. (2002) 'Perceived behavioral control, self-efficacy, locus of control, and the theory of planned behavior', *Journal of Applied Social Psychology*, 32: 665–83.

Bandura, A. (1997) *Self-efficacy: The Exercise of Control*, New York: Freeman.

Barry, M. (2006) *Youth Offending in Transition: The Search for Social Recognition*, Abingdon: Routledge.

Blomberg, G., Bales, W., Mann, K., Piquero, A. and Berk, R. (2011) 'Incarceration, education and transition from delinquency', *Journal of Criminal Justice*, 39(4): 355–65.

Brice Heath, S. (2008) 'Foreword', in A. O'Brien and K. Donelan (eds) *The Arts and Youth at Risk: Global and Local Challenges*, Newcastle upon Tyne: Cambridge Scholars Publishing, pp ix–xvi.

Carey, J. (2005) *What Good Are the Arts?*, London: Faber & Faber.

Crosweller, S., Stafford, M. and Bathgate, H. (2022) 'The education and social care background of young people who interact with the criminal justice system', London: ONS.

Day, L., Hanson, K., Maltby, J., Proctor, C. and Wood, A. (2010) 'Hope uniquely predicts objective academic achievement above intelligence, personality, and previous academic achievement', *Journal of Research in Personality*, 44: 550–3.

Detterman, D.K. (1996) 'The case for the prosecution: transfer as an epiphenomenon', in D.K. Detterman and R.J. Sternberg (eds) *Transfer on Trial: Intelligence, Cognition, and Instruction*, Norwood: Ablex Publishing, pp 1–24.

DfE (2022) 'Special educational needs and disability: an analysis and summary of data sources', London: DfE.

DfE and MoJ (2016) 'Understanding the educational background of young offenders: joint experimental statistical report from the Ministry of Justice and Department for Education', London: MoJ and DfE.

DfE and MoJ (2022) 'Education, children's social care and offending', London: MoJ and DfE.

Farrall, S. (2016) 'Understanding desistance in an assisted context: key findings from tracking progress on probation', in J. Shapland, S. Farrall and A. Bottoms (eds) *Global Perspectives on Desistance: Reviewing What We Know and Looking to the Future*, Abingdon: Routledge, pp 188–203.

Goodwin, S. (2022) 'Keeping busy as agency in early desistance', *Criminology & Criminal Justice*, 22(1): 43–58.

HMI Probation (2022) 'A joint inspection of education, training and employment services in youth offending teams in England and Wales', HMI Probation, Available from: https://www.justiceinspectorates.gov.uk/hmiprobation/inspections/ete-thematic

Hobcraft, J. (2002) 'Social exclusion and the generations', in J. Hills, J. LeGrand and D. Piachaud (eds) *Understanding Social Exclusion*, Oxford University Press, pp 62–83.

Hughes, J. (2005) 'Doing the arts justice: a review of research literature, practice and theory', Canterbury: Unit for the Arts and Offenders, Centre for Applied Theatre Research.

Hurry, J. and Moriarty, V. (2003) 'Youth Justice Board intervention programme: education, training and employment', Central Evaluators' Final Report, London: Youth Justice Board.

Hurry, J., Brazier, L. and Moriarty, V. (2006) 'Improving the literacy and numeracy skills of young people who offend: can it be done and what are the consequences?', *Numeracy and Literacy Studies*, 14(2): 61–74.

Jermyn, H. (2004) 'The art of inclusion: research report 35', London: Arts Council England.

Johnston, T.M., Brezina, T. and Crank, B.R. (2019) 'Agency, self-efficacy, and desistance from crime: an application of social cognitive theory', *Journal of Developmental and Life-Course Criminology*, 5(1): 60–85.

Klocke, A. and Stadtmuller, S. (2019) 'Social capital in the health development of children', *Child Indicators Research*, 12: 1167–85.

Lanskey, C. (2015) 'Up or down and out? A systematic analysis of young people's educational pathways in the youth justice system in England and Wales', *International Journal of Inclusive Education*, 19(6): 568–82.

Locke, E.A. and Latham, G.P. (2002) 'Building a practically useful theory of goal setting and task motivation: a 35-year odyssey', *American Psychologist*, 57(9): 705–17.

Margolis, H. (2005) 'Increasing struggling learners' self-efficacy: what tutors can say and do', *Mentoring and Tutoring*, 13(2): 221–38.

Maruna, S. (2001) *Making Good: How Ex-convicts Reform and Rebuild Their Lives*, Washington, DC: American Psychological Association.

McMahon, G. and Jump, D. (2018) 'Starting to stop: young offenders' desistance from crime', *Youth Justice*, 18(1): 3–17.

McNeill, F., Anderson, K., Colvin, S., Overy, K., Sparks, R. and Tett, L. (2011) 'Arts projects and what works: inspiring desistance?', *Justitiële verkenningen*, 37(5): 80–101.

Moore, R., Gray, E., Roberts, C., Merrington, S., Waters, I., Fernandez, R. et al (2004) 'ISSP: the initial report', London: Youth Justice Board.

Moreira, A., Yunes, M., Nascimento, C. and Bedin, L. (2021) 'Children's subjective well-being, peer relationships and resilience: an integrative literature review', *Child Indicators Research*, 14(5): 1–20.

Mowlah, A., Niblett, V., Blackburn, J. and Harris, M. (2014) 'The value of arts and culture to people and society: an evidence review', London: Arts Council England.

Palmer, E.J., McQuire, J., Hounsome, J.C., Hatcher, R.M., Bilby, C.A.L. and Hollin, C.R. (2007) 'Offending behaviour programmes in the community: the effects on reconviction of three programmes with adult male offenders', *Legal and Criminological Psychology*, 12(2): 251–64.

Paterson-Young, C., Bajwa-Patel, M. and Hazenberg, R. (2019) *The Social Impact of Custody on Young People in the Criminal Justice System*, Cham: Springer International.

Rex, S. (1999) 'Desistance from offending: experiences of probation', *The Howard Journal of Crime and Justice*, 38(4): 366–83.

Robertson, P.J. (2018) 'Developing career capabilities in "NEET" young people: experiences of participants in the Prince's Trust team programme', *British Journal of Guidance & Counselling*, 46(6): 752–64.

Schoon, I. and Cook, R. (2021) 'Can individual agency compensate for background disadvantage? Predicting tertiary educational attainment among males and females', *Journal of Youth and Adolescence*, 50: 408–22.

Schwarzer, R. and Jerusalem, M. (1995) 'Generalized self-efficacy scale', in J. Weinman, S. Wright and M. Johnston (eds), *Measures in Health Psychology: A User's Portfolio; Causal and Control Beliefs*, Windsor: NFER-Nelson, pp 35–7.

Schwarzer, R. and Luszczynska, A. (2006) 'Self-efficacy, adolescents' risk-taking behaviors, and health', in F. Pajares and T. Urdan (eds) *Self-efficacy Beliefs of Adolescents*, Charlotte: Information Age Publishing, pp 139–59.

Seddon, F., Hazenberg, R. and Denny, S. (2013) 'Effects of an employment enhancement programme on participant NEET', *Journal of Youth Studies*, 16(4): 503–20.

Stephenson, M. (2007) *Young People and Offending: Education, Justice and Social Inclusion*, Cullompton: Willan Publishing.

Stephenson, M., Adams, M. and Tarling, R. (2014) 'The art of engagement? Outcomes and impact of the Summer Arts College programme 2007–12', Norwich: Unitas.

Stephenson, M., Fleming, P. and Hargreaves, C. (2019) 'Examining the impact of the arts on educational engagement and desistance from offending through Summer Arts Colleges: final report', Arts Council England (unpublished).

Stevens, P., Lupton, R., Mujtaba, T. and Feinstein, L. (2007) 'The development and impact of young people's social capital in secondary schools', London: Wider Benefits of Learning Research Report no 24.

Strand, S. (2021) 'Ethnic, socio-economic and sex inequalities in educational achievement at age 16: an analysis of the Second Longitudinal Study of Young People in England (LSYPE2)', Commission on Race and Ethnic Disparities, Available from: https://www.gov.uk/government/publicati ons/the-report-of-the-commission-on-race-and-ethnic-disparities-sup porting-research/ethnic-socio-economic-and-sex-inequalities-in-educatio nal-achievement-at-age-16-by-professor-steve-strand

Wigzell, A. (2021) 'Looking forward, not Backwards', National Association for Youth Justice, Available from: https://thenayj.org.uk/cmsAdmin/uplo ads/explaining-desistance-briefing-feb-2021-final.pdf

Winner, E., Goldstein, T.R. and Vincent-Lancrin, S. (2013) 'Art for art's sake? The impact of arts education', Educational Research and Innovation, OECD Publishing.

Youth Justice Board (2006) 'Barriers to engagement in education, training and employment for young people in the youth justice system', London: Youth Justice Board.

11

Desistance through participatory practice: involving children in decision-making processes in youth justice

Sean Creaney, Samantha Burns, Anne-Marie Douglas, Andrew Brierley and Colin Falconer

Introduction

The purpose of this chapter is to explore children's involvement in the design and delivery of youth justice services and offer insight into how practitioners can promote children's voices to enable desistance. There are different forms of participation, underpinned by varied theoretical frameworks (Percy-Smith and Thomas, 2009; Cahill and Dadvand, 2018). Although variously defined, participation tends to be described and understood as involvement in an activity or an event. Co-production is about the design element of partnership working and can be characterised as a deeper or more substantive level of participation (Social Care Institute for Excellence, 2022). To facilitate children's active or meaningful involvement in processes, practitioners need to be transparent about their role and invite children to lead on agenda-setting, relinquish a degree of power and become a co-facilitator (Johns et al, 2022; Smithson et al, 2022). Despite there being no universal definition or single formula for co-production, key principles, necessary for the development of this approach, include collaborative working, power sharing, trust and safe spaces (Burns et al, 2023; Creaney et al, 2023a, 2023b). These principles have guided practices across the Greater Manchester youth justice sector. For example, a participation framework co-designed in collaboration with and for children has been adopted by key stakeholders (practitioners and case managers) to guide decision-making processes across the region (Smithson et al, 2022). This approach and associated guidance produced on the steps required to co-create practice has impacted on policy development and transformed practice. It is a clear illustration of how youth justice services can embrace children's voices to enable them to thrive in an environment that is conducive to the development of knowledge and skills partnerships (Smithson et al, 2020).

While such participation practices are dynamic and multi-faceted, harnessing children's strengths in particular is a vital element in the application of desistance principles. This can be beneficial in a setting where choices can be limited or there are constraints on opportunities for children to input into processes due to attending mandatory appointments and being required to complete certain activities or programmes as part of legal orders. Furthermore, despite the involuntary nature of their participation, for this practice to yield positive outcomes, there needs to be some acknowledgement of the inherent power dynamics that are present within the youth justice practitioner and child relationship. Arguably what is required is a sincere recognition, on the part of practitioners, that children have the ability to exert influence and constructively shape responses to their care needs, including how they will input into decision-making about supervision requirements (Smithson et al, 2022; see also CJCJ, 2022). Significantly, participatory practice was built into the Positive Youth Justice model and remains a fundamental feature of the Youth Justice Board's (YJB) Child First approach, which is a set of tenets around how to work with children and a clear shift to collaborative forms of service delivery (see YJB, 2021; Burns and Creaney, 2023).

The Child First approach endeavours to remove barriers to desistance by promoting a strengths-based use of language that avoids labelling children as problems to be solved. It also encourages a 'doing with' relationship, promoting inclusion and social justice, akin to a collaborative power-sharing process, by treating children as capable co-producers (Haines and Case, 2015; Smithson et al, 2022). Crucially, children under supervision and in receipt of interventions should be encouraged to discuss their needs, wishes or concerns with authority figures and feel empowered to contribute to the decision-making process. However, there have been concerns that processes remain tokenistic or non-consultative, what may be referred to as *faux* participation (Johns et al, 2022), whereby children 'go through the motions' to 'tick the box', as described in a study by Creaney (2020) about children's perspectives on the extent and nature of participatory practices in a youth offending team (YOT) in England, which includes key themes of power, voice, compliance and resistance. As was found in a report on desistance and young people by HM Inspectorate of Probation (2016), children may comply but not actively engage: "The YOT just make you go on these courses to show that you've done victim work. Then they say well done, you nod, smile and move on. I was just playing with them" (Child, HM Inspectorate of Probation, 2016, p 21).

Thus, while children may attend statutory appointments, be treated fairly, viewed as capable agents of change and complete the legal order successfully, the processes used may still be described as non-participatory, fostering forms of passive compliance (Barry, 2010; Hine, 2010). Models of participatory practices within the field of youth justice, which seek to challenge characterisations of children as passive objects, may go some way to addressing this issue of passive compliance and invoke a pathway of desistance (Peer Power Youth, 2021). Moreover, as a practice or approach it should not be uncritically valorised. It is worthy of being subjected to interrogation given that it covers a spectrum of meanings (Hilyard et al, 2001, p 56). As a result, there can be various models of participation and co-production in existence, including different frameworks and underpinning philosophical or guiding principles (Cahill and Dadvand, 2018). Understandings of these concepts can differ, and at times, the word is used interchangeably with other terminology, which may result in varied practices and create uncertainty of purpose for practitioners 'on the ground' navigating a series of demands from officialdom and working with children to enable positive outcomes (see Smithson et al, 2022). The authors of this chapter explore the concept of participation as a non-hierarchical continuum. This can involve quite diverse practices comprising varying degrees of reciprocity, ranging from consultation to active positions involving co-creation between children and practitioners (Peer Power Youth, 2021; Johns et al, 2022).

This chapter will critically discuss how and why an increased focus on participatory practices has prompted efforts to challenge power inequalities and tokenistic practices (non-participation or passive involvement). Crucially, it is argued that opportunities need to be created for children to occupy a level of influence over the agenda-setting and decision-making within youth justice settings and processes. This commitment to power-sharing opportunities and forms of reciprocity can be achieved by practitioners promoting the value of children's knowledge/insights and by nurturing opportunities for involvement in peer-led practices in youth justice. Following this, the chapter proceeds to offer insight into the purpose and key features of peer support and mentorship as a form of participation which can enable desistance. This involves children being recruited and trained to undertake peer support or navigator roles and motivated and inspired to educate and advise others by sharing their lived experiences of system contact (Peer Power Youth, 2021; Burns and Creaney, 2023). Youth Ink, who work in partnership with a youth justice service, facilitate participatory practices and involve peers in the development of interventions to enable pathways to desistance. The lived-experience charity offers many types of peer support from individual to group, including a peer-led conversation hub. Here, they create non-discriminatory and inclusive spaces and encourage children to talk about their lives and experiences with others who have been or are going through the youth justice system (Goodman and Porteous, 2022, p 3). How types of peer support can improve the self-esteem of both the mentor and mentee will vary depending on levels of involvement and the nature of interactions between stakeholders. Nevertheless, this form of peer-led practice is beginning to be described as a principled and potentially progressive approach (Burns and Creaney, 2023). This type of practice can help to shape a person's self-concept. It places value on children's 'experts by experience' status by treating children not as passive objects who are 'done to' (for example through non-consultative arrangements) but as co-producers whose insights can influence service design and delivery (Burns and Creaney, 2023). With this in mind, the authors proceed to define participation and unpack its relevance to a youth justice context, which involves children undertaking court orders under the supervision of a local youth justice service.

The authors of this chapter draw on desistance literature when offering insight into how peer-led practice can be viewed as a type of pro-social approach. The chapter then proceeds to explore the extent to which peer-led participatory practices can be a useful mechanism to facilitate processes of desistance. There are limitations to the approach, and these are outlined and reflected upon within the chapter. For example, justice-involved children have often described being in hardship or in deficit of economic and social capital (Yates, 2010). Thus, ensuring children have access to structural support systems is of importance if this approach is to enhance participation and maximise positive outcomes for those concerned. Significant numbers of justice-involved children have experienced abuse or loss prior to becoming involved in the justice system (see Spacey and Thompson, 2021). If any trauma experience remains unresolved, it can manifest at a different point in time and impact on levels of compliance with court-ordered requirements, notably their ability to reflect on and make sense of expectations: '[C]hildren and young people struggling with the effects of trauma may be caught in "survival mode" and find it very difficult to process and understand their own and other people's emotions. This can in turn affect their ability to conceptualise and understand the gravity of their actions' (Spacey and Thompson, 2021, p 20).

It is important to note that hearing the testimony of others can be traumatic and trigger vicarious/secondary trauma for children and practitioners (Lee, 2017). Another aspect that can impact on the child's involvement in processes (including motivation levels) is the extent to which children feel they are being treated fairly by those in positions of authority (Haines and Case, 2015). If children express a sense that they will *not* be listened to if they share their perspective or if they hold a distrust of practitioners and feel their ideas will not be considered worthy of being acted upon, these experiences can hinder their meaningful participation in decision-making (Myles, 2022). On the other hand, if children feel included and informed, and reassured that their suggestions for improvement or recommendations for change have a degree of influence on how practitioners operate, children may feel a sense of investment and be more likely to actively participate.

What participation means in youth justice

Participation is a contested concept, and there are different perspectives alluding to what it means in a youth justice context. Despite definitional problems, to participate is to be involved in matters that are of interest to a child or of relevance to the child's life or circumstances. It can also mean experiencing a sense of ownership over parts of the decision-making process, influencing change and contributing to debates (CYCJ, 2022; Day et al, 2023). If children are awarded a degree of power to exert influence, they may feel empowered to contribute as partners in the process of knowledge construction (Case et al, 2020; Johns et al, 2022). There has been burgeoning interest in developing or facilitating practices that challenge institutional power or dominant cultures by enabling children to shape decisions and outcomes (Smithson et al, 2020). Children undergoing court order requirements are mandated to attend appointments with practitioners and thus have limited choice over how to proceed. Yet, involving children in decision-making is not only morally and ethically right but a central tenet of the UN Convention on the Rights of the Child and a key element of effective practice (Lundy, 2007; Weaver et al, 2019; CYCJ, 2022, p 3). This was reiterated in a report by Peer Power Youth (in partnership with the YJB for England and Wales, 2021). The report was based on a project that audited participatory approaches and forms of co-creation across youth justice services in England and Wales. The authors suggest that a flexible and bespoke approach is required, adapted by age or circumstance, one that is fluid and dynamic dependent on the context or situation. Crucially, this involves acknowledging power inequalities and working towards inclusive forms of practice by being responsive to the child's specific needs and interests (see Peer Power Youth, 2021).

Although there are different approaches to practice, from multi-creative techniques to outright tokenistic processes where children are denied opportunities to input or are asked to confirm a decision that has already been reached, it can be argued that a defining feature of participation is the redistribution of power (Arnstein, 1969). Children can 'quickly become disinterested or disengage from interventions, if they do not feel valued or listened to' (YJB, 2008, p 8). That said, it is necessary to promote children's voices and facilitate opportunities for them to express perspectives. Participatory thinking has cohered around ideas about how to tackle power inequalities, develop trusting and non-judgemental child–practitioner relationships, project empathy and warmth, nurture safe spaces and facilitate meaningful opportunities for children to co-create youth justice practice (Douglas, 2022; Johns et al, 2022, p 135; Smithson et al, 2022). A key challenge has been how to ensure all children, particularly those from systemically marginalised groups, are provided with opportunities to participate in appropriate mechanisms and channels to provide feedback and engage in forums or consultation groups about organisational structures. When invited to take part in decision-making processes, children can offer comment on the efficacy of practice at the point of service delivery (Duke et al, 2022). Some services may implement feedback groups or co-create participation forums for children to participate in, which may lead to them sharing their experiences or viewpoints on matters (Weaver et al, 2019). Crucially, there must be careful reflection on whether children's voices do make a difference in terms of policy development and at the point of service delivery and, if so, to what extent (Peer Power Youth, 2021, p 50; see also Lundy, 2007). As Lundy (2007) has alluded to, children need to know the influence and/or impact of their participation, which can improve their experiences and as a by-product overcome potential barriers to desistance.

Barriers to desistance-informed participatory practices

At this point, it is key to note some barriers to participatory practices. Despite benign intent, it could be counterproductive to involve children in processes if there is not adequate focus on equal distribution of power within relationships or if there remains a lack of attention paid to ensuring children's voices have influence at an individual level or on how the workforce operates (Johns et al, 2022). Moreover, justice-involved children often have complex needs due to having experienced forms of adversity, neglect and abuse (Spacey and Thompson, 2021, p 20). These factors can impact on children's cognitive capacity to participate effectively in any process of decision-making (McMahon and Jump, 2017). Children in conflict with the law often have unmet health and social care needs and communication and literacy difficulties (Taylor, 2016). There may be a level of uncertainty about their abilities to express agency and influence procedures. Thus, children may require assistance to express their voice effectively and adopt active decision-making roles. In other words, children may need specialist or creative opportunities to articulate their feelings or communicate their wishes at each stage of the decision-making process, particularly with regard to those who have experienced adversities.

As Duke et al (2022, p 10) note, children often have 'complex and multiple needs which need to be prioritised first and foremost'. Drawing on the work of Cahill and Dadvand (2018), Duke et al (2022) refer to the difficulties in negotiating a balance between discourses of protection and participation. In other words, practitioners have a responsibility to strike a balance between judging whether a child is sufficiently competent to provide informed consent or whether it is necessary to invoke certain processes to protect vulnerable children from harm. Moreover, being respectful of children's participation rights may not be a priority for front-line practitioners in their day-to-day decision-making, especially when the main focus is on addressing unmet health and social care needs or managing concerns around harm: '[A]dult concerns about protecting children may get in the way of their participation rights, for example by reducing opportunities for them to associate freely or by preventing them from influencing decisions' (Percy-Smith and Thomas, 2009, p 358). While it is necessary to facilitate opportunities for children to discuss their needs or concerns and jointly participate in intervention planning, an undue focus on risk or the child's perceived deficits can undermine the power or potential of collaborative practice. Professionals have the power to open up or close down opportunities for children to input into service design and delivery at any point. As Myles (2022) has alluded to, professionals need to acknowledge the obstacles to child participation (including their own biases or preconceptions) and be willing to listen to children.

If professionals retain power and are reluctant to invite responses from children, this can prohibit a democratic process of co-learning and co-creation and maintain power inequalities within relationships (Day et al, 2023). There may be a disproportionate focus on children's past behaviour and an overly conscious effort to detect and monitor concerns about harmful behaviours, which may hinder 'possibilities for reciprocity, mutuality, genuine or equal partnerships' (Day, 2022; Johns et al, 2022, p 129; Creaney and Smith, 2023). Furthermore, while there may be differing strategies and philosophical underpinnings for models of participatory practice in existence, the practitioner may retain the status as expert, ultimately with the authority to decide a course of action, regardless of the views of children (Creaney and Burns, 2023). While it remains important to encourage children to actively participate in processes meaningfully, if professionals embrace the principle of defensible decision-making with a risk-averse mindset, this may stifle innovative and bespoke practices. This militates against power-sharing arrangements. Nevertheless, given that there has been an increased focus on collaborative practices, there is at least the minimum expectation that the child will be consulted on the nature of the interventions they will receive. At the point of service delivery, it is essential that youth justice practitioners demonstrate empathy, embrace children's voices and drive participatory agendas.[1] There are some projects that offer novel insights into the use and value of lived experience in a youth justice context.

Valuing lived experience: promoting peer support as key to desistance

Children within the youth justice system have often experienced adversity, including prior experiences of disruptive relationships with authority figures. This may curtail their ambitions, hopes for the future and hinder the prospect of desistance. It is of fundamental importance that practitioners seek to address fractured relationships with 'authority', rebuild trust and confidence in service systems and, in so doing, display an empathic understanding about their lifestyle or challenging situation they find themselves in (Drake et al, 2014; Cross, 2020; Wigzell, 2021; Day et al, 2023). Arguably, the principle of reciprocity should be observed between stakeholders (Johns et al, 2022). Relationship-focused practice can be a vehicle through which opportunities for children to participate in schemes, such as peer support and mentorship, can be maximised. Within such approaches to practice, practitioners can seek to embed desistance principles including the spirit of reciprocity, which can redress some of the power imbalances between children and practitioners. Peer support is one approach to practice that can promote children's participation within the youth justice system and facilitate the process of desistance. For example, this pro-social type of practice is relationship-based. It is conducive to a philosophy of forging a meaningful connection between those who have similar backgrounds and system experiences (Lopez-Humphreys and Teater, 2018, p 193; see also Buck and Creaney, 2020). At this point, the chapter will now explain how this type of approach can be realised in practice and then briefly reflect on some of the pitfalls and challenges of such practices.

Some youth justice services have either devised bespoke projects or partnered with third sector organisations – potentially viewed by children as more inclusive and less punitive than criminal justice agencies (see CYCJ, 2022) – to offer opportunities for children to undertake peer support, navigator roles or become peer advocates. As Thompson and Spacey (2023) note, this approach can encourage desistance through nurturing behavioural and attitude change. As a valuable pedagogical practice, it can enhance the self-efficacy of those undergoing court orders and those in mentor or helper roles. For example, Youth Ink (2024) work in partnership with a local youth justice service to co-design and co-deliver peer-led programmes in collaboration with and for justice-involved children. The lived-experience charity has created both peer-trainer and peer-support navigator roles. Individuals who undertake these roles are former service users. Peer navigators seek to promote participatory practices, foster non-hierarchical partnerships and build both empathic and trusting relationships with justice-involved children (Burns and Creaney, 2023). They promote pro-social attitudes and behaviours and help to facilitate healing and growth (Hazel et al, 2017). Peer navigators provide emotional and practical forms of support to young people experiencing difficulties. Crucially, they aim to be a positive influence.

Peer support involves those who share similar backgrounds and experiences acting as mentors to those in need of support or guidance. A key part of the process involves mentors, who have experiences of using justice services, acting as positive role models and igniting or nurturing a positive direction of travel for justice-involved children whereby they are encouraged to pursue law-abiding endeavours including pro-social hobbies (Maruna et al, 2015; Wilkinson et al, 2022). This involves building trusted relationships with children under youth justice supervision and connecting with those experiencing hardship. The mentee can feel inspired to make positive changes as a result of receiving support from a former service user who has lived experiences of overcoming difficulties (Creaney, 2018; Myles, 2022). Young people who have experienced challenges, overcome adversity and forged a positive path for themselves despite obstacles and unfortunate circumstances can accrue experiential knowledge and draw on these insights when supporting vulnerable children (Creaney, 2018; CYCJ, 2022; Duke et al, 2022; Myles, 2022). This approach holds international relevance. In the United States, a former justice leader recently called for a strategy to create credible messengers nationwide (Fuller and Goodman, 2020; Washington Post, 2022).[2] Credible messengers, like experiential peers (Lenkens et al, 2021), have first-hand experiences of system contact but have desisted from crime and are deemed capable of relating to and connecting with those in need who are experiencing personal, social or emotional difficulties.

Reflecting on the limits of these practices, mentors may instil in the mentee a desire to resist order or oppose authority, which may result in the mentee modelling such behaviours and disengaging from criminal justice processes. However, Youth Ink require that all mentors participate in training courses on how to model pro-social behaviours, share lived experiences and promote positive choices and law-abiding mindsets. This training could be pivotal in supporting the desistance process. The lived-experience charity also encourages mentors to work collaboratively and constructively with mentees and other practitioners to bring about changes in how the youth justice service operates by challenging the status quo or questioning the norms and values that underpin responses in the field, in progressive ways. Youth Ink embrace a commitment to drive participatory practices from the ground up (Johns et al, 2022, p 125). This is evident in both the philosophy they adopt and the principles that guide their approach, whereby they seek to transform practice through pressing for lived experience, including children's skills and knowledge, to be properly 'recognised and valorised as expertise' (Goodman and Porteous, 2022; Johns et al, 2022, p 125).

Youth Ink exemplify a commitment to valuing the perspectives of justice-involved children. Their commitment to inclusivity is evident through a drive to treat peer navigators as knowledge creators whose insights can positively influence pathways to desistance. Youth Ink is independent from the youth justice service and has relative freedom to involve young people in its strategy and approach. Thus, to a certain extent it is not necessarily vulnerable to its working practices being dismantled by the whims of 'someone at the top' getting 'cold feet' due to perceived concerns about risk of harm or anxiety surrounding potential safety concerns (Johns et al, 2022, p 128). That said, screening and selection processes are intended to be thorough. There are procedures in place to ensure that those occupying peer-navigator roles have been properly vetted and completed required training courses and induction programmes.

However, as Brierley (2023) notes, mentors may not have the required skills to undertake the role effectively and thus may not feel confident in their abilities to utilise child-centred techniques to assist those in need. Moreover, barriers to operationalising Child First or translating and applying desistance principles into practice include practitioners remaining wedded to the rhetoric of managing risk through a deficit-based lens. Resource constraints may hinder peer-support activities or apprenticeship schemes from being developed, there can be challenges acting in accordance with the principle of 'do no harm', and anxieties exist around managing safeguarding concerns (Creaney et al, 2023a, 2023b; Thompson and Spacey, 2023). Therefore, more focus on training courses and what they should entail is required for this type of approach to be effective. Furthermore, while presenting as being 'in need' of guidance from a positive role model, justice-involved children may not value the support of a mentor and thus be reluctant to engage in the process of mentor/mentee matching. This is why the focus on the relationship is important to ensure children see the value in building a connection with their mentor/practitioner. Moreover, as Day et al (2023, p 3) have pointed out, some commentators may aver that a disproportionate focus on children's lived experiences of adversity or disadvantage may result in accusations that there is insufficient focus of ensuring children are held accountable for at least some of their own actions or responses to situations, 'and that a focus on addressing criminogenic need should remain at the forefront of youth justice practice'. However, peer support as an approach must be needs-based and respectful of children's participatory rights, in line with Child First principles.

Conclusion

This chapter has sought to explore how to facilitate children's participation in decision-making processes to support desistance. The chapter has critiqued types of participatory practice, acknowledging the benefits and challenges of involving children in decision-making processes. Participation is a contested concept in that there are differences of opinion on what it means in a youth justice context. As discussed at the beginning of this chapter, to participate is to be involved in matters that are of interest to a child. It can also mean experiencing a sense of ownership of parts of the decision-making process. The chapter also offered insight into how and why an attempt to foster children's involvement in the design and implementation of participatory practices has prompted efforts to challenge power inequalities, to reposition practitioners as co-facilitators with justice-involved children. Such practices are forward-facing, a key feature of desistance-based practice and respectful of children's participatory rights, in line with a Child First ethos. There is an expectation that those undergoing court order requirements will be consulted on the nature of the interventions that are to be implemented. This chapter has argued that, as partners in the supervisory process, children can be empowered to share valuable insights during supervision into what support systems are required to enable children to maintain non-offending lifestyles and be given a platform to critique/disrupt harmful systems and influence or shape the development of strategies that impact on organisational priorities and how practitioners connect with children at the point of service delivery.

Leading on from this, the chapter has offered insight into the reason why there appears to be an increased interest in progressing types of peer support. Peer support projects can help to build children's pro-social identity and enhance access to the accumulation of social capital (positive connections with pro-social peers), which as a by-product can enable non-offending (Arthur et al, 2019; Ministry of Justice/Youth Justice Board, 2019). The work of Youth Ink, which appears to be in consonance with desistance-focused practice and closely aligned to the Child First collaboration principle, involves stakeholders with lived and those with living experience of crime or criminalisation working in partnership with one another. Peer navigators can offer unique perspectives, informed by experiences of system contact, and can offer suggestions to practitioners about how to avoid using techniques that may stymie genuine forms of participation. The authors reflected upon some concerns about how this unfolds in practice, which includes thinking about power dynamics, specific training requirements and attitudes towards 'criminogenic' behaviours. Despite this, it is argued that peer support is a type of desistance-informed participatory practice that has the potential to align with the current Child First ethos in youth justice and adhere to children's rights in this context.

Authors and Acknowledgements

Project Team, Peer Power Youth: Aaliyah, Alexys, Bashiie, Jack, Parishma, Ria, Yolanda, Joshua, Anne-Marie Douglas, Colin Falconer, Samantha Burns, Sean Creaney, Sarah Rockett (desk-based research in 2020), Nicola Kidston (coordination), Laura Kennedy and Jake Edwards (both for communications and design). Project Team, ClearView Research: survey report authors: Burphy Zumu, Sandra Hicks. Project Team, resource report design and sketchnotes: Lizzie Reid (lizzieslines.com) and Mandy Johnson (sketchnotes.co.uk).

Notes

[1] It is important to note that practitioners/those with power need to engage in a reflective process around the nature of involving children in decision-making to ensure that they have considered the extent to which they can 'decision make' in different areas of the service. This involves being clear from the outset with children. In other words, which part of the continuum does this project/decision sit? How do we talk about this with children from the start? (Peer Power Youth, 2021).

[2] The New York City Department of Probation launched the Arches Program in 2009. It is a group project that children and young people aged between 16 to 24 years old who are subject to legal orders can voluntarily participate in. Each session is led by a mentor (credible messenger) with lived experience of contact with the justice system who facilitates a range of activity-oriented exercises including spoken word and rap contests. Mentors also draw on personal experiences of overcoming difficulties and seek to connect and empathise with group participants. Credible messengers do this in a number of ways. For example, they enable honest conversations about lifestyles and perceptions of crime. They help participations to prepare for employment and 'build more capital' (Fuller and Goodman, 2020, p 74) via legitimate means. Participants attend invited talks and are taught life skills, including managing finances, and receive advice and guidance on possible routes into certain industries, including how to become a successful entrepreneur.

References

Arnstein, S.R. (1969) 'A ladder of citizen participation', *Journal of the American Institute of Planners*, 35(4): 216–24.

Arthur, R., Dunn, R. and Wake, N. (2019) 'Empowering young people: multi-disciplinary expressive interventions utilising Diamond9 evaluative methods to encourage agency in youth justice', *International Journal of Mental Health and Capacity Law*, 25: 79–196.

Barry, M. (2010) 'Promoting desistance amongst young people', in W. Taylor, R.W. Earle and R. Hester (eds) *Youth Justice Handbook: Theory, Policy and Practice*, Cullompton: Willan Publishing, pp 158–67.

Brierley, A. (2023) 'Experiential peers cultivate a participation culture in youth justice', *Safer Communities*, 22(2): 78–90, doi: 10.1108/SC-07-2022-0024

Buck, G. and Creaney, S. (2020) 'Mental health, young people and punishments', in P. Taylor, S. Morley and J. Powell (eds) *Mental Health and Punishments: Critical Perspectives in Theory and Practice*, Abingdon: Routledge, pp 143–58.

Burns, S. and Creaney, S. (2023) 'Embracing children's voices: transforming youth justice practice through co-production and Child First participation', in S. Case and N. Hazel (eds) *Child First: Developing a New Youth Justice System*, London: Palgrave Macmillan, pp 333–65.

Burns, S., Creaney, S., Hampson, K. and Case, S. (2023) 'Child First: seeing children as the solution, not the problem', CYCJ, Available from: https://www.cycj.org.uk/resource/info-sheet-110/

Cahill, H. and Dadvand, B. (2018) 'Re-conceptualising youth participation: a framework to inform action', *Children and Youth Services Review*, 95: 243–53.

Case, S. and Haines, K. (2014) 'Youth justice: from linear risk paradigm to complexity', in A. Pycroft and C. Bartollas (eds) *Applying Complexity Theory: Whole Systems Approaches to Criminal Justice and Social*, Bristol: Policy Press, pp 113–40.

Case, S., and Haines, K. (2021) 'Abolishing youth justice systems: children first, offenders nowhere', *Youth justice*, 21(1): 3–17.

Case, S., Creaney, S., Deakin, J. and Haines, K. (2015) 'Youth justice: past, present and future', *British Journal of Community Justice*, 13(2): 99–110.

Case, S., Creaney, S., Coleman, N., Haines, K., Little, R. and Worrall, V. (2020) 'Trusting children to enhance youth justice policy: the importance and value of children's voices', *Youth Voice Journal*, special issue: 25–40.

Children and Young People's Centre for Justice (CYCJ) (2022) 'Children and young people in conflict with the law: policy, practice and legislation', Available from: https://www.cycj.org.uk/resource/youthjusticeinscotland

Creaney, S. (2018) 'Children's voices: are we listening? Progressing peer mentoring in the youth justice system', *Child Care in Practice*, 26(1): 22–37.

Creaney, S. (2020) '"Game playing" and "docility": youth justice in question', *Safer Communities*, 19(3): 103–18.

Creaney, S. and Smith, R. (2023), 'Social work and youth justice', in J. Parker (ed) *Introducing Social Work* (2nd edn), London: Sage.

Creaney, S., Burns, S. and Day, A.-M. (2023a) 'Guest editorial', *Safer Communities*, 22(2): 73–7, Available from: https://doi.org/10.1108/SC-04-2023-053

Creaney, S., Burns, S. and Day, A.-M. (2023b) 'Guest editorial', *Safer Communities*, 22(3): 149–55, Available from: https://doi.org/10.1108/SC-07-2023-054

Cross, Z. (2020) 'The working relationship and desistance: what constitutes a good quality working relationship?', *Salus Journal*, 8(2): 77–99.

Day, A.M. (2022) '"It's a hard balance to find": the perspectives of youth justice practitioners in England on the place of "risk" in an emerging "Child-First" world', *Youth Justice*, 23(1): 58–75.

Day, A., Malvaso, C., Butcher, L., O'Connor, J. and McLachlan, K. (2023) 'Co-producing trauma-informed youth justice in Australia?', *Safer Communities*, 22(2): 106–20, doi: 10.1108/SC-08-2022-0030

Douglas, A.-M. (2022) 'Toward a system that heals: exploring empathy and its application to youth justice and children's education, health and social care services', Peer Power, Available from: https://www.peerpower.org.uk/wp-content/uploads/2022/02/PeerPower_EmpathyReport-2.pdf

Drake, D., Fergusson, R. and Briggs, D. (2014) 'Hearing new voices: reviewing youth justice policy through practitioners' relationships with young people', *Youth Justice*, 14(1): 22–39.

Duke, K., Gleeson, H., Dabrowska, K., Dich Herold, M., Rolando, S. and Thom, B. (2022) 'Building cultures of participation: involving young people in contact with the criminal justice system in the development of drug interventions in the United Kingdom, Denmark, Italy and Poland', *Youth Justice Journal*, 23(1): 97–116.

Fuller, C. and Goodman, H. (2020) 'The answer is in the community: credible messengers and justice system involved youth', *Social Work with Groups*, 43(1–2): 70–4.

Goodman, A. and Porteous, D (2022) 'An evaluation of Youth Ink interim report', London: Middlesex University, Available from: https://yjreso urcehub.uk/practice-based-evaluations/item/1057-interim-evaluation-report-of-youth-ink-child-first-pathfinder-middlesex-university-novem ber-2022.html

Haines, K. and Case, S. (2015) *Positive Youth Justice: Children First, Offenders Second*, Bristol: Policy Press.

Hampson, K.S. (2018) 'Desistance approaches in youth justice: the next passing fad or a sea-change for the positive?', *Youth Justice*, 18(1): 18–33.

Hart, R.A. (2008) 'Stepping back from "the ladder": reflections on a model of participatory work with children', in A. Reid (ed) *Participation and Learning: Perspectives on Education and the Environment, Health and Sustainability*, Dordrecht: Springer, pp 19–31.

Hazel, N., Goodfellow, P., Liddle, M., Bateman, T. and Pitts, J. (2017) 'Now all I care about is my future: supporting the shift; framework for the effective resettlement of young people leaving custody', Report, London: Beyond Youth Custody.

Hazel, N., Drummond, C., Welsh, M. and Joseph, K. (2020) 'Using an identity lens: constructive working with children in the criminal justice system', Nacro, Available from: https://www.nacro.org.uk/news/new-tool kit-using-an-identity-lens-constructive-working-with-children-in-the-criminal-justice-system

Hine, J. (2010), 'Young people's voices as evidence', in W. Taylor, R. Earl and R. Hester (eds) *Youth Justice Handbook: Theory, Policy and Practice*, Cullompton: Willan Publishing.

Hirschi, T. and Gottfredson, M. (1983) 'Age and the explanation of crime', *American Journal of Sociology*, 89(3): 552–84.

Hilyard, N., Hegde, P., Wolvekamp, P. and Reddy, S. (2001) 'Pluralism, participation and power: joint forest management in India', in B. Cooke and U. Kothari (eds) *Participation: The New Tyranny?*, London: Zed Books, pp 56–71.

HM Inspectorate of Probation (HMIP) (2016) 'Desistance and young people: an inspection by HM Inspectorate of Probation', Available from: https://www.justiceinspectorates.gov.uk/hmiprobation/inspections/desistance-and-young-people/

Johns, D., Flynn, C., Hall, M., Spivakovsky, C. and Turner, S. (2022) *Co-production & Criminal Justice*, Abingdon: Routledge.

Lee, R. (2017) 'The impact of engaging with clients' trauma stories: personal and organizational strategies to manage probation practitioners' risk of developing vicarious traumatization', *Probation Journal*, 64(4): 372–87, Available from: https://doi.org/10.1177/0264550517728783

Lenkens, M., Nagelhout, G.E., Schenk, L., Sentse, M., Severiens, S., Engbersen, G. et al (2021) '"I (really) know what you mean": mechanisms of experiential peer support for young people with criminal behavior; a qualitative study', *Journal of Crime and Justice*, 44(5): 535–52.

Lopez-Humphreys, M. and Teater, B. (2018) 'Peer mentoring justice-involved youth: a training model to promote secondary desistance and restorative justice among mentors', *The International Journal of Restorative Justice*, 1(2): 187–209, Available from: https://doi.org/10.5553/IJRJ/258908912018001002002

Lundy, L. (2007) '"Voice" is not enough: conceptualising Article 12 of the United Nation's Convention on the Rights of the Child', *British Educational Journal*, 33(6): 927–42.

Maruna, S., Coyle, B. and Marsh, B. (2015) 'Desistance from crime in the transition to adulthood', in B. Goldson and J. Muncie (eds) *Youth Crime and Justice* (2nd edn), London: Sage, pp 157–69.

McMahon, G. and Jump, D. (2017) 'Starting to stop: young offenders' desistance from crime', *Youth Justice*, 18(1): 3–17.

Ministry of Justice/Youth Justice Board (2019) 'Standards for children in the youth justice system 2019', London: HMSO.

Myles, K. (2022) 'Youth justice practice and lived experience: inclusion or exclusion?', Howard League for Penal Reform, Early Career Academic Network Bulletin 51, Available from: https://howardleague.org/wp-content/uploads/2022/08/ECAN-summer-2022-FINAL.pdf

Peer Power Youth (2021) 'Co-creation and participation in practice project', London: Peer Power/YJB.

Percy-Smith, B. and Patrick Thomas, N. (eds) (2009) *A Handbook of Children and Young People's Participation: Perspectives from Theory and Practice* (1st edn), Abingdon: Routledge, Available from: https://doi.org/10.4324/9780203871072

Smithson, H., Gray, P. and Jones, A. (2020) '"They really should start listening to you": the benefits and challenges of co-producing a participatory framework of youth justice practice', *Youth Justice*, 21(3): 321–37.

Smithson, H., Lang, T. and Gray, P. (2022) 'From rhetoric to reality: participation in practice within youth justice systems', in S. Frankel (ed) *Establishing Child Centred Practice in a Changing World, Part A*, Emerald Studies in Child Centred Practice, Bingley: Emerald Publishing, pp 111–22.

Social Care Institute for Excellence (2022) 'Co-production in social care: what it is and how to do it', Available from: www.scie.org.uk/co-pro duction/what-how

Spacey, M. and Thompson, N. (2021) 'Beyond individual trauma: towards a multi-faceted trauma-informed restorative approach to youth justice that connects individual trauma with family reparation and recognition of bias and discrimination', *British Journal of Community Justice*, 18(1): 18–35.

Stephenson, M., Giller, H. and Brown, S. (2010) *Effective Practice in Youth Justice*, London: Routledge.

Taylor, C. (2016) 'Review of the youth justice system in England and Wales', London: Ministry of Justice, Available from: https://assets.publishing.serv ice.gov.uk/government/uploads/system/uploads/attachment_data/file/ 577105/youth-justice-review-final-report-print.pdf

Thompson, N. and Spacey, M. (2023), '"I would want to see young people working in here, that's what I want to see ...": how peer support opportunities in youth offending services can support a Child First, trauma-informed, and reparative model of practice for youth justice', *Safer Communities*, 22(3): 200–16, Available from: https://doi.org/10.1108/ SC-08-2022-0031

Washington Post (2022) 'The mentoring movement that is expanding from D.C. to other cities', 17 September, Available from: https://www.washing tonpost.com/dc-md-va/2022/09/17/credible-messengers-juvenile-crime

Weaver, B. (2019) 'Understanding desistance: a critical review of theories of desistance', *Psychology, Crime & Law*, 25(6): 641–58.

Weaver, B., Lightowler, C. and Moodie, K. (2019) 'Inclusive justice: co-producing change; a practical guide to service user involvement in community justice', Glasgow: University of Strathclyde, Available from: https://pur eportal.strath.ac.uk/en/publications/inclusive-justice-co-producing-cha nge-a-practical-guide-to-servic

Wigzell, A. (2021) 'NAYJ briefing: explaining desistance; looking forward, not backwards', London: National Association of Youth Justice.

Wilkinson, D., Price, J. and Crossley, C. (2022) 'Developing creative methodologies: using lyric writing to capture young people's experiences of the youth offending services during the COVID-19 pandemic', *Journal of Criminological Research, Policy and Practice*, 8(2): 105–19.

Yates, J. (2010) 'Structural disadvantage: youth, class, crime and social harm', in W. Taylor, R. Earl and R. Hester (eds) *Youth Justice Handbook: Theory, Policy and Practice*, Cullompton: Willan Publishing, pp 5–22.

Youth Ink (2024) 'About us', Available from: https://www.youth-ink.org. uk/our-work/

Youth Justice Board (2008) 'Assessment, planning interventions and supervision: key elements of effective practice', London: Youth Justice Board.

Youth Justice Board (2021) 'Strategic plan 2021–24', Report, London: YJB.

12

Relationship-based work with children in the youth justice system

Roberta Evans and Kirstine Szifris

Introduction

Relationships sit at the centre of much of the work with children who come into conflict with the law. While the nature, purpose and intensity of these relationships can vary, there is a broadly accepted assumption that a level of trust between a professional and a child will have a positive effect on the outcomes for the child (Newman, 2004; Truth Hurts, 2006). In this chapter, we focus on the relationship between a child and a professional, how such relationships establish trust and how relationships can be affected by the professional's work being constrained by statutory frameworks.

Desistance theory has consistently emphasised the importance of relationships in supporting people out of crime: 'Former service users consistently identified having a trusting, open, and collaborative working relationship with a YOT [youth offending team] member of staff or one professional outside the YOT as the most important factor in helping them move away from offending' (HMIP, 2016, p 17). Some academics have suggested that even attempting to apply offending reduction/desistance supporting programmes to children in contact with the youth justice system is incongruent with the fact that offending is a normal part of adolescence (Pitts, 2003) and most grow out of crime (Goldson, 1997; Sampson and Laub, 2004). Further, McAra and McVie (2007) report that children are more likely to desist from offending when they are not formally processed through the youth justice system and argue for a 'maximum diversion approach' (p 338). Since their research, the number of first-time entrants in the youth justice system has reduced significantly, and most children formally processed in the youth justice system are receiving pre-court outcomes (YJB, 2022b).

This has resulted in a smaller cohort of children receiving post-court outcomes. They tend to be those with more serious levels of offending and/ or multiple court outcomes, and these children present with higher levels of vulnerabilities and chaotic lives (Taylor, 2016; Johns et al, 2017; YJB, 2020). Evans' work (Vlugter, 2009) found that there are 'notable differences in personal, family or social needs among those children that have high levels of offending compared to those with low levels of offending' (p 117). The Youth Justice Board's (YJB) national standards promote the use of desistance practice for all children (YJB, 2019). Applying desistance theory to the youth justice system ought to be done with caution as the underlying theories stem from research with adults (see Maruna, 2001; Giordano et al, 2002). There is, however, some emerging research that sheds some light into the desistance process for teenagers. While there is still a recognition that maturity plays a key role in trajectories out of crime (Robinson, 2014), McMahon and Jump (2018) found that successful desisters (male, under 18) were actively seeking to shed their old criminal identities, while persisters lacked confidence in doing so. Furthermore, desisters tended to have greater involvement in new pro-social activities than persisters, indicating the importance of self-understanding even at a young age. But how do we support children with higher and more serious levels of offending, particularly when the needs are complex and interwoven? We recognise that the sample cohort in this study is small and focused on serious and prolifically offending children. While this is representative of the small number of children on repeat court orders, it is worth nothing it is not representative of all children on court-ordered community sentences, as currently the majority are officially first-time entrants.

To explore these themes, we draw on research conducted by SHiFT, a charity in the UK that offers long-term, intensive support to children whom professionals consider 'high risk' and caught up in the 'cycle of crime' (Smith et al, 2022). SHiFT guides work intensively alongside a small number of children over a sustained timescale of at least 18 months. This longevity of support is seen by SHiFT as vital in building trust and engagement with children who have considerable previous experiences of trauma, neglect, abuse and poor attachment and have previously been passed in and out of different services according to various statutory thresholds.

SHiFT's model of working offers an opportunity to reflect on relationship-based working. Both of this chapter's authors were involved in a pilot of the SHiFT programme, with Evans as the Senior Manager overseeing the youth justice service in one of the pilot local authorities, and Szifris as SHiFT's Research and Evaluation Lead. With our 'insider-outsider' perspectives on the work of the SHiFT professionals, we use the research to reflect on trust- and relationship-based working in an attempt to draw out learning that can be applied across the sector. The work of SHiFT offers an insight into what a long-term, trusted relationship might look like and the importance of different ways of working with the children and their families.

Trusted relationships in a position of power

In the UK, there has been a growing interest, certainly since the 2010s, in the role of trusted relationships in working with children and adults with complex needs. Most notably, the Early Intervention Foundation was commissioned by the Home Office to review their trusted relationships policy, and the summary report provides the following definition: 'A professional "two way" relationship where the roles and boundaries around these are clearly understood; and where a young person or child feels comfortable about talking openly within this context' (White, 2017, p 4). The main report concludes that 'enabling trusted relationships within public services requires a nuanced and multi-dimensional approach, taking account of the fit between a childr's [sic] lived experience, the skills of the practitioners and the context in which the intervention is delivered' (Lewing et al, 2018, p 30). The authors describe contextual factors as longevity of the relationship, effective training and supervision and less demand on practitioners through reduced bureaucracy and improved autonomy. They describe practitioner factors as involving appropriate attitudes and values, the use of effective techniques and being responsive to the child. While the report did not highlight the importance of showing genuine care for the young person, this has been raised in other literature (Maruna et al, 2004; HMIP, 2016; Wigzell, 2020).

Literature from work in prisons offers some insight into the complexity of developing trusted relationships. Szifris's work (2021) implies that a person's behaviour being overseen and 'watched' by authorities can limit self-expression. In other words, when the person feels there are consequences for what they say, they do not speak openly. Further, Liebling et al (2011) emphasise the importance of 'prisoner voice' in legitimate interaction, with Crewe (2009) coining the phrase 'biro-power' to articulate the power professionals have to shape the future of people in prison. Therefore, certain contexts naturally incline against the emergence of trust.

While issues of trust within prisons cannot be directly translated to the world of youth justice, there are some insights that seem relevant. For example, Liebling with Arnold (2004) offers a definition of trust as 'reliance on the honesty, reliability, and good sense of a person; the level of responsibility or confidence invested in and experienced by individuals' (p 248). She argues that this is underpinned by respectful treatment and grows out of social relationships. Further, Szifris's (2021) work highlighted the importance in trust for the professionals' underlying motivations with open, non-judgemental and fair treatment being described as key to establishing trusted relationships. Having professionals, particularly with a role in the criminal justice system, recognising and praising evidence of desistance supports a non-offender identity (Maruna, 2001), and praise from 'on high' is key to delabelling and supporting desistance (Maruna et al, 2004).

How do we manage the professional relationship without breaking trust?

When considering the value of relationship-based approaches, a key question is: how can trusted relationships be created within a statutory youth justice setting? The case worker in a YOT could be seen to have the best opportunity to develop a strong relationship with a child receiving a formal outcome due to their responsibility to assess the child's needs, plan for their intervention and oversee the intervention's delivery for the duration of the outcome or order. However, the worker's role is bound by legal parameters. How does the youth justice practitioner develop and maintain the relationship from a position of power and without breaking trust when delivering the statutory requirements of the role?

The relationship is the most important part of supervision, particularly the ability to go beyond the supervisory role and show mutual care and communication (Wigzell, 2020). The professional has the ability to 'normal-smith' or 'deviant-smith' the child through their interactions, analysis, assessment and representation of them in the court or other professional settings (Maruna, 2001; Maruna et al, 2004; Lofland, 1969). The YJB introduced a reoffending project that looked at effective practice in reducing reoffending (Hayes, 2014). This found that teams with low reoffending had highly motivated and engaged staff who could enlist the support of the wider partnership and had sufficient resources available to deliver interventions (YJB, 2015). A later report outlined that children 'benefit from a stable, trusting and respectful relationship with at least one practitioner' (YJB, 2016). It also stated that the work should be broadly therapeutic and not overly focused on punishment, recognising desistance as an ongoing process and that the 'practitioners need the skills to engage [children], and to establish trust as well as boundaries' (YJB, 2016). The compulsory nature of statutory interventions can be a barrier to engagement and requires workers to be persistent, to look beyond whether a child attends the session or not, to promote the benefits of the intervention to the young person and focus on their relationship (Bateman and Hazel, 2013). Practitioners' skills in relationship building are demonstrated through an ability to 'get along', hold 'proper friendly conversations', 'being there' and 'going the extra mile' (Wigzell, 2020).

The use of boundaries can include enforcement for non-compliance, as set out in the Powers of Criminal Courts (Sentencing) Act 2000. In a study commissioned by the YJB, workers reported that enforcement is an effective method of encouraging compliance (Ipsos MORI, 2010). This can also present a particular tension point for workers focused on relationship-based practice (Morris, 2015). The case practitioner is bound by the YJB's national standards, first established in 2000. These outline the expectations for managers and youth justice practitioners, timeframes for completing an assessment or pre-sentence report and the standards for delivering each order available in the court. Until 2022, a strong feature of the standards was ensuring the child's compliance with their order and timely enforcement (also known as 'breach') for non-compliance.

The breach process gives a clear message to the child that they have 'failed' and they need to return to court, potentially for resentencing. This is regardless of whether the child has made excellent changes to various areas of their life – if they do not comply with the conditions of the order, and specifically do not attend planned face-to-face appointments, they face the courts. This goes against the guidance for desistance-based practice, which encourages society to take a chance on an individual who is trying to make an effort towards desistance, as not giving this chance could lead to further offending (Maruna, 2004). When boundaries are implemented from a perspective of support and setting the young person on the right track, this is seen to be more 'legitimate' by children (Johns et al, 2017).

When the Scaled Approach was introduced (YJB, 2010), the aim was to tailor the intensity of intervention based on the assessment of risk and therefore more effectively manage risk. A child presenting with more risk was required to attend and participate in more sessions and activities to reduce risk (YJB, 2010). So with more chaos in their life, they were expected to attend, on time, a higher number of appointments.

A decade later, we have a welcome fresh perspective on the national standards (YJB, 2019) whereby they reflected the principles of a Child First approach (Case and Browning, 2021). The focus is on relationship-based practice and promoting a child's desistance. The guidance promotes practice that is in the child's best interests, building their strengths and their means of developing a pro-social identity, where work is constructive and future-focused, built on supportive relationships that empower children to fulfil their potential and make positive contributions to society, and so on. This shift in approach has a promising tone that could support children away from the criminal justice system.

In 2022 the case management guidance that accompanied the national standards had also completely changed. This reflects the new way of working that encourages youth justice workers to make every effort to engage the child and their family and to adapt their work based on the child's various needs. The guidance is more flexible in how to set the frequency of appointments, and if the child is overwhelmed by expectations or struggling, the worker can reduce the frequency of appointments. Previously, such a change required management oversight. In the one reference to 'breach', the guidance clearly states that 'it is incumbent on you to make every effort to engage children in completing their order' (YJB, 2022a). The burden of overcoming barriers to achieving engagement is placed on the adults, not the child.

While this is a positive step in the right direction, it will take time to embed. Years after the establishment of YOTs, there was evidence of 'cultural hang-overs' and ongoing professional differences in opinion about welfare- versus risk-led approaches (Morris, 2015). Changes in guidance can have an impact, but inevitably practitioners will continue (to an extent) to apply their own principles of practice. This is particularly pertinent with the ongoing power dynamic of a statutory worker being required to assess and manage risk. With the previous assessment and intervention framework remaining, it will be difficult to move away from the isolated risk-based approach to the child (John et al, 2017). The tension of whether to breach a child for non-compliance on the basis of public protection (Morris, 2015) will also be an ongoing dynamic. As outlined by Wigzell (2020), case practitioners struggle with the increased paperwork and management expectations involved in more complex case work. The emotional impact is also significant. A relationship-based approach that supports desistance requires time, frequency and quality contact alongside a desire to engage young people and promote their positive development (Johns et al, 2017). Therefore, workers need to balance their ongoing risk-management statutory role and accompanying paperwork with a long-term relationship-based Child First approach.

Methodology

The findings presented in this chapter stem from an internal, process evaluation of SHiFT – a youth justice organisation which, at the time of the research, ran two practices in London and worked with a total of 43 children. Each SHiFT practice consisted of five Guides (one of whom is the Lead) and a practice coordinator and is supported by the SHiFT national team. SHiFT practices are run within local authorities, alongside or within the youth justice service. The research question which framed the data collection and analysis was: 'What does SHiFT look like when it is working well?'

By focusing on relationships where SHiFT *is* working, the research captured strong, positive, *trusted* relationships between children and Guides. This was determined by an initial analysis of quarterly returns and explicit selection for whom positive outcomes could be demonstrated (for example, a return to mainstream education, reduced missing episodes and improved accommodation for children in care, or reduced engagement with criminal activity and conflict with the law). These were discussed with the practice teams, and children who were seen as suitable were extended an invite.

The research methodology drew on contribution analysis (Mayne, 2008) and involved constructing a range of 'contribution stories' for eight of the 43 children working with a SHiFT Guide.

Data collection and analysis

The research was conducted by SHiFT's Research and Evaluation Lead (Dr Kirstine Szifris), who is also an author of this chapter. For the full evaluation, a range of data collection activities took place including theory of change workshops with SHiFT Guides, interviews with children and Guides, telephone interviews with parents, focus groups with professionals and examination of administrative data and SHiFT's 'exploration tools' (completed by Guides and children together to monitor progress). For the purposes of this chapter, we focus on data from timeline interviews with children and Guides and the telephone interviews with parents and family members. The eight children included in the research were identified in collaboration with SHiFT Lead Guides and their line managers. A shortlist of 25 provided the basis for analysis of administrative data, with 12 being invited to interview and seven successfully interviewed alongside their Guides.

Timeline interviews involved meeting with children and Guides together for between one and two hours. Szifris led the child and Guide through a series of questions to understand how their relationship has developed, key events over the course of their time working together and reflections on what has gone well and where the child needed support. Timelines were visual in nature, with a range of materials including coloured pens, Post-It notes, string and large pieces of paper being provided.

There are some limitations to interviewing the child and the Guide together, with an increased likelihood of a positive review of the work of the Guide. However, the Guide's presence brokered the relationship, helping to provide a safe space for the child to discuss different aspects of their lives with the researcher. Furthermore, it allowed Szifris to observe the relationship between Guide and child with follow-up notes taken on a standardised form to help understand the role of different Guides in the children's lives. Interviews followed a loose interview schedule (taking a semi-structured approach) developed in discussion with the Director of Practice and Lead Guides and were recorded and transcribed. The interviews were analysed using open coding and thematic analysis techniques to develop contribution stories.

Findings from SHiFT's evaluation

'So how am I supposed to trust them? That's like the first point of like ... that's where from Day One, the trust has not been formed with social workers. This is the problem. This is the Day One problem like.' (Archie, 18 years)

Longevity and flexibility

SHiFT Guides began working with children with a clear intention of building relationships, getting to know their circumstances and situations, and using this as a foundation to establish positive change for and with the child.

The contribution stories suggested that the Guides had the time to genuinely get to know the children, their personalities, interests and circumstances:

'I said to her that I have the goal to be a footballer when I grow up – normally I would just say it, but [my Guide] listened to me and without me knowing, she checked on Google for football stuff. And she showed me that for anything I need, she is there.' (Banquo Jr, timeline interviews)

In the interviews, many of the children discussed the importance of the relationship with the Guide, highlighting its intensive nature: "[Other workers] just give me a phone call every two weeks. But I meet him [his Guide] every week. Sometimes twice a week" (James, timeline interview).

Both children and Guides talked about simply turning up and spending time in the child's home, getting to know them and their families. In many cases, the child was wary of a new professional making promises and being part of their lives. The Guides understood the need to take their time to find a way to connect with the child. This also meant the Guides could tailor the work to the child in a meaningful way. Each Guide set individualised goals with the children.

The SHiFT model emphasises *flexibility*, encouraging Guides to meet children in their own environment and to tailor the work to the child's needs. This means Guides can spend time with a child in the way the child feels comfortable without the time pressures of a short, targeted programme.

The children spoke enthusiastically of time spent doing interesting activities – basketball, horse-riding, music clubs, football and water sports – but also that these activities provided a safe and secure foundation to engage in meaningful conversation – often in the car on the way there:

James:	But the car journey is actually pretty good when it comes to us just talking and getting to know each other. Even on the journey here …
SHiFT Guide:	Yeah on the journey here we were talking about emotional regulation, and parents' emotional regulation.
James:	We talk a lot, it helps a lot, just the talking. Instead of doing all of this all the time (pointing at the timeline exercise they were doing), it's good like but not all the time. It's nice to sit in the car, go get a coffee, and talk.

Jaimie and her Guide began by simply going out for food. They used this time to get to know each other and to understand different influences in Jaimie's life, including her grandmother, the only relative with whom Jaimie has regular contact. It became apparent that Jaimie has had few reliable adults in her life and has a sense of independence: "Put it like this ... I haven't been told what to do in a very long time."

Guides demonstrated their ability to spend significant time with the children, flexibly and in their own contexts, including with family members. Guides, children and parents discussed how the Guide took a flexible and creative approach to engaging the children. With only a small number of children to work with, Guides were able to get involved in the children's lives in a meaningful way. Children highlighted small ways in which Guides were flexible – such as agreeing to a time that suited the child.

There are various examples within the stories of a Guide's ability to be flexible in the moment. When different issues arise, instead of being moved to different services and the child having to work with a new professional, the SHiFT Guide works with them on whatever aspect of their lives they currently need support on.

Genuinely interested and committed

Several of the children discussed how the Guides engaged them in a much more meaningful way than other workers. SHiFT Guides seemed more open and willing to develop genuine relationships with children, who described them as 'open' and 'available'. Their Guides 'got them': they listen and take the time to understand their point of view.

Children emphasised the importance of the time the Guides took just to sit and listen, letting them vent their frustrations, articulate their thoughts and explore their feelings when the children needed to do this:

> 'I mean, a lot of the time, he's very like ... he will sit there and listen like. Even if I sit there and be chatting so much shit; "Oh I hate the world! I hate my family! I wish everything's ...", mad talk. But he still sits there and listens, you know. Not a lot of socials really do that.' (James)

The conversation is different: "You get the, like, social workers, they're always asking this, asking that. It seems like they're trying to dig for information and like da da da da. But [my SHiFT Guide] like was a bit more relaxed. And more times, he's coming just to chat with me innit like" (Archie). For others, time spent with the Guides provided opportunity for meaningful conversation. As described by James, the 'car conversation' can be a safe way to engage in discussions about various topics.

With a trusted relationship, these conversations could also be openly challenging. For example, working with her Guide, Jaimie does not go unchallenged. In these moments in the interview, when Jaimie's Guide asks her to explain what happened, she listened without judgement and then challenged Jaimie to think about a different way of responding. There are some indications that it is working as, a week or so after the timeline interview, Jaimie's Guide and Jaimie's social worker reported that Jaimie had independently chosen to write a formal email to explain her concerns within the placement instead of "kicking off".

The interviews highlighted the importance of workers following through on their promises:

> 'Whereas he's proven ... to a certain degree, he's proven a lot. Like what he's said he's going to do, he's actually done it. Like he said he was going to sign Kieran up to a gym and went and done that. Meetings like, things like that. He does it.' (Kieran's mother)

For Banquo Jr, his Guide following through with a conversation and taking the time to find out how to support him in his interests (in this case football) was key to him believing she was on his side. Whether or not a professional follows through with a promise is important to parents too:

> 'The relationship with professionals broke down, because there was a lot of things getting promised, and never ... no matter what me or Kieran was doing. Cause it got to the point where I thought ... I was on the order. It was me that was in trouble as well.' (Kieran's mother)

Importantly, having established rapport and good relationships with children and families, Guides then followed through with actions. Guides have driven children to music clubs, using car journeys to talk about emotions and how to regulate them (James and his Guide), or acted as an emergency contact, vouching for the child when they wanted to go back to college and get their education back on track (Archie and his Guide). Guides have turned up at the police station when children got arrested (Sam and his Guide), accompanying them to court, speaking in support of them (Rob and his Guide) and continuing to work with them if they go into custody, are moved to a placement outside of the borough and after they turn 18 (the broader group).

In four out of the seven interviews with children, there was an opportunity to discuss past experiences with professionals and services and compare them with their experience of working with their SHiFT Guide. These discussions highlighted the importance of authentic care from the first introduction: "A lot of these social workers, they'll say they'll care, but they won't like" (James);

"The way he introduced himself to me, without digging for information, and without being a classic social worker, which makes me want to actually chat to him more. Then there, by definition, when he tells me things, I'm going to listen more" (Archie).

Jaimie explained that she felt her voice wasn't being heard in the system because there wasn't anyone who wanted to listen:

Researcher: What needs to change in the system?
Jaimie: I needed someone to listen to me and what I actually wanted.

The interviews also identified the importance of the SHiFT Guide being realistic about the child's context. Archie's experience of his Guide was different from his previous interactions with professionals, which he was clearly frustrated about and felt let down. The SHiFT Guide respected his views and understood the lifestyle he had been involved in. This enabled him to find a way to challenge some of Archie's views and to encourage him towards going "legit": "[The Guide] teaches Archie how to protect and support himself with the reality of Archie's world. That is probably the key difference that I have seen compared to any other previous support" (Archie's parent).

The interviews highlighted the value in working alongside the family. With a Guide working alongside Kieran's mother, she was able to engage with the professional network in a way that meant they began to understand Kieran's story – the trauma that he was dealing with and the needs that she felt were underpinning his behaviour.

Kieran's Guide worked closely with his mother while he was in prison, developing a deep understanding of his situation and life circumstances. By doing this, the Guide was able to be alongside Kieran within the professional network, supporting him and his family to understand requirements and advocate for his specific needs.

While the children have highlighted key differences between the Guides and statutory professionals, they also outline ways in which a social worker or youth justice professional can approach their role, such as taking time to listen, being interested in the child themselves, meeting the child where they are, engaging them in fun activities and allowing the child to bring forward the information when ready.

Shifting the adultification bias

In many cases, the SHiFT worker gets involved with a child who has worked with services for many years. The Guides take an insider-outsider role with these services, working with the network of professionals to change the narrative around the child. The following examples articulate a key issue in working with children caught up in the cycle of crime, in that for those that might want to move forward, their past behaviours are used as a factor in judging risk and their needs. This is not a problem confined to the youth justice space, as evidenced in the adultification literature (Davis and Marsh, 2020).

In the interviews, children and parents discussed how professionals would discuss children's 'problem behaviours' but would not engage in a discussion about the reasons for this behaviour. In the following exchange, a Guide and child discuss how 'the system' has treated Oscar primarily as a 'criminal' instead of a 'victim' despite Oscar having been involved in county lines activities since the age of eight:

Interviewer:	What I'm finding interesting is that, right from the outset, you've very much been treated as …
Guide:	A criminal
Interviewer:	Why do you think that is?
Oscar:	I feel like it's a little bit, because of all these professionals and that.
Interviewer:	How do you see yourself?
Oscar:	Just like a normal person, innit.
Guide:	I think that's a very good point though. That … and I think that can be profession-wide in terms of the terminology that we use and the language that we use … in meetings, the lens should be; the young person is a victim.

Kieran's mother also highlights the issue of professionals seeing the offending first:

'And my biggest concern was, when he come home [from custody], was the professionals. I'm not going to lie. I think I was more concerned about what the professionals were going to say, what they were going to try and put in place, and things like that. … And I've always felt to a certain degree that the youth offending and other professionals have made things difficult for me and [Kieran] to move forward.' (Kieran's mum)

For Archie's Guide, a key part of working with him was to address the professional narrative. He is known within the local authority as being one of the 'ring leaders' of criminal activity, responsible for recruiting others and deeply entrenched in the 'roads' lifestyle. Archie's mother explains how this was also experienced in Archie's school journey:

'I think he is undiagnosed ADHD and severe dyslexia. So he was really, really struggling, and that came out as bad behaviour, a massive round of exclusions, he moved schools, he was locked in rooms while in school, he was running away and his attendance was less than 30 per cent. I feel like I tried to speak to people to get him diagnosed, instead of looking at him as being really naughty and getting him out of our school. I feel like if that had been gone down at an early age, that would have been different. If they had understood the naughty behaviour as a symptom rather than who this person is.' (Archie's mother)

By getting to know the child and taking the time to understand the reasons behind their behaviour, Guides were able to get alongside the child and focus on their goals rather than behaviour.

Furthermore, key to the work of the Guides is their ability to 'get alongside' the other professionals involved in their lives as well as the child and family. To support the child's journey, all of the Guides worked alongside the children's professional network. They would begin by looking at the records and talking with their social workers and YOT workers to understand the child's situation. This was a benefit of the 'insider-outsider' role.

Conclusion

Children need supervision and someone who is looking out for them (Schaefer-McDaniel, 2004; Smith, 2004), whereby good communication and looking out for them reduce risk of further offending (Osgood and Anderson, 2004). For this to have the best impact, it needs to be with positive regard and care, praising each positive step towards reform (Maruna et al, 2004; Wigzell, 2020). When it comes to the statutory order and the requirements to be completed in the order, to the point when a worker has to breach for non-compliance, there is a tension present. This is perhaps similar to the role of an authoritative parent, which is still an important role for adolescents (Hanson and Holmes, 2014).

The worker's approach to the child in the court system needs to be a balance of positive outlook, showing care and interest, developing a trusting relationship and also holding authority (HMIP, 2016). The YJB supports a relationship-led, balanced approach to support children through a change process, responding to children as individuals with trust and respect without ignoring personal responsibility (YJB, 2016). Desistance can be supported when workers have a desire to engage young people and show an interest in their development and are clear about the boundaries and expectations when seeking to develop a trusted relationship (Johns et al, 2017).

Where youth justice practitioners are applying the same interested, open, caring and flexible approach as SHiFT Guides alongside the principles of the new national standards (YJB, 2019) and case management guidance (YJB, 2022a),they support a pathway of change and an exit path out of the criminal justice system. Where a worker focuses on the child as a person, discusses their interests, rather than focusing on what they have done wrong, the child will be more likely to engage and trust the worker's advice. The worker has a responsibility to move beyond the behaviour, recognise the trauma and find the child behind the behaviour – to be genuinely interested and friendly, 'get along' and care about them and go the extra mile (Wigzell, 2020). They need to get into a habit of praising the child for every success as that is what will also likely change their behaviour (Maruna et al, 2004).

The worker is now responsible to the child for their attendance and reviewing their approach in how they engage a child (rather than only expecting a child to attend to them and judge their reasons for non-attendance). The worker can go out to the child and wait for them to be ready or change the time that suits them. They could consider the child's learning and development needs when considering if the reason for being late or not attending is reasonable. They could create sessions that are of interest to the child so they are more likely to be present, as well as having fun and 'car conversations' as avenues for a safe space to talk. By responding creatively and flexibly, the worker's relationship will be more like an advocate or mentor than an authoritarian worker in a position of power. This would more likely increase engagement, reduce the need for enforcement and support a 'normal-smithing' process out of crime (Wigzell, 2020).

How youth justice practitioners (or social workers) and managers take this on board and apply it within their statutory setting will be an ongoing discussion, which needs to be supported by the YJB (and Ofsted) and local authorities. This needs to be more than an offer of training and reflective supervision, although these will complement the new steer from the 2019 national standards and 2022 case management guidance. The difference with SHiFT was that the workers could take the time to build the relationship – a lot of time – both in the length of their involvement and due to their small caseload. The SHiFT Guides had less paperwork and bureaucracy. They had flexibility and could go outside of the boundaries of a start or end date in an order or social work plan. Therefore, rather than attempt to make the most of every interaction in the time limits of a court order (Johns et al, 2017), youth justice services may need to consider working beyond the parameters of these timeframes. Accepting the importance of a trusted relationship and recognising the time this requires may have more impact on the child and their behaviour than focusing on the paperwork and court timeframes. Furthermore, when a worker has the opportunity to get to know a young person and 'what makes them tick', they will likely require less time to complete the paperwork when this eventually comes.

Children have told us how important the worker's engagement and approach is to their behaviour, outcomes and wellbeing; this means having a worker 'be there', be flexible, be persistent and stay with them throughout. So now, with the permission of a Child First approach, it's time to listen.

References

Bateman, T. and Hazel, N. (2013) 'Engaging young people in resettlement', London: Beyond Youth Custody.

Case, S. and Browning, A. (2021) 'Child First justice: the research evidence-base', Full report, Loughborough University.

Crewe, B. (2009) *The Prisoner Society: Power, Adaptation and Social Life in an English Prison*, Oxford: Oxford University Press.

Davis, J. and Marsh, N. (2020) 'Boys to men: the cost of "adultification" in safeguarding responses to Black boys', *Critical and Radical Social Work*, 8(2): 255–9.

Giordano, P.C., Cernkovich, S.A. and Rudolph, J.L. (2002) 'Gender, crime and desistance: toward a theory of cognitive transformation', *American Journal of Sociology*, 107(4): 990–1064.

Goldson, B. (1997) 'Children, crime, policy and practice: neither welfare nor justice', *Children & Society*, 11(2): 77–88.

Hanson, E. and Holmes, D. (2014) 'That difficult age: developing a more effective response to risks in adolescence', Devon: Research in Practice and ADCS.

Hayes, D. (2014) 'YJB toolkit aims to cut youth reoffending rates', Children and Young People Now, 26 March, Available from: https://www.cypnow.co.uk/news/article/yjb-toolkit-aims-to-cut-youth-reoffending-rates

HMIP (2016) 'Desistance and young people: an inspection by HM Inspectorate of Probation', Available from: https://www.justiceinspectorates.gov.uk/hmiprobation/wp-content/uploads/sites/5/2016/05/Desistance_and_young_people.pdf

Ipsos MORI (2010) 'A review of techniques for effective engagement and participation', London: Youth Justice Board.

Johns, D.F., Williams, K. and Haines, K. (2017) 'Ecological youth justice: understanding the social ecology of young people's prolific offending', *Youth Justice*, 17(1): 3–21.

Liebling, A. and Arnold, H. (2004) *Prisons and Their Moral Performance: A Study of Values, Quality, and Prison Life*, Oxford: Oxford University Press.

Liebling, A., Arnold, H. and Straub, C. (2011) 'An exploration of staff–prisoner relationships at HMP Whitemoor: 12 years on', Cambridge University, Prisons Research Centre, London: National Offender Management Service, Ministry of Justice.

Lewing, B., Doubell, L., Beevers, T. and Acquah, D. (2018) 'Building trusted relationships for vulnerable children and young people with public services', Early Intervention Foundation, London: Home Office.

Lofland, J. (1969) *Deviance and Identity*, Englewood Cliffs: Prentice-Hall.

Maruna, S. (2001) *Making Good: How Ex-convicts Reform and Rebuild Their Lives*, Washington, DC: American Psychological Association.

Maruna, S., Lebel, T.P., Mitchell, N. and Naples, M. (2004) 'Pygmalion in the reintegration process: desistance from crime through the looking glass', *Psychology, Crime and Law*, 10(3): 271–81.

Mayne, J. (2008) 'Contribution analysis: an approach to exploring cause and effect', Institutional Learning and Change (ILAC) Initiative.

McAra, L. and McVie, S. (2007) 'Youth justice? The impact of system contact on patterns of desistance from offending', *European Journal of Criminology*, 4(3): 315–45.

McMahon, G. and Jump, D. (2018) 'Starting to stop: young offenders' desistance from crime', *Youth Justice*, 18(1): 3–17, Available from: https://doi.org/10.1177/1473225417741223

Morris, R. (2015) '"Youth justice practice is just messy": youth offending team practitioners; culture and identity', *The British Journal of Community Justice*, 13(2): 45–57.

Newman, T. (2004) *What Works in Building Resilience*, Ilford: Barnardo's.

Osgood, S. and Anderson, A. (2004) 'Unstructured socialising and rates of delinquency', *Criminology*, 42(3): 519–50.

Pitts, J. (2003) 'What do we want? The "SHAPE" campaign and the reform of youth justice', *Youth Justice*, 3(3): 134–51.

Robinson, A. (2014) *Foundations for Youth Justice: Positive Approaches to Practice*, Bristol: Policy Press.

Sampson, R.J. and Laub, J.H. (2004) 'Life-course desisters? Trajectories, of crime among delinquent boys followed to age 70', *Criminology*, 41(3): 301–39.

Schaefer-McDaniel, N.J. (2004) 'Conceptualizing social capital among young people: toward a new theory', *Children, Youth and Environments*, 14(1): 140–50.

Smith, D. (2004) 'Parenting and delinquency at ages 12–15 years: the Edinburgh Study of Youth Transitions and Crime Number 3', Centre for Law and Society, University of Edinburgh.

Smith, S., Mann, G. and Lewis, J. (2022) 'SHiFT feasibility study', Youth Endowment Foundation, Centre for Evidence and Implementation, Available from: https://youthendowmentfund.org.uk/wp-content/uploads/2022/09/SHiFT-YEF-Feasibility-Study-Sep-22.pdf

Szifris, K. (2021) *Philosophy behind Bars: Growth and Development in Prison*, Bristol: Bristol University Press.

Taylor, C. (2016) 'Review of the youth justice system in England and Wales', Ministry of Justice.

Truth Hurts (2006) 'Report of the national inquiry into self-harm among young people: fact or fiction?', Mental Health Foundation and Camelot Foundation.

Vlugter, R. (2009) 'Too little, too late: parenting orders as a form of crime prevention', unpublished PhD thesis, University of Bedfordshire, Available from: http://hdl.handle.net/10547/326354

White, C. (2017) 'EIF trusted relationships summary report', Clarissa White Research.

Wigzell, A. (2020) 'Ethnographic perspectives on youth justice supervision and the supervisory relationship', unpublished PhD thesis, University of Cambridge, Available from: https://doi.org/10.17863/CAM.57144

YJB (Youth Justice Board) (2010) 'Youth justice: the scaled approach; a framework for assessment and interventions', YJB England and Wales.

YJB (2015) 'Reducing reoffending: furthering our understanding', YJB England and Wales.

YJB (2016) 'Understanding and improving reoffending performance: a summary of learning from the YJBs reoffending programme with implications for practice', YJB England and Wales.

YJB (2019) 'Standards for children in the youth justice system 2019', YJB England and Wales.

YJB (2020) 'Enhanced case management guidance: implementing the approach', YJB England and Wales.

YJB (2022a) 'Case management guidance', YJB England and Wales.

YJB (2022b) 'Youth justice statistics in England and Wales 2021–22', Available from: https://www.gov.uk/government/statistics/youth-just ice-statistics-2021-to-2022/youth-justice-statistics-2021-to-2022-accessi ble-version

13

Through a youth justice practitioner's lens: would a sentencing alternative to a criminal conviction be a small change with a big impact on children's desistance?

Steven Carr

Introduction

Learning through experience and sharing this learning is central to reflective practice (Finlay, 2008). This chapter encompasses the reflective thoughts of a practitioner who has worked in youth justice for a quarter of a century and, notably, has had the opportunity to work on the 24 picturesque square miles of Guernsey as a Youth Justice Officer. Prior to working in Guernsey, I had experience as a youth offending service (YO[S]) social worker in England, as well as working within the criminal justice service on the shores of the Shetland Islands. Based on this experience, this chapter proposes that a remittal be added to the youth court sentencing framework that is not a conviction and refers children to a specialist environment. This offers the opportunity to reframe thinking away from an adversarial youth justice system and instead promote greater collaboration that aligns more closely with current Child First thinking about supporting the child's development of a positive identity.

The chapter begins with my critical reflections from practice, with my proposition that the youth court process blocks children's desistance through its adversarial structure, which induces oppositional identities between children and youth justice agencies. The chapter goes on to show the evolutionary shape of youth court sentencing and suggests an alternative structure that supports collaborative working and positive identity development, which could play a valuable role in enabling children's desistance. Specifically, I provide an overview of the Guernsey Model, where the youth court sentencing structure includes remittals without convictions that are received by the Office of the Children's Convenor (OCC), and, then, propose that the existing structures of the Children's Hearing System (CHS) in Scotland, diversionary Swansea Model in Wales and Youth Referral Order Panels) are already in place to receive youth court non-conviction remittals like the Guernsey Model which could reshape youth court sentencing.

I conclude by acknowledging that although the reshaping of youth court sentencing may promote a collaborative philosophy and an improved environment between children and youth justice agencies that are conducive for children's desistance, it is the interaction and relationship between children and youth justice practitioners that will facilitate real change. With this in mind, 'The Barcode of Desistance' (BoD) model is presented as a practitioners' aide-mémoire to balance risk parameters by promoting 'benefit thinking' with children. This model could be incorporated within assessments and court reports as assets to nurture the development of children's non-offending identity, furthering the tertiary stage of desistance, with practitioners advocating positive change in children and in so doing enriching the philosophy and culture of children's justice.

Critical reflections from practice

Is justice best served through the sentencing of a child to a criminal conviction? The Sentencing Council's view is that in many cases, there will be advantages to diverting children away from court:

> In most cases a young person is likely to benefit from being given greater opportunity to learn from mistakes without undue penalisation or stigma, especially as a court sanction might have a significant effect on the prospects and opportunities of the young person, and, therefore, on the likelihood of effective integration into society. (Sentencing Guidelines Council, 2009, p 7)

Although everyone may have a different interpretation of justice, the United Nations Convention on the Rights of the Child (1989) as endorsed by the UK states in Article 40, 3(b) that

> [s]tates parties shall seek to promote the establishment of laws, procedures, authorities and institutions specifically applicable to children alleged as, accused of, or recognised as having infringed the penal law, and in particular: whenever appropriate and desirable, measures for dealing with such children without resorting to judicial proceedings, providing that human rights and legal safeguards are fully respected.

The Convention (1989) is fundamental in setting out the process for dealing with children without resorting to judicial proceedings therefore promoting the identity of children as children; whereas children [n the UK who enter court, potentially experience a change in identity; the identity of the child changes from entering court as a child, receiving a 'court order' and leaving court with a conviction and the label of a child criminal (Haines and Case, 2015). While this creates challenges for the child, there are possible] alternatives where a child in court could be remitted without a conviction to a tribunal, clinic, hearing, panel or similar process outside of court. This allows a child to leave court without a criminal record and so facilitates the continuum towards a more 'Child First' doctrine (Haines and Case, 2015). In this case, the state demonstrates that it is aligning itself with the UN Convention on the Rights of the Child, valuing the needs of the child.

The Independent Parliamentarians' Inquiry (Carlile, 2014, p 49) into the operation and effectiveness of the youth court quotes youth magistrate David Chesterton:

> I am of the view that the greatest failure of our youth justice system is the adversarial approach we have adopted. It seems to me this approach is about 'establish who did it and punish them'. In contrast, the inquisitorial system adopted by our European neighbours seems to me to be about 'find out what went wrong and fix it'. ... Our focus on punishment rather than problem solving contributes to our high levels of reoffending.

From a practitioner's perspective, I endorse Chesterton's sentiment regarding the youth justice system's adversarial approach and give consideration as to where the youth court framework and sentencing structure can be enhanced. I believe in promoting desistance at every available opportunity, which requires the whole system to share a collaborative identity of a child-friendly/ Child First approach for children's justice. Although children's criminal justice is annexed from the adult criminal justice system, it remains too closely connected through sharing adult structures and therefore ideology. There are exceptions within the children's criminal justice system that have scope to be further developed and thus expand children's criminal justice towards a more distinctive system and ultimately with its own unique identity, such as Referral Orders which make meaningful steps towards collaborative thinking.

As a practitioner in England, I was frequently informed by First Time Child Entrants (FTCEs) in youth court in England that they felt removed, disempowered and confused at court. The court was considered authoritarian and punitive, defining children as criminals and adversely impacting upon desistance through a process of stigmatisation and labelling. Conversely, children and families have informed me that Referral Order panels make them feel more involved, giving them a voice and therefore invested in the better able to value the process in making amends (restoratively). Having previously worked as a Referral Order Co-ordinator, I have witnessed children engaging in this inclusive process and gaining a clarity of understanding of the restorative ideology of putting things right and constructively moving on. This collaborative process made sense to children, parent(s)/carer(s), panel members and victims alike. Although this can be viewed positively, the Referral Order carries a conviction that defines the child as a criminal (albeit just for the duration of the order), and therefore the process remains linked to youth court. In my experience, the Referral Order is aligned to the Social Discipline Window (IIRP 2007, p 5) of working 'WITH' children (see Figure 13.1) rather than 'NOT' doing things or doing things 'FOR' children. Yet, with its conviction status and potential for breach proceedings that involve going back to court, the 'TO' Social Discipline Window is also at play, making the Referral Order a hybrid of internal and external means of control. The Referral Order process with 'Panels' held outside of court and typically in a YOT offer the potential to reframe identity through a healthier environment that enables the child, the panel and professionals not to define the child by their offence(s) but instead may foster an identity that works with the child in their entirety and in so doing establish positive working relationships and thinking that is favourable to desistance.

As noted earlier, the process of court carries adversarial limitations, labels children and therefore lessens the principal aim of the Crime and Disorder

Figure 13.1: Social Discipline Window

	Low support	High support
High Boundaries	**Adversarial/authoritarian approach** 'Doing to' = Stigmatising **TO** Emotional status: Anxious vigilance Oppositional Defensive Marginalised	**Collaborative/restorative approach** 'Doing with' = Inclusive **WITH** Emotional status: Relaxed alertness Cooperative Reflective Connected
Low Boundaries	**Uninvolved/neglectful approach** 'Doing nothing' = Apathetic **NOT** Emotional status: Reflective defensive Ignored Isolated Disconnected	**Proscriptive/permissive approach** 'Doing for' = Avoidance **FOR** Emotional status: Passive enabled Continuance Reinforcement Disempowered

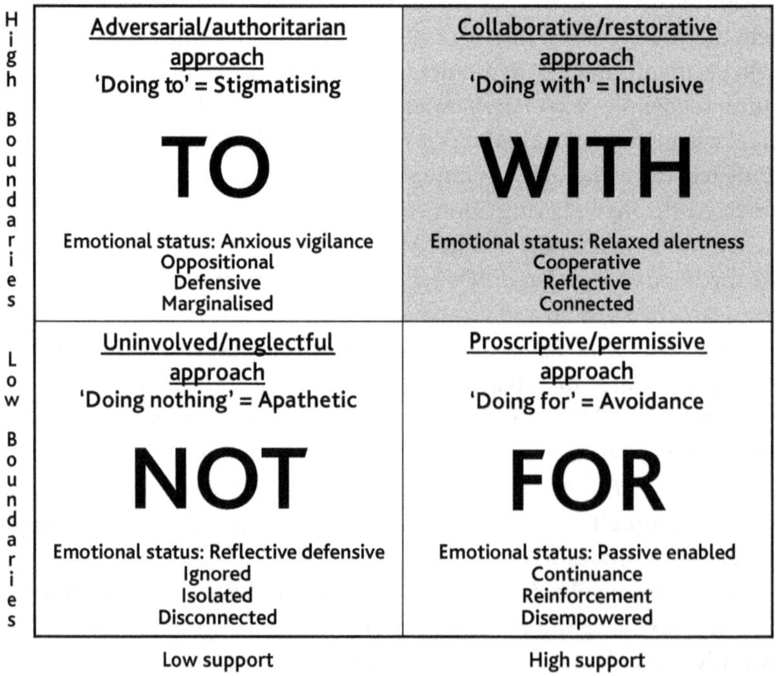

Act 1998, namely 'preventing offending by children and young people'. This is because in court children learn 'external means of control', an authoritarian style of criminal justice with an adversarial dynamic that in my experience is omnipresent in the criminal justice system, experienced at the point of arrest, police interview, in court, via community and custodial sentencing and is compounded by its connection with the adult criminal justice system. The learnt adversarial stance from children is perhaps more observable in a child involved in 'persistent' offending, as they may be better acquainted with the adversarial system. Indeed, as a practitioner, I have attended Appropriate Adult interviews at the police custody suite with children I am acquainted with and witnessed their characters transform when they patently tell mistruths in police interviews. Similarly, I have witnessed people give false names to the court. An adversarial process encourages children to adopt an oppositional approach that does not align them to law and order but instead side-lines the child from mainstream social norms. This oppositional approach can marginalise children, who may go on to construct anti-establishment identities, including a child, now an adult, that I worked with some years ago, who self-tattooed 'Fuck Feds' on to his arm, illustrating his adversarial position at that time.

The prominent self-tattoo asserts a strong anti-establishment identity that not only alienated him from the police as a child but also moved him closer to a criminal subculture, who endorsed the sentiment of his tattoo. The tattoo was explicit, displaying an individual child's oppositional identity, yet it was aimed at a collective, projecting an adverse identity of the social structure of the police. Identities then are not just restricted to individuals but are ubiquitous to places, organisations and cultures; they are not interpreted universally and, instead, are dependent upon your role and interaction with them. If we are looking to promote desistance at every available opportunity, then social structures, including environments, processes and the people within them, should all attune to the 'WITH' Social Discipline Window.

Remittals without convictions changing the shape of youth court sentencing

Professor Neal Hazel (cited in Carlile, 2014, p 51) states that the criminal justice system should seek to

[s]hift their [children's] understanding of themselves to something more positive, so that you stop people thinking of themselves as street kids, as criminals and so on, and start to think of themselves as progressive members of the community, as engaged and so on. You can't, it's very difficult to do that within the type of criminal justice system that we have at the moment, with the processes and with disposals that we have.

Figure 13.2: Simplified schematisation of the changing shape of sentencing for children

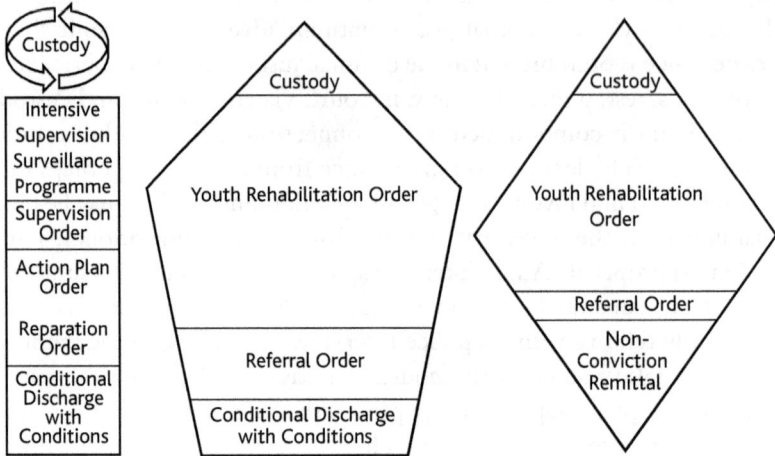

Custody

Intensive
Supervision
Surveillance
Programme

Supervision
Order

Action Plan
Order

Reparation
Order

Conditional
Discharge
with
Conditions

Custody

Youth Rehabilitation Order

Referral Order

Conditional Discharge
with Conditions

Custody

Youth Rehabilitation
Order

Referral Order

Non-
Conviction
Remittal

Through the lens of a youth justice practitioner, I have witnessed the reshaping of youth court sentencing, from the oblong matchstick shape (see Figure 13.2) that saw the escalation of children sentenced to the next tier of the ladder, culminating in the revolving door of custody; to the current pentagon shape (see Figure 13.2), extending the incremental ladder of the oblong matchstick sideways with the Youth Rehabilitation Order (YRO) that gives breadth to community sentences and widens the sentencing shape, and in so doing suppresses children's progression into custody.

The incorporation of a non-conviction remittal to a support agency offers the potential to reshape youth court sentencing again, possibly reaching the diamond standard, by diverting children away from a youth court conviction and suppressing the label of child criminal, then maintaining the existing shape with YRO's widening community penalties for those children with convictions and tapering numbers into custody, as shown in Figure 13.2.

The Guernsey Model maps on to the diamond shape of sentencing as the court has the option of making a remittal without a criminal conviction (yet it is still recorded on the Police National Computer and some Disclosure and Barring Service checks) to the OCC.

OCC

The Guernsey and Alderney Criminal Justice Law 2008 led to the implementation of the OCC and the Child Youth and Community Tribunal (the Tribunal) in 2010. The OCC is the gatekeeper to the Tribunal, which replaces youth court as a diversionary measure in most cases of child offending, and like Referral Orders take a less formal approach than court, geared towards discussion with both the child and family. The OCC addresses offending through voluntary intervention or compulsory measures (Care Requirement) under Section 35(1) of the law where 'there is, or appears to be, no one able and willing to exercise parental responsibility so as to provide adequate care protection or control to the child'. Whether voluntary intervention or compulsory measures, there is no 'conviction'. The court system for children in Guernsey and the Bailiwick continues for high-gravity offences, children who contest charge(s) against them (for a resolution of innocence or guilt) and children who persistently offend. A court remittal to the OCC for children is an option available at youth court, and when this occurs a child attends a Tribunal and does not incur a conviction, shown in Figure 13.3.

The OCC workflow follows six marked steps:

1. Referral: following arrest and after charge, the police/Border Agency refer all cases to the OCC (except for high-gravity offence[s] where the child is detained to the next available court and the OCC is notified). The Custody Officer explains the OCC referral process to the child and their appropriate adult, bailing the child until Step 2 or Step 3.
2. The OCC investigates: the OCC undertakes an assessment process, known as the Convenors Referral Meeting (CoRM), utilising information from a wide range of sources including: police, youth justice service (YJS) (who supply an Initial Enquiry Report [IER]), social services, school, Child and Adolescent Mental Health Services, health and the voluntary or third sector. All the information is studied, and if not 'Jointly Reported', then the OCC may determine an action from the following list without referring to the prosecution law officers:
   - No further action.
   - Convenor's Interview: a child and their parent(s)/guardian(s) or carer(s) attend a meeting with an OCC representative, YJS representative and/ or a representative(s) from other agency(s). The CoRM investigation may show for example that a child is leaving school and wishes to pursue employment; the Convenor's Interview can then be a proactive sign-posting opportunity where an agency representative (for example Guernsey Employment Trust) is introduced to the child and the resource is explained; there is no obligation for the child to engage with that agency.
   - Restorative Measures: restorative intervention is checked as viable by the YJS (reparation may be incorporated within restorative measures).
   - Request an Initial Convenor's Report (ICR), undertaken by the YJS to explore more fully than the IER further family details, circumstances of

Figure 13.3: Guernsey's OCC criminal offence referral and investigation workflow

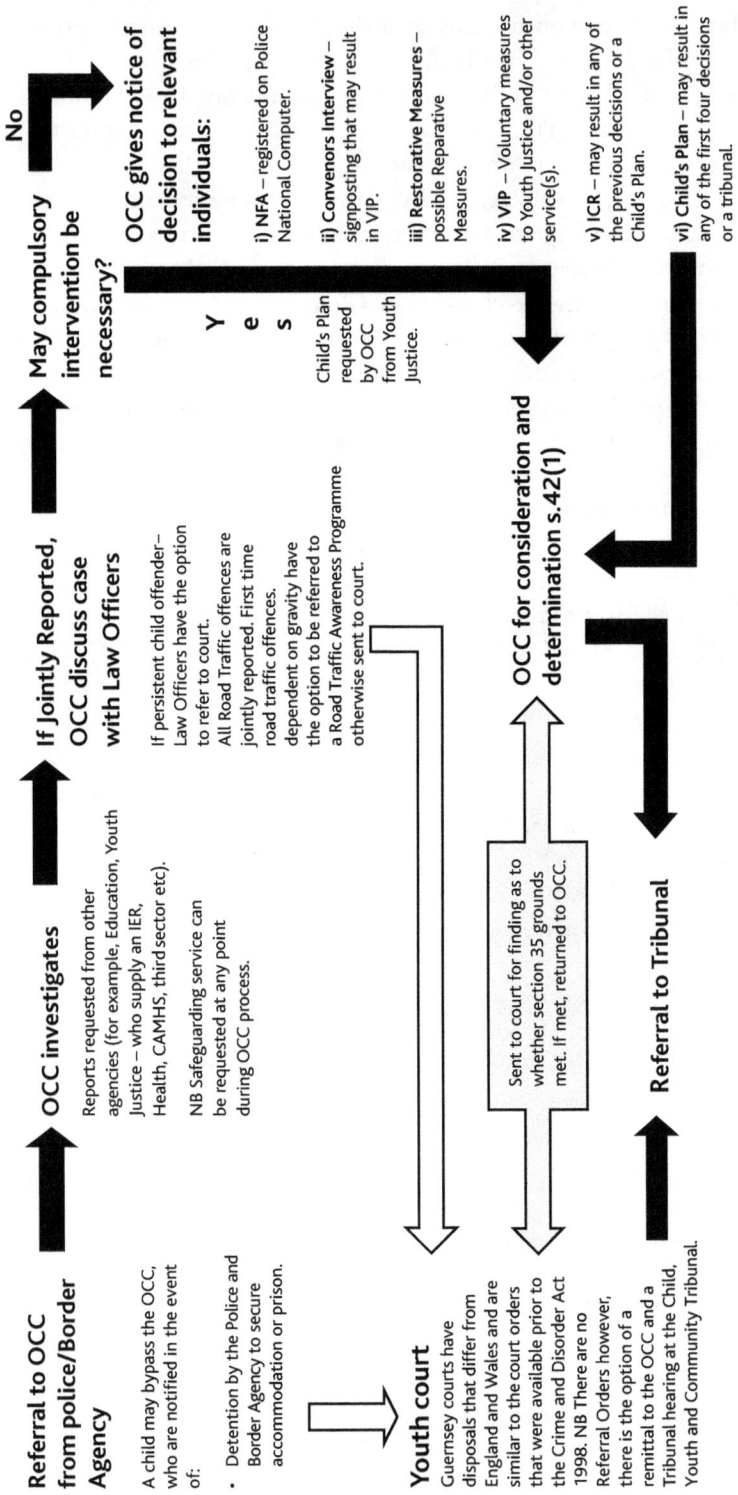

Referral to OCC from police/Border Agency

A child may bypass the OCC, who are notified in the event of:

- Detention by the Police and Border Agency to secure accommodation or prison.

OCC investigates

Reports requested from other agencies (for example, Education, Youth Justice, Health, CAMHS, third sector etc).

NB Safeguarding service can be requested at any point during OCC process.

If Jointly Reported, OCC discuss case with Law Officers

If persistent child offender – Law Officers have the option to refer to court.

All Road Traffic offences are jointly reported. First time road traffic offences. dependent on gravity have the option to be referred to a Road Traffic Awareness Programme otherwise sent to court.

May compulsory intervention be necessary?

Yes

No

OCC gives notice of decision to relevant individuals:

i) **NFA** – registered on Police National Computer.

ii) **Convenors Interview** – signposting that may result in VIP.

iii) **Restorative Measures** – possible Reparative Measures.

iv) **VIP** – Voluntary measures to Youth Justice and/or other service(s).

v) **ICR** – may result in any of the previous decisions or a Child's Plan.

vi) **Child's Plan** – may result in any of the first four decisions or a tribunal.

Child's Plan requested by OCC from Youth Justice.

OCC for consideration and determination s.42(1)

Referral to Tribunal

Sent to court for finding as to whether section 35 grounds met. If met, returned to OCC.

Youth court

Guernsey courts have disposals that differ from England and Wales and are similar to the court orders that were available prior to the Crime and Disorder Act 1998. NB There are no Referral Orders however, there is the option of a remittal to the OCC and a Tribunal hearing at the Child, Youth and Community Tribunal.

the referral, school, significant issues for the child and family, child's and family's views and a conclusion. The report makes a recommendation, which maps on to the OCC actions outlined earlier with the addition of a Voluntary Intervention Programme (VIP) or a Child's Plan (CP).

- VIP agencies such as the YJS engage with the child and family in a voluntary capacity, which is agreed with the child and family to support them in the areas that are identified in the ICR. If the VIP is considered not viable following a change in circumstances (that is, it is considered Section 35[1] of the law has been met), then a referral to the OCC for a CP may be requested.
- CP: this is requested when preliminary investigations identify a likelihood of 'Compulsory Intervention' being required; or if a child is on a VIP or other support action and circumstances have changed such that the threshold of Section 35(1) of the Children Law (Guernsey and Alderney) is likely to be met; or the case is remitted from court. The youth justice practitioner or identified agency undertakes a comprehensive assessment for the OCC, which is provided to those attending a Tribunal (see Step 6).

3. Jointly reported cases discussed with the prosecution law officers: similar to Step 2, with the exception that the offence(s) have a higher-gravity score and/or the child is identified as a persistent offender or have committed a road traffic offence. Dialogue between the OCC and the prosecution law officers results in cases either being sent to youth court or kept with the OCC. If kept with the OCC, then the range of actions are as identified in Step 2 with the addition of a referral to an educative Road Traffic Awareness Programme (RTAP) for first-time road traffic offences; repeat road traffic offences are typically sent to court.

4. Compulsory intervention is necessary: referral to the Tribunal where Section 35(1) of the Children Law (Guernsey and Alderney) and Section 35(2)(f) 'the child is 12 or over and has committed a criminal offence' are met (the age of criminal responsibility in the Bailiwick of Guernsey and Alderney is two years older than in England and Wales). If Section 35 grounds are not met, then the range of actions identified in Step 2 are available.

5. OCC for consideration and determination: where a case is referred to the Tribunal, and before the Tribunal meets, the parents, child and others entitled (child supporter and/or legal advocate) are given full details of the reasons for the referral and asked whether they agree with them. Before the Tribunal meets, there will be a Convenor's meeting, with the parents, child and others required to establish whether the conditions for referral are accepted. If they are not, then the matter is sent to court to determine whether Section 35 conditions are met. If the court decides they are, the case will go back to the Tribunal for a decision on whether compulsory intervention is necessary.

6. Referral to Tribunal: the Tribunal is made up of a lay panel of three people drawn from the local community. Guided by the basic principles of the Bailiwick of Guernsey and Alderney Children Law, with the welfare of the child as the paramount consideration, the Tribunal sits with the child, child's parent(s)/carer(s), youth justice social worker and other relevant agencies, aided by a CP, to consider whether a child is at risk or in need of compulsory intervention to ensure they receive sufficient care, protection, guidance or control. Within the criminal law, there are four other considerations when dealing with offending behaviour: the interests of any victim, the welfare of the child, the alternatives to criminal proceedings (except when these considerations conflict with public interest and safety) and the desirability of ensuring the child remains in the community.

Conviction and remittal differences between the Guernsey Model and frameworks in Scotland, England and Wales

The framework of the CHS in Scotland is comparable to the OCC, with the 'Hearing' structure like the OCC 'Tribunal' consisting of three lay panel members, social worker, professionals, child, child's family/carer(s) and optional child supporter and legal advisor. A hearing like a tribunal requires an admission of guilt, which if disputed is similarly referred to court for a proof hearing. The main disposal available to the hearing panel is a supervision requirement based on the needs of the child.

The Swansea Model again has similarities to the OCC framework. The police determine a referral on key principles including acknowledgement of guilt, low gravity of offence and criteria around FTCE into the youth justice system. A Bureau Co-ordinator requests information from an array of sources, which is analysed by the YOT Pre-Court Team Officer, who undertakes an assessment with the child that also incorporates the victim's needs. A multi-agency panel discuss the report and make a provisional decision for the 'Clinic' that consists of the members of the panel plus the child and their parent/carers to reach a mutually agreed decision of either:

- Non-criminal disposal, accompanied by a support package if required for the child and/or parents/carers on a voluntary basis (support packages and services are child- rather than offence-focused)
- Police reprimand or final warning
- Prosecution at court

The youth court in England and Wales does not have the means to remit a child without a conviction. A difference between the Referral Order and the Swansea Model is that the latter is a court diversionary measure with the youth court unable to remit to the Swansea Model unless through a

Conditional Discharge with conditions; however, this would include a conviction. A difference between the Referral Order and the Guernsey Model is that the Referral Order carries a conviction. In both Guernsey and Scotland, remittals are available to the OCC and the CHS respectively; however, in Scotland, the remittal includes a conviction from court. I propose that a remittal sentencing option like the Guernsey Model Tribunal could be incorporated in Scotland, England and Wales through the existing structures of Referral Order panels, the Swansea Model Clinics and in the CHS. Such an addition should change the shape of sentencing towards the diamond standard, improving desistance by reframing identities away from being labelled as criminals and instead towards seeing the child first. The inclusion of a sentencing remittal without a conviction to a panel, clinic or hearing should provide youth courts parity when initially considering whether they have sufficient powers to sentence children; if they do not, then they are remitted to a higher court that has weightier penalties. The addition of a remittal without a conviction to a Tribunal or similar provides balance to the scales of justice since consideration is also given to whether the child must be sanctioned to an intervention with a criminal conviction.

The impact of reshaping youth court sentencing to include non-conviction remittals upon the philosophy and culture of children's justice

The Referral Order, as noted earlier, currently carries a conviction. This might be considered by some as an advantage insofar as there are consequences for non-adherence, with the child returned to court. However, the sanction of breach furthers an adversarial engagement, effectively complicating relationships between the child and the YOT. The Youth Justice Board (YJB) case management guidance recognises that 'evidence indicates the more frequently a child is taken to court, the more negative the outcomes for that child are likely to be. This means that breach action should only be taken as a last resort' (YJB, 2022). Imagine then that the Referral Order is restructured so that no conviction is attached; in this context, if a child fails to adhere to a Referral Order, the YOT would follow current practices, with the exception of not breaching the order and returning the child to court. The youth justice inspectorate should examine engagement of YOT practice, and the development of successful engagement practices should be furthered. YOTs could potentially shift away from the threat of returning the child to court for non-engagement, nurturing a collaborative culture that shifts the thinking towards a problem-solving philosophy to gain a better understanding as to why a child has not engaged at this time.

The existing structures of the Swansea Model, CHS and Referral Order panels would require nominal alteration for remittals without a conviction from youth court. The narrative and the thinking behind the order is modified along with the identity of the youth court, the sentence, the YOT and the child. The YJB's case management guidance recognises the contradictory interests a conviction has upon engagement between a child and YOT practitioner, and guidance is given to circumnavigate these contradictory interests:

- it is a breach of the order if the child, without reasonable excuse, fails to do what they are required to; so positive activities may be better delivered on a non-mandatory basis;
- maximising opportunities for voluntary engagement may be more effective than requirements which contain compulsory attendance;
- therapeutic work which helps to lessen the likelihood of future harmful behaviours such as counselling is actively undermined by compulsory status;
- children who are forced to attend sporting or other positive activities are likely to engage less than those who attend by choice.

A non-conviction remittal may ease these contradictory interests.

A dualistic Referral Order is also an option where the existing Referral Order with criminal conviction remains and the addition of a Remittal Referral option without a criminal conviction is introduced. In the case of the latter, the Police National Computer will not show a conviction but would show a referral to the YOT. Should the child return to the youth court in future for another offence, the YOT would be able to inform the youth court of the child's engagement on the non-conviction remittal. Indeed, it may be instrumental in the youth court considering another non-conviction remittal or an alternative sentence.

The addition of a non-conviction remittal to a supporting agency acknowledges a child welfare ethos and raises the profile of community involvement through tribunals and panels or other community-based elements. This would align more closely to the proposal by the Children's Commissioner for Wales and YJB that 'youth proceedings be convened outside of formal court buildings to improve young people's engagement and encourage local community justice' (Carlile, 2014, p 52).

Practitioner relationships with children and the enablement of desistance identities

The addition of a youth court remittal without a conviction to a supporting agency does not detract from practitioners' interactions with children within tribunals, clinics, hearings, panel meetings and alike. Practitioner relationship building continues to remain pivotal in setting the basis of engagement with children and enabling desistance. Relationship dynamics occur in every interaction and can become a learned expectation of behaviour, like the relationships between student and teacher, police and suspect, court and defendant, YOT practitioner and offender and YOT practitioner and child. The final two examples being one and the same, yet each projecting different relationship identities with the latter being under the auspices of a youth court remittal without a conviction. The relationship skills of practitioners with children remain key, and a shift from an adversarial premise should assist how practitioners are perceived.

Within an adversarial framework, YOT practitioners may be seen as external agents of social control monitoring court orders and initiating breach proceedings, despite practitioners working hard to reframe this narrative to children who in my experience can be wary of the dual role of the YOT practitioner as being both child advocate and perceived informant for the court. Practitioners continue to balance such identities through working with children transparently, with an honest and genuine approach. The perspective of enforcement is a controversial means of achieving compliance and may reinforce oppositional attitudes that centre on power and control. In my experience, the perspective of enforcement in and of itself may lead children to adopt strategies of thinking for self-preservation reasons. Practitioners working from an enforcement paradigm ensure that orders are complied with through the influence of penalties to deter children from breaking orders. However, when practitioners recognise that children are becoming adept at learning how to control their situations, the enforcement rationale may interpret this as 'they're only telling you what they think you want to hear'. Such statements encourage the notion of deceit, are unproductive and hamper the practitioner–child relationship. Yet they stem from a system of enforced compliance, which lends itself to children learning to mask and feign a compliant identity in order that they may successfully, albeit superficially, complete their court order. Similarly, a visible oppositional identity may be heightened from the enforcement paradigm, which may be seen as challenging and invariably lends itself to children being marginalised, disengaged and failing to complete their court order. Either of these child–practitioner engagements can increase a child's risk profile and are derivatives from an adversarial framework. In my experience, the Guernsey Model may enhance practitioner–child relationships through a sentencing framework distanced from working with children within adversarial parameters, which in turn enhances the collaborative process. The Guernsey Model places the child at the heart of the assessment in requiring the views of the child and thus enabling the youth justice practitioner to cultivate the role of child advocate.

Following the inclusion of a youth court remittal without a conviction to a supporting agency, assessments may evolve that are less inclined to adopt an enforcement and deficit model and favour a collaborative and strengths-based model, moderating a child's risk profile. The Tribunal's philosophy of inclusivity, engaging children and families in a process that is participative and in an environment that is less formal than court sees 'the approaches professionals adopt affecting their perceptions of children' (Bovarnick, 2010, pp 80–96). It is with this and the knowledge that 'engagement wanes when there is an emphasis on risks and deficits rather than strengths' (Carlile, 2014, p 51), that the BoD, inspired by AssetPlus, is presented as a practitioner's visual aide-mémoire to assist agencies within children's criminal justice to build constructive relationships with children through strengthening positive identities in demonstrating that children have successfully desisted. Rather than focusing upon the risk factors of offending, the BoD model can be utilised to encourage visualisation with the child in locating occasions when things worked well and identify what was happening at this time with a view to develop these assets and therefore maintain desistance; reinforcing a positive non-criminal identity and may be incorporated within the pre-sentence report format heading 'Factors which will support positive outcomes for the child and promote public safety'.

The BoD model

Classifying children within a collective measurement framework such as conviction rates does little to take into consideration the multitude of complex variants that are peculiar to each individual child, including the severity and time between offences. A refined measure shown within (Figure 13.4), in what I have termed the BoD, where the vertical lines indicate an offence event, the boldness of the line the gravity of the offence, the gap between each line the time elapsed between offences, with the numbers underneath the timeline (in this instance the age of the child) giving a visual representation of an offending career and looks similar to a barcode:

This visual representation of a child's criminal history could easily be termed the 'Barcode of Offending', and historically the youth justice service have expertly examined the offence bars to understand a child's chronology of offending behaviour and informed the youth court of the risks associated with it and how to externalise control through programmes and groups available that specifically address the risk of reoffending.

The BoD model invites youth justice agencies to see the gaps between the lines as a 'period of desistance' which require as much understanding as the bars in perpetuating desistance. By recognising and elongating these gaps, the lines in the illustration disappear and the child can figuratively escape their bars of offending through the gaps between them.

Figure 13.4: Barcode of Desistance

In the illustration, there are four bar lines around the child's 14th birthday, and the BoD timeline can be adjusted by reducing it from years to months, weeks or a timeline that best exemplifies periods of desistance, enabling the child and the practitioner to identify within those gaps the positive building blocks that will extend the desistance timeline to months, years and beyond.

The gaps in the BoD can be missed as attention is drawn towards 'offence-centric' domains that evaluate and attempt to control risk, exemplified when youth justice agencies are required to enforce a court order, as for example when a child fails to adhere to the conditions of a community order and returns to the court for breach of proceedings, it creates another line in the BoD. To differentiate a breach proceeding within the BoD illustration, the line is designated with hatched shading as in Figure 13.5.

This BoD again demonstrates how difficult it is to see the gaps between the bars, despite the gaps taking up more of the space on the page than the lines. In Figure 13.6, the gaps are made solid suggesting that this is important space worthy of investigation and indeed recognises the child first.

The BoD maps on to the age–crime curve, demonstrating that with maturation the proclivity of offending diminishes. The youth court in England and Wales has knowledge of this correlation disparity involving age and offending shown by the Sentencing Guidelines Council: 'Offending by a young person is frequently a phase which passes fairly rapidly and therefore the reaction to it needs to be kept well balanced in order to avoid alienating the young person from society.' Through fully exploring the gaps in the BoD model, youth justice agencies should help to balance pro-social identities with children by observing the positives and turning points in a child's development rather than promoting intervention upon an offending identity.

Conclusion

The Independent Parliamentarians' Inquiry into the operation and effectiveness of the youth court chaired by Lord Carlile of Berriew (2014)

Figure 13.5: Barcode of Desistance (with breach)

Note: The hatched lines indicate with breach

Figure 13.6: Barcode of Desistance (emphasising desistance gaps)

'asked for submissions on alternative models to the current system'. As Carlile noted: 'The overwhelming contention of respondents was that England and Wales should look to move to a more or fully non-adversarial approach, with the Scottish CHS the first amongst others referenced as an alternate model' (Carlile, 2014, p 54). The promotion of desistance within an adversarial child criminal justice system may remain problematic in neutralising a criminal identity and therefore preventing offending by children. Introducing a youth court remittal like the Guernsey Model within England and Wales that is not a conviction may provide impetus in broadening existing collaborative youth justice structures for children. The decline of children masking compliance or visibly opposing an adversarial child criminal justice system should occur as structures and their processes become aligned towards nurturing internal means of control through encouraging a strengths-based practice that focuses upon the child and their context, not just on the offence(s) but on the gaps when they desist.

References

Bovarnick, S. (2010) 'How do you define a "trafficked child"? A discursive analysis of practitioners' perceptions around child trafficking', *Youth and Policy*, 104: 80–96.

Carlile, A. (2014) 'Independent parliamentarians' inquiry into the operation and effectiveness of the youth court', chaired by Lord Carlile of Berriew CBE QC, Available from: https://michaelsieff-foundation.org.uk/cont ent/inquiry_into_the_operation_and_effectiveness_of_the_youth_court-uk-carlile-inquiry.pdf

Haines, K. and Case, S. (2015) *Positive Youth Justice: Children First, Offenders Second*, Bristol: Policy Press.

International Institute for Restorative Practices (2007) 'Restorative practices: facilitator skills training students course workbook', Available from: https://www.iirp.edu/images/pdf/rjevidence.pdf

Islands Safeguarding Children Partnership (2010) 'The short guide: children law; Guernsey and Alderney; 27', Available from: http://iscp.gg/childrenLaw

Sentencing Council (2009) 'Overarching principles: sentencing youth, definitive guideline', Sentencing Guidelines Council, Available from: https://www.sentencingcouncil.org.uk/wp-content/uploads/web_overarching_principles_sentencing_youths.pdf

United Nations (1989) 'Convention on the Rights of the Child', Treaty Series 1577, 3, Available from: https://www.unicef.org.au/united-nati ons-convention-on-the-rights-of-the-child

Youth Justice Board (2022) 'Case management guidance', Available from: https:// www.gov.uk/guidance/case-management-guidance/how-to-work-with-children

14

Innovative and theoretically informed intervention programmes for children who offend: The Compass Project

Neema Trivedi-Bateman

Introduction

There is an important need for more robustly designed crime reduction intervention programmes for children. Rigorously designed interventions might include evidence-based and theoretically informed programme content, highly skilled and trained research staff, the inclusion of a control group and a thorough process and impact evaluation (Ariel et al, 2022). Many of the programmes that do exist have been criticised for adopting a seemingly scattergun approach to trying to fix the problem of crime, characterised by the absence of a sound theoretical underpinning (Roach, 2023). This chapter explores whether desistance can be achieved by introducing children to a range of psychological strategies that are designed to develop law-abiding morality and emotions. Law-abiding morality can be measured with the belief that it is wrong to commit acts that break rules or laws (Wikström and Treiber, 2009), and it can be achieved by demonstrating conformity to rules (Bottoms et al, 2004). The link between low law-relevant morality, low emotional functioning and regulation and child antisocial behaviour and crime is well evidenced (Wikström et al, 2012; Pauwels et al, 2018; Trivedi-Bateman, 2021). What is less understood is the ways in which these traits can be strengthened in adolescence by participation in intervention programmes.

In this chapter, an applied perspective is used to outline the links between the current child crime desistance literature and law-abiding morality. It is suggested that child crime desistance can be achieved by reorienting the focus to support morality and emotional development. By building on existing work about the roles of self and social identity (Laub and Sampson, 2001; Maruna, 2001), it is proposed that morality, moral emotion and emotionality are integral components of the ways in which self-identity and the perspective of the self and others are expressed in relation to criminal behaviour. Next, evidence of the relationship between morality, emotion and child antisocial behaviour and crime is presented alongside a theoretical framework for this work. Situational Action Theory (SAT) takes an evidence-led approach to deem morality to be of central importance to explanations of why crime occurs and provides potential mechanisms and explanatory processes for the relationship between law-abiding morality and law-abiding behaviour (Wikström, 2004). This theoretical model purports that whether crime is selected from an array of perceived action alternatives is dependent on the inputs to a 'moral filter'. This moral filter is influenced by the individual (that is, whether they think crime is wrong and whether they feel bad about it) and the immediate setting (that is, whether the environment is crime-conducive, such as whether there are provocations, deterrents or monitors present) (Wikström and Treiber, 2009).

Taking inspiration from these theoretical concepts that are empirically found to be related to involvement in crime, The Compass Project (TCP) intervention programme, the first to fill a gap in intervention testing and apply SAT in practice, will be introduced. Careful consideration of the evidence base serves as a preparatory foundation for the development of TCP. The Compass pilot study, a nine-week programme delivered in 2022 to children at a youth work charity in Cambridgeshire, UK, will be introduced. The intervention comprised a set of newly developed group activities to encourage children to use a range of psychological strategies and tools to develop law-abiding morality. The intervention background, rationale and methodology development will be presented. While TCP served to pilot test the programme content, main or interaction analyses of pre- and post-data could not be performed due to sample size restrictions. Since then, post-pilot adjustments to the methodology and study design have been made, and Compass is being implemented in other contexts (such as schools), where attrition is expected to be lower (SAT NAV Compass study, https://www.lboro.ac.uk/research/compass-project/project-delivery/school/). In future, other contexts in which programmes of this nature can be administered will be identified (such as youth offending teams and pupil referral units). The central proposition is that there is potential for programmes of this kind to give children the opportunities to develop law-abiding tools, strategies and perspectives in relation to their attitudes, feelings and behaviours as they relate to crime. Ultimately, this could contribute to the shared goal of the youth justice system to achieve desistance and equip children to live a life free of sanctions, punishments and barriers to their development, all of which are unsatisfactory elements of the ways in which the youth justice system currently operates.

The application of traditional and modern desistance theories to child crime

This work operationalises 'desistance' using broader definitions of cessation or permanent stopping of offending (secondary desistance) as well as significant crime-free gaps, or primary desistance (Bottoms et al, 2004). Both traditional desistance theories and modern desistance theories, while varying in their inclusion of agency and/or structural factors (Ugwudike and Raynor, 2017; Farrall, 2019), tend to focus primarily on adult offending, as noted in Chapter 1. The importance and complexity of explaining why desistance occurs is apparent, in which programmed potential, structures, culture and habitus (or individual dispositions arising from shared cultures), situational contexts and agency are all deemed to be key in explaining desistance, as outlined in the interactive framework offered by Bottoms et al (2004).

It is suggested that approaches often label children and pathologise their offending behaviour, and this is not fruitful in achieving desistance (Allen, 2012; Shapland et al, 2012). The notorious use of harsh discipline and lack of support and safety for children who offend needs to become a historical approach, and we must unwaveringly walk alongside children and take the pace they set while we encourage their narrative to change to become law-abiding (Lösel et al, 2012). Laub and Sampson (2001) suggest that explanations of low-severity child crime may not be worth pursuing since in many cases the offending stops in early adulthood, such as is the case for adolescent-limited offenders (Farrington, 1986; Moffitt, 1993). While this seems logical, there is reason to believe that the factors that lead to the onset of (mild-severity) adolescent crime are relevant in understanding why desistance is and is not achieved later in life (Bottoms et al, 2004). Further to this, the financial and emotional harms of low-severity crimes, although difficult to quantify, are vast and substantial (Heeks et al, 2018).

The sociogenic account proposes that the deceleration of criminal behaviour in the early 20s can be explained by major life events that often occur on the cusp of moving from childhood to adulthood (Lösel et al, 2012). While research explores possible reasons, such as the roles of cognitive maturation, abatement of risky behaviour and the development of empathy, it generally skips over the precise mechanisms or specific explanatory processes at play. Possible drivers for change that have been highlighted include job stability (Sampson and Laub, 1993), meaningful romantic relationships, responsibility for dependants, stability of housing, support from others and less time spent with peers in crime-conducive settings. It is suggested that the consequences of rule-breaking are amplified when there is something – a job and legitimate source of income – or someone – a romantic partner or a child – to lose. What is clear is that life events (or 'turning points' as they have been referred to) themselves do not have a causal relationship to crime (they do not cause people to stop committing crime), but rather that it is factors such as limitations on one's time to offend, and the broad psychological stability resultant from those events and associated relationships, that provide the actual mechanisms of interest (Maruna, 2001). For example, stable relationships and employment are likely to be associated with improved emotional functioning, which encourages rule-abiding behaviour (Trivedi-Bateman, 2022).

Laub and Sampson (2001), in qualitative interviews with young adult offenders, report that a new sense of self and a new identity is commonly found in those who desist from crime. The ideas proposed in this chapter align with some of the principles of Shover's (1996) accounts of crime as a (sometimes limited) choice likely to be made under certain circumstances, and Gove's (1985) ideas in relation to psychological maturation and increases in cooperativeness with age. This work also draws parallels with the condemnation script proposed by Maruna (2001), in which the self is actively reconstructed. TCP attempts to fill a research gap to explore how children engage in such reflection on their own behaviour by facilitating moral debates, discussions and activities for children, alongside repeated reflections on past, current and future thoughts, feelings and behaviours. By placing morality at the forefront of understanding why people commit acts that break rules, we can encourage offenders towards future compliance with rules (Bottoms et al, 2004).

Crime-desistance theories have also highlighted social bonds with others, such as pro-social relationships, to be important (Sampson and Laub, 1993). However, the skills and attributes required to initiate and maintain those relationships have not received as much attention. The neglect of individual subjective processes such as the emotional components of one's identity is a missed opportunity to better understand desistance (Maruna, 2001). By considering the value of pro-social morality, empathy, shame and guilt as core and functional parts of identity in relation to building and maintaining relationships with others, we can gain a fuller understanding of why children start and stop committing crime. Pro-sociality is recognised as one of the core tenets of the fast-emerging and impactful work of the Child First approach (Case and Hazel, 2020) and in Maruna's (2001) extensive work developing desistance theory. Individual-level cognitive processes are indeed found to be integral to the desistance process (Giordano, 2016). Furthermore, desisters are more likely than offenders to report more positive affective states, and one interpretation of this is that enhanced wellbeing facilitates the desistance process (Healy, 2016). This approach aligns with the psychological maturation concepts that are very widely cited in relation to desistance (Moffitt et al, 2002; Mulvey and Schubert, 2016). For example, current research argues that perspective-taking, relationships with others, acceptance of societal values and concern for others can play a key role in law-abiding behaviours. The pertinent question is: for what reasons do most children stop offending once they enter young adulthood, and what is it about the individuals that do not stop offending and the environments they find themselves in that differs from desisters?

By encouraging or strengthening the relevant psychological capabilities in childhood, early interventions can address the processes that are found to be related to the general stopping of crime in early adulthood. This can be achieved by considering the childhood development of emotional faculties and morality, which are largely found to be influenced by imitation and modelling of caregivers, siblings and peers as outlined in social learning theory (Akers and Jennings, 2019; Trivedi-Bateman and Crook, 2022). Identity development is a continual and iterative process throughout the life course. Emotion regulation, among other factors, continues to mature in adulthood (Mulvey et al, 2004). For those with particularly low law-abiding morality and moral emotion, intervention programmes can help provide the strategies and tools to build on these attributes in childhood before the adolescent peak of offending occurs. This section has presented evidence to suggest that traditional and modern desistance theories do not necessarily apply in the same way to children as to adult offenders and suggests an alternative child–desistance paradigm that views morality as being of central importance. The Youth Justice Board (YJB) have recently adopted the Child First approach as part of all strategic goals moving forward. By encouraging practitioners in the youth justice system to demonstrate and model their own empathy in their interactions with children who offend while simultaneously considering the potentially disrupted empathic abilities of children who offend, children can be seen and heard with compassion.

SAT: the relationship between law-breaking morality and crime involvement

SAT is a general theory of all crime types and can be applied to why people stop offending as well as to why people start offending. The key theoretical and empirically tested insights from SAT purport that changes in morality statistically correspond to significant changes in crime at the individual level (Wikström et al, 2018). SAT proposes that all acts of crime are acts of moral rule-breaking and, crucially, finds substantial evidence that morality is the key contributor to crime when testing against many other factors, such as self-control (Pauwels et al, 2018). Emotions contribute to overall moral outlook, and more specifically, low empathy is found to be associated with subsequent low shame and guilt, all of which play a primary role in violence decision-making (Trivedi-Bateman, 2021). Cognitive and affective empathy (understanding and responding to others' emotional states) are vital skills in the underpinning of moral ability (Masto, 2015). Empathy plays a central role in the crime decision-making process (Bach et al, 2017) and is consistently found to be positively associated with rule-abiding and pro-social behaviours.

It is rare to find repeated studies of theoretical and empirical knowledge combined in this way, and interventions based on these concepts have the potential to reduce reoffending (Lösel et al, 2012). Since evidence suggests that the development of morality in childhood, adolescence and adulthood is continual and malleable, this provides an opportunity to intervene using intervention programmes (Ongley and Malti, 2014). Accordingly, this means that interventions that focus on addressing learning and rehearsing moral rules (how right or wrong one thinks illegal action is) and associated emotions (empathy, shame, guilt) should lead to changes in decision-making and subsequently reductions in crime and improvement in pro-social behaviour. As such, law-resistant morality presents fertile ground for crime-desistance intervention development.

Existing crime reduction research and interventions: morality, empathy and emotional functioning

This section summarises findings from a literature review of morality, empathy and emotion interventions to identify what has been effective in achieving positive behavioural (including desistance) outcomes. It is imperative to note that no intervention has addressed morality and emotion as they relate to a theoretical explanation of crime, and studies tend to include part of or one or more (but not all) of the several concepts of interest. To my knowledge, a review with this subject focus and depth has not been carried out to date. The methodologies and findings from the studies in this literature review were instrumental in the development and design of TCP intervention programme activities. The findings provide some promising support for the use of morality, empathy and emotion content in crime-reduction interventions with children who offend, although whether these concepts combined in one programme can reduce crime remains to be seen in the upcoming schools' delivery impact evaluations.

Starting with morality interventions, a moral dilemma discussion intervention increased moral reasoning and found greater pro-social behaviour in incarcerated children (Claypoole et al, 2000). Another moral reasoning development programme found increased moral reasoning and was associated with decreased behavioural issues, including referrals, absenteeism, contact with police and increased academic performance in children (Arbuthnot and Gordon, 1986). A group morality intervention for young adults resulted in increased moral judgement and was associated with increased greater social responsibility and higher inclination to contribute to society (Comunian and Gielen, 2006).

Empathy training can increase empathy and is associated with decreased bullying behaviours in children (Şahin, 2012; Van Ryzin and Roseth, 2019). Dadds et al (2012) find that exposure to empathic-emotion recognition training increased empathy and was associated with decreased conduct problems in children with high callous-unemotional traits. The effect of empathy is also seen with other crime types. For example, a child cyberbullying-focused empathy intervention increased empathy and reduced cyberbullying perpetration (Schultze-Krumbholz et al, 2016), as did a child virtual reality bullying prevention intervention (Ingram et al, 2019). A diffusion of benefits to other pro-social behaviours can also be seen: for example, anti-bullying interventions are associated with increased peer intervention upon witnessing others being bullied (Ingram et al, 2019). Increased cognitive empathy after taking part in the Violence Prevention Programme in Singapore (which partly focuses on empathy development) is associated with decreased proactive aggression and total aggression in children (Zhou et al, 2018), particularly for those with low pre-intervention empathy.

Emotion regulation can be defined as the capacity to 'monitor, assess, understand, and modify emotional reactions with appropriate functioning' (Lotfali et al, 2017, p 115). The following studies demonstrate that emotion regulation is associated with morality, rule-abiding and positive behaviours. Wyman et al (2010) administered an emotion regulation intervention and found decreased rates of child disciplinary referrals and suspensions and improved behaviour control, learning and assertiveness in the classroom. Elsewhere, an emotion management programme for children with attention deficit hyperactivity disorder (ADHD) increased emotion regulation and was associated with increased appropriate social behaviour, social ability (including initiative and cooperativeness) and empathy, as well as improved general psychological wellbeing (Choi and Lee, 2015). A different emotion regulation training intervention (involving practising expression of emotions in verbal and non-verbal modes) for child anger management is associated with increased emotion regulation, decreased expression of anger and increased anger control (Lotfali et al, 2017). Carroll et al (2020) report that increased social and emotional competence (including measures of self-awareness, self-management, social awareness, relationship skills and responsible decision-making) in children is associated with a reduction in internalising and externalising difficulties over time when compared with control participants. More recently, Beelmann and Lösel (2021) report that improved social skills (following social skill training interventions targeting interpersonal and communication abilities) are associated with reduced aggressive, delinquent and related child behaviour problems.

Looking at specific emotions, there is much evidence to indicate that there is a relationship between shame and guilt and child delinquency and crime (see Trivedi-Bateman, 2015, 2021 for a literature review). Restorative justice focuses on building shame in offenders (Braithwaite and Braithwaite, 2001) to prevent further offending, and others have argued that guilt and empathy play just as critical a role (Tangney and Fischer, 1995). Guilt and shame processing are found to be negatively associated with involvement in antisocial behaviour, aggression and crime (Tangney et al, 2007; Svensson et al, 2013; Trivedi-Bateman, 2021). Low guilt is found to be negatively associated with antisocial goals and aggressive responses, measured using vignette methodology (Mazzone et al, 2021). However, there are some contrasting findings that evidence that the relationship between shame, guilt and crime is complicated (Tangney and Fischer, 1995; Elison et al, 2014). Children that commit rule-breaking behaviour are found to lack guilt from three to four years of age (Frick et al, 2013); if early interventions can offer children the tools to assess the impact of their behaviours on themselves and others, they could serve as a handbrake on rule-breaking behaviour.

TCP: background, rationale and methodology

TCP is innovative and ground-breaking because, to date, an evidence-based morality-strengthening programme of this kind has not been administered with children anywhere in the world.[1] Prominent criminologists, such as Bottoms (2002, p 24), have argued that "[i]f they are to be true to their calling, all criminologists have to be interested in morality", but crucially, it remains to be explored in depth in intervention research. The Compass pilot feasibility research encompasses one of the first interventions to explicitly focus on increasing law-relevant morality as a way of encouraging pro-social behaviour. It explores how the practical application of academic morality theories can spark change in moral behaviours in daily life (Wright et al, 2020). A central purpose is to develop confidence of individual agency and conflict resolution to equip young adults to manage risk of future involvement in criminal activity. If found to be successful, morality-enhancing workshops of this kind could reduce the overall proportion of children with a criminal record and play a role in other general positive outcomes, such as quality of relationships with others.

For this work, moral action is defined in accordance with the law, and moral attitudes that condone breaking the law are labelled as law-resistant morality, elsewhere referred to as weak or low morality (Wikström and Treiber, 2009; Trivedi-Bateman, 2021). By defining morality as it corresponds to the laws in a given jurisdiction, value judgements about 'good' and 'bad' behaviour and subjective views on whether laws should be in place can be avoided. Instead, the focus can be on law-abiding and law-breaking moral attitudes and subsequently how to address law-resistant morality. In doing so, little room remains for sociocultural interpretation, for example consideration of religious and cultural facets. Morality-associated emotional factors are found to contribute to moral identity: for example, empathy is critical for the assessment of the consequences of crime to others to take place, and shame and guilt indicate the extent to which one cares about the laws (Tangney et al, 2007).

The means by which we can teach and learn morality must be tested, applied and refined. This is especially relevant for children who have experienced unstable or inconsistent parental modelling, parental attachment and disciplinary style, all of which are crucial to morality development in childhood (Trivedi-Bateman and Crook, 2022). Morality-strengthening programmes can bridge the gap and potentially reduce future antisociality and criminality. The central contention of the Compass pilot was to test the methodology and allow research design strategies to be refined as a result. The longer-term objective in the current SAT NAV Schools study when an adequate sample size is achieved is to test whether morality can be strengthened to align with law-following (compared to a control group) and whether the effects remain on a longer-term basis and across different samples and geographical locations. Findings will be discussed in the context of desistance from crime and interpreted within multiple theoretical frameworks as introduced in the earlier sections of this chapter.

Turning to the methodology, TCP Randomised Controlled Trial pilot involved nine once-weekly 90-minute group sessions for 11–16-year-olds (programme group) at a youth work centre in Cambridge, UK.[2] The randomly selected programme group (N = 51) attended the programme sessions, in which they carried out various practical activities, debates and discussions, alongside their usual youth work activities, and the control group (N = 52) solely attended their usual youth work activities (see Trivedi-Bateman and Martingano [2023] for more information). The philosophy behind the TCP methodology is not dissimilar from that of cognitive-behavioural programmes that are based on social learning and moral reasoning, many of which have reduced violent and general offending in past programmes (Lösel, 2012). However, the content is novel. The intervention comprises activities, discussions and tasks based on a 160-study literature review of previous intervention programmes. For the pilot, trained fieldwork research assistants delivered the interventions at five different sessions per week, and all activities and researcher instructions can be found in a detailed fieldwork handbook (Trivedi-Bateman, 2023).[3] The activities cover five topic strands of interest (see Table 14.1). There was a significant amount (60 per cent) of attrition throughout the programme, and substantial barriers to carrying out such intervention research have since been identified alongside strategies to overcome such barriers in future research (Trivedi-Bateman and Martingano, 2023).

Conclusion

The Compass intervention technique has the potential to support children in multiple contexts and samples, and to achieve desistance by making law-abiding, positive and fulfilling action choices in long-lasting ways. The approach described takes a child-specific orientation and aims to avoid stigmatisation and reinforcement of negative identities, thereby contributing to the development of innovative forms of child justice practice. Children

Table 14.1: The Compass Project topic strands and corresponding example activities

Topic focus	Example activity
Empathy	Putting oneself in others' shoes by hearing their life stories, looking at images, listening to music, watching emotive videos and acting out scenarios (for example, bullying)
Morality	Moral dilemma group discussions and debates (hypothetical situations and real-life news stories)
Emotion recognition and management	Defining and categorising emotions, identifying constructive and distorted thinking patterns, drawing oneself in the past, present and future
Shame and guilt	Identifying feelings of shame and guilt in scenarios and discussing their appropriateness in certain situations
Peer resistance	Group discussions on experience of peer pressure, role playing hypothetical scenarios, learning peer refusal techniques

should be treated as such: they do not have the neurological capabilities to take full responsibility for their actions, and, as if often the case, features of the environments around children have let them down – for example, unstable or absent caregiver nurturing, difficulty maintaining school attendance, witnessing crime events in family or peer groups or crime victimisation. The often-difficult predicament of the child can be very difficult to weigh up against the potentially devastating consequences of child offences to victims, and I believe this is the reason so much controversy remains around how child offenders should be treated. If we can move towards a 'delabelling' ((Maruna et al, 2004, p 275)), strength-based approach to replace the current negative labelling and risk-based approach, we may see more and more children lessen their conflict with the law and achieve desistance in coming years.

It is acknowledged that this chapter incorporates some positivist assumptions about the relationship between developmental factors, child crime and desistance which might be open to critique. For example, some theorists (such as Polizzi, 2015) purport that child crime is a social construct rather than an objective form of behaviour towards which children may be inclined. While the proposed explanations of crime in this chapter centre on individual-level factors, it should be noted that environmental and social factors are imperative to consider in tandem. The extent to which the social context – including relationships with others, and reduced provocations – can provide support that is conducive to achieving desistance is critical. The coupling of the opportunity to reflect on one's behaviour actively and purposefully, reinforced by the reassurance and recognition by supportive others, has been noted in existing desistance theory (for example Bottoms et al, 2004). As such, TCP intervention has the potential to meaningfully contribute to child development and the process of maturation as an interactive process between the child and their wider environment.

Acknowledgements

The Compass pilot was funded by The British Academy, Anglia Ruskin University (Faculty of Arts, Humanities and Social Sciences) and Loughborough University. With thanks and appreciation to Romsey Mill youth work charity, fieldwork research assistants Emma Crook and Sam Malik-Bhatti and the rest of the project team, and project advisors Dr Alex Sutherland and Dr Beth Hardie.

Notes

[1]   https://www.lboro.ac.uk/research/compass-project/
[2]   The Compass pilot was funded by The British Academy (Small Grant, SRG21\210039, £9,980) the Faculty of Arts, Humanities and Social Sciences, Anglia Ruskin University (£27,453), and Loughborough University (£1,637). The project was approved by the Loughborough University Ethics Review Sub-Committee on 14 April 2022. The trial was registered before the trial start date at osf.io on 6 May 2022 (https://osf.io/t638j/?view_only=0a57c19ec6744ce2aa3f06d6204cb5dd).
[3]   While TCP delivery served to pilot test the programme content and main or interaction analyses could not be tested due to sample size restrictions, 14 outcome variables, measured using standardised questionnaire scales pre-study and post-study, were collected. The outcome variables are: empathy, emotion regulation, mindfulness, moral rules, wellbeing, callous-unemotional traits, self-control, self-esteem, shame and guilt, quality of relationships, peer resistance, legitimacy of the law, contact with the police, and self-reported crime and victimisation. Programme enthusiasm and engagement data were also collected (programme group only).

References

Akers, R.L. and Jennings, W.G. (2019) 'The social learning theory of crime and deviance', in M. Krohn, A. Lizotte and G. Hall (eds) *Handbook on Crime and Deviance*, New York: Springer, pp 113–29.

Allen, R. (2012) 'Young adults in the English criminal justice system: the policy challenges', in F. Lösel, A. Bottoms and D.P. Farrington (eds) *Young Adult Offenders: Lost in Transition?*, London: Willan Publishing, pp 171–85.

Arbuthnot, J. and Gordon, D.A. (1986) 'Behavioral and cognitive effects of a moral reasoning development intervention for high-risk behavior-disordered adolescents', *Journal of Consulting and Clinical Psychology*, 54(2): 208–16, Available from: https://doi.org/10.1037/0022-006X.54.2.208

Ariel, B., Bland, M. and Sutherland, A. (2022) *Experimental Designs*, London: Sage.

Bach, R.A., Defever, A.M., Chopik, W.J. and Konrath, S.H. (2017) 'Geographic variation in empathy: a state-level analysis', *Journal of Research in Personality*, 68: 124–30, Available from: https://doi.org/10.1016/j.jrp.2016.12.007

Beelmann, A. and Lösel, F. (2021) 'A comprehensive meta-analysis of randomized evaluations of the effect of child social skills training on antisocial development', *Journal of Developmental and Life-Course Criminology*, 7: 41–65, Available from: https://doi.org/10.1007/s40865-020-00142-8

Bottoms, A. (2002) *Ideology, Crime and Criminal Justice*, Cullompton: Willan Publishing.

Bottoms, A., Shapland, J., Costello, A., Holmes, D. and Muir, G. (2004) 'Towards desistance: theoretical underpinnings for an empirical study', *The Howard Journal of Crime and Justice*, 43(4): 368–89.

Braithwaite, J. and Braithwaite, V. (2001) 'Shame, shame management and regulation', in E. Ahmed, N. Harris, J. Braithwaite and V. Braithwaite (eds) *Shame Management through Reintegration*, Cambridge: Cambridge University Press, pp 3–58.

Carroll, A., McCarthy, M., Houghton, S. and O'Connor, E.S. (2020) 'Evaluating the effectiveness of KooLKIDS: an interactive social emotional learning program for Australian primary school children', *Psychology in the Schools*, 57(6): 851–67, Available from: https://doi.org/10.1002/pits.22352

Case, S. and Hazel, N. (2020) 'Child First, offender second: a progressive model for education in custody', *International Journal of Educational Development*, 77: 102244.

Choi, E.S. and Lee, W.K. (2015) 'Comparative effects of emotion management training and social skills training in Korean children with ADHD', *Journal of Attention Disorders*, 19(2): 138–46, Available from: https://doi.org/10.1177/1087054713496460

Claypoole, S.D., Moody, E.E. and Peace, S.D. (2000) 'Moral dilemma discussions: an effective group intervention for juvenile offenders', *Journal for Specialists in Group Work*, 25(4): 394–411, Available from: https://doi.org/10.1080/01933920008411682

Comunian, A.L. and Gielen, U.P. (2006) 'Promotion of moral judgement maturity through stimulation of social role-taking and social reflection: an Italian intervention study', *Journal of Moral Education*, 35(1): 51–69.

Dadds, M.R., Cauchi, A.J., Wimalaweera, S., Hawes, D.J. and Brennan, J. (2012) 'Outcomes, moderators, and mediators of empathic-emotion recognition training for complex conduct problems in childhood', *Psychiatry Research*, 199(3): 201–7, Available from: https://doi.org/10.1016/j.psychres.2012.04.033

Elison, J., Garofalo, C. and Velotti, P. (2014) 'Shame and aggression: theoretical considerations', *Aggression and Violent Behavior*, 19(4): 447–53.

Farrall, S. (ed) (2019) *The Architecture of Desistance*, Abingdon: Routledge.

Farrington, D.P. (1986) 'Age and crime', *Crime and Justice*, 7: 189–250.

Frick, P., Ray, J., Thornton, L. and Kahn, R. (2013) 'Annual research review: a developmental psychopathology approach to understanding callous-unemotional traits in children and adolescents with serious conduct problems', *Journal of Child Psychology and Psychiatry, and Allied Disciplines*, 55(6): 532–48, doi: 10.1111/jcpp.12152

Giordano, P.C. (2016) 'Mechanisms underlying the desistance process: reflections on "a theory of cognitive transformation"', in J. Shapland, S. Farrall and A.E. Bottoms (eds) *Global Perspectives on Desistance*, Abingdon: Routledge, pp 27–43.

Gove, W.R. (1985) 'The effect of age and gender on deviant behavior: a biopsychosocial perspective', in A.S. Rossi (ed) *Gender and the Life Course*, New York: Aldine de Gruyter, pp 115–44.

Healy, D. (2016) '"I've always tried but I hadn't got the willpower": understanding pathways to desistance in the Republic of Ireland', in J. Shapland, S. Farrall and A.E. Bottoms (eds) *Global Perspectives on Desistance*, Abingdon: Routledge, pp 27–43.

Heeks, M., Reed, S., Tafsiri, M. and Prince, S. (2018) 'The economic and social costs of crime' (2nd edn), Home Office Research report 99.

Ingram, K.M., Espelage, D.L., Merrin, G.J., Valido, A., Heinhorst, J. and Joyce, M. (2019) 'Evaluation of a virtual reality enhanced bullying prevention curriculum pilot trial', *Journal of Adolescence*, 71: 72–83, Available from: https://doi.org/10.1016/j.adolescence.2018.12.006

Laub, J.H. and Sampson, R.J. (2001) 'Understanding desistance from crime', in M. Tonry (ed) *Crime and Justice: A Review of Research*, vol 28, Chicago: University of Chicago Press, pp 1–69.

Lösel, F. (2012) 'What works in correctional treatment and rehabilitation for young adults?', in F. Lösel, A. Bottoms and D.P. Farrington (eds) *Young Adult Offenders: Lost in Transition?*, London: Willan Publishing, pp 90–128.

Lösel, F., Bottoms, A. and Farrington, D.P. (eds) (2012) *Young Adult Offenders: Lost in Transition?*, London: Willan Publishing.

Lotfali, S., Moradi, A. and Ekhtiari, H. (2017) 'On the effectiveness of emotion regulation training in anger management and emotional regulation difficulties in adolescents', *Modern Applied Science*, 11(1): 114–23, Available from: https://doi.org/10.5539/mas.v11n1p114

Maruna, S. (2001) *Making Good: How Ex-convicts Reform and Rebuild Their Lives*, Washington, DC: American Psychological Association.

Maruna, S., Lebel, T.P., Mitchell, N. and Naples, M. (2004) 'Pygmalion in the reintegration process: desistance from crime through the looking glass', *Psychology, Crime & Law*, 10(3): 271–81.

Masto, M. (2015) 'Empathy and its role in morality', *The Southern Journal of Philosophy*, 53(1): 74–96.

Mazzone, A., Yanagida, T., Camodeca, M. and Strohmeier, D. (2021) 'Information processing of social exclusion: links with bullying, moral disengagement and guilt', *Journal of Applied Developmental Psychology*, 75: 1–10, Available from: https://doi.org/10.1016/j.appdev.2021.101292

Moffitt, T.E. (1993) 'Adolescence-limited and life-course persistent developmental behavior: a developmental taxonomy', *Psychological Review*, 100(4): 674–701.

Moffitt, T.E., Caspi, A., Harrington, H. and Milne, B.J. (2002) 'Males on the life-course-persistent and adolescence-limited antisocial pathways: follow-up at age 26 years', *Development and Psychopathology*, 14(1): 179–207.

Mulvey, E.P. and Schubert, C.A. (2016) 'Issues to consider in future work on desistance from adolescence to early adulthood: observations from the Pathways to Desistance Study', in J. Shapland, S. Farrall and A. Bottoms (eds) *Global Perspectives on Desistance: Reviewing What We Know and Looking to the Future*, Abingdon: Routledge, pp 142–59.

Mulvey, E.P., Steinberg, L., Fagan, J., Cauffman, E., Piquero, A.R., Chassin, L. et al (2004) 'Theory and research on desistance from antisocial activity among serious adolescent offenders', *Child Violence and Juvenile Justice*, 2(3): 213–36.

Ongley, S.F. and Malti, T. (2014) 'The role of moral emotions in the development of children's sharing behavior', *Developmental Psychology*, 50(4): 1148–59.

Pauwels, L., Svensson, R. and Hirtenlehner, H. (2018) 'Testing situational action theory: a narrative review of studies published between 2006 and 2015', *European Journal of Criminology*, 15(1): 32–55.

Polizzi, D. (2015) *A Philosophy of the Social Construction of Crime*, Bristol: Policy Press.

Roach, J. (2023) 'Psychology and crime prevention', in J. Roach, *Practical Psychology for Policing*, Bristol: Policy Press, pp 78–92.

Şahin, M. (2012) 'An investigation into the efficiency of empathy training program on preventing bullying in primary schools', *Children and Child Services Review*, 34(7): 1325–30, Available from: https://doi.org/10.1016/j.childyouth.2012.03.013

Sampson, R.J. and Laub, J.H. (1993) *Crime in the Making: Pathways and Turning Points through Life*, Cambridge, MA: Harvard University Press.

Schultze-Krumbholz, A., Schultze, M., Zagorscak, P., Wölfer, R. and Scheithauer, H. (2016) 'Feeling cybervictims' pain: the effect of empathy training on cyberbullying', *Aggressive Behavior*, 42(2): 147–56, Available from: https://doi.org/10.1002/ab.21613

Shapland, J., Bottoms, A. and Muir, G. (2012) 'Perceptions of the criminal justice system among young adult would-be desisters', in F. Lösel, A. Bottoms and D.P. Farrington (eds) *Young Adult Offenders: Lost in Transition?*, London: Willan Publishing, pp 144–61.

Shover, N. (1996) *Great Pretenders: Pursuits and Careers of Persistent Thieves*, Boulder: Westview Press.

Svensson, R., Weerman, F.M., Pauwels, L.J., Bruinsma, G.J. and Bernasco, W. (2013) 'Moral emotions and offending: do feelings of anticipated shame and guilt mediate the effect of socialization on offending?', *European Journal of Criminology*, 10: 22–39, doi: 10.1177/147737081245439

Tangney, J. and Fischer, K. (1995) *Self-conscious Emotions: The Psychology of Shame, Guilt, Embarrassment, and Pride*, New York: Guilford Press.

Tangney, J.P., Stuewig, J. and Mashek, D.J. (2007) 'Moral emotions and moral behavior', *Annual Review of Psychology*, 58: 345–72.

Trivedi-Bateman, N. (2015) 'The roles of empathy, shame, and guilt in violence decision-making', PhD thesis, University of Cambridge.

Trivedi-Bateman, N. (2021) 'The combined roles of moral emotion and moral rules in explaining acts of violence using a Situational Action Theory perspective', *Journal of Interpersonal Violence*, 36(17–18): 8715–40.

Trivedi-Bateman, N (2023) 'Access information for The Compass Project programme handbook', Educational resource, Loughborough University, https://doi.org/10.17028/rd.lboro.24131649.v1

Trivedi-Bateman, N. and Crook, E.L. (2022) 'The optimal application of empathy interventions to reduce antisocial behaviour and crime: a review of the literature', *Psychology, Crime & Law*, 28(8): 796–819.

Trivedi-Bateman, N. and Martingano, A.J. (2023) 'Addressing challenges to carrying out intervention programmes with youth populations: successes and strategies', *Journal of Research on Adolescence*, 33(4): 1435–46, doi: 10.1111/jora.12886

Ugwudike, P., Raynor, P. and Annison, J. (eds) (2017) *Evidence-Based Skills in Criminal Justice: International Research on Supporting Rehabilitation and Desistance*, Bristol: Policy Press.

Van Ryzin, M.J. and Roseth, C.J. (2019) 'Effects of cooperative learning on peer relations, empathy, and bullying in middle school', *Aggressive Behavior*, 45(6): 643–51, Available from: https://doi.org/10.1002/ab.21858

Wikström, P.-O. H. (2004) 'Crime as alternative: towards a cross-level situational action theory of crime causation', in J. McCord (ed) *Beyond Empiricism: Institutions and Intentions in the Study of Crime*, New Brunswick: Transaction, pp 1–37.

Wikström, P.-O. H. and Treiber, K. (2009) 'Violence as situational action', *International Journal of Conflict and Violence*, 3(1): 75–96.

Wikström, P.-O. H., Mann, R.P. and Hardie, B. (2018) 'Children's differential vulnerability to criminogenic exposure: bridging the gap between people- and place-oriented approaches in the study of crime causation', *European Journal of Criminology*, 15(1): 10–31.

Wikström, P.-O. H., Oberwittler, D., Treiber, K. and Hardie, B. (2012) *Breaking Rules: The Social and Situational Dynamics of Young People's Urban Crime*, Oxford: University Press.

Wright, J.C., Weissglass, D.E. and Casey, V. (2020) 'Imaginative role-playing as a medium for moral development: Dungeons & Dragons provides moral training', *Journal of Humanistic Psychology*, 60(1): 99–129.

Wyman, P.A., Cross, W., Brown, C.H., Yu, Q., Tu, X. and Eberly, S. (2010) 'Intervention to strengthen emotional self-regulation in children with emerging mental health problems: proximal impact on school behavior', *Journal of Abnormal Child Psychology*, 38(5): 707–20, Available from: https://doi.org/10.1007/s10802-010-9398-x

Zhou, Y.Q., Gan, D.Z.Q., Hoo, E.C.C., Chong, D. and Chu, C.M. (2018) 'Evaluating the Violence Prevention Program: group and individual changes in aggression, anger, self-control, and empathy', *The Journal of Forensic Psychiatry & Psychology*, 29(2): 265–87, Available from: https://doi.org/10.1080/14789949.2017.1375541

15

What next for desistance and youth justice?

Alexandra Wigzell, Claire Paterson-Young and Tim Bateman

Introduction

The roots of this book lie in conversations about desistance and children in early 2021 that originated following an online event with academics, practitioners and policymakers who energetically critiqued and commented on the relevance and application of desistance theories to youth justice-involved children. While the purpose of the online event was to launch a briefing paper on desistance and youth justice, and thus mark the culmination of the National Association for Youth Justice's (NAYJ) work on the topic, the discussions led to a number of reflections and questions. What helps children to move away from offending? To what extent is the concept and theorisation of desistance useful to explaining this during childhood and adolescence? Does the application of desistance theories risk problematising rather than normalising children's behaviour? How is desistance thinking understood, interpreted and implemented in youth justice policy and practice?

We issued an open call inviting contributions from practitioners, academics and researchers on these questions and, more broadly, around critical perspectives on desistance and children. We asked all contributors to consider how structural factors and inequalities impact children's ability to move away from offending and their healthy longer-term development in their area of discussion. Just over two years and 14 chapters later, we have a rich and varied collection of insights on this theme, covering a diverse range of topics. It provides insights into the applicability and implementation of desistance thinking in youth justice; issues of gender, race and faith; and the role of the arts, participation and co-production, caring relationships, the court system and moral emotions in children's desistance journeys. While the collection approaches the topic of desistance and children through a national lens, these topics will have global relevance.

We acknowledge that this volume does not cover all issues on desistance and children. For example, the collection does not explicitly consider: the role of international children's rights frameworks (although these are drawn upon in many chapters); the implementation of desistance approaches in custodial settings; the particular needs of neurodiverse children in moving away from offending; or if and how restorative justice fits within the context of desistance and Child First (a topic of debate, see, for example, Cuneen and Goldson, 2015; Hodgson, 2020). Further, the contributions in this volume attest to the importance of examining perspectives on desistance (and indeed Child First) among professionals in other sectors who may play a significant role in children's lives, shaping their development and pathways in and out of the justice system; as well as exploring the extent to which cultural norms and values impact on desistance with children (that is, a global perspective). In this regard, we hope this collection is treated as an invitation for further debate and discussion about desistance and children.

Our aim in this concluding chapter is not to summarise all the insights of each contribution – an enormous task – but to reflect on the central themes that have emerged from the collection. We then consider the implications and challenges that may lie ahead.

Desistance as a social justice issue

Several chapters of the book have emphasised that the barriers and enablers to children's desistance – and wellbeing and healthy development – lie far beyond youth justice. In Chapter 5, Sharpe writes powerfully about girls' and young women's experience of school, the UK welfare system and criminal justice labelling as intersecting and at times mutually reinforcing sites of punishment. She contends that these cumulative experiences of negative labels, exclusion and othering cause profound harm to girls' sense of self and future prospects. Focusing on Black and mixed-heritage boys, Wainwright (Chapter 7) argues that intersecting experiences of poverty, racism, educational exclusion and contested spaces are essential to understanding their disproportionate criminalisation and opportunities for desistance. Staines et al (Chapter 6) draw attention to the 'triple whammy' of stigma that girls in care who offend are liable to experience, noting that state and institutional responses – across children's social care, residential care providers, mental health services, the police, the courts and youth justice – often increase the likelihood of their involvement in offending behaviour and inhibit their ability to move away from it. On a more positive note, Stephenson (Chapter 10) focuses on the wide-ranging benefits of an arts-based educational programme with youth justice-involved children, demonstrating the potential power of arts in education. Thus, a significant insight threaded through all these chapters is the critical role of institutions and experiences *outside of* youth justice in shaping children's sense of self-identity, self-belief and self-efficacy.

Desistance as a youth justice-wide issue

There can be a tendency in discussions about 'youth justice' to treat it as a monolithic system: that is, of there being a uniform youth justice arena (for an extended discussion, see Phoenix, 2016). But as a number of chapters attest, there are diverse youth justice actors and environments that play a role in whether children's desistance is helped or hindered. Interwoven throughout the collection is the recognition that contact with the youth justice system can often hamper desistance, in reflection of the strong evidence base to this effect (see, for example, McAra and McVie, 2007, 2010). Thus, Little and Haines (Chapter 4) contend that whether or not a child is labelled as an 'offender' or considered to be a 'desister' has as much to do with the system's (and particularly, police enforcement) behaviour as it does the child's actions. On a similar theme, Staines et al (Chapter 6) note that despite increased awareness among the police and care providers of the importance of diverting children away from the youth justice system, practice remains inconsistent.

For Carr (Chapter 13), the environments in which children are sentenced and the structure of those sentences are important factors in shaping a child's opportunities to move away from crime. He argues that whether or not there is a conviction (and the possibility of breach) attached to the sentence has significant implications for how children think about themselves, regard the system (as there to help or not) and the supervisory relationship. Hampson (Chapter 9) notes that other agencies and professionals, such as the police and magistracy, play a significant role in enabling the development of desistance-informed youth justice, highlighting the importance of providing desistance training to these groups. His Majesty's Inspectorate of Probation (HMIP) is another important influence in this regard, with some noticeable recent movement towards Child First thinking (Chapters 2 and 9), but arguably further progress to be made too.

The centrality of caring relationships

The significance of the relationship between the child and their worker is commented on by virtually every chapter in this collection. This is perhaps no surprise: the importance of the professional relationship is a long-standing feature of scholarship and the effective practice literature. More recently, there has been a renewed emphasis on the professional relationship at a policy level: it is a key focus of the Youth Justice Board case management guidance (2022) and national standards (2019), and HMIP's inspection framework (2021). And yet, for all the talk of the importance of the professional relationship, there is little discussion about what it *means* to have a positive professional relationship or the factors that help and hinder the development and maintenance of such relationships (with some exceptions; see, for example, Fullerton et al, 2021). Prior and Mason (2010, p 219) note that 'the quality of the relationship between practitioner and the young person and the associated knowledge and skills – has rarely been the topic of rigorous research investigation'. Thus, there remains a 'significant lacunae in our understanding of the minutiae of the practitioner–young person relationship' (Drake et al, 2014, p 26). The insights about the professional relationship in this collection comprise a step toward bridging this gap.

A key message is that relationships must involve genuine care for the child, a feature that is often left out of definitions, as Evans and Szifris point out in Chapter 12. In Johns' (Chapter 3) words, 'justice demands care and caring'. Such 'caring justice' values empathy, building trust and responding to actual needs (Held, 2010), and importantly genuine care must be perceived as such by service users too (Tronto, 2010). Several chapters draw our attention to the important role of the structural frameworks in shaping the professional relationship (Chapters 6, 7, 9, 11, 12 and 13). In Chapter 6, Staines et al note that caring relationships will be potentially harder for children in care due to frequent movement between settings and counties; and high staff turnover related to inadequate employment conditions can further exacerbate such difficulties. Evans and Szifris (Chapter 12) reflect on the importance of *taking time* to genuinely connect with the child (see also Chapter 6), which is constrained within time-limited statutory youth justice supervision and by high levels of paperwork (see also Hampson, Chapter 9). Staines et al (Chapter 6), while pointing out the benefits of long-term, consistent relationships with youth justice professionals, note that contact with the youth justice system can be criminogenic and support must be provided earlier and outside of the justice system. Improving relationships is no easy task, but, in Chapter 13, Carr argues that a key potential benefit of introducing a community sentence without conviction is that it may improve relationship-based working by shifting the relationship away from its adversarial premise (that is, through the threat of breach) towards one of cooperation and wellbeing. Trivedi-Bateman (Chapter 14) writes persuasively about the importance of attending to children's moral emotions, such as empathy, moral reasoning and emotional regulation to support their desistance; as she notes, empathetic interactions with practitioners and strong relationships are crucial in this regard.

Supporting identity development, not identity reform

Identity is a recurrent feature across the contributions to this volume. Several authors highlight the harmful effects that exclusionary and stigmatising experiences of school and society have on children's self-identity and self-worth (Chapters 5, 6 and 7). Several chapters offer insights into the role of identity in children's pathways away from offending (Chapters 1, 2, 3,

4, 7, 8, 13 and 14; see Chapter 10 for discussion of the related concept of self-efficacy). In this regard, Little and Haines (Chapter 4) argue that desistance thinking cannot apply to children since it necessitates an established 'offender identity' which they may not have. Hazel and Case (Chapter 2) conceive of this topic differently, contending that supporting children's pro-social identity development is of central importance to their realisation of positive outcomes and does not presuppose the existence of a criminal identity. This accords with the findings of empirical research on desistance and children, as discussed in the opening chapter. There is, however, also ongoing debate about whether pro-social identity development ought to be a principal focus of practice, particularly in a justice context, with two of the editors of this volume arguing elsewhere that practice should be centred on fostering children's long-term healthy development through caring professional relationships, what they term *progressive desistance practice* (Bateman and Wigzell, forthcoming, 2024).

Seeing through the child's lens

A key aim of this collection has been to create a space for critical reflection about the relevance of desistance thinking to children, encompassing both contributors who contest *and* develop its application to children. What is evident across all contributions is the importance of approaching such questions through a child's lens or by 'inhabiting children's worlds' (Chapter 3). This involves doing much more to facilitate children's participation within services (Chapters 7 and 11) and co-produced action research, as outlined by Wainwright (Chapter 7). The professional relationship is significant here too: genuine empathy is required to understand the reality of the child's 'lived experiences' (Eadie and Canton, 2002, p 22) or 'to sense the client's private world as if it were your own, but without ever losing the "as if" quality' (Rodgers, 1957).

Seeing youth justice in this way highlights the significance of *time* for children, a feature of several chapters (Chapters 3, 6, 12 and 13). Both Johns (Chapter 3) and Carr (Chapter 13) discuss the value in focusing more on the 'gaps' in between in children's offending, focusing on these periods as positive blocks to build on. And as noted earlier, relationships of genuine care take *time* to build and requires the involvement of children in activities that are meaningful (Chapters 6 and 12). Meaningful participation for children is discussed by Creaney et al (Chapter 11), with focus on how to facilitate children's participation in decision-making processes. Participatory approaches can prove beneficial if a meaningful process is embedded within youth justice, and, more importantly, if this approach is translated effectively into practice. This is not to say that meaningful participation is not complex, with challenges in balancing practicalities, tokenistic participation and inter-agency tensions.

Implications and challenges

Here we consider the implications and challenges to realising these themes (inspired by Hazel and Case's [2023] postscript).

For research

We are reluctant to conclude a book rich with insights and learning calling for *more* research. And yet, our understanding of how children move away from offending during childhood and adolescence remains underdeveloped, too often treated as a poor cousin to adult justice scholarship rather than a field in its own right. Several authors in this volume have, in our view rightly, called for further research about how children move on from crime, particularly focusing on what helps different 'groups' of children (while recognising that each child is unique). Wainwright (Chapter 7) argues for co-creative action research with Black and mixed-heritage boys 'as it is only by understanding their experience ... that there can be genuine opportunity to bring about changes that lead to desistance'. In this regard, it is essential that the growing interest in participatory and co-designed practice (Chapter 11) is reflected in research funders' support for such approaches, since genuinely participatory research requires resources (Torre et al, 2018).

In the opening chapter, we highlight the need to learn more about children's pathways away from crime across the spectrum of youth-justice involvement (given that, to date, research has typically focused on children leaving custody and/or who have committed serious or high-frequency crimes). Rosier (Chapter 8) advocates for research that considers the role of spirituality in children's pathways from crime – a concept that has received increasing attention in criminal justice literature with adults but has been limited with under 18s. His chapter reminds us that, notwithstanding the debate about the applicability of adult-based desistance theories with children, there are valuable insights from this literature that merit consideration in relation to under 18s.

Hampson (Chapter 9) is one of a small number of scholars who have examined *how* desistance thinking is being implemented in youth justice (see also Day, 2022), importantly highlighting some of the barriers and training gaps. More such research will be needed as desistance approaches, and their links with Child First, continue to develop in youth justice. This will need to be conducted within and across youth justice services and youth custodial establishments, as well as the police, referral order panels, youth proceedings and the inspectorates, in reflection of the range of stakeholders and the varying penal models and cultures (Smith and Gray, 2019, Gray, 2020; Goldson and Briggs, 2021) that make up youth justice in England and Wales. This is an ambitious programme of research, but it is essential if we are to understand and advance the ways in which research and policy is translating into practice with children. In sum, practice with children in the youth justice system must be informed and supported by research with and for children.

For practice and policy

We discuss practice and policy together, since many of the implications and challenges, perhaps unsurprisingly, straddle both arenas and cannot be easily separated. The key areas discussed here are 'caring relationships', 'training' and 'people and participation'.

Caring relationships

As noted, one of the dominant themes in the book is the central importance of caring relationships between children and practitioners. While policy and practitioners agree on this, it is clear there are challenges to realising the centrality of the relationship in practice. A number of authors point to the *lack* of time practitioners spend *with* children associated with lengthy AssetPlus assessments and paperwork (Chapters 9 and 12), time-limited youth justice supervision (Chapter 12), unstable care placements and high staff turnover (Chapter 6). Several chapters (Chapter 9, 10 and 12) note the importance of meaningful activities for relationship building and broadening children's horizons (Drake et al, 2014), but Hampson (Chapter 9) reports that lack of funding is a significant barrier. There are no straightforward solutions to these issues, but if consistent and caring relationships are 'pivotal' to children's desistance and wellbeing (YJB, 2022), policymakers together with practitioners need to do much more to realise this in the system's structure and support.

In the meantime, several contributors offer ideas on immediate-term changes that would enable more time to be spent with children and better support relationship-based practice. Hampson (Chapter 9) argues that AssetPlus requires review by policymakers but also points to an example where local practitioners worked together to make the intervention plan more child-friendly – she is hopeful that the introduction of Child First case management guidance will, in time, further support such innovation. Training (discussed further in the following section) is another central feature of realising caring relationships (Chapters 6 and 12); in this regard, it is encouraging that the Effective Practice Certificate includes content on attachment theory, trauma-informed or trauma-aware practice and relationship building, despite some concern about the content remaining risk-oriented (Chapter 9). Yet reflective practice is also a critical component (Chapter 12) of relationship-centred practice; anecdotal evidence suggests that this is too often missing or infrequent. On this point, while Child First thinking rightly encourages us to responsibilise adults rather than children (Hazel and Case, 2023), if we want practitioners to build caring relationships with children, we must also care for our practitioners.

Training

Lack of training is a recurrent challenge highlighted across chapters. Many authors in this volume (Chapters 5, 6, 7, 8, 9, 11 and 12) argue that if we are to support children's wellbeing and desistance, we need to better equip the workforce within and beyond youth justice to recognise and respond to their needs. Sharpe (Chapter 5) emphasises the need for increased awareness of and mental wellbeing provision in schools to identify girls' needs and provide support at an early stage. Staines et al (Chapter 6) recommend that further training is required across the police, care providers and other relevant agencies about diversion and trauma-aware approaches to prevent girls from entering the system, as well as mental health support and trauma-informed training to help them move away from it. Hampson (Chapter 9) notes the need for child-friendly desistance training – across youth justice services, the police and youth courts. Rosier (Chapter 8) compellingly writes about the importance of religious literacy training and reflective practice to better enable practitioners to talk with children about religion, faith and spirituality. Drawing on Dingham (2016), he proposes that such training should encourage critical thinking, equip one to identify and challenge potential prejudices (our own and others) and underlying emotional assumptions, and foster openness to knowledge. As Rosier argues, religious literacy goes beyond understanding the foundations of religion and 'is a key life skill which is central to the effective, peaceful functioning of a plural democracy'. One can imagine that such training tenets may have wide application across the child penal realm.

People and Participation

Wainwright (Chapter 7) and Creaney et al (Chapter 11) discuss the value of involving those who have experience of the system as peer mentors. Wainwright contends that Black and mixed-heritage boys listen and respect peer mentors with similar experiences and that they are ideally placed to challenge their involvement in offending 'from a prism of Blackness' and through a long-term working relationship. Both chapters point to the challenges of realising the involvement of peer mentors. Wainwright highlights exclusionary Disclosure and Barring Service checks and potentially poor financial remuneration as key barriers to members of the Black and mixed-heritage community committing to such roles. Creaney et al (Chapter 11) note that professional concerns about the children's past behaviour and defensible decision-making can militate against power sharing. They hold up the charity Youth Ink's work with youth justice services as an exemplar of meaningful participatory practice, involving trained peer mentors who work flexibly with youth justice-involved children, through a trusting relationship, alongside statutory supervision. They argue that this can promote children's genuine participation in decision-making, positive outcomes and desistance.

At the system-wide level

Many of the contributions to this collection have underlined the need for change across and throughout a range of services if children's wellbeing and desistance is to be supported. This includes improved mental health support in schools and the community (Chapters 5 and 6); greater provision of youth services and housing (Chapters 6 and 7); a more compassionate and inclusive educational system (Chapters 5 and 7); the development of a supportive rather than penalising welfare system (Chapter 5); and bespoke services that understand and are responsive to the needs of Black and mixed-heritage families (Chapter 7) and marginalised girls (Chapter 6). Staines et al (Chapter 6) want to see Child First principles applied across the care system, as well as within youth justice. The overwhelming current challenge is that the financial climate mitigates against additional funding for such services, resulting in children being further neglected and marginalised.

Others have invited us to look beyond statutory services for solutions. Stephenson (Chapter 10) encourages the development of partnerships between arts organisations and youth justice services to give more children the opportunity to develop skills and self-agency. Creaney et al (Chapter 11) and Evans and Szifris (Chapter 12) highlight some of the benefits of involving the charitable sector in youth justice, including the flexibility to work with children beyond the confines of time-limited youth justice supervision and with potentially less of a power imbalance. This will not be easy within the current system, but investment in such provision is required if we are to reduce negative outcomes for children.

Sharpe (Chapter 5) reminds us that we cannot discuss desistance and children without acknowledgement of our age of criminal responsibility in England and Wales, which at ten years of age remains 'extremely low'. As she argues, raising it offers the potential to significantly reduce the number of criminalised children and would improve their employment prospects. It should be noted that the United Nations Committee on the Rights of the Child (Children's Rights Committee, 2019) has recently raised its recommended minimum age of criminal responsibility from 12 to 14 years on the basis of the neurodevelopmental evidence:

Documented evidence in the fields of child development and neuroscience indicates that maturity and the capacity for abstract reasoning is still evolving in children aged 12 to 13 years due to the fact that their frontal cortex is still developing. Therefore, they are unlikely to understand the impact of their actions or to comprehend criminal proceedings. (Children's Rights Committee, 2019, para 22)

The NAYJ has long argued that the minimum age of criminal responsibility should be raised significantly, not least given that the large majority of children grow out of crime (NAYJ, 2019). Yet, at the time of writing (late 2023), with an impending General Election and 'law and order' seemingly mobilised once again as a key territory in which it will be fought,[1] the likelihood of reform remains to be seen.

This discussion perhaps inevitably raises questions about whether youth justice is configured in a way that best supports children's wellbeing and desistance. Little and Haines (Chapter 4) contend that we should adopt an oblique approach (Canton, 2012) to youth justice, focusing on fostering children's universal positive outcomes based on a Child First philosophy (notably *instead of* desistance thinking), rather than directly aiming to reduce offending. Hazel and Case (Chapter 2) explain that similar ideas are at the core of the Child First conceptual framework and a key impetus for it. As they state: '[F]ocusing interventions directly on offending behaviour and desistance from it, risk-based youth justice brings "negative", punitive features. These include (inadvertent) labelling and stigmatisation of children ... "net-widening" ... and over-emphasising the prevention of negative outcomes.' They go on to argue that 'this model points to the need for the YJS to focus primarily on achieving positive child outcomes. The aim of "desistance" is best considered as a secondary outcome, which reduces the negative consequences of it being a direct focus'.

In the prelude to this collection, Wigzell (2021) similarly argued that child-friendly desistance entails a central focus on children's positive outcomes, beyond reducing offending. She questioned how such aspirations will translate into youth justice practice when preventing offending remains the statutory aim of youth justice (Crime and Disorder Act 1998), noting that '[i]f preventing offending and managing risk remain the modus operandi of the system ... there is a danger that practice will inevitably be orientated towards these goals, regardless of child first aspirations' (2021, p 16). These concerns continue to be salient. The statutory aim of youth justice sits unchanged; reoffending (the binary and frequent rate) continues to be a key performance indicator (KPI) for youth justice services in reflection of this aim (albeit alongside an expansion of KPIs relating to supporting children's wellbeing) (YJB/MoJ, 2023); and the effectiveness of work to reduce offending remains a central focus of HMIP youth justice inspections (HMI Probation, 2021). This is not to detract from the positive developments made in implementing Child First, which Bateman (2023) describes as a 'seismic shift which deserves to be applauded'; or to underestimate the pragmatic considerations involved in positioning Child First in a way that appeals to ministerial and civil service concerns (Chapter 2).

Hazel and Case (Chapter 2) suggest that the advancement of Child First 'will inevitably raise challenging questions' about the political preoccupation with (re-)offending and perhaps the appropriateness of a justice system for supporting children's positive outcomes. Perhaps, then, we need change before we can fully realise the possibilities for reform and thinking beyond current configurations of youth justice. This is not to call into question the need for a specialist workforce and resources for children in conflict with the law, which are of vital importance for this so often marginalised group (Wigzell, 2021). But, ultimately, if we understand children's desistance as a *social justice* issue, indirectly realised by nurturing children's *healthy development* through *long-standing caring relationships* and *non-stigmatising socio-structural support*, then surely a justice response is not the answer.

Note
[1]   See, for example, Labour's recent advertisements accusing Prime Minister Rishi Sunak of being 'soft' on crime (Allegretti, 2023); and the Conservative promise of a 'crackdown on antisocial behaviour' (Crew, 2023).

References

Allegretti, A. (2023) 'Labour strategists to press on with Sunak attack ads despite criticism', *The Guardian*, 7 April, Available from: https://www.theg uardian.com/politics/2023/apr/07/labour-defends-ad-claiming-sunak-doe snt-think-child-sex-abusers-should-be-jailed

Bateman, T. (2023) 'Challenging punitive youth justice', in S. Case and N. Hazel (eds) *Child First: Developing a New Youth Justice System*, Cham: Palgrave Macmillan.

Canton, R. (2012) 'The point of probation: on effectiveness, human rights and the virtues of obliquity', *Criminology and Criminal Justice*, 13(5): 577–93.

Children's Rights Committee (2019) 'General comment no. 24 on children's rights in the child justice system', Available from: https://www. ohchr.org/en/documents/general-comments-and-recommendations/ general-comment-no-24-2019-childrens-rights-child

Crew, J. (2023) 'Rishi Sunak promises antisocial behaviour crackdown', BBC News, 27 March, Available from: https://www.bbc.co.uk/news/uk-65077271

Cunneen, C. and Goldson, B. (2015) 'Restorative justice? A critical analysis', in B. Goldson and J. Muncie (eds) *Youth, Crime and Justice* (2nd edn), London: Sage, pp 137–56.

Day, A.-M. (2022) '"It's a hard balance to find": the perspectives of youth justice practitioners in England on the place of "risk" in an emerging "Child First" world', *Youth Justice*, 23(1): 58–75, Available from: https://journals. sagepub.com/doi/epub/10.1177/14732254221075205

Drake, D., Fergusson, R. and Briggs, D.B. (2014) 'Hearing new voices: re-viewing youth justice policy through practitioners' relationships with young people', *Youth Justice*, 14(1): 22–39.

Eadie, T. and Canton, R. (2002) 'Practising in a context of ambivalence: the challenge for youth justice workers', *Youth Justice*, 2(1): 14–26.

Fullerton, D., Bamber, J. and Redmond, S. (2021) 'Developing effective relationships between youth justice workers and young people: a synthesis of the evidence', REPPP Review, University of Limerick.

Goldson, B. and Briggs, D. (2021) 'Making youth justice: local penal cultures and differential outcomes; lessons and prospects for policy and practice', Howard League for Penal Reform.

Gray, P. (2020) '"Rights-based" and "children and young people first" approaches to youth justice', in P. Ugwudike, H. Graham, F. McNeill, P. Raynor, F.S. Taxman and C. Trotter (eds) *The Routledge Companion to Rehabilitative Work in Criminal Justice*, London: Routledge, pp 743–54.

Hazel, N. and Case, S. (2023) 'Postscript: progress and challenges for progressing progressive Child First youth justice', in S. Case and N. Hazel (eds) *Child First: Developing a New Youth Justice System*, Cham: Palgrave Macmillan, pp 367–85.

Held, V. (2010) 'Can the ethics of care handle violence?', *Ethics and Social Welfare*, 4(2): 115–29.

HM Inspectorate of Probation (2021) 'Inspection standards for youth justice services', Available from: https://www.justiceinspectorates.gov.uk/hmiprobation/wp-content/uploads/sites/5/2021/05/Youth-Offending-Inspection-Standards-May-2021-v1.1.pdf

Hodgson, J. (2020) 'Offending girls and restorative justice: a critical analysis', *Youth Justice*, 22(2): 166–88.

McAra, L. and McVie, S. (2007) 'Youth justice? The impact of system contact on patterns of desistance from offending', *European Journal of Criminology*, 4(3): 315–45.

McAra, L. and McVie, S. (2010) 'Youth crime and justice: key messages from the Edinburgh Study of Youth Transitions and Crime', *Criminology & Criminal Justice*, 10(2): 179–209.

National Association for Youth Justice (2019) 'Manifesto 2019/2020', Available from: https://thenayj.org.uk/manifesto-2019-final.pdf

Phoenix, J. (2016) 'Against youth justice and youth governance, for youth penality', *The British Journal of Criminology*, 56(1): 123–40.

Prior, D. and Mason, P. (2010) 'A different kind of evidence? Looking for "what works" in engaging young offenders', *Youth Justice*, 10(3): 211–26.

Rodgers, C.R. (1957) 'The necessary and sufficient conditions of therapeutic personality change', *Journal of Consulting Psychology*, 21(2): 95–103.

Smith, R. and Gray, P. (2019) 'The changing shape of youth justice: models of practice', *Criminology and Criminal Justice*, 19(5): 554–71.

Torre, M., Stoudt, B., Manoff, E. and Fine, M. (2018) 'Critical participatory action research on state violence: bearing wit(h)ness across fault lines of power, privilege, and possession', in N.K. Denzin and Y.S. Lincoln (eds) *The SAGE Handbook of Qualitative Research*, London: SAGE Publications, pp 492–516.

Tronto, J.C. (2010) 'Creating caring institutions: politics, plurality, and purpose', *Ethics and Social Welfare*, 4(2): 158–71.

Wigzell, A. (2021) 'Explaining desistance: looking forward, not backwards', National Association for Youth Justice, Available from: https://thenayj.org.uk/cmsAdmin/uploads/explaining-desistance-briefing-feb-2021-final.pdf

Youth Justice Board (2022) 'Case management guidance', Youth Justice Board for England and Wales, Available from: https://www.gov.uk/guidance/case-management-guidance/how-to-work-with-children

Youth Justice Board (2019) 'Standards for children in the youth justice system 2019', Available from: https://assets.publishing.service.gov.uk/government/uploads/system/uploads/attachment_data/file/1115435/Standards_for_children_in_youth_justice_services_2019.doc.pdf

Youth Justice Board/Ministry of Justice (2023) 'Key performance indicators for youth justice services', 8 March, Available from: https://www.gov.uk/guidance/key-performance-indicators-for-youth-justice-services

Index

References to figures and photographs appear in *italic* type;
those in **bold** type refer to tables.

A

aboriginal peoples 68
abuse and trauma 117, 134, 215, 229
  and offending behaviour 10
  victims of 81, 83, 85, 97
  young women and 100
adultification 130–1, 239
adults 199
  Black men and masculinity 138, 141
  Black men serving long sentences 80
  care-experienced adults 112
  and desistance 38, 63, 77, 176
  and difference with children 7–16, 175–8
  ex-prisoners self-construction 4–5
  and labelling 41
  representations of women 102
  and time 57–8, 62, 68
  women with criminal records 101
  women's desistance narratives 5
adversial environment 245, 247, 249, 280
African Caribbean boys
  see Black and mixed heritage boys
age
  age-crime curve 4, 259
  of criminal responsibility 77, 106, 285–6
  see also maturation
agency 16, 39, 43, 49, 77, 176, 205,
  268, 285
Akomolafe, B. 65
Allnock, D. 100
anger control 267
antisocial behaviour 8, 178, 202, 205,
  261, 267
art, engagement through
  see Summer Arts Colleges (SAC)
assessment framework 1, 17, 18, 39
  and investigations 251
ASSET 17, 18, 39–40
  AssetPlus 18–19, 22–3, 24, 178–80, 283
  training and evaluation 182–7
attention deficit hypractivity disorder
  (ADHD) 267
attitudinal change and SAC
  programme 201–2, 205–6
austerity 104, 188
Australia 12, 61–2, 66, 67–8

B

Barcode of Desistance (BoD) 246, 258–9,
  258, 259

Barry, M. 6, 10, 11
Bateman, T. 287
Beelmann, A. 267
behaviour, reasons for 6, 84, 239–40
belief
  see faith
Beyond Youth Custody (BYC) 44, 46–7,
  49, 51
Black and mixed heritage boys 278, 282,
  284, 285
  adultification of Black boys 130–1
  Black boys and desistance 134–6
  desistance and CRT 136–42
  experiences with YJS 84
  lives and racism 128–30
  racialisation and CRT 131–2
  spaces/communities 132–4
  youth development 61
Black Lives Matter (BLM) 137–8, 142
Black people 159, 199
  Black children 84, 87
  Black masculinity 138
  Caribbean girls and exclusion 100
  men 84–5
  men serving long sentences 80
  spaces/communities 132–4
  see also Black and mixed heritage boys
Bottoms, A. 6, 8, 13, 268
Bowling, B. 9
boys and young men 7, 9, 13
  and powerlessness 11
  school exclusion 84, 99
  and time 65–6
  see also Black and mixed heritage boys
Brazil, research in 6, 14
breach/non-compliance 232, 255, 256, 279
Brierley, A. 221
British Asian girls and restorative
  justice 116
Bronfenbrenner, U. 58, 60–1
Brown, K. 84
Bugnon, G. 14
bullying 101, 106, 267
Burgess, W.A. 161–2
Bushway, S. 5

C

Cahill, H. 217
Cambridgeshire 27, 262
care system 285

care work 103
care-experienced girls 10, 97–9, 102, 123, 199
  diversion and restorative justice 114–16
  independent living 121–2
  positive relationships 118–20
  and stigma 116–17
  victimisation and mental health 117–18
  and the youth justice system 112–14
caring justice 280
caring relationships
  see relationships
Carlile, Lord 259
Carr, S. 280, 281
Carroll, A. 267
Carvalho, H. 97
Case, Stephen 21, 77, 286, 287
cautions
  see pre-court disposals
change, theory of
  see theory of change
charitable sector 285
Child First approach 10, 23, 113, 221, 232
  and desistance 19–21, 37, 178, 187, 213
  framework 43
  and HMIP 82–3
  and joined-up policies 123
  and non-conviction remittals 247
  and positive outcomes 286–7
  and pro-sociality 264
  and theory of change 48–50, 50–2
children
  and agency 176–7
  benefits of desistance 82–6
  best interests of 20, 37, 48
  child rights 59–60
  childcare 98, 105, 106
  and desistance narratives 84–6
  exploitation and vulnerability 41, 75, 83, 84–6, 195, 217, 229
  faith journeys of 153
  lives and experiences 17–18, 81–2
  and an offender identity 74–6
  responsibilisation of 21, 38, 77–8, 86
  SEND and disabled children 99
  see also boys and young men; children's perceptions; girls and young women; maturation
Children's Hearing System (CHS) 245–6, 254–5
children's perceptions 6, 16, 17–18, 213, 281
  of being listened to 216, 236, 238
  children's voices 217, 218
  of court delays 79
  fugitivity 63–5
  of selves 8, 12, 44, 47
  of time 60–2, 63–6, 67, 68
  view of support 21

Chile 6, 13
chronosystem 58, 60–2
citizenship 103–4
civil servants and religious literacy 157–8
Clarke, B. 134
class 18, 98, 105, 130, 135
  working-class people 99, 105
co-creative action research 140–1
cognitive change
  see maturation
collaborative work
  see participatory practice
collective responsibility 60, 81
colonial histories 61–2
community resources, for Black boys 140–1
Compass Project (TCP) 262, 264, 268–9, 270, **270**
compliance 213–14, 257
Constructive Working (CW) 38, 44–8
co-production 212, 215, 218, 282
'county lines' 80, 85, 134, 239
courts and sentencing 185–6, 232, 246, 279
  children in court 247–8
  community sentences 1, 229, 280
  convictions 106, 250, 258, 279
  court delays 79
  court orders 26, 139, 215, 216, 222, 229, 257
  magistrates 186, 279
  non-conviction remittals 249–53, 255–6
  sentencing and children 250
  young women in court 102–3
  see also Guernsey Model; remittals
COVID-19 114, 156, 187
Coyle, B. 8
Creaney, S. 213, 281, 284, 285
Crewe, B. 230
Crime and Disorder Act 1998 15, 37, 39
criminal justice system
  and Black people 84
  and Black/mixed heritage boys 10, 128–31, 135–6
  care-experienced children 112
  and care-experienced girls 114, 120
  children in 25, 41
  and desistance thinking 230, 232, 241
  journeys through 73, 78
  see also youth justice service (YJS)
criminal records 101–3
  disclosure of 98, 106
criminal responsibility 6, 77, 106, 285–6
criminalisation, reducing 114–16
criminogenic labels
  see labelling
Critical Race Theory 128, 131–2, 136–42
cultural associations 129–30
custody 40, 47, 67, 180, 181
  Beyond Youth Custody (BYC) 11–12, 44, 46–7, 52

Black children in 128
care-experienced children in 10
care-experienced girls in 97–8, 112
Constructive Working (CW) 44
and education 195, 207
and Guernsey Model 250–1
training for Black boys 135
Youth Custody service 51–2

D

Dadvand, B. 217
Day, A.M. 23, 83–4
decision-making 43, 212, 215, 216–17,
    221, 281
delinquents 13, 38, 58, 267
  peer groups 9, 195, 203, 204
demonisation
  of Black people 129
  of women 102
desistance
  about/what is desistance 1–6
  Barcode of Desistance (BoD) 246
  and Black/mixed heritage boys 134–6,
    136–42, 140–1
  and care-experienced girls 112–16
  and Child First 19–21
  and children 87–8, 277–8
  concepts and confusion 175–8, 188
  desistance thinking 73–6, 76–82
  differences between children and adults 7–8
  and education 195
  and the evidence base 4–6
  and faith 151–3
  and identity 12–15
  implementation and obstacles 21–4,
    178–82, 282
  and maturation 8–11
  and non-conviction remittals 245–6, 260
  and participatory practices 221–2
  and peer support 218–21
  primary/secondary desistance 150
  and psychological strategies 262
  and rehabilitation 78–81
  and relationships 11–12, 228, 240
  research on children and desistance 5–7
  and resilience 15–16
  and risk management 38–40
  and SAC programme 195, 202–6
  as a social justice issue 278–9
  tertiary desistance 16
  theories of 3–6, 62, 74–6, 86, 149–51,
    262–5
  training 182–7
  and YJS decision-makers 78–9
  and youth justice 16–19
Dinham, A. 157, 158–9
disability 99, 103, 105
disadvantaged groups
  see marginalised groups

Disclosure and Barring Service 101, 284
discrimination 46
  see also race and racism
disempowerment 5, 10, 26, 116, 138, 213,
    216, 247
diversionary practices 49, 114–16, 123,
    203, 279
drift 76, 177, 179
drugs, illegal 80, 85, 133, 134
Duke, K. 217

E

Early Intervention Foundation 230
Edinburgh Study of Youth Transitions and
    Crime 99, 176
education 9, 98, 116, 183, 195, 207, 237
  Arts qualification 200, 203
  and desistance 195
  failing Black boys 132, 136, 139
  inclusive system 285
  literacy/numeracy 197, 199, 200, 217
  SEND and disabled children 99
  see also school
Ellison, C.W. 161–2
emotional development 264–5, 267
employment 4, 9, 77, 133, 263, 280
  and criminal records 102, 106
  and education 195
  low pay 104, 138
  precarious employment 104
engagement 43, 46, 199–200, 235, 258
  engaged staff 231
  with ETE 196–7
  voluntary engagement 256
  see also Summer Arts Colleges (SAC)
ETE
  engagement with 196–7, 200, 201
  tracking 198, 206
ethnicity 7, 117
Evans, R. 280, 285
everyday life 61, 113, 214, 216
  of Black boys 140
  life events 48, 77, 121, 263
  limited life choices 77
  lived experience 218–21, 230, 238, 281
  lives of little value 106
  postcolonial *Other* 132
  racism 129–30, 131, 137
  real issues 85
exclusion 130, 138

F

faith
  children's journeys of 153
  and desistance 151–3
  Faith, Spirituality and Religion model *148*
  Faith Development Model **154**
  faith terminology 147–9
  and Generation Z 153–6

and generational change 156
knowledge and skills 159–63
religious literacy 156–9
spirituality frameworks 161–2
see also religion; spirituality
families
and Black/mixed heritage boys 128, 130, 138, 139
family violence 97, 100, 104, 270
generational disadvantage 138
and girls and young women 104–5, 122
and Guernsey Model 251, 253
and harm/violence 112, 117
importance of 4, 9, 10, 232
instability in 268
and SHiFT 229, 235, 237, 238, 240
supportive relationships in 10
Farrall, S. 3, 5, 14, 150
Ferguson, Ann 65–6
'FICA' assessment tool 162–3
financial security 105, 106
First Time Child Entrants (FTCEs) 247, 254
Fitzpatrick, C. 15
Fitzpatrick, E. 11
Fowler, J.W. 152, 153, 159
free school meals 99
fresh 'AIR' 45, 50
fugitivity 58, 63–5
funding 186, 187, 283, 285
Furness, S. 161

G

gangs 83, 84–5, 133–4, 138
gender
gendered judgements 117
punishment 105
generation theory 153, 156
Generation Z, the faith of 153–6
Gilligan, P. 161
Giordano, P.C. 5
girls and young women 7, 9, 46, 116, 278
aspirations of 123
criminal records 101–3
impact of welfare system on 103–5
media representation 101–3
mental health 284
needing early support 124
punishment at school 99–101
punishment by the state 97–8
see also care-experienced girls
Giroux, H.A. 64
Good Lives model 175, 176, 178
Gove, W.R. 264
government
APPG on Religious Education 157, 159, 160
Coalition government 18
Conservative government 188

HMIP 19, 21, 23, 52, 181, 213, 279
Home Office 122, 130
Independent Parliamentarians' Inquiry 259
law and order mantra 286
Ministry of Justice 6, 81, 122, 157, 198
New Labour 23
welfare in Britain 103–5
see also police
Graham, J. 9
Gray, P. 10, 21
Greater Manchester 212
growing out of offending 1, 4, 5
see also maturation
Guernsey Model 250
Barcode of Desistance (BoD) 258–9
Office of the Children's Convenor (OCC) 245–6, 250–5, *252*
guilt 27, 80, 81, 251, 254, 267–8
Gypsy Roma children 100

H

Haigh, Y. 12
Haines, Kevin 21, 77, 279, 281
Hampson, K.S. 22, 83, 279, 282, 283, 284
Hazel, N. 249–50, 286, 287
health needs 217, 218
health workers and spirituality frameworks 162
HM Inspectorate of Probation (HMIP) 21, 23, 52, 213, 279
desistance concept confusion 19, 181
Hodgson, J. 116
Home Office 122, 230
'hooks for change' 5, 153
housing 121, 132, 136, 138, 263
Hulley, S. 80

I

identity 8, 19, 247
Black identity 138
building identities 256–8
complex ethnic identities 135
development of 280–1
and emotions 264–5, 267
fluid identities 130, 140, 141
future selves 12, 13, 14
identity change 4–5, 12–15, 207, 264
identity change and faith 151–2
interactional identity 5, 45–6, 49, 150
and morality 261
offender identity 74–5, 76–7, 86, 281
self-worth 19, 20, 138, 183
sense of self 97, 101, 215
see also pro-social behaviours
incapacitation and SAC programme 202–3
independent living after care 121–2
Independent Parliamentarians' Inquiry 259
indigenous peoples 68
concepts of time 65, 66

individualisation and responsibilisation 77–8
inequalities 10, 18, 81, 84, 88, 103
  experienced by girls 116
  see also Black and mixed heritage boys
inspections 23, 83, 180–2
institutions outside youth justice 278
interventions 51, 124, 135, 141, 149,
    176, 213
  Child First approach 19–21, 48–50
  Children's Hearing System (CHS) 245–6
  Compass Project (TCP) 261–2, 269
  Constructive Working (CW) 44–8
  and desistance 20–3
  Early Intervention Programme 230
  and Guernsey Model 251–3
  and law-abiding morality 266–8
  participatory practice 213–14, 218
  Positive Youth Justice (PYJ)
    model 38, 41–3
  psychological strategies 27
  Summer Arts Colleges (SAC) 194, 205, 207
  Swansea Model 245–6

J

Johns, D. 11, 77, 78, 280, 281
Johnson, K. 3
'joint enterprise' 80
Jump, D. 9, 12, 229
Just for Kids Law 80

K

Key Elements of Effective Practice
    (KEEPS) 17, 39
knives 49, 133, 140

L

labelling 10, 38, 47, 75, 116, 247,
    270, 279
Lammy, D. 135
Laub, J.H. 77, 176, 263, 264
LGBT+ girls 120
Liebling, A. 230
life events
  see everyday life
literacy/numeracy 197, 199, 200, 217
Little, Ross 279, 281
London gangs 134
lone parents
  see parenthood
long-term development 15–16,
    50, 281
  see also identity; maturation
Lösel, F. 267
Love, Bettina 67–8
Lundy, L. 217

M

magistrate training 186, 279
Mann, R. 82

marginalised groups 46, 103, 216
  Black boys 132
  children 99, 195
  girls and young women 97, 102, 106, 285
Maruna, S. 4, 8, 63, 82, 150, 151,
    258–29, 264
masculinity 85, 135, 138
Mason, P. 280
maturation 7–8, 8–11, 149, 177, 229, 259, 264
McAra, S. 58, 84, 99, 228
McGuire, M.B. 160
McMahon, G. 9, 12, 229
McNeill, F. 3, 74, 81, 113, 115,
    150, 178
McVie, L. 58, 84, 99, 228
media representations of women 101–3
men
  see adults; boys and young men
mental health 106, 284, 285
  and girls in care 117–18
  services 121–2
mentors 219–20, 221
  peer mentors 139–40, 216, 284, 285
Miller, P. 100
Miller, W. 163
minimal intervention 58, 69
Ministry of Justice 6, 81, 122, 157, 198
minority ethnic communities 5, 10, 46,
    87, 102, 103, 120, 199
misogyny 98, 103
mixed heritage
  see Black and mixed heritage boys
Mockler, N. 82
moral panics 102
morality, law-abiding 261–2, 264–5
  morality-strengthening programme 268–9
Moten, F. 64
mothers, young 9, 98, 101, 103, 106, 122
  and welfare benefits 104
motivating children 19, 46
Mulvey, E.P. 8
Murray, Cathy 13–14
Muslim children 159
Myles, K. 218

N

narratives 8, 47, 62, 150
  for Black boys 137
  desistance narratives 82–4
National Association for Youth Justice
    (NAYJ) 2, 6, 277, 286
national standards 20, 229, 232, 241, 279
needs, unmet 217, 218, 232, 241, 280
  tailoring to needs 236
neglect 100, 217, 229
neurodevelopment 285
neurodiverse children 278
normative offending 1, 5, 18
Nugent, B. 3, 6, 150

O

offending
  binary view of 13, 60
  and Black boys 139
  gaps between offences 63, 258–9, 263, 281
  not identifying as an offender 13–14
offending, prevention of 45, 52, 78, 81–2, 231, 286
  ASSET/KEEPs 17
  and Child First 43–4
  Child First approach 20, 49–50
  and Guernsey Model 249
  and PYJ 41
  and resilience 15
  RFPP 38–9, 73
  and SAC programme 194, 203
  and YJS 37
  see also desistance; interventions
Office of the Children's Convenor (OCC) see Guernsey Model
Osler, A. 99, 100
Othering 83–4, 128, 129, 132, 134, 137, 139
over-representation concept 57, 84–5, 87

P

parenthood 11, 122, 263
  lone/absent parents 103, 104, 105, 138
  mothers 9, 98, 101, 103, 106, 122
participatory practice 212–16, 281
  barriers to 217–18
  and desistance 221–2
  meaning of participation 216–17
Paternoster, R. 5
peer support 139–40, 214
  and desistance 218–21
personal deficits 38–9, 115, 175, 207, 218, 258
Phillips, J. 74
physical appearance 129
Piaget, J. 153
placements, changing 118, 120, 237, 280
places/spaces 136, 137, 138, 140, 141, 214
  dangerous communities 133
  of worship 152
police 131, 137, 140, 185, 237, 279, 284
  and Black boys 134
  child interviewees 80, 249
  Met Police 'gangs matrix' 83
  PACE 1984 78
  PNC 256
  policing and racism 57
  stop and search 78, 134, 140
Police, Crime, Sentencing and Courts Act 2022 181, 188
political economy in Britain 103–5
Posick, C. 77
positive work 49, 183, 240, 256, 266
  and faith 156
  positive outcomes 50, 51, 286

Positive Youth Justice (PYJ) model 38, 41–3, 51, 213
postcolonialism and Othering see Othering
poverty 10, 18, 85–6, 88, 99, 132, 134, 138
  welfare in Britain 103–5
power dynamics 213, 214, 216, 217, 218, 230
Powers of Criminal Court (Sentencing) Act 2000 231
practitioners/professionals
  assessments 17–18
  and child relationship 213, 216
  communication and training 178–80
  and desistance 82–4, 83–4
  failing children 239–40
  good practice 122
  inconsistent practice 279
  and participatory practices 221–2
  reflections of a 245–6
  relationships 11–12, 43, 118, 123, 231–3, 256–8, 279–80
  and religious literacy 158–9, 159–63
  and risk paradigm 17
  and structural obstacles 78
  time/funding issues 186–7
  and training 21–2, 182–7, 187–8
pre-court disposals 1, 7, 75, 101, 116, 249
Prevent 159
primary desistance 150
Prior, D. 280
prison 135, 230, 238
programmes/training about offences 49
pro-social behaviours 38, 51–2, 152, 219, 281
  identity development 44–8, 177–8, 232
  and morality 266
  and peer groups 195
  and relationships 264
psychological strategies 261, 262
public sector workers and religious literacy 158–63

Q

quantitative judgements 40, 81–2, 178

R

racism 57, 61–2, 68, 84–5, 128
  and Black boys 129–32, 134–6, 136–8
  racial violence 67
redemption scripts 4, 150
Referral Orders 247–8, 254–5
reflective practice 159, 283
rehabilitation 78–81
Reid, E. 85
relationships 18–19, 20
  caring relationships 11, 279–80, 283–4
  and desistance 256–8
  in faith settings 152

importance of 263
improved by SAC programme 204–5
long-term relationships 280
positive relationships 10, 43, 118–20
professional 11–12
relationship-based work 219, 228–33,
  236–8, 256–8, 280
stable relationships 46
trusting relationships 16, 230–3, 240, 241
religion
  and desistance 151–3
  Faith, Spirituality and Religion
    model 148
  religion and belief framework 161
  Religious Commitment Inventory
    (RCI) 163
  religious literacy 284
  religious literacy training 156–9, 159–63
  religious terminology 147–9
  see also faith; spirituality
remittals 245
  and conviction differences 254–5
  non-conviction remittals 249–53, 255–6
resettlement/re-entry
  Beyond Youth Custody (BYC) 11–12,
    44, 46–7
  and care-experienced girls 97–8,
    121–2, 123
  Constructive Working (CW) 38, 44
  and education 195, 207
  rehabilitation 78–81
restorative approaches 19, 114–16, 251
rights 37, 43, 59–60, 69, 216, 246–7
risk paradigm 17–19, 22–3, 37,
  175–6, 232
  HMIP and risk/desistance
    concepts 181–2
  risk management and desistance 38–40
  and theory of change 40–1
road traffic offences 253
Rocque, M. 77
Rodriguez, L.J. 68
role models 43, 120, 136, 139, 220, 221
Rosier, T. 282, 284

S

Sampson, R.J. 7, 77, 176, 263, 264
sanctions, welfare 104–5
Scaled Approach 17, 232
Schinkel, M. 3, 150
school 9, 284
  bullying 98, 101, 106
  exclusion 84, 98, 99, 101, 139, 195, 199
  mental health provision 285
  need for wellbeing support 106
  punishment of girls 99–101
  pupil referral units (PRU) 139
  see also education
Schubert, C.A. 8

Scotland 6, 10, 11, 13–14, 176
  Children's Hearing System (CHS) 245–6,
    254–5, 260
  school exclusion study 99–100
secondary desistance 150
secure care 98
secure schools 67
self-control 8
self-efficacy 197, 198, 202, 205–7, 219
self-worth 19, 120, 138, 183
sense of belonging 99, 150, 151, 152–3
serious/persistent offenders 7, 102, 115,
  134, 139, 228–9, 251
sexual offences 100, 102, 115, 117, 175
  sexual exploitation 113
shame 13, 27, 62, 85, 101–3, 116,
  264, 267–8
Shapland, J. 5, 6, 8, 13, 14
Sharpe, G. 6, 101, 278, 284, 285
Shaw, M. 157
Sheffield 8, 13
SHiFT 229, 233–40, 241
Shover, N. 264
Situational Action Theory (SAT) 5, 207,
  262, 265–6, 269
Smith, R. 21
social capital 133, 136, 222, 267
  and SAC programme 203–5
social context 4, 8, 18, 19, 270
Social Discipline Window 248, 248
social inclusion 49, 50, 99
social justice 278, 287
social media 88, 102
social networks 12, 195
social responsibility 156
  see also morality, law-abiding
social work 245
  and spirituality framework 161
  staff turnover 118, 119
socio-economic factors 10, 39, 77, 85–6,
  97, 112, 132, 270
  social background 98
socio-structural support 24, 25–6, 287
  see also structural contexts
Spacey, M. 219
special educational needs (SEND) 99, 199
spirit murder 67–8
spirituality 147–8, 148, 282
  and desistance 151–3
  of Generation Z 156
  professional frameworks 161–2
  Spiritual Criminology 147, 163
  see also faith; religion
stability 263
Stacey, M. 82
staff turnover 118, 119, 280, 283
Staines, J. 278, 279, 280, 284, 285
Stephenson, M. 278, 285
Stern, J. 61

stigmatisation 10, 49
  and care-experienced girls 116
Stone, N. 103
stop and search 78, 134, 140
strengths-based working 18, 19, 20, 22, 213
  BYC/CW model 46
  and Child First 43, 48
  and desistance approaches 175–8,
    180, 182
structural contexts 11, 76, 77, 80, 97, 112,
    150, 263
  structural barriers 10, 20, 21, 48, 61,
    106, 114, 195
  structural racism 129, 131, 132
  structural support 43, 45–6, 215
Summer Arts Colleges (SAC) 194, 196
  attitudinal change/shifts 201–2, 205–6
  and desistance 202–6
  participants and outcomes 198–202
  success of the 206–7
  and theory of change 196–8
supervisory relationships
  see practitioners/professionals
support 280
  for girls in care 119–20
  lack of for Black boys 263
  long-term support 229
  outside justice system 280
  provided by faith 151, 152
  providing support across services 285
  support principles 46, 49, 98
  see also structural contexts
Swansea Model 245–6, 255
Szifris, K. 229, 230, 234, 280, 285

T

Taylor, Charlie 19–20
temporal ecologies 60–3
Thatcher, Margaret 103
theory of change 38, 48–50, 50–2, *197*
  developing a pro-social identity 44–8
  and risk management 40–1
  and SAC programme 196–8, 202
Thompson, N. 219
time 280, 281, 283, 285
  and desistance thinking 4, 58–9, 69
  escaping adult time 65–6
  fugitivity 63–5
  and human development 60–2
  perceptions of 57, 66–8
  spent on AssetPlus completion 184
Timpson review of school exclusion 99
Toor, S. 116
training 17, 21–2, 116, 136, 279, 284
  lack of for Black boys 135
  in religious literacy 157–9
  see also practitioners; youth justice service
    (YJS)
'trap life' 83, 85

trauma 120, 215, 229, 238, 241, 283, 284
  and Black/mixed heritage boys 134–6, 137
  generational trauma 138
  and mental health support 117–18
  witnessing crime 270
Trivedi-Bateman, N. 280
trust and relationships
  see relationships

U

Ukrainian War 187
Unitas training 187
United Nations 285
  Convention on the Rights of the
    Child 37, 59, 216, 246–7
  on UK welfare system 103
United States 6, 39
  credible messengers 221
  serious offenders study 8
Universal Credit 104
Unlock 102

V

Vaneigem, R. 57–8
victimisation 11, 25, 116, 123, 127, 239, 270
violence 100, 101, 102, 133, 134, 136, 140
  faced by Black boys 137
  perceived violence of Black boys 131

W

Wainwright, J. 278, 281, 282, 284
Wales 10, 11, 19–20, 22, 256
  research in 77
  Swansea Model 246, 254–5
  training in 182–7
Warner, K. 81–2
Weaver, B. 74
welfare system 278, 285
  anti-youth system 98
  welfare in Britain 103–5
  and young women 97, 106
wellbeing 153, 264, 284
  see also faith
Western understandings of time 66
White people 5, 129, 130, 131
  exclusion from White society 132
  girls and exclusion 100
Wigzell, A. 21, 75, 76, 233, 286
Williams, P. 134
Williams, R. 21
women
  see adults; girls and young women
workload 241, 280, 283
Wyman, P.A. 267

Y

Young, T. 80
youth culture 64
Youth Ink 214, 219, 221, 222, 285

youth justice 277, 279–80, 285–7
youth justice service (YJS)
  adversial approach of 245, 247
  and arts programme 194, 207
  Black boys experience with 84
  and care-experienced girls 112–14, 123
  and 'cultural blindness'; 83
  decision makers in 78–9
  and desistance concepts 16–19, 175–8
  and desistance confusion 178–80
  desistance in practice 21–4, 83
  desistance thinking 1–2, 73–8
  desistance training 182–7
  diversionary and restorative practices
    114–16

and inspections 179–82
and non-conviction remittals 255–6
and participatory practices 212–18
policy and children's lives 84–6
practice and policy 283–4
PYJ/CW 37–8, 41–3, 44–4
reflections of a youth justice officer
    245–9
relationship-based work 228–33,
    240–1
and religious literacy 159–63
training 24–287, 182–7
YOTs 19, 120, 198, 233, 255, 256
YOTs and desistance 83–4
see also ASSET; Child First approach

www.ingramcontent.com/pod-product-compliance
Lightning Source LLC
Chambersburg PA
CBHW062113040426
42337CB00043B/3758